'Highly readable and a great introduction to the dynamic
thinking used in many natural sciences.'
The Post-Crash Economics Society (UK)

'Read this book!'
Indonesian Society for Social Transformation (INSIST, Indonesia)

'Entertaining, informative and highly recommended.'
MDB Insight (Canada)

'Terrible, willfully ignorant, deeply anti-intellectual ... there
is nothing an interested layman could possibly learn from
this book.'
Professor of Economics, University of Victoria

'Just random – sort of like Malcolm Gladwell without the insight.'
Professor of Economics, Carleton University

Praise for *Truth or Beauty*

'Fascinating ... Orrell is an engaging and witty writer, adept at
explaining often complicated theories in clear language.'
Ian Critchley, *Sunday Times*

Praise for *The Money Formula*
(with Paul Wilmott)

'This book has humor, attitude, clarity, science and common
sense; it pulls no punches and takes no prisoners.'
Nassim Nicholas Taleb

Praise for *The Evolution of Money* (with Roman Chlupatý)

'Perhaps the best book on money I have ever read ... A reasonable and benign dictator might demand that those engaged in activities relating to economic management should, as a condition of employment, be compelled to read *The Evolution of Money* and pass a written examination based on an understanding of its contents.'

Colin Teese, former deputy secretary of the Department of Trade, *News Weekly* (Australia)

Economyths

Economyths

11 Ways Economics Gets it Wrong

DAVID ORRELL

ICON

This edition published in the UK in 2017 by
Icon Books Ltd, Omnibus Business Centre,
39–41 North Road, London N7 9DP
email: info@iconbooks.com
www.iconbooks.com

Previously published in the UK in 2010 and 2012 by Icon Books Ltd

Sold in the UK, Europe and Asia
by Faber & Faber Ltd, Bloomsbury House,
74–77 Great Russell Street,
London WC1B 3DA or their agents

Distributed in the UK, Europe and Asia
by Grantham Book Services, Trent Road,
Grantham NG31 7XQ

Distributed in the USA
by Publishers Group West,
1700 Fourth Street, Berkeley, CA 94710

Distributed in Canada
by Publishers Group Canada,
76 Stafford Street, Unit 300,
Toronto, Ontario M6J 2S1

Distributed in Australia and New Zealand
by Allen & Unwin Pty Ltd, PO Box 8500,
83 Alexander Street, Crows Nest, NSW 2065

Distributed in South Africa
by Jonathan Ball, Office B4, The District,
41 Sir Lowry Road, Woodstock 7925

ISBN: 978-178578-229-9

Typeset in Minion by Marie Doherty

Printed and bound in the UK by
Clays Ltd, St Ives plc

Contents

For Beatriz

David Orrell is an applied mathematician and author of popular science books. He studied mathematics at the University of Alberta, and obtained his doctorate from Oxford University on the prediction of nonlinear systems. His work in applied mathematics and complex systems research has since led him to diverse areas such as weather forecasting, economics, and cancer biology. His most recent book is *The Money Formula: Dodgy Finance, Pseudo Science, and How Mathematicians Took Over the Markets*, written with Paul Wilmott. He lives in Toronto.

Foreword to the 2017 edition

When I first read *Economyths* during my undergraduate studies, I was just beginning to get acquainted with the economic world outside neoclassical economics. Disenamoured and frankly bored with my economics degree, I had been reading books and blogs which offered more critical perspectives on what I was being taught, especially given the failure of the discipline following the 2008 financial crisis. I enjoyed many of these but *Economyths* was so readable, and such a comprehensive critique, that I read it in a single day.

What was so interesting about the book was that it combined knowledge of the history of mathematics, mathematics itself, and crucially the limitations of mathematics. Economists largely disregard the first (and the history of their own subject), pride themselves on the second and often seem completely unaware of the third. Indeed, a common response to critics of mainstream economic theory is that they are complaining simply because they dislike or do not understand mathematics, which is assumed to be inherently more rigorous than qualitative techniques. But here was an applied mathematician – with a much more in-depth grasp of mathematics than most economists – telling them they had got it wrong.

Another positive thing about *Economyths* is that the critique is not only negative. David Orrell draws examples from areas of maths such as complexity theory, network theory and chaos theory to offer up alternatives to models which are dominated by notions of individualism, equilibrium and optimality – straitjackets which constrain realistic analysis of the economy, particularly financial crises. At the same time he appreciates that *no* mathematical approach, however sophisticated, can substitute for what are fundamentally ethical discussions about the environment, the role of economics and what the good life is.

But despite the flurry of critical works like *Economyths* following the crisis, what we were learning at undergraduate level had not changed. I discovered I was not the only one to think this when some fellow economics students set up the Post-Crash Economics Society at Manchester to campaign for changes to our economics education to make it more critical, pluralistic and connected to the real world. I went along to their first event and soon applied for the committee, of which I am still a member today (now as a PhD student instead of an undergraduate). Over the years the society and others like it have received media coverage and (hopefully) contributed to the debate about how economics education should change following the financial crisis.

The response of the discipline has sometimes been reasonable, with new curriculums like CORE (Curriculum Open-access Resources in Economics) being tested at universities (CORE does not answer all of the students' critiques, but it is a step in the right direction). It has sometimes been less so, as certain reviews of *Economyths* have made abundantly clear. But these debates are not just academic; economics affects everyone. With many of the problems identified by David Orrell lingering on and in some cases intensifying, we cannot afford for economics to remain stuck in the same habits of thought which led to the crisis. Hopefully those economists who are willing to read this book – and others like it – with an open mind will appreciate the progress that can come from embracing new ideas.

Cahal Moran, PhD economics student at Manchester,
Chair of the Post-Crash Economics Society and co-author of
The Econocracy: The Perils of Leaving Economics to the Experts
(Manchester University Press, 2016)

Preface to the 2017 edition

Economyths, like a host of other books, was born from the financial crisis. I first started working on it in 2009, a few months after Lehman Brothers went bankrupt, and the first edition was published in 2010. In a way it was a reaction to events at the time; but it was also about broader questions that I had been working on for a while, such as how we use numbers and mathematical models to simulate and understand the world, and how this was being affected by new approaches such as complexity science.

Since the book first came out, a lot has happened. In March 2011 the Canadian magazine *Adbusters* printed an extract from Chapter 10 urging students of economics to take a chance on 'speaking up, questioning your teachers, being open to disruptive ideas and generally acting as an agent of change'. The publisher Kalle Lasn added: 'Ten years from now, as the blowback from the externalities of their way of doing business repeatedly hammers us and global warming kicks in with a vengeance, we'll look back [at neoclassical economists] and wonder what it was about these logic freaks and their money narratives that so mesmerized us.'[1]

A few months later, Lasn wrote a blog post calling for a peaceful occupation of Wall Street, beginning on 17 September (his mother's birthday), to protest against issues such as wealth disparity and the involvement of financial companies in politics. Quite a few people turned up to the event, which became known as Occupy Wall Street. It grew into a movement that soon spread around the world.

The same *Economyths* extract, which was reprinted in the November issue of *Adbusters*, as well as the *Adbusters* team's book *Meme Wars: The Creative Destruction of Neoclassical Economics*, had noted that elite institutions including Harvard University were grooming students for work in the financial sector. It was therefore cheering when that month, as part of what was by then the global Occupy movement, Harvard students staged a walk-out from Gregory Mankiw's Economics 10 class. According to Gabriel Bayard, one of the organisers, 'Ec 10 is a symbol of the larger economic ideology that created the 2008 collapse'.[2] (I am not claiming *Economyths* played any role in all of this, but it certainly came out at a receptive time.)

One of the students' complaints was that the course offered 'very little access to alternative approaches to economics'.[3] A similar concern motivated the founding of the World Economics Association in May of that year. Its manifesto called for an emphasis on attributes such as a plurality of approaches, diversity in membership, relevance to the real world, and ethics. More than 3,600 people from 110 countries joined in the first ten days.

In the UK, Manchester University economics students started the Post-Crash Economics Society, posting a petition to revise the economics syllabus in November 2013 (with what was then the second edition of *Economyths* on its list of recommended reading). The following year, students from a Quebec group – part of the International Student Initiative for Pluralist Economics – wrote a petition noting that the field leaves 'little room for ethical, epistemological, philosophical, political and historical reflection, which would allow the discipline to reflect on itself and renew continuously'.[4] The umbrella organisation known as Rethinking Economics soon represented over 40 groups around the world.

Students and others had made similar calls for reform in the past, most famously perhaps in the 'post-autistic economics' movement initiated at the École Normale Supérieure in Paris in 2000; but the financial crisis had now added a much greater impetus. In May 2014, Cambridge University economists Ha-Joon Chang and Jonathan Aldred noted that their subject 'is the only academic discipline in which a significant and increasing number of students are in an open revolt against the content of their degree courses'.[5]

The number of people protesting about economics, and proposing or calling for new ideas and approaches, did not therefore quietly decline as the economy slowly healed – instead it continued to explode. Economics, it seemed, had finally passed the tipping point. The field would never look the same again.

Unless, of course, you were an economist.

Third time lucky

From this survey, one might assume that the collapse of mainstream economics under the strain of its insularity, rigidity, and general dysfunction would be nearing its completion a decade after the crisis, with the field primed for glorious rebirth after an agonising but necessary stage involving rampart-storming by students, public displays of contrition, show trials of former leaders, the purge of members who don't 'get it', etc. Of course, nothing is so simple – and if things had really changed so much, there wouldn't be a need to reissue this book. But as shown later in the updates made to individual chapters, progress has been fitful at best, and the core concerns of the book are as relevant as ever.

Some universities have begun to reform their curriculum – in the UK, Greenwich, Goldsmiths and Kingston stand out. Techniques described in this book, from areas such as complexity theory, network theory, and so on, continue to make inroads, and there is increasing recognition of the need to address the underlying causes of the crisis. Organisations such as the Institute for New Economic Thinking (INET) are funding some exciting new work.[6] But in general, according to a 2015 INET talk by Marc Lavoie from the University of Ottawa, 'nothing has changed in the classrooms or in academic journals'.[7] Keith Harrington from the *Adbusters*-affiliated group Kick It Over told *Yes!* magazine the same year: 'Despite its enormous failings in the face of the financial crash, the mainstream of the profession has by and large failed to embrace self-criticism or open itself up to different approaches.'[8]

Notre Dame's David Ruccio wrote in 2016: 'as anyone who teaches or studies economics these days knows full well, the mainstream that has long dominated economics (especially at research universities, in the United States and elsewhere) is not even beginning to let go of their almost-total control over the curriculum of undergraduate and graduate programs.'[9] Rethinking Economics did a survey of UK university courses in 2016 and concluded that 'Economics education currently teaches only one perspective, neoclassical economics: of the 172 module course outlines we analysed, only 17 mentioned alternative perspectives. Tomorrow's economists are taught that neoclassical economics provides the single correct and universal explanation of how the economy functions.'[10]

In early 2017 the Bank of England's chief economist Andrew Haldane described it as a 'fair cop' to say that the profession was in crisis, adding that 'Out of this crisis, there could be a rebirth of economics'.[11] Anne Pettifor – who had warned of the financial crisis in two books – agreed, writing that economics has failed to move on in part because it remains 'dogged by ideology' including an 'almost religious belief' in ideas such as efficiency (Ha-Joon Chang also speaks of the 'almost religious mentality' of mainstream economists).[12] Journalist Simon Jenkins noted that what has been missing following the financial crisis is an 'official or professional inquiry. No one took any responsibility or blame for a forecasting failure that led to a policy disaster ... The essence of any science is relentless self-criticism. Economics should suffer what the [UK] intelligence community did after Iraq. It should be asked, in public, to explain how it came to make so blatant a professional error.'[13] A Bloomberg editorial said that given its 'spectacular failures, you'd think the profession would have gone back to the drawing board. It hasn't.'[14] As with the bailed-out bankers, there has been neither a reckoning nor a proper rethink – only what another Bloomberg piece called a 'waning of economists' prestige and influence'.[15]

Business schools are no better: a 2016 paper called 'Business schools in crisis' began: 'Let's not mince words: Our MBA graduates marched out and destroyed the world financial system. Few in academe have stepped up to take responsibility. We have yet to hear a professor say, "I taught those people, and I'm sorry."'[16] Areas such as quantitative finance remain similarly unmoved. This is despite the fact that related issues raised by this book, from financial instability, to the environmental crisis, to wealth inequality leading to possible social unrest, haven't exactly gone away.

Economists have proved remarkably resistant to new ideas, for three reasons. (When I say 'economists' I am generally referring to mainstream, as opposed to *all* economists including the heterodox ones; the distinction should be obvious from context. Also, I will have something to say about these labels in the final chapter.) The first has to do with institutional effects; the second is deeper and is related to our entire scientific worldview; the third, hidden in plain sight, is the focus of the new Chapter 11 in this edition. Economics can't stand true reform, because true reform does not just entail incremental change: instead it represents an existential threat.

The institutional reasons became apparent quite early. Most readers who contacted me seemed to enjoy the book (and I greatly appreciated the many warm messages of support), and it received generally favourable reviews in at least ten countries, from economists and others.[17] But not everyone was so enthusiastic – especially, as it turns out, Canadian economists, perhaps because my home country survived the crisis rather well so they were still feeling smug (sample review quote: 'terrible, willfully ignorant, deeply anti-intellectual … there is nothing an interested layman could possibly learn from this book'[18]). In general, it seemed the book was received best by people (and in countries) with more direct experience of the crisis. Academic economists were largely insulated from its effects – unlike many other people at the time, they didn't have to worry about losing their job.[19] And their critiques had nothing to say about how they failed to foresee or even make sense of what might be the biggest event in their profession's history.

The most troubling part of the reaction by many economists to the crisis was that they couldn't see the connection between it and their work or teachings. The world was in the depths of a global financial crisis, and economists couldn't understand why they should care about a critique of the subject that in many ways was at the heart of it. But in a way it makes sense when viewed in psychological terms. It has made for fascinating, if at times uncomfortable viewing to watch the still-ongoing process as economists come to terms with their role in the crisis. For those who are interested, this process is charted separately in the new Appendix on 'The five stages of economic grief'.

The institutional faultlines of economics were put into a religious context by the late economic historian Frederick Lee, who in his 2009 book *A History of Heterodox Economics* described how 'mainstream economists have attempted to suppress the economic ideas and arguments of blasphemous economists'; he defines those blasphemers as people who are calling for 'the total rejection of a body of ideas and their replacement with ideas that are completely different'. He relates how mainstream economists have 'used organizational power to prevent the hiring of blasphemous economists, to deny them tenure, or to directly get them fired for teaching blasphemous material'.[20] No wonder some economists sounded like they wanted to burn copies of this book – and why I felt at times as if I had stumbled into a rather one-sided religious war.

Thinking in opposites

The second reason why the old guard clings on, and why the topics raised in the book are still relevant, is because they refer not to particular theories or fashions, but to general principles which form the foundation of economic thought, and much science in general.

Consider for example the idea that markets are self-stabilising, or that the economy can be viewed as a collection of atomistic individuals, or that it is an essentially linear system. All of these assumptions are embedded in key theories and techniques, from risk-management tools to the models used by policy-makers; and abandoning them is not easy, because they are related rather than independent. As mathematician Benoît Mandelbrot noted, for example, 'market efficiency is an aspect of economic equilibrium'.[21] The assumption of equilibrium relies in turn on things like rationality, independence, and so on. The result forms what author James Hannam called 'a complete system of reality' so that 'rejecting any significant chunk of it would cause the whole edifice to collapse' (though he was talking not about economics but about Aristotelian philosophy, which continued to dominate in the Middle Ages even as empirical evidence piled up against it).[22]

These principles are also not limited to economics, but instead reflect deep and interconnected aspects of our scientific aesthetic. As explored in more detail in my 2012 tome *Truth or Beauty* (published by Yale and Oxford university presses, so doubly academic), they are nicely expressed by the Pythagorean list of opposites presented in Chapter 5, which like twin strands of viral DNA have installed themselves in our minds and shaped our worldview. In fact, the original ten topics covered in *Economyths* were inspired by this list – not because I think economics is directly based on them, but because of the way they continue to resonate with our patterns of thinking, as they have since the dawn of Western science. This aesthetic is being slowly overturned in other areas of science, with economics lagging well behind. (The standard line on Pythagorean mysticism is that it was 'dross' which had nothing to do with their mathematical insights, but I would say that it is one of the most influential and interesting parts of their philosophy.[23] And if they can peg a doctrine on it, then I can peg a book on it.)

In this revised edition I have added a box to each chapter, showing the relation to the Pythagorean list where that might not be obvious, and discussing how the field has (or has not) moved on since the book first came out. However, I have kept the rest of the text mostly unchanged from the previous edition. After all, these principles have been around for two and a half millennia, and apply just as well today as they did several years ago. And it's interesting to revisit that post-crisis vibe when revolution was in the air – like pretending you're back in Zuccotti park, with the tear gas and police dogs and the chaos and the bearded European philosophers shouting out lectures on Marxism, only a lot more comfortable.

Have I missed anything?

I wrote the original *Economyths* in a hurry. I had a full-time job, a commute, a family, a deadline, and something to say. I worked early in the mornings or on weekends. After researching a chapter I would sometimes write a draft in a couple of sessions.

After the book had come out, I did wonder whether I had been completely fair to economists, whether I could have made mistakes, or missed something important. Of course no book is perfect, and I may have got a bit carried away in places, but had I goofed up in a major way? This weighed upon me. Perhaps I needed to *reach out* to economists, and expose myself more fully to their culture and their way of thinking.

After seeing the rather extreme reaction to the book from some economists, though, I decided to put off the listening tour.

(However, I appreciated all comments from economists and have incorporated them where appropriate, if sometimes for illustrative purposes.) I did have the renowned Czech economist Tomáš Sedláček over for a cup of coffee one morning in 2010, along with the journalist Roman Chlupatý, to share ideas about the state of economics, and we got along very well. Thanks to Tomáš's fame, our musings got turned into a small book called *Soumrak Homo Economicus*, or 'The Twilight of Economic Man', which was published in four languages, including two audio versions, though none of them in English. Still not sure what we said.[24] More recently, I also collaborated on another book called *The Money Formula: Dodgy Finance, Pseudo Science, and How Mathematicians Took Over the Markets* with Paul Wilmott, the mathematician/finance expert who literally wrote the book, or books, on quantitative finance.[25] Again, I didn't need to convince him of how mathematical models are misused in finance – he was well ahead of me on that score, having been one of the first to warn against the dangers of the Gaussian copula model discussed in Chapter 6.

For this revised edition of *Economyths*, Cahal Moran kindly agreed to write the foreword and take a look at the draft manuscript. I first encountered Cahal back in 2011 when, as an undergraduate economics student at Manchester, he wrote to inform me of his efforts to defend the book against a particularly comprehensive assault he'd come across online (he seemed to know what he was talking about, so I left him to it). I was very impressed by the breadth of his knowledge even then, so it didn't surprise me to find that he has now co-authored an excellent book (*The Econocracy: The Perils of Leaving Economics to the Experts*, cited below), and I am grateful for his comments. I think that he and the other student organisers at the Post-Crash Economics Society and at Rethinking Economics will be people to watch as this story unfolds. Usual (non)disclaimer applies: all mistakes and omissions are my own.

Economists need a few more jesters looking in from outside, tapping on the walls and making faces. Also, as one sympathetic reviewer pointed out, 'We should not forget that Smith and Marx were trained in philosophy, Ricardo was a stockbroker, and von Neumann, a mathematician'.[26]

Still crazy

Of course, I understand that most economists would not see themselves in the bald phrasing of these 'economyths', especially coming from an outsider; and will be keen to distance themselves from the ideas that the economy is perfectly rational or stable or efficient or fair, or that economic growth is always good. Others labouring in a specialised area may see little connection with their own work. They may even be unaware of the role that these often unexamined ideas play – Keynes famously said that 'Practical men who believe themselves to be quite exempt from any intellectual influence, are usually the slaves of some defunct economist', but he might as well have been talking about economists.[27] But as I argue throughout, what counts is the core teachings of their models, and how these models are interpreted when used to make decisions. If they don't agree with the models, then they should point that out – at least they will now have plenty of company. As we'll see, the role that these myths has played in economic thought has only become clearer in the last several years, as the voices of insiders join those of students, heterodox economists, and non-economists in calling for fundamental reform.

As anticipated in the first version, many economists have also argued that these economyths are an unfair caricature of their field – a 'straw man' I am setting up to easily defeat. Four things to add. First, this argument is a little over-used. 'Read any review of a heterodox book by an economist', noted Cahal Moran in 2011, and 'you will find the exact same rhetoric': the author is 'attacking straw men, he doesn't understand economics, etc.'[28] An external investigation into the economics department at the University of Manitoba in 2015 found that 'the insistence by the mainstreamers that the heterodox are attacking a straw man could be labelled "gaslighting" [i.e. psychologically manipulating someone into doubting their own sanity]. Even as some heterodox are subject to unfriendly discrimination, ridicule, hostility, and censure, some mainstreamers simply deny it and insist the others are making it all up.'[29] Call me crazy, but I think they have a point.

Secondly, economists have long deflected criticism by claiming that key assumptions such as the rational behaviour of 'economic man', as Lionel Robbins put it in 1932, are 'only an expository device – a first approximation used very cautiously at one stage in the development of arguments'.[30] (As seen in the Appendix, economists repeat the identical argument today.) But that same 'economic man' – which as a view of human behaviour is less a first approximation than a severe distortion – reached perhaps its most gloriously exaggerated form in the Arrow–Debreu model (Chapter 5) well after Robbins dismissed it as a 'bogey' (the expression 'straw man' was not yet in vogue), and remains at the heart of much economic modelling, which is why eight decades later we could name a book after its impending twilight with no fear of redundancy.

Thirdly, there is also a longstanding tradition in which, as Moran and his co-authors Joe Earle and Zach Ward-Perkins put it in *The Econocracy*: 'The concerns of critics are said to be addressed when economists find some way of incorporating their critiques into existing frameworks. The result is often a highly stylised version of what the critic had in mind, and may drop the things that are most important while conforming to certain assumptions that the critic may reject.'[31] When economists consider small departures from something like equilibrium – they would have to, wouldn't they? – or arrange patches for the more egregious examples of 'market failure' – such as the environmental crisis – they are like the ancient astronomers who added extra epicycles to their geocentric models of the cosmos to better fit observations, while still assuming that the universe was based on circles and the sun went around the earth. In fact it is economists who have set up a highly simplified version of the real world – but instead of destroying it, they hold it up as an ideal to which real economies can only aspire.[32] (And if that is a 'caricature' or a 'straw man', we will stop attacking it when it stops threatening to blow up the world.)

Finally, I take pains in the book to show that the arguments apply not just to this pure textbook version of the theory, but to anything near it, epicycles and all. And as we'll see, supposedly sophisticated models may deviate from these foundational assumptions, but they can never stray too far without losing internal consistency – which is exactly why the field finds itself in a state of crisis.

Define economyth

It might help, though, if I define my terms a little more accurately. According to the *Oxford Dictionary*, the word *myth* has two main meanings.[33] The first and original sense is 'A traditional story, especially one concerning the early history of a people or explaining a natural or social phenomenon, and typically involving supernatural beings or events'. An example is the story of Apollo in Greek mythology (or in economics, as we'll see). This meaning is often endorsed by rulers and priests, and closely linked to religion.[34] It is less a straw man than an idol. The second, more trite meaning, often used as a shallow put-down, is 'A widely held but false belief or idea'.[35] These meanings are obviously different, and I mean a bit of each, but mostly the former. I therefore offer the following definition.

> economyth [noun] *A belief or story that shaped the foundations of economics, and continues to play a key role in economic practice, for example in the models used by economists, though sometimes in weakened form. It is usually linked to an essentially supernatural view of the economy, which is characterised for example by the 'invisible hand', 'efficient markets', hyper-rationality, changes caused by mysterious 'external shocks', and so on. And it's wrong.*

In May 2010, the heterodox economist James K. Galbraith testified to the US Senate: 'Economic theory, as widely taught since the 1980s, failed miserably to understand the forces behind the financial crisis. Concepts including "rational expectations", "market discipline", and the "efficient markets hypothesis" led economists to argue that speculation would stabilize prices, that sellers would act to protect their reputations, that caveat emptor could be relied on, and that widespread fraud therefore could not occur. Not all economists believed this – but most did.'[36] Those were the economyths in action.

Today many economists will realise that, in our modern connected world of big data and dynamic networks, most of these economyths look rather corny. (For example, the idea of progress towards an increasingly rational and efficient world might have sounded convincing, up until the moment when computer scientists hooked up the internet to create the global brain, only to find that it was a *delinquent teenage* brain with no attention span, hooked on games, videos and random browsing.) They therefore won't take them as general truths, but – at least if they want to belong to the mainstream – will spend their careers either treating them as a 'good enough' approximation, or testing what happens when they are relaxed or distorted slightly. Even here, though, the economyths form a central point of reference as a representation of an idealised economy, which we mortals can aspire to but never attain. One finding of this revised edition is how mainstream economists have become increasingly artful as they attempt to disassociate themselves from some of these core ideas, while not quite letting them go.

The tables turn

Anyway, even given the many attractions of these economyths from an aesthetic or institutional standpoint, it still seemed strange to me how economics was so stuck in the past. Sure, other areas have been influenced by classical ideals of symmetry, stability, and so on, but most don't take them quite so literally. Organisations of all sorts resist change (one of the main purposes of an institution, after all, is to maintain itself) but somehow genuine progress is made. And it gradually dawned on me that I had, in fact, missed something terribly important. I had neglected to fully discuss what might be seen as the central idea which holds the whole complex of economic thought together. How could I possibly have given it so little attention? Yes, I mention it here and there, but it surely demands an entire chapter to itself. What was I thinking? If only I had talked to more economists, maybe I would have twigged on it sooner.

But in order to fill the void, it wouldn't be enough just to point it out, to stand back and criticise, to suggest that economists should be using different tools. No, I would have to propose something new. I would have to come up with *original economic ideas* of my own. And in order to convince people, or at least obtain a thin veneer of credibility, I would have to publish them in reputable academic outlets, as opposed to popular publishers (no offence, Icon). It would entail researching (with Roman Chlupatý) a book about the *entire history of money* from Mesopotamian clay tablets to bitcoins for Columbia University Press, and submitting research papers to obscure journals. And that would mean subjecting my work to peer review from economists. It was a short and slippery slope to actually *becoming* an economist, at least of the unloved heterodox sort, without any actual pay or position. This, it seemed, was my fate.

But that is all for later. The upshot is that here in this new, revised, extended, and repainted version are not ten, but eleven ways that economics gets it wrong. All thoroughly checked out and road-tested.

I would also like to add an extra dedication for this book: to all those students and others around the world who are taking a risk, standing up, and demanding a new economics. I'm pretty sure it will be more fun than the last one.

Now, prepare to travel back in time, to an era after Lehman but before Occupy, when the world was in the depths of the Great Recession, and it was time to have a serious talk about economics. Further updates at the end of each chapter and throughout.

INTRODUCTION

Every dogma must have its day.
Aphorism dating to late 19th century

The year 2008 was going to be a prosperous one for the financial markets, according to forecasters polled by Bloomberg.com at the start of the year. None foresaw a loss, and the average prediction was for a gain of 11 per cent. They were blissfully unaware that one of history's biggest financial earthquakes was already taking shape beneath their feet. By year-end the S&P 500 index was down 38 per cent, $29 trillion had slipped through the cracks appearing in global markets, and many of the foundations of the world economy lay in ruins.[1]

The credit crunch had a number of phases, but perhaps the pivotal event was the collapse of the financial services firm Lehman Brothers in September 2008. With over $600 billion in assets, this was the largest bankruptcy in US corporate history. Lehman was also one of the key nodes in the financial network, and its extinction sent the crisis into a new and extremely dangerous phase. Many feared that the entire global financial system would break down completely. That didn't happen, and markets eventually recovered from their near-death experience, but the aftershocks of those events are still being felt around the world, in sovereign debt crises and street protests.

The failure of economists to predict the credit crunch or the ensuing world recession was not atypical. As shown later, financial forecasts have an extremely poor track record of success, even when based on sophisticated mathematical models. This time, though, not only did the models fail to predict the crash – they actually helped cause it.

In the years preceding the crash, financiers had become increasingly reliant on quantitative mathematical models to make their decisions. Even if models couldn't predict what exactly would happen in the future, they were supposed to be able to calculate risk. For example, in order to figure out how much risk a package of loans incurred, they needed only to make a statistical calculation using a simple formula or risk model, based on standard economic theory. This appeared to work well – so well that quantitative analysts began to use the models to take bigger and more sophisticated bets.

Even before the crisis was in full swing, though, there were signs that the models were failing to capture the true risks of the economy. On 11 August 2007, a year before Lehman Brothers went bust, some unexpected market turbulence brought on by a decline in US house prices led one of their employees to remark that 'Events that models predicted would happen only once in 10,000 years happened every day for three days.'[2]

While that sounds most unusual, the chief financial officer at Goldman Sachs went even further: 'We were seeing things that were 25-standard deviation moves, several days in a row.'[3] To unpack that statement, a 25-standard deviation event is something that is not expected to happen even once in the duration of the universe – let alone each day of a week.

You don't need to be a mathematician to see that the models that lay at the core of the world financial system had something seriously wrong with them. But how could so many highly-paid experts have turned out to be completely mistaken about the workings of the economy? As Queen Elizabeth said on a visit to the London School of Economics: 'Why did no one see it coming?'[4]

Storm warnings

Actually, not everyone was as surprised by the crisis as were the quantitative analysts and their mathematical models. In 2005 Raghuram Rajan from the International Monetary Fund warned his audience of central bankers including Alan Greenspan and Ben Bernanke that financial innovation had introduced new risks into the financial system, only to be called a 'Luddite' by Larry Summers.[5] In January 2007 Jean-Claude Trichet, the European Central Bank president, observed that 'We are currently seeing elements in global financial markets which are not necessarily stable ... we don't know fully where the risks are located.' (Though just weeks earlier officials at the Federal Reserve had congratulated Alan Greenspan on an economy that looked, according to Janet Yellen, 'a lot like a tennis racquet with a gigantic sweet spot.'[6]) Some, such as author Nassim Taleb, mathematician Paul Wilmott, and economists William White, Ann Pettifor, Steve Keen and Nouriel Roubini, to name a few, were more specific in their warnings; however, their voices were ignored or even ridiculed in the rush for profits that characterised the boom years (though not by a small number of traders who went short and profited from the collapse).[7]

As with preceding crashes, the causes of the credit crunch have been much analysed and debated. The obvious lightning rod for criticism was of course the bankers themselves, who were earning fabulous salaries, and even more fabulous bonuses, for taking risks that turned out to have cataclysmic consequences for the real economy when the bets went wrong. Other culprits were the regulators, who failed to keep up with the pace of innovation in financial products; the American homeowners who took out subprime loans they could never afford to repay; the central banks, who (Trichet's comments aside) often seemed to be in denial about the extent of the problem; and the economists who designed the flawed mathematical models in the first place.

This still leaves the question of how so many people in the financial industry could have been misled about the risks they were running and unaware of the dangers. The reason, I believe, is that the fundamental assumptions that form the basis of economic theory are flawed. This means that not just the mathematical models, but the actual mental models that most economists have of the economy are completely wrong.

This problem goes well beyond the calculation of financial risk. The main problem with our economic system is not that it is hard to predict, but that, despite its enormous productivity and creativity, it appears to be in a state of ill health. The economy is unfair, unstable, and unsustainable. But economic theory has no way of dealing with these issues either.

The economy is unfair. Economic theory is supposed to be about optimising the allocation of resources. However, the reality is that the rich really do get richer. In 2009 one hedge fund manager earned over $2 billion, while over a billion people earned less than $1 a day.[8] As discussed later, mainstream economics is a theory aligned with the interests of the very rich – which is one reason it has been so well-funded.

The economy is unstable. According to theory, the 'invisible hand' should keep asset prices at a stable level. But in reality, assets including oil, gold, and hard currencies are subject to enormous gyrations. In late 2007 the price of oil surged to over $120 a barrel, then plunged to under $40, all in the space of a few months. Oil is often called the lifeblood of the economy, but our own blood supply is much better regulated. For a while it seemed the economy was having a cardiac event.

The economy is unsustainable. The central aim of economics has long been to maximise long-term growth. However, we are now bumping up against hard constraints due to things like overcrowding, climate change and environmental degradation. As author and environmentalist Edward Abbey pointed out, 'Growth for the sake of growth is the ideology of the cancer cell'.[9]

Together, these problems far exceed the importance of an event like the credit crunch. The debt that the global economy is building up with the environment, or the debt of rich countries to poor countries, are of much greater concern than the debt of banks to governments or shareholders. Indeed, it may turn out that this crisis was a blessing in disguise, if it provides the impetus for us to rethink our approach to money.

Just as economic theory fails to address the shortcomings of the economy, it also fails to properly account for its good qualities, of which there are many, including enormous dynamism and productivity. A model that emphasises stability isn't very good at capturing the market's creativity – as any artist or student of rock history will know, these two qualities rarely go hand in hand. So why do we persist with an economic theory that is so obviously unfit for purpose?

Counterfeit coin

Economics is a mathematical representation of human behaviour, and like any mathematical model it is based on certain assumptions. I will argue, however, that in the case of economics the assumptions are so completely out of touch with reality, and with the needs and behaviour of most people, that the result is a highly misleading caricature. The theory is less a science than an ideology. The reason why so many people are conned into thinking the assumptions reasonable is that they are based on ideas from areas like physics or engineering that are part of our 2,500-year scientific heritage dating back to the ancient Greeks. Superficially they have the look and feel of real science, but they are counterfeit coin.

To make progress, it's not enough to adjust or revise these assumptions. Much work has already been done in exploring minor variations. Instead, we need to reinvent the subject from the bottom up. While economics has traditionally modelled itself after physics and mechanics, the economy has more in common with a living organism than it does with a machine. This book will show how a new generation of economists, mathematicians, ecologists and other scientists are applying lessons and techniques from areas such as complexity science to develop a more realistic model of the economy.

Each chapter begins with one of the misconceptions or 'economyths' (defined in the Preface) behind orthodox economic theory. It then goes back into the history to see where the idea came from, explains how it affects our everyday life, finds out why it persists despite evidence to the contrary, and proposes how we can change or replace it. The specific ideas are:

- The economy can be described by economic laws
- The economy is made up of independent individuals
- The economy is stable
- Economic risk can be easily managed using statistics
- The economy is rational and efficient
- The economy is gender-neutral
- The economy is fair
- Economic growth can continue for ever
- Economic growth will make us happy
- Economic growth is always good

And new in this edition:

- The economy boils down to barter

These ideas form the basis of orthodox economic theory and affect decision-making at the individual, corporate, and societal level; but the book will show they are mistaken and will present alternatives. We will find out how the economy is the emergent result of complex processes that defy reduction; how the value of your home or pension is affected by unpredictable economic storms; why the economy is not rational or fair; and why economic growth is not automatically desirable, either for our own well-being or for that of the planet.

Before proceeding, I should address a few concerns. The first is that, faced with the above list, most economists would protest that it is an over-simplified straw man, and that economics is far more sophisticated than that. Defenders of the theory have been hiding behind this argument for too long. No one thinks that markets are perfectly stable, or that investors are perfectly rational, or that markets are fair and everyone has access to the same information. But what counts is the calculations that are actually performed – and key components of theory such as the efficient market hypothesis are explicitly based on exactly these assumptions. Peer under the hood of the risk models used by banks, or the models used to allocate your pension funds or determine government policy, and you will find the same assumptions there, with at best small modifications. As we'll see, a number of so-called heterodox economists, who make up perhaps 10 per cent of economists,[10] have been arguing against these assumptions for years, but until now their voices have carried little weight. We will go beyond a critique of these ideas, to explore where they came from in the first place and how they can be replaced. (I am also told that many economists do not really believe the mainstream theory, but play along in order to get publications and tenure – in which case they should enjoy this book.)

Some readers might find it hard to believe that mainstream economics is as flat-out wrong as I describe it here. After all, the great strength of science is that it is supposed to be self-correcting.

If a theory is flawed, then it will be replaced by a better one. Even Newton's laws of motion had to be modified with the development of quantum theory. A problem occurs, however, when no alternative is demonstrably better at making predictions, which is traditionally the acid test for a new theory. The new approaches discussed here do not yet amount to a single, unified replacement for orthodox theory, and nor do they claim to be much better at predicting the economy – in fact they openly acknowledge the uncertainty inherent in complex systems.

Another possible concern is that this book is written from the perspective of an applied mathematician, whose day job is in the area of systems biology (come to think of it, I never studied biology either). Some readers will prefer to get their economic analysis from economists, but I would argue that having a training in economics is actually a liability (which some particularly gifted people are capable of overcoming). If, as I believe, economics encodes a particular ideology, then being trained in it is effectively a way of closing your mind. Many of the new ideas that are revitalising economics come from diverse areas such as complexity, network theory, psychology, and indeed systems biology which are far outside the standard economics curriculum. When a field is in as poor a state as economics, being an outsider is a distinct advantage because it allows you to analyse the problems without having to justify previous theories that you were exposed to early in your career and feel compelled to defend.

Enough justification. Economics, as already stated, is a mathematical model of human behaviour. The next chapter offers a brief tour through the history of such models, and asks whether there is any such thing as an economic law.

CHAPTER 1

THE ANARCHIC ECONOMY

Above, far above the prejudices and passions of men soar the laws of nature. Eternal and immutable, they are the expression of the creative power; they represent what is, what must be, what otherwise could not be. Man can come to understand them: he is incapable of changing them.
Vilfredo Pareto (1897)

Spread the truth – the laws of economics are like the laws of engineering. One set of laws works everywhere.
Lawrence Summers (1991)

Economics gains its credibility from its association with hard sciences like physics and mathematics. But is it really possible to describe the economy in terms of mathematical laws, as economists including Larry Summers – former economics advisor to President Obama – claim? Isaac Newton didn't think so. As he noted in 1721, after losing most of his fortune in the collapse of the South Sea bubble: 'I can calculate the motions of heavenly bodies, but not the madness of people.'

To see whether the economy is law-bound or anarchic, bear with me first for a little ancient history. It turns out that many of the ideas that form the basis of modern economics have roots that stretch back to the beginnings of Western civilisation. That's one reason why they are proving so hard to dislodge.

The first economic forecaster, in the Western tradition, was probably the oracle at Delphi in ancient Greece. The most successful forecasting operation of all time, it lasted for almost a thousand years, beginning in the 8th century BC. The predictions were made by a woman, known as the Pythia, who was chosen from the local population as a channel for the god Apollo. Her predictions were often vague or even two-sided and therefore hard to falsify, which perhaps explains how the oracle managed to persist for such a long time (rather like Alan Greenspan).

Our tradition of numerical prediction can be said to have begun with Pythagoras. He was named after the Pythia, who in one of her more famous moments of insight had predicted his birth. (She told a gem-engraver, who was actually looking for business advice, that his wife would give birth to a boy 'unsurpassed in beauty and wisdom'. This was a surprise, especially because no one, including the wife, knew she was pregnant.)

As a young man, Pythagoras travelled the world, learning from sages and mystics, before settling in Crotona, southern Italy, where he set up what amounted to a pseudo-religious cult that worshipped number. His followers believed that he was a demi-god descended directly from Apollo, with superhuman powers such as the ability to dart into the future. Joining his inner circle required great commitment: candidates had to give up all material possessions, become vegetarian ascetics, and study under a vow of silence for five years.

The Pythagoreans believed that number was the basis for the structure of the universe, and gave each number a special, almost magical significance. They are credited with many mathematical discoveries, including the famous theorem about right-angled triangles and the square of the hypotenuse which we are all exposed to at school. However, their major insight, which backed up their idea that number underlay the structure of the universe, was actually about music.

If you pluck the string of a guitar, then fret it exactly half-way up and pluck it again, the two notes will differ by an octave. The Pythagoreans discovered that the notes that harmonise well together are all related by the same kind of simple mathematical ratio. This was an astonishing insight, because if music, which was considered the most expressive and mysterious of art forms, was governed by simple mathematical laws, then it followed that all kinds of other things were also governed by number. As John Burnet wrote in *Early Greek Philosophy*: 'It is not too much to say that Greek philosophy was henceforward to be dominated by the notion of the perfectly tuned string.'[1] (And modern physics; see string theory.)

The Pythagoreans believed that the entire cosmos (a word coined by Pythagoras) produced a kind of tune, the music of the spheres, which could be heard by Pythagoras but not by ordinary mortals. And their interest in number was not purely theoretical or spiritual. They developed techniques for numerical prediction, which remained secret to the uninitiated, and it is also believed that Pythagoras was involved with the design and production of the first coins to appear in his area. Money is a way of assigning numbers to things, so it obviously fit with the Pythagorean philosophy that 'number is all'.

Rational mechanics

If the cosmos was based on number, then it could be predicted using mathematics. The ancient Greeks developed highly complex models that could simulate quite accurately the motion of the stars, moon and planets across the sky. They assumed that the heavenly bodies moved in circles, which were considered to be the most perfect and symmetrical of forms; and also that the circles were centred on the earth. Making this work required some fancy mathematics – it led to the invention of trigonometry – and a lot of circles. The Aristotelian version, for example, incorporated some 55 nested spheres. The final model by Ptolemy used epicycles, so that planets would go around a small circle that in turn was circling the earth.

The main application of these models was astrology. For centuries astronomy and astrology were seen as two branches of the same science. In order for astrologers to make predictions, they needed to know the positions of the celestial bodies at different times, which could be determined by consulting the model. The Ptolemaic model was so successful in this respect that it was adopted by the church, and remained almost unquestioned until the Renaissance.

Classical astronomy was finally overturned when Isaac Newton combined Kepler's theory of planetary motion with Galileo's study of the motion of falling objects, to derive his three laws of motion and the law of gravity. Newton's insight that the force that made an apple fall to the ground, and the force that propelled the moon around the earth, were one and the same thing, was as remarkable as the Pythagorean insight that music is governed by number. In fact Newton was a great Pythagorean, and believed Pythagoras knew the law of gravity but had kept it secret.

Newton held that matter was made up of 'solid, massy, hard, impenetrable, movable particles', and his laws of motion described what he called a 'rational mechanics' that governed their behaviour. It followed, then, that the motion of anything, from a cannonball to a ray of light, could be predicted using mechanics. His work therefore served as a blueprint for numerical prediction – reduce a system to its fundamental components, discover the physical laws that rule them, express as mathematical equations, and solve. Scientists from all fields, from electromagnetism to chemistry to geology, immediately adopted the Newtonian approach, to enormously powerful effect. You can hear the whisper coming from the Pythagoreans: 'Spread the truth – one set of laws works everywhere.'

Rational economics

Among those to hear the whisper, if somewhat belatedly, were the new group of people calling themselves economists in the late 19th century. If Newtonian mechanics was proving so successful in other areas like physics and engineering, maybe it could also be applied to the flow of trade.

The theory they developed is known as neoclassical economics. Today it still forms the basis of orthodox theory, and makes up the core curriculum taught to future economists and business leaders in universities and business schools around the world.[2] As a set of ideas, it might be the most powerful in modern history.

Neoclassical economics is based on an explicit comparison with Newtonian physics. Just as Newton believed that matter is made up of minute particles that bump off one another but are otherwise unchanged, so neoclassical theory assumes that the economy is made up of unconnected individuals who interact by exchanging goods and services and money but are otherwise unchanged. Their behaviour can be predicted using economic laws, the human analogue of the laws that govern the cosmos.

To calculate the motions of the economy, one must determine the forces that make it move around. The neoclassical economists based their mechanics on the idea of utility, which the philosopher Jeremy Bentham described in his 'hedonic calculus' as the sum of pleasure minus pain. For example, if an apple gives you three units of pleasure, and paying for it gives you only two units of pain, then purchasing the apple will leave you one utility unit (sometimes called a util) in profit.

Leaving aside for a moment what units of measurement a util is expressed in, an obvious problem is that different people will assign different utility values to objects such as apples. The early neoclassical economists got around this by arguing that all that counted was the average utility. It was then possible to use utility theory to derive economic laws. As William Stanley Jevons put it in his 1871 book *Theory of Political Economy*, these laws were to be considered 'as sure and demonstrative as that of kinematics or statics, nay, almost as self-evident as are the elements of Euclid, when the real meaning of the formulae is fully seized'.

Thus was born the economyth that the economy can be accurately described by economic laws; which to quote the English economist Lionel Robbins – who famously defined economics in 1932 as the science of scarcity – were 'as universal as the laws of mathematics or mechanics'.[3] Chief among these universal laws were what Jevons called the 'unquestionable truth of the Laws of Supply and Demand'.

Imaginary lines

If economics has an equivalent of Newton's law of gravity, it is the law of supply and demand. Economist Brad DeLong calls it the 'one real law of economics'.[4] According to Arnold Kling, 'the law of supply and demand always operates, even though markets have different institutional structures'.[5] Christopher Ragan and Richard Lipsey state in a textbook that 'The term "law" in science is used to describe a theory that has stood up to substantial testing'; and in this case 'the predicted behaviour occurs sufficiently often that economists continue to have confidence in the underlying theory'.[6] Rather like the law of gravity, 'The theory of the determination of price by demand and supply is beautiful in its simplicity' but is 'powerful in its wide range of applications'.

The law is illustrated in Figure 1, which is a version of a graph first published in an 1870 essay by Fleeming Jenkin. It has since become the most famous figure in economics, and is taught at every undergraduate economics class. The figure shows two curving lines, which describe how price is related to supply and demand. When price is low, supply is low as well, because producers have little incentive to enter the market; but when price is high, supply also increases (solid line). Conversely, demand is lower at high prices because fewer consumers are willing to pay that much (dashed line).

The point where the two lines cross gives the unique price at which supply and demand are in perfect balance. Neoclassical economists claimed that in a competitive market prices would be driven to this point, which is optimal in the sense that there is no under- or over-supply, so resources are optimally allocated. Furthermore, the price would represent a stable equilibrium. The market was therefore a machine for optimising utility.

Figure 1. The law of supply and demand. The solid line shows supply, which increases with price. The dashed line shows demand, which decreases with price. The intersection of the two lines represents the point where supply and demand are in balance.

For example, suppose the equilibrium price for a house is 500,000 (currency units of your choice), but for some reason (perhaps recent volatility) the market is not currently at equilibrium and the price is instead 550,000. The quantity supplied at this price would be higher than the quantity demanded, so to entice consumers the sellers would have to reduce the price until it reached the equilibrium level where the quantity demanded matched the quantity supplied. The net effect would be to pull prices down to their resting place, as sure as the force of gravity. Conversely, if prices were too low, then supply would drop, demand would increase, and prices would bob back up again.

However, if demand were to increase for some structural reason, such as population growth, then the entire demand curve in Figure 1 would shift up, so the equilibrium price would be higher. If supply permanently increased, say because new land opened for development, then the equilibrium price would shift down along with the supply curve.

This is for just one good, and the situation becomes considerably more complicated when multiple goods and services are included, now and in the future, since consumers then have a choice on where and when to spend their money. One of the supposed triumphs of neoclassical economics in the 1960s was to mathematically prove that the entire economy will still be driven to a stable and optimal equilibrium, again subject to certain assumptions. This was seen as mathematical proof of Adam Smith's 'invisible hand', which maintains prices at their 'natural' level, and formed the basis of General Equilibrium Models that are used to simulate the economy today.

The visibly shaking hand

We are all familiar and comfortable with the law of supply and demand, and it is often used to explain why prices are what they are. A strange thing, though: historical data for assets like housing just doesn't look that stable or optimal. In fact it seems the invisible hand has a bad case of the shakes.

As an illustration, the top panel in Figure 2 shows a plot of UK house prices over about three decades. The numbers have been corrected for inflation. It shows the large ramp up in house prices from 1996 until 2009. Similar behaviour was seen in other leading economies.

It appears from this figure that houses were much more affordable before 1985 than after 2000. However, the figure is a little misleading because affordability is a function not just of real house prices but also of mortgage rates, which were about twice as high in 1985 as they were in 2000. To correct for this, the lower panel shows the estimated typical mortgage payment, based on the prevailing interest rates. This reveals a distinct boom/bust pattern.

In 2008, at the peak of such a housing boom, when prices appear to have been grossly inflated, it was frequently argued that prices were high because of the balance between supply and demand: the UK is a 'small, crowded island' so the supply of housing is constrained. But the UK was also a small, crowded island in 1995, when homes were relatively affordable. So were prices really optimal in 2008, as the law of supply and demand would seem to imply, so change was due to other factors? Or was something else going on?

The lines and the unicorn
In one sense, the law of supply and demand captures an obvious truth – if something is in demand, then it will usually attract a higher price. The problem arises when you decide to go Newtonian, express the principle in mathematical terms, and use it to prove optimality or make predictions.

Figure 2. Top panel shows the real growth in UK house prices from 1975 to 2009. Prices are in 1975 currency, adjusted for inflation.[7] Lower panel is the estimated relative mortgage payment. The scaling is relative only.

In order to translate the relationship between supply and demand into a mathematical law, neoclassical economists had to make a number of assumptions. In particular, the curves for supply and demand needed to be fixed and independent of one another. This was justified by the idea that the utility for producers and consumers should not change over the time period considered.

But here we come to one of the differences between economics and physics. The particles described in physics are stable and invariant, so an atom of, say, carbon on earth is indistinguishable from one in the sun, and has the same gravitational pull. The law of gravity therefore applies the same here on earth as it does elsewhere in the cosmos, which is why it is such a powerful tool. However, people are not atoms; they vary from place to place, and they also change their opinions and behaviour over time. The housing market is also linked to the rest of the global economy, which itself is in a state of ceaseless flux.

The law of supply and demand implies that if prices increase above their 'equilibrium' value then demand should decrease. This works reasonably well for most goods and services (if you omit things like luxury goods whose cachet increases as they become less affordable). If a baker overcharges for bread, he will come under pressure from competitors (unless he can distinguish his services, for example by advertising); charge too much for your labour and you'll find it hard to get a job (unless, as seen in Chapter 7, you're a CEO or movie star). However, the relationship breaks down completely when you consider assets, such as real estate or gold bars, which are desired in part for their investment value. Both supply and demand are a function not just of price, but of the rate and direction at which prices are changing (this is explored further in Chapter 3). The perceived utility of owning a home is much greater when house prices are seen to be rising than when they are falling off a cliff. Soaring prices can therefore lead to reduced listings, as owners decide to hold on to their suddenly valuable property, and increased demand, as buyers are afraid of missing out.

Supply and demand are also a function, not just of price changes, but of each other; a shortage of supply, for example, can lead to increased demand (marketers call it exclusivity). Matters become even more tenuous in today's networked economy, where what is being supplied or demanded is often not a physical object at all, but something less tangible or constrained like information, a brand, or access to a network, which are shared rather than exchanged, so supply is essentially infinite.

Supply and demand also depend in intricate ways on the exact context and history, even for basic goods. Suppose for instance that the price of bread is everywhere uniformly raised by 5 per cent. Let's consider three cases, all of which lead to different structural changes in the relationship between supply and demand. In the first case, the government announces that the price rise is due to a new bread tax being applied. People will likely react by buying less bread (see box, page 34, for a non-hypothetical example of this). In the second case, a rumour goes out that the price change is because of a drought that has affected wheat prices. Whether the rumour is true or not, demand may increase because some people will buy extra loaves and store them in the freezer before prices increase further; i.e. perceived high demand leads to hoarding and reduced supply. In a third, hypothetical case, suppose that shoppers are given a drug so that any memory or preconception they have about the price of bread is rather hazy, so they respond only to big price changes (a lot of people are like this anyway). Then they would probably not notice the difference and just go ahead and buy the bread as usual. There is also a dynamic, time-sensitive element, because it is hard to know whether a change in demand will be long-lasting or short-lived.

To summarise, because supply and demand are coupled, in flux, and context-dependent, it doesn't make sense to treat them as stable and independent curves. (Economists sometimes try to get around this by saying their curves hold *ceteris paribus* – other things held constant – but the point is they aren't held constant.[8]) In fact the idea that something like 'demand' can be expressed in terms of neat lines at all, as in Figure 1, is a fiction. As econophysicist Joe McCauley observed, there is no empirical evidence for the existence of such curves. Despite that, 'intersecting neo-classical supply–demand curves remain the foundation of nearly every standard economics textbook.'[9] Like unicorns, the plot of supply and demand is a mythological beast that is often drawn, but never actually seen.

This helps explain why large economic models, which involve many such supply–demand curves, fail to make accurate predictions (traditionally the test of reductionist theories). As an example from something even slippier than house prices, Figure 3 shows the price of crude oil over a third of a century, along with predictions from the Energy Information Administration (EIA), which is part of the US Department of Energy. The computations are performed by estimating the global levels of supply and demand, using their World Oil Refining, Logistics, and Demand (WORLD) model. In the 1980s, the predictions called for prices to increase, probably because the models incorporated memory of the 1970s oil price shock. Prices instead fell and remained low for the next couple of decades. The forecasts eventually learned that prices were not going to return to previous levels, and flattened out; but as soon as they did, prices spiked up to $128 per barrel. Then plummeted to $36. Then doubled again.

This oil price spike played a large part in exacerbating the credit crunch, but went completely unpredicted by the experts. One reason is that, according to the EIA, world oil supply actually *rose*, and demand *dropped*, in the six-month period preceding the spike.[10] So why did prices go up? Well, the demand for actual oil

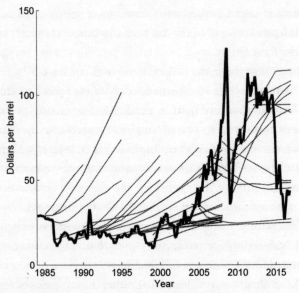

Figure 3. Price of crude oil (solid line), along with central predictions (dashed lines). Source: Energy Information Administration.

– the black, gooey stuff they get out of the ground – wasn't getting stronger. But as discussed in Chapter 8, oil futures – contracts giving the right to buy oil at a set price and future date – were all the rage in 2008. The spike in oil was a classic speculative bubble, with the same dynamics as a real estate bubble, except that it was played out in months instead of years.

The economic weather

Our poor record of foresight might still seem counter-intuitive: how can it be that specialists can't predict the future of the economy given their immense expertise, huge amounts of data, and access to high-speed computers? Surely we know more than the Delphic oracle? One reason is that the economy is made up of people, rather than inanimate objects. But it's interesting to note that the same problem is seen in other areas that appear more amenable to a Newtonian approach. Much can be learnt from a comparison with weather forecasting.

In a 2009 speech, the Federal Reserve chairman Ben Bernanke, that year's version of the oracle, discussed his institution's long-standing involvement in economic forecasting as follows: 'With so much at stake, you will not be surprised to know that, over the years, many very smart people have applied the most sophisticated statistical and modelling tools available to try to better divine the economic future. But the results, unfortunately, have more often than not been underwhelming. Like weather forecasters, economic forecasters must deal with a system that is extraordinarily complex, that is subject to random shocks, and about which our data and understanding will always be imperfect.'[11]

As an illustration of Bernanke's point, the top panel of Figure 4 is a plot of sea-surface temperature in a zone of the Atlantic ocean, which indicates the presence of El Niño events. I have chosen a timespan such that the fluctuations match quite closely the plot of housing price affordability from Figure 2, shown rescaled in the lower panel (unfortunately the timescale is different, so, no, we can't use El Niño to predict UK housing prices). El Niño drives global weather patterns that have a huge economic impact on everything from agriculture to insurance, so there is even more incentive to predict it than there is to predict house prices. And yet our most sophisticated weather models still do a poor job of predicting El Niño.[12] As with housing prices, it is possible to discern a distinct pattern, but it is almost impossible to call the exact timing of the next peak or trough. The reason is that both El Niño and housing markets are part of complex, global systems that elude reduction to simple rules or laws.

Indeed the whole idea of a fundamental law, given by a simple equation, is applicable only to certain specialised cases, such as

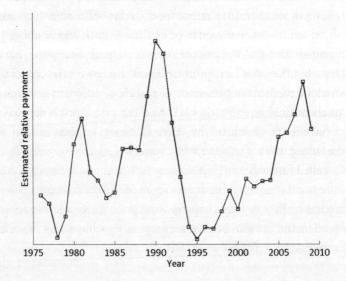

Figure 4. Top panel is a plot of sea-surface temperature anomalies.[13] Above 0.5 indicates an El Niño event, below –0.5 La Niña. Lower panel is a rescaled plot of estimated mortgage payments from Figure 2.

gravity. In weather forecasting, one of the main challenges is to predict the formation and dissipation of clouds, which drive much of the weather and determine precipitation. However, there is no law or equation for clouds, which are formed in a complex process whereby droplets of water congregate around minute particles such as salt, dust or pollen in the air. In fact, clouds are best described as *emergent properties* of the atmospheric dynamics.

The definition of an emergent property is somewhat hazy, and depends on the context; but in general it refers to some feature of a complex system that cannot be predicted in advance from knowledge of the system components alone. An early description was supplied by philosopher and economist John Stuart Mill, who wrote in 1843 that while all organic bodies are composed of parts, 'no mere summing up of the separate actions of those elements will ever amount to the action of the living body itself' (though he was talking about chemistry rather than 'the law of demand and supply, which is acknowledged to be applicable to all commodities').[14] Scientists know a lot about the parts of a cloud – air, water, particles – but they still can't produce a realistic one on the computer, let alone predict the behaviour of real clouds. Engineers know a lot about fluid flow, but they still find it hard to model the effects of turbulence, which is why Formula 1 racing teams are among the largest users of wind tunnels. Some scientists even believe that so-called fundamental physical laws – including the law of gravity – are just the emergent result of a more complex dynamics. As we'll discuss further in later chapters, economic forces such as supply and demand are also best seen as emerging from a mix of social, economic, and psychological factors.

Emerging economy

The concept of emergence did play an important role in the history of economics, especially in the theories of Austrian economists including Carl Menger, who used it to describe the spontaneous emergence of money as a way to facilitate transactions; and F.A. Hayek, who used it to describe the self-organisation of the economy.[15] While interest in the area was sidelined by the neoclassical focus on reductionist equilibrium approaches – Ricardo Caballero, for example, wrote in 2004 that 'economics is, and is likely to remain, fundamentally reductionist (that is, it seeks to understand the behavior of the whole from that of the parts)' – it is now making a comeback under the influence of complexity scientists, who use techniques such as cellular automata and agent-based models to study emergent phenomena.[16]

Cellular automata are computer programs that typically divide the screen into a grid of cells. The evolution of the system is governed by simple rules that describe how one cell affects its neighbours. While the laws are simple at the local level, the emergent behaviour at the global level can be extremely complex, and can't be modelled directly using equations. Cellular automata have been used to study a wide range of phenomena, including turbulent fluid flow, avalanches, the spread of forest fires, and urban development.

Agent-based models consist of multiple software 'agents' that could represent, say, investors in the stockmarket. The agents are allowed to influence each other's behaviour, just as in reality investors communicate with those around them. They make decisions based not on uniform laws, but on fuzzy heuristics or rules of thumb. Agents can also learn and adapt their behaviour, in the same way that investors become more conservative after being burned by a market fall. It is therefore impossible to assign them a fixed and independent demand curve of the sort required by the 'law of supply and demand'.

The collective effect of the agents is again to produce emergent behaviour that is often quite surprising, and that can lead to useful insights about how the system works. Agent-based models have been used to reproduce the boom/bust behaviour of markets, and have found many other applications in areas from transport to cancer therapy.[17] Programmes in complexity are starting to appear at some universities and institutions like the London School of Economics. The first way to revive economics, then, is to encourage this trend, and in the process rid the field of its quasi-Newtonian pseudo-laws.

One drawback of this type of research is that it has none of the icy glamour and prestige of great Newtonian mathematical laws. Nor does complexity theory offer a single unified approach. Models are seen more as patches, each of which captures an aspect of the complex reality.

Also, while the complex systems approach is useful for simulating many aspects of the economy, it is unlikely that it will prove to be much better than orthodox theory at predicting the course of something like the housing markets. The reason is that the exact behaviour of a system depends on all the exact details, and the only way to predict a system would be to reproduce it on the computer. That's the point of emergent properties: they can't be predicted by a simple equation. Instead, complexity scientists search for pockets of predictability – aspects of the system that are amenable to prediction.[18]

Complexity research has many implications for economics (most of the conclusions of this book are based on a complexity viewpoint), but its most devastating consequence is that it destroys the economyth – sometimes promoted, sometimes denied, but mostly just tacitly assumed – that 'the laws of economics are like the laws of engineering', as Larry Summers expressed it (echoing a long series of economists such as Lionel Robbins, Frank Knight, and of course the subject's neoclassical founders). This in turn throws a spanner in the entire mechanistic approach for modelling complex systems like the economy. Newton's blueprint for numerical prediction, again, was to reduce a system to its fundamental components, discover the physical laws that rule them, express as mathematical equations, and solve. But this reductionist method doesn't work for emergent properties. There are no fixed laws – only general fuzzy principles that can be roughly captured by rules of thumb but rarely conform to neat mathematical equations. The message of the Pythagoreans – that all can be reduced to number – turns out not to be true.

In the next chapter, we consider the behaviour of groups of people as they engage in the economy – and ask whether they behave as independent individuals, as theory tells us, or more like the components of a cloud.

Supply and demand update – fact or fiction?

When I first wrote this chapter I had to look quite hard to find criticisms of something as basic as the law of supply and demand. One professor even remarked in 2010, rather rigidly, that 'There are only one or two exceptions to this rule that have ever been documented', which would certainly put it up there with a fundamental law of the universe.[19] Another academic pointed out that my 'amazing' treatment of the law would see me 'flunked out of Economics 101' (true) and proved that I do 'not understand even the most basic economic ideas' (also true – because they don't make sense – though as an image-control tip, economist Noah Smith did advise his peers in a 2017 Bloomberg piece that they should avoid talking down to others, and 'should definitely never tell people that they "flunked Econ 101"').[20] Indeed it does seem rather extreme to say that what is commonly referred to as the main law of economics is an *unobservable fictional unicorn* – if that were really the case, then how could economists use it to argue for example that market forces drive prices to a stable equilibrium?

Now, though, some mainstream economists suddenly seem to be happily agreeing that *of course* it's not real! Which might seem to be an epiphany of sorts, were it not for the fact that at the same time they are saying it's not a problem. It is the economics equivalent of admitting that the best bits of your bestselling, supposedly fact-based memoir were actually *all made up*, while refusing to apologise because it's such a great story.

Consider for example the 2015 paper 'A Neoclassical Curmudgeon Looks at Heterodox Criticisms of Microeconomics', in which Donald Katzner notes that while the explanation of supply and demand 'has passed from the realm of academic economics into the public domain', it is 'nevertheless all based on a fiction' with 'a fictitious market, a fictitious commodity and price, and fictitious functions'. That sounds rather like an economyth. However, he still concludes that it is a 'reasonable start'.[21] Which it was, 150 years ago.

Even the *Economist* magazine felt fit in 2016 to ponder the elusive lines of supply and demand. 'Drawing these lines is necessary to answer many big economic questions', it worried, but unfortunately the 'lines themselves are unobservable' because every data point represents a single measure of two quantities, supply and demand, neither of which is fixed in time.[22] Cue other economyths: 'many economists cling to stark, crude theories about market efficiency or rational behaviour precisely because it helps them pin down all those slopes and other parameters. If they did not care about these defining numbers, they could afford to entertain messy, homespun beliefs about human nature and market institutions. But then they would be called sociologists.' Or storytellers.

Finally, let's tune in to a 2016 *Freakonomics* podcast, with journalist Stephen J. Dubner probing the mind of Chicago economist Steve Levitt on the subject of demand curves. It opens with Levitt relating how, as a student and then a university professor, he had 'never questioned anything about demand curves' (this must be what Jevons meant by the theory's 'unquestionable truth').[23] While researching his 2012 textbook *Microeconomics*, though, he thought he should include a demand curve to show what one 'really looks like in the real world'. Unfortunately he 'looked and looked and in the end we didn't really have a very good example'.

Dubner: 'So you're saying that the demand curve as it exists in economics and economic literature is kind of a fiction or an invention of economists to explain the rest of the transactions around it?' Levitt: 'Exactly.' Though, as he quickly points out, 'we aren't faking it … we know they exist because we define them and they're there'. It's like in physics 'when the models had figured out something about protons and electrons, but we hadn't actually figured out how to literally see an electron'. (This is actually not a bad comparison, if you substitute supersymmetric particles for the electron.)

Levitt then discusses a working paper he co-authored which estimated a 'real-life demand curve' based on data from Uber's dynamic pricing system.[24] Dubner: 'So sounds like you found the unicorn … You found in the natural world the perfect demand curve. Yes?' Levitt: 'I wish that that were really true.' Unfortunately the curve only describes a typical customer's response to spot changes as the price adjusts in front of him, as opposed to longer-term price shifts. It's not a unicorn, it's a pony with a party hat.

So how do we square all this – by which I mean the 'unobservable' (*Economist*) 'fictional' (Katzner) 'unicorn' (Dubner), or as I put it, the 'mythological beast that is often drawn, but never actually seen' – with the claim in a globally bestselling textbook (Samuelson and Nordhaus) that 'the law' that demand curves always slope downward has been 'empirically tested and verified for practically all commodities' (though the example given is labelled as hypothetical)?[25] Well, economists have actually been estimating demand curves for things like agricultural commodities since at least the 1920s, but to do it properly you would need to hold supply constant for each point, while in the real world supply and demand are in a constant dance with one another. The idea of a fixed curve is a mental construct that we are imposing on the data – and as discussed in this chapter it quickly breaks down when applied to things like financial assets (and that includes oil, houses, stocks, etc.).

Of course, all models are made up to a degree – they are all mental constructs – but the danger here is that, because of the way supply–demand is presented as being empirically based, scientifically proven, etc., an impressionable student might come across it and decide to devote their career to the quest for a perfect equilibrium model based on these imaginary curves. So to be on the safe side, at least until they are amended, can we suggest that these textbooks be filed in the fiction section, along with the poems about unicorns?

Right versus left

As mentioned in the Preface, the chapter topics were loosely based on the Pythagorean list of opposites. Most don't require much explanation, but the theme for this chapter – deterministic economic laws versus emergent properties – was inspired by the pair Right versus Left. The Pythagoreans associated the left hand with weakness and mutability (maybe they were all right-handers). The right side of the body is controlled by the left side of the brain, which is associated with a style of thinking that according to psychiatrist and literary scholar Ian McGilchrist is 'rigid, rarified, mechanical, governed by explicit laws'.[26] It is prose instead of poetry; non-fiction instead of fiction.

With their assumptions of rational behaviour and stability, emphasis on mechanistic cause-and-effect, impression of mathematical precision, and claims of generality, the 'laws' of economics seem to be the embodiment of the right-handed (left-brained) view of the world. As money manager and economist Zachary Karabell observed in a 2013 piece, 'Increasingly, our debates about – and our solutions to – pressing issues such as immigration, budgets and debt are framed in the context of all-powerful economic laws that dictate what is and is not possible'.[27] This belief in 'ironclad rules', and the corollary that economics is a mathematical problem with only one correct answer, explains why heterodox approaches don't get more of a hearing in university courses: Pontus Rendahl from Cambridge University, for example, told the *Financial Times* in 2016 that because economics has 'immutable laws' it makes no more sense to teach heterodox economics than it does to teach 'heterodox engineering or alternative medicine' (he later said he was referring to accounting principles, but that would imply heterodox economists can't add).[28] It also explains why ethical issues are similarly ignored, as discussed further in Chapter 10.

As seen above, though, even some mainstream economists are admitting that these 'immutable laws' are less fact than fiction. Of course all models are stories, but modellers have an ethical responsibility to be transparent about their limitations, especially when the models are being used to make important decisions. 'Referencing "the laws of economics" as a way to refute arguments or criticize ideas has the patina of clarity and certainty', notes Karabell, but this is 'simply another way to justify beliefs and inclinations'. A first step is to amend textbooks by cutting the associations – explicit or implied – with physical laws, and being clear about what has or has not been empirically validated.

The lack of an empirical tether also leads to a kind of intellectual stasis. When something like the law of supply and demand comes under question, its defenders first say that of course it's not perfect, but it is justified by its use in making predictions. When forced to admit that the equations have little or no empirical backing, they insist that they are nevertheless correct. When provided with counter-examples, they say that such exceptions can be addressed using epicycles. When the complicated model based on these ideas is then shown to have no predictive power, they appeal to something like external shocks or the efficient market hypothesis. The theory is therefore unfalsifiable, and economists can continue to rigidly stand by it no matter what evidence is presented.[29] This type of confabulation is again a specialty of the left hemisphere: according to McGilchrist, researchers have shown how the left hemisphere, when isolated in clever experiments, will not only 'insist on its theory at the expense of getting things wrong, but it will later cheerfully insist that it got it right'.[30]

As discussed in this book, the fascination with clarity, certainty, and fixed rules is being challenged by the growing use of alternative approaches – including data analysis of the sort used by Steve Levitt (see box above) – which take into account the fact that not everything is reducible to neat equations, and tell a rather different story. The right hand is still in control, but it is starting to lose its grip.

One issue raised in this chapter was that of context sensitivity (which is a specialty of the right hemisphere).[31] As another example, in mid-2016 average house prices in the city of Vancouver were increasing at something like 30 per cent a year. Demand still appeared strong right up until August, when the provincial government suddenly imposed a 15 per cent tax that applied only to foreign buyers – and average prices reacted by plunging a record 19 per cent in just one month.[32] So if houses become more expensive to buy, that makes people excited about houses and drives more price appreciation, unless the cause is a tax on a small number of purchases, in which case it panics them to sell. For an example where supply decreases as price increases, meanwhile, we have the February 2017 headline 'Toronto Home Sellers Vanish as BMO Warns of Housing Bubble'.[33]

As discussed later, money is confusing because it fuses (confuses?) the properties of an owned thing, located in the real world, with those of abstract number; stories with calculations; left with right. These properties feed through to objects being bought, such as houses, which are seen both as a 'real' home, but also as a financial asset (so real estate). The relationship between these two aspects is fundamentally unstable, which leads to complicated dynamics that cannot be reduced to simple laws. One of the examples used in the first edition of the book was the UK housing market, circa 2010. To bring these statements up to date, just replace 'UK' with 'Canadian', circa 2017.

Finally, in 2017 the Bank of England's Andrew Haldane described the 2008 crisis as the profession's 'Michael Fish moment', referring to the BBC weather forecaster's famous

1987 prediction that the UK would avoid a hurricane (it didn't).[34] He blamed more recent forecasting misses, such as the Bank's miscalculations of the effects of the Brexit vote (they predicted the UK would be hit by an economic storm – it wasn't), on models that 'were ill-equipped to making sense of behaviours that were deeply irrational'. But maybe again it is more about context. The response of people to something like Brexit depends on how they perceive it. The Bank had assumed that consumer demand would collapse, but instead it remained mostly unchanged – perhaps because, having voted for Brexit, and not being governed by rational economic laws, the majority saw it as an OK thing. Now, if only we could stop real hurricanes in their tracks through the power of positive thinking.

CHAPTER 2

The connected economy

*The pernicious love of gambling diffused
itself through society, and bore all public
and nearly all private virtue before it.*
Charles Mackay, *Memoirs of Extraordinary Popular
Delusions and the Madness of Crowds* (1848)

There is no such thing as society.
Margaret Thatcher (1987)

Economists are taught that the economy is the net result of the actions of individual investors, who act independently of one another to maximise their own utility. This view of the economy – similar to the atomic theory of physics – sees the individual as all-important, and downplays the role of society (which according to one of Margaret Thatcher's more famous statements doesn't even exist). The reality, however, is that we influence one another all the time. We buy houses not just for a roof over our head, but also because everyone else is buying one and we are afraid to be left off the 'housing ladder'. This chapter shows how mainstream economists ignore or downplay the herd behaviour of markets, and therefore fail to predict or properly prepare for economic crises.

One of Pythagoras' most famous disciples – though he was born after the master's death – was the philosopher Democritus. His biographer Laertius wrote that he derived all his doctrines from

Pythagoras, to the point that 'one would have thought that he had been his pupil, if the difference of time did not prevent it'. Today, Democritus is best known for his theory that matter is made up of atoms, named after the Greek word *atomos* for indivisible.

The idea that a system can be broken down into its smallest components is a key plank of our reductionist scientific tradition. Today, scientists are still following this quest at facilities like the Large Hadron Collider near Geneva, by flinging small pieces of matter together at nearly the speed of light and analysing the debris. The atomic theory has also had enormous influence in other areas, including economics.

Democritus arrived at his idea by imagining that you could take an object – say a page from this book – and cut it into two pieces, then cut it again, and again, and so on. At some point, he argued, you would have to come to a smallest possible piece, because otherwise you could continue for ever and that would make no sense (the Greeks didn't cope well with the notion of infinity). That smallest unit is an atom. Substances had different properties because of the shape of their atoms – the atoms of oil, for example, had to be very smooth so that they would slide over one another easily.

The atomic theory never really caught on at the time, in part because Aristotle didn't like it, and it came into favour only much later when scientists such as Galileo and Newton lent their support. When Newton said that matter was made up of 'solid, massy, hard, impenetrable, movable particles', he was describing atoms.[1]

Because no one could actually see atoms, they remained a mostly theoretical construct until 1905, when Albert Einstein convincingly demonstrated their existence and even managed to estimate their size and velocity. It had long been known that, when viewed under a microscope, particles such as dust or pollen in a suspension tended to jostle around in a random fashion almost as if they were alive. This Brownian motion – named after the Scottish botanist Robert Brown, who was the first to investigate it – was something of a mystery, but Einstein showed that it could best be explained by assuming that the particles were constantly buffeted by individual atoms in the suspension. Atoms were small, but sometimes they could make themselves felt.

Particle theory

While physical atoms may have been just a theory in the late 19th century, the concept was eagerly adopted by neoclassical economists such as William Stanley Jevons, with the difference that the atoms of the economy were individual people (or firms). An advantage was that people were larger than atoms so you could see what they were doing; a disadvantage was that they showed considerable variability. But as Jevons argued in his *Theory of Political Economy* (1871), it was necessary only to model 'the single average individual, the unit of which population is made up'.

One of Newton's key insights was that, to compute the gravitational pull of a spherical body like the earth, it wasn't necessary to compute the effect of each individual part of the earth – each atom in a lump of rock or blade of grass. Instead it sufficed to assume that a single point mass, equal to the mass of the earth, was located at its centre. In the 19th century, physicists working in the new field of statistical mechanics had also shown that states such as temperature were governed not by what was happening with individual atoms, but by the statistical average. Jevons believed in the same way that it was possible to ignore the fact that people are different, and take into account only the population average. Indeed, this is exactly what modern economic models do to estimate the demand for a commodity like oil: it is impossible to take into account each person or company, so they make guesses for aggregate demand over a country or sector.

By equating the aggregate supply with the aggregate demand, the economists could in principle predict the equilibrium level of the economy, where supply and demand were in perfect agreement. But what explained the apparent day-to-day fluctuations in prices, of the sort seen, for example, on financial markets for stocks and bonds?

In 1900, even before Einstein's explanation of Brownian motion, the French economist Louis Bachelier came up with a similar theory for the economy. In his Ph.D. thesis, he proposed that financial markets are always close to equilibrium, but are buffeted around by the actions of individual investors as they respond in different ways to news or just the market's current state. Any change in price is therefore essentially random. As with a piece of pollen undergoing Brownian motion, the market might look like it's alive and has a sense of purpose, but that's just an illusion.

Bachelier's work initially made little impact, perhaps because it appeared to say that forecasting was a waste of time (never popular with forecasters). However, Bachelier had also pointed out that it should still be possible to evaluate the probability of the market changing by a certain amount over any given period. Price movements could be modelled using the normal distribution, or bell curve, which had long been used by astronomers and other scientists to account for the effect of random errors in their observations. In the 1950s and 60s, this aspect of his thesis was picked up on by economists, who used it to develop an elaborate theory of risk using the same mathematics as that used to describe Brownian motion.

Atomic markets

The atomic theory of the economy – and the economyth that the economy is made up of independent, atomistic individuals – reached its point of highest glory in 1965 with the efficient market hypothesis, which was proposed, in another Ph.D. thesis, by Eugene Fama of the University of Chicago. He described the market as made up of 'large numbers of rational profit-maximizers' who had access to all relevant information and were in active competition with each other. Given these assumptions, Fama argued, prices of any security would automatically adjust to reflect its 'intrinsic value'. Any deviations from that level would be small and random.

While Bachelier's work never gained popularity until after his death, Fama became something of a celebrity among economists. The reason was that he had taken the same idea – that market movements were random – and created a new story around it. Instead of the market being as dumb and lifeless as a piece of dust, it was granted a semi-divine status: a deity with a tag machine that can stick the correct price on anything.[2] The reason we can't predict it is that no forecaster can possibly outwit this god.

The efficient market hypothesis also granted we ordinary mortals various special properties, such as rationality, an obsession with reading the news, and an intense focus on making money. However, the most striking thing about it is that, like inert atoms, its people never interact except by bouncing off one another in the marketplace. No one ever gets together to talk about the price of houses or oil or the stock market; they all have to make their own mind up. They are truly independent. (Weaker versions of the hypothesis exist that account for effects such as private information and insider trading.[3])

As a mathematical model of how people make economic decisions, this theory is extremely strange. I still find it bizarre that it is taught at universities and colleges where other departments that teach social sciences like sociology, or humanities like drama or literature, presumably take the opposite stance that people do actually affect each other's lives. And yet, as author and investment strategist George Cooper wrote in 2008, the hypothesis 'remains the bedrock of how conventional wisdom views the financial system, the key premise upon which we conduct monetary policy and the framework on which we construct our financial risk systems'.[4] George Soros describes it as 'The prevailing interpretation of financial markets'.[5]

It's interesting to ask whether the influence could extend even further. Western society has been slowly atomising itself and breaking down into smaller units for many centuries – our sense of individuality has flourished at the same time as our sense of community has shrunk – and if anything that process has accelerated since the 1960s.[6] According to one survey, most Americans saw others (but not apparently themselves) as 'increasingly atomized, selfish, and irresponsible'.[7] An economic worldview that puts those qualities at its centre – and that ties in with our deepest scientific traditions – is bound to have an influence on the society that it purports to resemble. Perversely, we seem intent on conforming ourselves to fit the model. More on this in Chapter 9.

Random motion

One reason for the enduring popularity of the efficient market hypothesis is that it does make one correct prediction, namely that the markets are unpredictable. Even big institutions such as the International Monetary Fund (IMF) or the Organisation for Economic Cooperation and Development (OECD), which have access to large computer models and enormous quantities of data, turn out to be no more prescient in their predictions than the forecasters from Bloomberg cited in the introduction.

The heavy line in Figure 5 shows changes in US gross domestic product (GDP) over a two-decade period before and after the financial crisis. The narrow lines are predictions from the US Energy Information Administration. The model is tuned in such a way that it favours moderation: whether the economy is surging

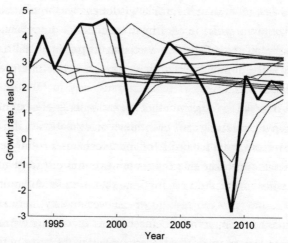

Figure 5. Predictions for GDP growth in the US.
Source: Energy Information Administration.[8]

or depressed, the model always points to a growth of around 2 or 3 per cent.

The track record of models at other institutions like the OECD or IMF is no better.[9] In April 2007, for example, the IMF said that: 'Notwithstanding the recent bout of financial volatility, the world economy still looks well set for continued robust growth in 2007 and 2008.' A later study showed the consensus of forecasters in 2007 was that not one of 77 countries considered would be in recession the next year (49 of them were).[10] A 2010 report from the US Federal Reserve found that their models 'are very poor in forecasting, but so are all other approaches' and concluded that 'forecasting ability is not a proper metric to judge a model' (though this didn't discourage anyone from using the models to make forecasts).[11]

The efficient market hypothesis would explain this lack of foresight by pointing out that, if a forecaster could correctly predict that the economy would go up or down, that would imply that he or she knew more than the market. Price changes would therefore not be random, which according to the theory is forbidden.

It's possible to convince yourself that the plot of GDP is a meaningless and unpredictable squiggle that just reflects the actions of independent investors reacting randomly to random news. However, while the efficient market hypothesis agrees that markets are unpredictable, one can't take this as confirmation of the theory (snowstorms are unpredictable, but no one claims they are efficient). Rather than postulate that the economy is some kind of god-like entity with a miraculous eye for prices, it is simpler and more realistic to assume that forecasts go wrong because they are based on a faulty reductionist premise. Our economic models are the modern equivalent of the circle-based Greek models of the cosmos: they are large and complicated and can be made to fit past data, but that doesn't mean they are an accurate reproduction of the real thing.

Indeed, as discussed later, efficient market theory is proved wrong by the fact that it does not correctly predict the observed frequency of sudden, extreme changes. In the economy described by the efficient market hypothesis, there can be no interesting weather patterns, no storms or droughts, because the only changes are small and random. Things are never too cold, never too hot, always just right. The economy would therefore also be almost entirely without risk, or for that matter any interesting features. And yet, as experience shows, the economy is as varied and changeable as the real weather.

Changeable, with a risk of crashes

One reason for this variability is that people do not behave like Newtonian atoms, but interact and affect each other's behaviour. Markets are largely driven by things like rumours and trends. These in turn affect the larger economy, and ultimately measures of activity like the gross domestic product.

Consider again the case of the UK housing market (Figure 2). The UK has a high rate of home-ownership, and houses are traditionally valued not just for their ability to provide shelter, but also as an investment. As house prices appreciated in the late 1990s, many people bought second homes, viewing the rental income as their pension. Banks began to offer special buy-to-let mortgages at attractive interest rates. Some amateur investors built up substantial portfolios with tens of properties, using one home as collateral to buy the next. House prices continued to climb, and people were getting seriously rich. Anyone with a decent house in a major city was making more money from that, at least on paper, than they probably were in their job. Property-related industries such as construction and real estate were also booming.

All of this did not go unnoticed by those who didn't yet own a home – particularly young people who were desperate to get on the housing ladder before it was too late. They therefore stretched their finances to the limit to buy whatever studio basement flat next to a railyard was available. Their anxiety was stirred up further by a constant barrage of TV shows about property: buying it, fixing it up, and above all, making money out of it. Anyone who didn't own a home was under constant social and psychological pressure to get one, fast – and banks were bending over backwards to help make it happen.

Behavioural psychologists describe this kind of thing as herd behaviour. Everyone senses which way the wind is blowing, and thunders off in the same direction. This process – well documented in 1848 by Charles Mackay in his *Memoirs of Extraordinary Popular Delusions and the Madness of Crowds* – does not look very rational, and indeed there is plenty of evidence to show that emotion plays a large role in decision-making. However, the question here is a little different, because in many ways first-time buyers were just responding to the best information from their peers and from the media, which was that prices were going to keep going up.

Efficient market theory is sometimes justified by the idea that groups of people can make better judgements than individuals. Experiments have shown that in certain situations, such as guessing how many pennies there are in a jar, the average of a number of independent guesses from different people is surprisingly accurate.[12] But when group dynamics take over, this 'wisdom of crowds' can quickly break down.

One might think that the banks supplying the mortgages would be more sophisticated and immune to such pressures, yet they were also caught up in the process. Just as people competed with each other to buy the best properties, which usually attracted multiple offers, so the banks competed with each other by offering cut-price deals in their quest for a larger share of the rapidly growing mortgage market. Often they were willing to forgo the need for a significant deposit, or even proof of employment.

In September 2007 – a month after the employee at Lehman Brothers had complained of 'once in 10,000 years' disturbances in the credit markets – the UK bank Northern Rock (aka 'the Rock') asked the Bank of England for some short-term support with a liquidity problem. With the share price dropping like a stone, the government immediately moved to reassure the Rock's customers that there was no need to worry about their mortgages or bank accounts. The customers listened, and the next morning formed an orderly queue outside the bank branches to get their money out. It was the first run on a British bank in more than a century.

Suddenly the information being passed around at the morning coffee break, down the pub, or in the media, took on a different tone. Concern was fuelled by disturbing news about a serious US housing crash developing on the other side of the Atlantic. People grew nervous about making large investments, and house prices flattened. Banks began to withdraw some of their more extravagantly cheap mortgage deals. The winds were turning direction.

According to the atomic theory of economics, individual people or businesses are supposed to be independent of one another, so they are uninfluenced by each other's decisions. In this picture, our desires and preferences therefore remain fixed. But in fact every decision we make is affected by what is going on around us – and not just during financial booms and busts. Our group behaviour can resemble that of a herd of animals, blindly following the same lead. But more generally it is as complex and ever-changing as the weather. Like El Niño, our actions reflect the fact that we are part of a global network – connected socially and financially to friends, community, the media, and even remote events on the other side of the world, in the farms or factories or booming business centres of China, India or Brazil.

Economics might gain its credibility from its association with engineering and physics; however, it is the physics of the 19th century. Some properties of a material, such as its temperature, are a function of the average behaviour of atoms or molecules, but today we know that many others are the emergent feature of the interaction between these components. Even something as ubiquitous and apparently simple as water turns out to elude reductionist analysis: its state (for example, whether it is water, ice, or vapour) depends on the complex interactions between molecules, which are engaged in a constant quantum-mechanical dance with their neighbours. That is one reason why clouds, and large-scale effects like El Niño, remain so hard to model or predict; and it is also why we need to update our views of the economy.

Electrical storm

If we think of housing markets as similar to large-scale atmospheric phenomena like El Niño, then the banking system is more like the electricity grid. Most of the time it works fine and we don't even think about it – but every now and then it lets us down. And when that happens, it can be a catastrophe.

One such event occurred during the electricity blackout of 14 August 2003. People waking up that morning in the north-east United States, or the province of Ontario, Canada, would have noticed nothing peculiar about their electricity supply. The shaver worked; the lights didn't flicker; the coffee machine functioned as it was supposed to. No one would have supposed that they would be trying to make their way home that evening without the benefit of traffic lights.

The trigger for the event was actually weather-related. Temperatures in the region were high (as shown in Figure 4, 2003 was an El Niño year) and people were switching on the air conditioners. The high demand caused power cables to overheat, so they expanded in length and sagged lower than usual between towers.

According to an official report, it seems that the blackout started when a generating plant outside Cleveland, Ohio went offline around 1.30pm, due to a technical problem.[13] High-voltage power lines in rural areas had to carry extra current to compensate. Sagging under the burden, one of them came into contact with trees, which had been inadequately trimmed. Power switched to another line, which also sagged and hit a tree. Further lines collapsed, putting the rest of the Ohio system under increased strain.

Finding itself suddenly short of power, Ohio drew two gigawatts from the neighbouring state of Michigan. In response, transmission lines in both states tripped out. The network was soon overwhelmed by huge fluctuations, caused by cuts in demand in some areas due to blackouts, and surges of power from other stations. Local grids separated from each other to try to control the damage, but to no avail. Failures cascaded through the system, and by the end 256 power plants were offline, and over 50 million people were without power.

Like the electricity grid, the banking system is a vital utility that we all rely on. It is also a huge connected network that controls the flow of money rather than electrons. When one bank or financial institution fails, it puts other nodes in the network under increased stress. Not only must they make up the financial slack, but they also come under increased scrutiny themselves. A run on one bank makes customers at other banks twitchy; and sagging lines of credit may cause a fire.

The credit crunch was like a power outage rolling around the world in slow motion. The first institutions to go offline were over-leveraged lenders like Northern Rock in the UK and Countrywide in the US. In March 2008 the investment bank Bear Stearns, on the verge of collapse, was taken over by JPMorgan Chase. During the course of the crisis, household names like Merrill Lynch, Fannie Mae, Freddie Mac, Lehman Brothers and the giant insurer AIG all failed, were taken over under duress, or were rescued by the government.

The credit blackout did not respect national borders: entire countries, such as Iceland, found themselves in the dark, their bank supplies cut off. Some of the worst affected were Eastern European nations that relied on financing from Western banks, such as Hungary, Lithuania and Latvia. The latter saw an annual house price decline of almost 60 per cent in the year following the crisis.[14] In the Middle East, Dubai experienced a similar decline in real estate prices, causing the company Dubai World to freeze payments on its debt in late 2009, with knock-on effects on international markets.[15]

So is there anything we can do to protect ourselves from such failures – or will we always be vulnerable to electrical storms?

The science of networks

The banking and electrical systems are two examples of technological networks. Others are the transportation network, the telecommunications network, and the world wide web. Similar networks are ubiquitous in nature: biological systems are characterised by complex networks of interacting genes and proteins, ecosystems by predator–prey relationships. And sociologists use social networks to investigate the transmission of ideas and trends through society.

Researchers in the field of network science view such systems in terms of nodes, which represent individuals or agents in the network, and links, which join the nodes and represent interactions of some kind. In a biological model the nodes could represent proteins or cells; in an ecosystem model they could represent species; in a social network they could represent people; in a model of the electrical grid they could represent power stations or consumers; in a model of the economy they could represent firms. For example, one paper published by Domenico Delli Gatti from the Catholic University of Milan and colleagues in June 2008 observed that: 'The complex pattern of credit relationships is a natural research issue to be dealt with by means of network analysis. It is straightforward to think of agents as *nodes* and of debt contracts as *links* in a *credit network* ... the default of one agent can bring about an *avalanche of bankruptcies* [their italics].'[16] If the authors had delayed publication a few months, they could have used Lehman's as an example.

Researchers have found that such networks – be they technological, biological, ecological, social, or economic – often have much in common, and can be divided into certain categories. One is the small-world network, where the connections between individual nodes are arranged in such a way that it takes only a small number of steps to link one node to another. The world wide web has this property, and search companies such as Google exploit it to derive their algorithms. Another category is scale-free networks. The term 'scale-free' means that there is no typical or expected number of connections for any node: most nodes have few connections to other nodes, but a small number of hubs are highly connected. An example is the air traffic network: some airports such as Heathrow are global hubs, while smaller regional airports may fly to only a few destinations. Artificial networks with these and other properties can easily be produced and studied on the computer.

Economists have long thought of the money system as a simple centralised network, with the central bank acting as what the 19th-century financial journalist Walter Bagehot called a 'lender of last resort', ready to step in with emergency liquidity in times of crisis. But the network topology or structure is far more complicated. Network modelling of the economy has become an active research area, in academia and institutions including the Bank of England. One of the key questions that engineers and network scientists are concerned with is network robustness, which often depends strongly on the way in which the network is arranged. Much can be learned from natural systems, such as ecosystems or biological systems, simply because they have been around for a long time so have presumably learned a trick or two. Some 'design principles' shared by robust networks – but not currently by our financial system – include modularity, redundancy, diversity, and a process for controlled shut-down.[17] Together they provide clues on how we can reduce the chance of another disaster.

Modularity   A network's modularity refers to its degree of compartmentalisation. In, for example, a small-world network, each node is connected to any other node by a small number of connections. This is good if the aim is communication, but in other cases it can be a problem. Scientists have studied the spread of epidemics using detailed network models of artificial societies in which nodes represent individuals, and connections between nodes represent the potential spread of the disease from one person to another. It turns out that one of the main factors determining the rate of spread is the transport network – the 2009 swine flu pandemic, for example, spread so quickly because of long-distance connections through air travel.

The banking system too has become increasingly integrated, and therefore vulnerable to contagion of a different sort. After the Great Depression, the Glass–Steagall Act was introduced in the US to separate commercial banks, responsible for day-to-day consumer banking, from investment banks, which were primarily involved in speculation. The repeal of this act in 1999 by the Gramm–Leach–Bliley Act dissolved the wall, and allowed banks like Citigroup to go nuts with derivatives, lose billions, and get rescued by the US government. (The same act also led to deregulation of electricity markets and the Enron saga.) On an international level, the degree of financial connectivity between major markets has increased dramatically in recent decades – meaning that if one catches a cold, they all get it.[18] Complex living organisms, or natural systems such as food webs, tend to be built up of smaller, weakly connected sub-networks, which reduces the probability of contagion from one area to another.[19]

The overall structure of the network architecture is also important. A common motif in biological and engineering networks is the 'bow-tie' structure, in which multiple inputs (one side of the bow) feed into a central control unit (the knot) to produce multiple outputs (the other side of the bow). An example again is the internet, where a wide variety of material such as web pages, emails, video and so on, is first compressed into a homogeneous, standardised computer language before expanding again as output on a user's screen. According to control theorists, who study the control of dynamical systems in engineering, the bow-tie structure has evolved in both natural and man-made systems because it allows a balance between robustness and efficiency.[20] The system is quite efficient, because it uses a standardised language to handle all the diverse inputs and outputs, but at the same time it is easy to monitor events and correct mistakes. In finance, the equivalent to a central control module would be a public exchange for instruments such as derivatives. These are currently often sold over-the-counter, which makes it impossible to measure or control systemic risk.

Redundancy   Another trick that nature employs to improve robustness is keeping something in place for backup. If one node or link in the network fails, another can take its place. That extra kidney might seem a waste to carry around until your other kidney fails (or you need to donate one). In financial terms, this supports the idea that banks should retain a higher minimum level of cash reserves, which could be adjusted up for large institutions or investment strategies that pose systemic risk.

Much of the appeal of the complex financial products developed in the last decade is that they enabled financial institutions to get around reserve requirements. Investment banks such as Lehman Brothers were leveraged at extremely high ratios (over 30 to 1), so they were essentially gambling with other people's money. The danger, as chairman of the US Federal Deposit Insurance Corporation Sheila Bair told a conference in June 2007, is that 'Without proper capital regulation, banks can operate in the marketplace with little or no capital. And governments and deposit insurers end up holding the bag, bearing much of the risk and cost of failure. ... The final bill for inadequate capital regulation can be very heavy. In short, regulators can't leave capital decisions totally to the banks. We wouldn't be doing our jobs or serving the public interest if we did.'[21] Canadian banks survived the credit crunch relatively unscathed, in large part because they had tougher lending requirements than their American counterparts.[22]

Diversity   A degree of diversity in a system can help it adapt to change. In an ecosystem this equates to a range of species; in the financial system it equates to diversity of trading strategies. On the surface, our financial system would appear to be highly diverse. However, one surprise to come out of the crisis was that everyone appeared to be employing the same strategies. Even adventurous hedge funds, which are supposed to come up with innovative ways to make money, were susceptible to group-think. Intense competition between institutions meant they were afraid of under-performing their peers, so were actually more likely to adopt the same techniques. As one trader put it, they 'talk to each other and have many of the same trades. These are people who say, "I see a pattern, and I've got to jump on."'[23]

The trend was exacerbated by the fact that funds often use quantitative rule-based strategies, which are inherently easy to copy. Banks also adopted near-identical risk models, even though they were known to be flawed, exactly because they were widely accepted by the industry. Complexity scientists are starting to monitor these different strategies, and the relationships between them, in the same way that ecologists monitor species in an ecosystem.[24]

Controlled shut-down   When cells in the human body are damaged beyond repair – say after exposure to toxins or radiation – they are usually targeted for a form of controlled death known as apoptosis. In this process, the constituents of the cell are taken apart and recycled for use elsewhere in the body. In cancer cells, the apoptotic machinery is disabled, and cells at the interior of the tumour become necrotic – they burst, disgorging their contents in a fashion that harms nearby cells.

When Lehman went bankrupt, its death was necrotic rather than apoptotic. In the US alone, it had over a million derivatives transactions outstanding with some 6,500 trading partners. Figuring out the mess has kept hundreds of lawyers employed for years. Banks also often structure themselves in a deliberately labyrinthine manner in order to avoid taxes, which makes them hard to wind up. In 2009, proposals for 'living wills' for banks were being considered by institutions including the UK's Financial Services Authority.[25]

To improve the robustness of our financial system it therefore follows that we should increase modularity, redundancy and diversity, and provide a mechanism for controlled shut-down. This applies not just to banks, but to other industries such as agriculture or retail, which, as discussed later, exhibit many of the same problems. There's only one problem: none of these measures would be seen as desirable according to orthodox dogma. The reason is again related to the idea of efficient markets.

Fixing the grid

According to theory, markets are made efficient if each atom (e.g. individual or company) pursues its own self-interest. Here self-interest refers usually to short-term interest, because if a company neglects the short term it will be taken over by competitors. And what happens after it dies is irrelevant. Economics likes to live only in the present, which sounds very Zen, but isn't.

Companies, including banks, therefore spend a lot of time worrying about their own short-term risk, but much less on systemic risk.[26] Governments and regulatory institutions have also generally gone along with the idea that markets are self-regulating. (In 2008, Alan Greenspan admitted that this idea was 'a flaw in the model

... that defines how the world works', but in 2011 he was back to warning against over-regulation, writing that 'With notably rare exceptions (2008, for example), the global "invisible hand" has created relatively stable exchange rates, interest rates, prices, and wage rates'.)[27] The financial network is therefore allowed to evolve towards a state that appears highly efficient in the short term, but is constantly accumulating systemic risk.

Introducing modularity, for example by separating speculative activities from ordinary commercial banking activities, or dividing large global banks into clearly defined national components, would probably reduce short-term efficiency, as would building extra slack and capacity into the system, e.g. by increasing the amount of money that banks need to keep on reserve.[28] Such measures can therefore be taken only by a strong regulatory agency. Some progress is now being made – there is certainly a desire for reform in the air – but changes will occur only under protest by the banks, whose main lesson from the crisis was that they can rely on taxpayer bail-outs. Indeed with the collapse of many players, the banking industry is more concentrated than it was before the crisis.

It is interesting to ask whether the credit crunch would ever have happened if politicians and risk experts at banks had been trained or educationally shaped in fields like complexity and network theory rather than orthodox economics.[29] When the US government took the decision to let Lehman fail in an uncontrolled manner, it seems that the administration was taken aback by the knock-on effects. It was like an untrained apprentice engineer wandering into the control room and unplugging the thick cable with the 'DO NOT DISCONNECT' sign above it.[30] And the result was nearly lights out for the economy. Three days after Lehman's bankruptcy, on 18 September, the Federal Reserve had to intervene to stop an electronic bank run on US money market accounts.

As Representative Paul Kanjorski of Pennsylvania explained, they feared that if it were allowed to continue, '$5.5 trillion would have been drawn out of the money market system of the US, which would have collapsed the entire economy of the US, and within 24 hours the world economy would have collapsed. It would have been the end of our economic system and our political system as we know it.'[31]

The next way to revive economics, then, is to educate our cadre of highly-paid 'financial engineers' in the principles and codes of real engineering. This includes building in firebreaks and safeguards to help prevent systemic failure, and developing diagnostic tools for the collection and analysis of network data. 'At present,' notes the Bank of England's Andrew Haldane, 'risk measurement in financial systems is atomistic. Risks are evaluated node by node. In a network, this approach gives little sense of risks to the nodes, much less to the overall system. It risks leaving policymakers navigating in dense fog when assessing the dynamics of the financial system.'[32]

Disasters and breakdowns will always occur, but the effects can be minimised and procedures put in place to get the system up and running as quickly as possible (the blackout in the US north-east was repaired in most places in under a day). New ideas and tools from mathematical areas like network theory and complexity can help to frame the problems, test and refine hypotheses, explore and communicate solutions, and motivate changes. As shown by the influence of neoclassical economics, models can have a large effect on the design of financial structures.

So far we have seen that economics derives its authority from its use of mathematical equations, and ideas such as atomism, that are core to our tradition of reductionist scientific thought. In the next chapter, we look at another topic beloved of the ancient Greeks and modern economists alike – the notion of stability.

One versus plurality

Since the crisis there have been some architectural improvements made to the financial network. In the US, for example, the Dodd–Frank Act moved some over-the-counter derivatives trading to third-party clearing houses (as opposed to public exchanges) where exposure can at least be better monitored.[33] Banks now need to hold larger reserves, and 'systemically important financial institutions' are required to develop those 'living wills' (though how credible these are is a matter of debate).[34] However, these measures fall well short of the response after the Great Depression – which is why some politicians including Bernie Sanders and Elizabeth Warren continue to call for reinstating the 1933 Glass–Steagal Act. And of course it is unclear, at the time of writing, how regulations will fare under a Trump presidency – though when the director of Trump's National Economic Council, Gary Cohn, whose previous job was President and co-COO of Goldman Sachs, states that he plans to 'attack all aspects of Dodd Frank', one can assume he doesn't mean it is for being too easy on banks.[35]

At the same time, network effects have ramped up in intensity with the explosion of high-frequency trading. Markets are often dominated by algorithms that race against each other to make trades based on price shifts that occur over periods measured in microseconds. Since these moves are usually dictated by other algorithms, the result is a hall-of-mirrors system that is more susceptible to herding effects than any human group. This was demonstrated in May 2010 when the Dow Jones index dropped by about 9 per cent in just half an hour, before quickly bouncing back almost to where it started. Similar 'flash crash' events have become disturbingly commonplace in a variety of markets.[36] Many people including Sanders and Warren have argued for a financial transactions tax, which would slow high-frequency trading, but the idea is of course opposed by the financial sector.

While the complexity viewpoint has been making steady progress in economics, the atomistic, efficient market model discussed in this chapter still lies at the heart of the mathematical models used to simulate risk in the markets.[37] Eugene Fama was even awarded the 2013 economics Nobel for his work (though to be fair they also gave one to behavioural economist Robert Shiller, who once called the conflation of unforecastability with efficiency 'one of the most remarkable errors in the history of economic thought').[38] One might think that people who have direct experience of the markets would be more sceptical, but in a poll of the quantitative finance community organised by Paul Wilmott and myself at the leading quant forum wilmott.com, 43 per cent agreed with the statement that the efficient market theory is basically true, even though it should in principle put them out of a job.[39] These core ideas have been around a long time, and they won't go easily.

Equally concerning is the way that the atomistic model – perhaps the ultimate manifestation of Schopenhauer's *principium individuationis* (principle of individuation) for which Nietzsche described Apollo as the archetype – still dominates the public discourse, in a time when our modern economy is characterised by extremely strong corporations and a divided and distracted populace.[40] As journalist George Monbiot notes: 'Though our wellbeing is inextricably linked to the lives of others, everywhere we are told that we will prosper through competitive self-interest and extreme individualism.'[41] One result, as Monbiot points out, is loneliness; another is that

many of the rights which previous generations fought and
unionised for, such as decent salaries, limited working hours,
paid vacations, and so on, are being slowly eroded. Workers
of the world, reunite!

CHAPTER 3

THE UNSTABLE ECONOMY

To understand what is going on we need a new paradigm.
The currently prevailing paradigm, namely that financial
markets tend towards equilibrium, is both false and
misleading; our current troubles can be largely attributed
to the fact that the international financial system has
been developed on the basis of that paradigm.
George Soros (2008)

There is nothing in this world constant but inconstancy.
Jonathan Swift (1707)

Economists are taught that the economy is intrinsically stable
– price changes are small and random, so perturbations are rap-
idly damped out by the 'invisible hand' of market forces. This
assumption would be fine, except that it is contradicted by all
of financial history. Booms and busts aren't exceptions, they
are the standard course of things. This chapter shows how the
assumption of stability has been a feature of scientific modelling
of natural systems since the time of the ancient Greeks – and
why we need to better account for the dynamic, unpredictable,
and reflexive nature of the economy.

If there are three words that characterise the orthodox view of the
economy, they are efficiency, stability, and rationality. Economists
seem compelled to convince the rest of us that the market is some
kind of magnificent technological machine that automatically

allocates resources with mathematical precision and is immune to shakes, wobbles, or outbreaks of craziness or delirium.

In the 19th century, when neoclassical economics was invented, the assumption of stability was required because without it, it would have been impossible to solve the equations using the mathematics of the time. However, this excuse is no longer relevant, now that we have computers to do the work. It is therefore strange, as physicist and quantitative analyst J.-P. Bouchaud noted, that 'classical economics has no framework through which to understand "wild" markets, even though their existence is so obvious to the layman'.[1] This seems to be a grave omission – especially since the credit crunch put the Eek! back into economics. So why is it that mainstream economists cling to the notion of stability? To find the answer, and understand the role that this key economyth plays in economic thought, we must again delve into the historical context.

The highest aim of mathematics has always been to find that which is timeless and unchanging in a world that appears to be in a constant state of flux. The beauty of the Pythagorean theorem about right-angled triangles is that it applies not just to some right-angled triangles, or most right-angled triangles, but to all right-angled triangles, now and at any time in the future. Of course, if you actually draw a right-angled triangle, and measure the sides, and compare the sum of squares of the two sides with that of the hypotenuse, then you will not get a perfect match, but that is because the triangle you drew is slightly flawed, and the measurements have a small error. The law applies only to perfect triangles, which like numbers themselves are mathematical abstractions.

Plato generalised this idea with his theory of forms. According to Plato, every object, such as a table or a chair, is an imperfect version of the Table form or the Chair form, which exist in some higher plane of reality. Everyday objects are subject to change, but their forms live for ever. We perceive the world using our senses, but forms can be known only through the intellect – and only they can lead to genuine knowledge.

As discussed in Chapter 1, the quest for unchanging laws still drives much of science. Even if the cosmos is in a constant state of flux, the laws that govern it are considered permanent and immutable.[2] Mathematics is a way of fixing nature, a kind of photography device to capture the eternal.

In Arthur Koestler's classic history *The Sleepwalkers*, he criticised Plato for what amounted to a fear of change: 'When reality becomes unbearable, the mind must withdraw from it and create a world of artificial perfection. Plato's world of pure Ideas and Forms, which alone is to be considered as real, whereas the world of nature which we perceive is merely its cheap Woolworth copy, is a flight into delusion.' (Woolworths lent poignancy to this quote by itself disappearing into bankruptcy as an early victim of the credit crunch in the UK.)

Efficiency, stability, and rationality

Like the ancient Greeks, neoclassical economists saw the economy as a 'world of artificial perfection' that was governed by order and stability. Three of the key figures who built the foundations of neoclassical theory were William Stanley Jevons (1835–82), Léon Walras (1834–1910) and Vilfredo Pareto (1848–1923). Although they all pursued an abstract vision of placid stability in their work, it is ironic that they were all strong characters who led interesting and not particularly stable lives. My impression is that they would have collectively run screaming from most present-day university economics departments.

We have already met William Stanley Jevons, who first translated utility theory into mathematical form. Jevons was a true polymath, with interests in chemistry, physics (he published two papers on Brownian motion), botany, meteorology (a paper on cloud formation), economics, social policy, and music.

Born in Liverpool in 1835, Jevons attended University College London for two years, but after the collapse of his father's iron business he was forced for financial reasons to look for work. Offered a position at the new mint in Australia, he moved to Sydney, where he spent five years, continuing his scientific investigations on the side. He then returned to the UK to complete his university degree. While supporting himself as a tutor and lecturer at Owens College, Manchester, he wrote several papers on logic, then in 1865 won a degree of fame with his treatise *The Coal Question*, which compellingly argued that the country was on the verge of running out of coal. Promoted to professor, he at first spent most of his time working on logic. He was spurred to return to economics after Fleeming Jenkin sent him a copy of a paper including a geometric interpretation of supply and demand (Figure 1) that resembled Jevons' own theories.

His 1871 book *Theory of Political Economy* drew explicit comparisons between utility theory and physics. The aim was to replace the fuzzy, qualitative descriptions of classical economists like Adam Smith with the mathematical language of numbers and equations. Like a physicist working on abstract problems where effects like friction or turbulence are ignored, Jevons analysed only idealised markets, in which each individual makes decisions based on 'a pure regard to his own requirements or private interests', the 'intentions of exchanging are known to all', and there is 'perfectly free competition' between participants. He compared the price mechanism to the motion of a pendulum, which comes to rest at the ideal balance between supply and demand.

In 1876 Jevons moved back to University College London, but he found his professional duties too stressful and time-consuming and resigned after four years. He was plagued throughout his life by poor health, insomnia and depression (mental health problems ran in his family, and his older brother and closest sister went insane). He died in a swimming accident near Hastings at the age of 46, leaving behind several thousand books, a huge stock of blank writing paper (he was anticipating a shortage), and an enduring reputation as one of the most influential economists in history.[3]

Fixed point

Next came Léon Walras. Born in France in 1834 to an economist father, he enrolled at the Paris School of Mines. However, he didn't enjoy engineering, so he tried a number of other careers including romance novelist, journalist, clerk at a railway company, and bank manager. Influenced by his father, he wrote some papers on economics, and in 1870 he was offered a chair in political economy at the Academy of Lausanne in Switzerland. He later said that economics had provided him with 'pleasures and joys like those that religion provides to the faithful'.[4]

Walras is best known for his *Elements of Pure Economics*, which is considered the founding text of equilibrium theory, a major plank of orthodox economics. While Jevons had considered only simplified examples, Walras simulated the workings of markets for multiple goods, where the price of one good (say wheat) could have knock-on effects on other goods (e.g. bread). He realised that the economy had to be modelled as an interconnected whole, like a solar system in which each body exerts a gravitational force on the others. To do this, he wrote out a set of equations that modelled the interactions between sellers and buyers for a range of products. Drawing on the mathematician Louis Poinsot's book *Éléments de Statique* (Static Elements), a copy of which he is said to have kept nearby at all times, Walras argued that because the number of unknowns equalled the number of equations, it was possible to solve the equations. He couldn't actually solve them himself, but in principle a solution should exist.

Walras' ideas made rather little impact during his lifetime, but his reputation has increased steadily ever since. In 1954 the economist J.A. Schumpeter wrote that 'Walras is in my opinion the greatest of all economists. His system of economic equilibrium, uniting, as it does, the quality of a "revolutionary" creativeness with the quality of classic synthesis, is the only work by an economist that will stand comparison with the achievements of theoretical physics.'[5] His equilibrium model was the forerunner of the ones used in macroeconomics today (see box, page 81).

When Walras retired, he was succeeded by his disciple, the Italian economist and sociologist Vilfredo Pareto. Pareto's father was an exiled Italian aristocrat and civil engineer. Pareto studied engineering in Turin, and came top of his class with his thesis on *The Fundamental Principles of Equilibrium in Solid Bodies*. On graduation he became director first of an Italian railway company, then a steel company in Florence. He was also involved in politics, railing in favour of liberalism and against government regulation.[6]

After the death of his parents in 1889, the 41-year-old quit his job, married a young Russian girl, and moved to a villa in the country, where he began writing and giving public lectures on economics. The government reacted to his provocative speeches by having him tailed and closing down his lectures when they could. Pareto was unintimidated (he was an expert marksman and swordsman, which probably helped). His work eventually got the notice of Léon Walras – with whom he shared a background in engineering – and through him the position at Lausanne.

In 1906 Pareto published his *Manual of Political Economy*, which elaborated on Walrasian equilibrium and extended its mathematical base. It also introduced the idea of Pareto optimality, defined as a state in which any change that makes a person better off will reduce the wealth of someone else. Pareto is more famous today, though, for his empirical discovery of the so-called 80–20 rule. He observed that in Italy and other countries, 20 per cent of the people held about 80 per cent of the wealth. Furthermore, wealth followed a scale-free distribution, which as mentioned earlier means that there is no typical degree of wealth: most people have little money, but a few are fabulously rich.

Along with other neoclassical economists, Jevons, Walras and Pareto laid the stable base on which modern economics could erect its impressive and imposing structures. In the 1960s, the economists Kenneth Arrow and Gérard Debreu rigorously demonstrated the first welfare theorem, which states that under certain conditions, free markets lead to a Pareto optimal outcome. Any change such as government regulation will only detract from this ideal Walrasian equilibrium. Of course, the theorem makes many assumptions, including perfect competition, perfect knowledge for market participants, negligible transaction costs, and so on. But as Dani Rodrik observes, the theorem was 'a big deal because it actually proves the Invisible Hand hypothesis. That is, it shows that under certain assumptions, the efficiency of a market economy is not just conjecture or possibility; it follows logically from the premises.'[7] During the Cold War, the first welfare theorem – or the invisible hand theorem, as economists refer to it colloquially – was promoted as mathematical proof that capitalism, and not communism, was the final fixed point of human development.

The market pendulum

Neoclassical equilibrium theory did not actually assume that the economy is *completely* stable. The market is constantly perturbed, for example, by political events, which it quickly adjusts to. There are also effects due to technological growth, and the so-called business cycle. However, their contributions were assumed to be relatively small and slow-acting, so that for practical purposes they could be ignored when everyday prices were being considered.

Jevons was actually very aware of the business cycle – members of his family had been bankrupted by the 'railway boom' crisis of 1847 – and he was one of the first economists to study it in detail. Inspired by his meteorological research, he believed that it was a periodic phenomenon driven by sunspots. Sunspots affect the weather, which affects agriculture, which affects the rest of the economy. Or as he put it: 'If the planets govern the sun, and the sun governs the vintages and harvests, and thus the prices of food and raw materials and the state of the money market, it follows that the configurations of the planets may prove to be the remote causes of the greatest commercial disasters.'[8] The fact that the average business cycle, which he put at 10.5 years, didn't match perfectly with the sunspot cycle led him into a long argument with astronomers over the quality of their solar observations. (An enduring feature of neoclassical economics is that if the data doesn't fit the theory, then the data must be wrong.)

While Jevons et al. imported the concept of stability from physics and engineering to the new subject of economics, they couldn't actually prove that the solutions to their equations would be stable. It was taken as a given that free markets would adjust prices to a particular level, which once attained would remain unchanged, apart from small perturbations. In a sense they were forced to make this assumption, because the mathematical tools available to them were suited only for studying static systems, or at best, systems that varied in a periodic fashion. And as Jevons wrote, it is 'much more easy to determine the point at which a pendulum will come to rest' than to compute its general motion.

However, it doesn't necessarily hold that, even if a system has a theoretical equilibrium, it will actually be attained in practice; or if it is attained, that it will remain stable. For example, a pen balanced vertically on a table might be at equilibrium, but the equilibrium isn't very stable since the slightest nudge will cause the pen to topple over. Such questions are the subject of nonlinear dynamics, and the related engineering field of control theory, which also have roots that go back to the 19th century.

The governor

At the same time that economists were painstakingly constructing their theory of a stable economy, physicists were trying to discover what exactly it was that made a system stable in the first place. A leader in this area was the Scottish theoretical physicist and mathematician James Clerk Maxwell (1831–79).

Maxwell was Jevons' elder by four years, and like Jevons died too young at the age of 48 (of cancer). His greatest achievement was his mathematical formulation of the laws of electromagnetism, known as Maxwell's equations, which showed that electromagnetic waves propagated through space at the speed of light. He concluded that electricity, magnetism and light were just different aspects of the same underlying phenomenon – a discovery that Einstein described as the 'most profound and the most fruitful that physics has experienced since the time of Newton'.

During his short but amazingly productive academic career, Maxwell also made important contributions to statistical mechanics, astronomy and engineering, and found time to produce the first colour photograph (of a tartan ribbon, not his holidays). But the aspect of his work that concerns us here is his classic 1876 paper, 'On Governors', which is still taught in introductory classes on control theory.

The title referred to mechanical devices bolted onto steam engines to regulate their speed. The invention of these governors played a vital role in the industrial revolution, because they made it possible for an engine to keep running smoothly, even under different mechanical loads. An example of a governor from the period is shown in Figure 6. If the engine is running too fast, then the two metal balls, which spin around with the motor, are spread apart by centrifugal force. This actuates a lever that slows the speed. Conversely, when the speed is too low, the balls descend, and the speed picks up.

Figure 6. A centrifugal governor.[9]

If the governor is correctly designed, with the weight of the balls and the length of the arms and so on adjusted correctly, then the system keeps the engine at a speed that is roughly constant; any small disturbance is quickly damped out. However, this wasn't the only possibility. Maxwell classified the different responses as follows:

1. The disturbance increases.
2. The disturbance diminishes.
3. An oscillation of increasing amplitude.
4. An oscillation of decreasing amplitude.

In the first case, any slight increase in the speed would cause the engine to run out of control. In the second, speed would adjust itself to a stable level, as desired. In the third, the speed would wildly oscillate between slow and fast, until the machine fell apart. In the fourth, the speed would oscillate but eventually stabilise.

Stability was therefore just one of the available options, and the system had to be carefully designed in order to achieve it – making the balls too heavy, for example, could actually make things worse. Engineers who assumed stability, without doing the necessary calculations, could end up with costly repair bills.

But if a system as simple as two metal balls attached to a steam engine could show such a range of behaviour, how could economists assume that the economy would instantly achieve a state of perfect equilibrium? Wasn't it possible that it too would run out of control, or oscillate violently until it was shaken apart, like an unregulated steam engine?

Harmony of tensions

The reason that steam engines with governors show such complex behaviour, Maxwell found, is because of the presence of feedback loops. A positive feedback loop is one in which a small disturbance is amplified. The classic example is a microphone pointed at a speaker; any sound picked up by the microphone gets sent to the speaker, which sends it back to the microphone, which sends the amplified signal back to the speaker, and so on. A negative feedback is one, like the governor, that tends to resist change.

In Maxwell's analysis of the governor/steam engine system, cases (2) and (4) represent situations in which negative feedback has the upper hand: a change from the set speed is either diminished directly, or the speed oscillates around the set point but the size of the swing shrinks in magnitude. In cases (1) and (3), positive feedback has the upper hand: any disturbance either just grows in size, or it swings between fast and slow in a highly unstable fashion.

Feedback is a concept that came out of control theory and engineering, but feedback loops are ubiquitous in any kind of organic complex system. In the climate system, for example, clouds have a particularly important and sensitive effect on temperature. If the temperature goes up during the day, then water vapour increases due to evaporation, which increases cloud cover, which cools the atmosphere (negative feedback on temperature). But at night, the cloud cover warms the atmosphere (positive feedback). The dual role of clouds makes them extremely hard to simulate, because a small change in the model can lead to a very different balance between these opposing effects.

Biological systems too are characterised by positive feedback loops that allow a rapid response, coupled with negative feedback that provides control. For example, if you cut your finger, a positive feedback loop triggers the rapid production of proteins to create a blood clot and stop the bleeding. These same reactions are normally tightly controlled, because otherwise they would lead to thrombosis. In fact any living system seems to contain this kind of internal tension, a balance between opposing forces. The Greek philosopher Heraclitus, who was a contemporary of Pythagoras, said it best: 'What is at variance comes to terms with itself – a harmony of opposite tensions, as in the bow or the lyre.'

Now, if we assert, as the neoclassicists did, that the economy is constantly at equilibrium, then that is the same as saying that the dynamics are completely dominated by negative feedback. In fact, according to efficient market theory, at least in its purest form, any perturbation isn't just damped out over a period of time – it is removed *instantaneously*. The main source of negative feedback is assumed to be the law of supply and demand (Chapter 1). If the price of a good is too high, supply outstrips demand and the price will fall to equilibrium (and the converse).

Another example of negative feedback in the economy is the 'law of diminishing returns'. If a factory increases its workforce by 20 per cent, it probably won't get 20 per cent more product out the other end, because the factory will become overcrowded. Similarly, if you have a job, then getting another one will not double your productivity because you won't be able to work as hard. This can be seen as a kind of stabilising force on the economy, because it limits the amount that any single person or company can do or acquire.

Since academic economists are still teaching undergraduate students that the economy is inherently stable; and since the current economic paradigm assumes, as George Soros points out, that 'financial systems are self-correcting and tend towards equilibrium'; and since, as seen later, the risk models used by banks also implicitly assume that markets are stable and self-correcting, as do modern macroeconomic models (see box, page 81); then one might assume that any positive feedback loops must be either extremely weak or very hard to find.[10] So let's go for a careful search and see if that's the case.

The reflexive economy

One source of positive feedback was discussed in Chapter 1. When prices of an asset like housing or a particular stock are going up, they attract a class of investors known as momentum buyers, who see people making money and decide to jump on the bandwagon. That acts as positive feedback by bidding prices up even further. If prices are instead decreasing, then momentum investors will sell the asset, thus again amplifying the change in price. A market dominated by momentum investors would be like Maxwell's class (3), in which the system is subject to increasingly large swings until it loses control altogether.

Another kind of positive feedback is due to the network effects seen in Chapter 2. Investors are not independent, but are in constant communication with one another. When people started making money from UK house price rises in the late 1990s, those who were benefiting didn't keep it as a closely guarded secret. Word got out, and fast. The media amplified the effect by increasing their coverage the more that prices rose. There were far more property shows on TV in 2007 than there were in 1995. So people who might not have considered themselves momentum buyers in 1995 ended up changing their positions.

Of course house prices couldn't have increased unless banks were willing to lend the necessary funds. The amount of money a bank is prepared to lend will depend on its balance sheet. Since the loans are backed by home equity, if house prices go up then their balance sheets improve, so they put even more money to work by lending it out. This in turn drives house prices further. In the same way, borrowers with large mortgages find that their own balance sheets – i.e. their personal net worth – has increased accordingly, so they can borrow even more money to get a bigger house or improve their lifestyle. As discussed further below, the same credit dynamic affects the economy as a whole.

Again, these feedbacks also work on the way down. Downward movements in house prices are quickly magnified by momentum sellers, media reports, and tightening of credit as banks try to withdraw from the mortgage market. According to the comparison site Moneysupermarket.com, the number of mortgage deals available from UK banks reduced from 27,962 in 2007 at the boom's peak, to only 2,282 in July 2009.[11]

Another source of positive feedback is risk management tools such as Value at Risk (VaR). Banks are required by regulators to use VaR to compute their maximum expected losses, based on the volatility of the relevant assets over the past year or so. The number determines how much capital they are required to hold in reserve. If markets are calm and operating smoothly, then the computed risk is low, and banks are free to leverage up; but if markets are stormy, then computed risk goes up and banks have to sell assets to bring their VaR back within an acceptable limit.

Because banks all use the same formula, with only minor adjustments, a consequence is that when volatility increases they are all required to sell assets at the same time. This creates further volatility, which again increases VaR, which means that more assets need to be sold to meet the regulatory requirement, and so on. The well-intended risk formula can then end up making the markets more risky. This type of synchronised de-leveraging was one of the causes of market turbulence in 2007.[12] As discussed in the next chapter, the VaR method has many other problems; but the point here is that *any* such numerical formula that computes risk based only on past price fluctuations will destabilise the markets, so long as it is uniformly adopted.

Bank runs such as the one that hit Northern Rock are the ultimate example of destructive feedback. Banks can function only if they have the trust and confidence of their customers, and of other banks. If a rumour gets out that a bank is in trouble, for whatever reason, then two things will happen: its customers will start trying to get their money out, and other banks will suddenly stop answering their calls. Even if the bank wasn't in real trouble, it soon will be. Its shares don't decline in an orderly fashion – the market for them just suddenly disappears. One of the main roles of central banks, as mentioned earlier, is to step in and act as the lender of last resort in such situations.

Positive feedback is also apparent in the wild swings of the currency markets, which often have little or nothing to do with what is going on with the actual countries involved. A favourite occupation of currency traders is the so-called carry trade. This involves borrowing in a low-yield currency, such as the Japanese yen, or (at the time of writing) the American dollar, and investing the funds in a high-yield currency. The trader pockets the difference in interest rates. The only risk is that the high-yield currency will depreciate relative to the loan currency, thus making the loan harder to pay off. If, for example, one of the governments involved adjusts its interest rates, then what can happen is that traders rush to unwind their positions, the high-yield currency depreciates in response, the trade becomes even less attractive, and the currencies suddenly jump to a new level.

Positive feedback is therefore an intrinsic and pervasive feature of the economy that appears in many different forms. It has been the driving force in asset price bubbles and crashes throughout financial history, with only the theme changing. The Dutch tulip mania of 1637 saw the newly introduced bulb become one of the hottest commodities of all time, as prices grew to insane heights before suddenly wilting. In 1720, the South Sea bubble was driven by speculation in shares of the South Sea Company, which had a monopoly to trade in Spain's South American colonies. Not much trading was going on, but rumours of access to unlimited supplies of South American gold meant that the stock rose from £175 to over £1,000 in a few months. It then collapsed to £135. In the 1840s, it was the railway crisis; at the end of the 20th century, we had the dot-com bubble.

Such manias and their accompanying crashes are dramatic; however, the presence of positive and negative feedback loops means that even in more apparently stable times the market is constantly reacting to itself. In part this is because markets are composed of people who reflect on current conditions and respond to them, but it's interesting to note that this reflexivity is a property of complex organic systems in general. Biological systems like our own bodies, or ecosystems, or indeed the biosphere as a whole, are also constantly evolving and adapting. In fact, a characteristic of such systems is that they operate at a condition far from equilibrium, in the sense that their components are constantly being churned around rather than relaxing to a state of stasis. The only systems that achieve stability are inert objects, but the economy is very much alive.

Having a Minsky moment

In comparing the achievements of Jevons et al. with those of Maxwell, it is easy to see why economics is often accused of suffering from 'physics envy'.[13] It is a bit of a stretch to compare, as Schumpeter did, the 'classic synthesis' of Walras with the synthesis of the laws of electromagnetism. At the same time, though, I have a good deal of admiration for the founders of neoclassical economics. They were smart, energetic, politically engaged, interested in different disciplines. They wanted to use techniques from science and engineering to understand the economy and make a better world. The tragedy is that mainstream economics did not develop much beyond their initial vision of a stable economy governed by simple mechanical laws.

The idea that markets might be inherently unstable goes back at least to Frederick Soddy's work from the 1920s (discussed later). Perhaps its best-known proponent, though, was the American economist Hyman Minsky. Before he died in 1996, Minsky was one of the few economists to speak out against deregulation and the risk of expanding credit. According to his Financial Instability Hypothesis, there are three types of borrowers: hedge, speculative, and Ponzi. Hedge borrowers can make payments on both the interest and the capital. A person with a traditional mortgage is a hedge borrower. Speculative borrowers can only service the interest payments, like a homeowner with an interest-only mortgage. Ponzi borrowers (named for the famous swindler Charles Ponzi) can't service interest payments but rely on the asset increasing in value. They are like a subprime mortgage-holder with no income, no job, but plenty of hope.

According to Minsky, in prosperous times debt tends to accumulate, first among hedge and speculative borrowers, and finally with Ponzi borrowers, as a result of positive feedback: 'Success breeds a disregard of the possibility of failure.'[14] However, debt becomes increasingly unsustainable, until finally the economy reaches a crisis point, now known as the Minsky Moment. The first to crash are the Ponzi borrowers, then the speculative borrowers, and finally even the hedge borrowers may be brought down. In the language of nonlinear dynamics, the Minsky Moment is the point where feedback changes direction to drive the markets down.

Minsky was considered an outsider and a maverick in the economics profession. In 1996, one reviewer wrote that his 'work has not had a major influence in the macroeconomic discussions of the last thirty years'.[15] Until 2008, most economists probably thought that Minsky Moment was a synth pop group from the 80s.

Control theory and nonlinear dynamics are becoming better known in economics circles – there is now a Society for Nonlinear Dynamics and Econometrics, with its own journal – but they have perhaps had their greatest impact in the area of business forecasting.[16] As mentioned in Chapter 1, one reason why the economy is so hard to predict is because of emergent properties that defy reductionist analysis. An equally important problem for forecasters is the interplay between positive and negative feedback loops. For every trend, it seems, a counter-trend soon develops; for every driver of a new technology, there is a blocker.

The difficulty for business forecasters is trying to guess how this balance between positive and negative feedback will play out – and what will be the next big thing. Precise forecasts are impossible; but studies and model simulations can still be useful to explore possible future scenarios and find ways to improve performance.[17]

Out of control

It might seem strange that control theory has not had wider influence on neoclassical theory, given that they were both founded at the same time; and that market economies are famed for their creativity and dynamism, which often seems the opposite of stability. It makes sense only when you think of economics, not as a true scientific theory, but as an encoding of a particular story or ideology about money and society. Viewed this way, equilibrium theory – and the economyth that the economy is inherently stable – is attractive for three reasons. Firstly, it implies that the current economic arrangement is in some sense optimal (if the economy were in flux, then at some times it must be more optimal than at others). This is a nice thing for professors at, say, Harvard Business School to teach their students before they head out into the upper echelons of the business world.

Secondly, it keeps everyone else in the game. As discussed further in Chapter 7, the benefits of increased productivity in the last few decades have flowed not to workers, but to managers and investors. If academics and the government were to let out the fact that the economy is unstable and non-optimal, then the workers might start to question their role in keeping it going.

Thirdly, it allows economists to retain some of their oracular authority. If the market were highly dynamic and changeable, then the carefully constructed tools of orthodox economics would be of little practical use. Efficient market theory, for example, rests on the assumption of an underlying stable equilibrium.[18] This is especially important in the quantitative finance industry, where the impression of accuracy and reliability is paramount.

The belief in stability leads to a kind of myopia about markets. During the 1990s and the early 2000s, the world economy appeared to be growing in a smooth, steady and sustainable way. Markets, it seemed, could regulate themselves. In the UK, chancellor (and future prime minister) Gordon Brown announced 'the end of boom and bust'. In the United States, there was talk of the 'Great Moderation'. The triumvirate of Federal Reserve chairman Alan Greenspan, and successive treasury secretaries Robert Rubin and Larry Summers, successfully opposed the regulation of financial derivatives on the grounds that 'this would cause chaos', according to one insider.[19] But as shown by Maxwell's less famous set of equations, chaos is a feature of many dynamical systems. The economy was running fast and free, like a steam engine with the governor removed, careering out of control towards its date with the Minsky Moment.

As systems biologist Hiroaki Kitano notes: 'Robustness can only be controlled with a good understanding and thorough analysis of system dynamics.'[20] He was speaking of cancer biology, but the statement applies to that larger biological system known as the economy. Regulatory feedback loops are necessary for control, and without them the result can be dangerous instability.[21] One lesson from the recent crisis is that central banks need to pay as much attention to the destabilising effects of excess credit and asset price growth as they do to things like inflation. Available instruments include margin requirements and minimum capital requirements on banks, which can be dynamically controlled in response to market conditions and feedback. When markets are euphoric, both can be tightened; when markets are depressed, they can be loosened (note that this is the exact opposite of what happens with VaR).[22] Use of the controls should be flexible, instead of rule-based, to avoid being gamed for commercial advantage. Of course financial institutions will resent having such regulatory constraints imposed upon them, which is a problem because they have an incredible amount of political influence.

The main message for investors is to remember that trust and risk are coupled together in an inherently unstable way. When trust is high, firms take on more leverage, and investors get drawn into the market. The economy appears strong, but risk is growing. After a disaster, trust evaporates, but risk may actually be at its lowest. It's impossible to time the markets, but one can avoid over-leveraging during the good times, or becoming overly cautious during the bad times.

A property of complex systems like the economy is that they can often appear relatively stable for long periods of time. However, the apparent stability is actually a truce between strong opposing forces – those positive and negative feedback loops. When change happens, it often happens suddenly – as in earthquakes, or financial crashes. As seen in the next chapter, it is when considering risk that the assumption of equilibrium can be particularly misleading and dangerous.

At rest versus in motion

The idea that the economy is at rest, rather than in motion, still permeates many aspects of economic thought. One example is the macroeconomic models known as Dynamic Stochastic General Equilibrium (DSGE) models, which as discussed further in Chapter 5 are the modern versions of Walras's equilibrium model. These see the economy as an inherently stable system that is subject to random (stochastic) perturbations or 'external shocks' but that tends to return to equilibrium. The 'dynamic' in the name is therefore misleading, since the only dynamic considered is restoration to stability. In recent years, these equilibrium models have come under increasing criticism from a variety of quarters, in what amounts to a veritable Greek chorus of woe. The situation serves as a graphic illustration of the tragic but slow-motion collapse of mainstream economics, as one if its key economyths collides with reality, and fails, but still somehow struggles on.

In his 2013 book *Never Let a Serious Crisis Go to Waste*, Philip Mirowski – a long-time critic of mainstream economics – pointed out that logically, based as it was on equilibrium, DSGE modelling could 'serve no useful function once the crisis hit, because it essentially denied that any such debacle could have materialized'.[23] In an article the same year, William White of the OECD agreed that 'such crises were literally ruled out in DSGE models by the assumption of self-stabilization'.[24] (A related issue is the already mentioned fact that these models, as White notes, 'make no reference to money or credit, and they have no financial sector'. This seems bizarre, but as discussed in Chapter 11 it actually makes perfect sense.)

In a 2014 piece for the Post-Crash Economics Society, the Bank of England's Andrew Haldane wrote that macroeconomic models typically incorporate an equilibrium which is 'unique, stationary and efficient' and a view of the economy which is 'ordered and rational'.[25] A consequence is that the models 'have failed to make sense of the sorts of extreme macroeconomic events, such as crises, recessions and depressions, which matter most to society'.

In 2015, Stephen King from HSBC told the British Academy: 'If one looks at standard dynamic stochastic general equilibrium (DSGE) models that are used by policy makers, it is easy to spot important factors which are excluded: the financial sector, the rest of the world, oil prices and innovation, to name a few. Excluding these factors facilitates the modelling of a long-run return to a steady state of equilibrium, but at the expense of reality.'[26] In his 2015 book *Economics Rules*, Harvard's Dani Rodrik stated: 'I cannot think of an important economic insight that has come out of such models. In fact, they have often led us astray.' In 2016 the prominent macroeconomist Paul Romer, now chief economist at the World Bank, admitted the whole area was basically 'pseudoscience' (see Appendix).

Now, it won't come as a surprise to readers of this book that, some 140 years after Walras first proposed them, and following untold man-hours of expensive development by academics, central bank researchers, and others in what MIT economist Ricardo Caballero described as 'an enormous collective effort' involving 'an increasing number of bells and whistles', these equilibrium models – the workhorses of macroeconomics, the trusted stalwarts of policy-makers – turn out to *not actually work* (because there is no equilibrium).[27] But it might seem puzzling that they are still in widespread use; or that when a team led by Steve Keen wanted to develop an alternative software package, appropriately called Minsky since it can model the nonlinear buildup of credit which characterises financial bubbles, they had to partially fund it on Kickstarter.[28]

One reason, as Wolfgang Munchau observed in the *Financial Times* in 2015, is that 'The mainstream invested a life's work' in developing their equilibrium models. 'They will not let go easily, but continue to tinker with their models, and hope that no policy maker will ever use them.'[29] (Unfortunately, as he pointed out, they of course already have, a lot.) He predicted that 'the successful challenge will come from outside the discipline, and that it will be brutal'. Another reason, as Romer noted, is that economists have been afraid to point out defects in models championed by leaders in their field for fear of provoking an 'unpleasant reaction' (though presumably that fear has begun to wear off). But the main reason is that the equilibrium economyth goes right to the heart of mainstream economics, so it can't be dispensed with easily. And calling it a caricature or a straw man won't make it go away either.

Steve Keen, in a 2016 article, argued that 'the continued use of the construct of equilibrium by economists is, without doubt, *the* major barrier to progress in the field'.[30] Approaches that do not assume equilibrium, including agent-based models and system dynamics programs such as Minsky, are broadening the range of models used in economics. Another perspective on non-equilibrium behaviour is provided by the field of evolutionary economics. A relative of other areas such as complexity economics and ecological economics, it borrows ideas from evolutionary biology to study the evolution of firms and other institutions within the economy, where forces of what Schumpeter called 'creative destruction' are constantly disrupting the old order. Even, if very slowly, in economics.

CHAPTER 4

THE EXTREME ECONOMY

*The same flaw found in risk models that helped
cause the financial meltdown is present in economic
models invoked by 'experts'. Anyone relying on
these models for conclusions is deluded.*
Nassim Nicholas Taleb and Mark Spitznagel (2009)

*There is no more common error than to assume
that, because prolonged and accurate mathematical
calculations have been made, the application of the
result to some fact of nature is absolutely certain.*
A.N. Whitehead (1911)

Economists are taught that risk in the economy can be managed using well-established scientific techniques, unless of course something really unusual happens. The problem is, such so-called extreme events aren't quite as unusual as theory would suggest: in the last thirty years we've had Black Monday, the Asian financial crisis, the Russian financial crisis, the dot-com bust, and the great financial crisis of 2007–08. This chapter looks under the hood of the risk models used by banks and other financial institutions, and finds that they rely on dangerous assumptions – stability, independent investors, and so on – that put our savings, pensions, and businesses in danger.

In October 2008, investors stared into the abyss. For a while it appeared that the entire financial system was on the verge of collapse. It was as if the whole world had gone to the cash machine, typed in the PIN, hit withdraw, and seen a blinking sign – INSUFFICIENT FUNDS.

Were we going to lose our jobs? Our houses? Our retirement nest-eggs? Would there be a complete breakdown, a return to the stone age? Would all social order come to an end? Would we end up scavenging for food in the forest and living off worms and grubs?

Of course, the situation soon improved, at least for most. Those who had scavenged for food prematurely had to return to their homes, looking sheepish. But the near-death episode was enough to shake anyone's faith in the financial system. And people soon started to ask how it was that the economy, which for years had been doing so well, could have been building up such unseen risks. Pensions and homes that had appeared to be safe and boring investments actually turned out to be quite exciting gambles. Who knew? Could it happen again? And didn't something like that happen before, come to think of it?

To answer those questions, and see what the future might hold, we'll again need to look back into the past, and in particular the history of risk. Most risk models are based on a 350-year-old mathematical object, first developed for gamblers. Unfortunately it gives the wrong answers, but we'll show how that can be fixed.

Games of chance

Our desire to predict the future is mirrored by a desire to control it. The reason we want to foresee events is so that we can position ourselves correctly, and even influence the future.

Pythagoras is said to have taught predictive techniques based on divination through number. His student Empedocles earned the name Alexanamos, or 'Averter of Winds', for his ability to predict and control the weather. However, in general the Greeks maintained a dichotomy between the abstract world of mathematics, which was governed by stability and symmetry, and the everyday world, which was governed by a bunch of squabbling gods. Mathematics was about beauty and precision and eternal forms, not messy, provisional reality. To get insights into the future you consulted the oracle, who had a hotline to Apollo, the god of prediction.

This separation is strange, because in many respects mathematics and risk appear to be made for each other, at least when it comes to games of chance. Just as astronomy needed to await Renaissance figures like Copernicus to shake off the static hold of Greek philosophy, so mathematics had to await the arrival of those same free-thinkers to get a grip on risk. The first person to write a text on probability was an Italian mathematician, physician, astrologer, and dedicated gambler named Girolamo Cardano (1501–76).

Cardano sounds like the sort of person for whom 'risk management' would have been a useful concept. He was born the illegitimate son of a mathematically talented lawyer, whom Leonardo da Vinci had consulted on mathematical problems. Trained in medicine, Cardano was refused entry into the College of Physicians in Milan. The official reason was his illegitimate birth, but more likely it was because of his argumentative nature. To pay his way he turned to full-time gambling. That didn't go well – he pawned his wife's belongings and ended up broke – but once out of the poorhouse he started treating patients privately and soon grew famous for some astonishing cures. Eventually the College accepted him, and around the same time he started publishing his books on mathematics.

Cardano is best known today for his books on algebra, and for inventing the universal joint, but he also wrote a text, *Liber de Ludo Aleae* (Book on Games of Chance), which showed how to calculate the chances of obtaining different combinations at dice, such as rolling two sixes. As an addicted gambler who always carried a knife and once slashed the face of a cheat during a game of cards, he knew a thing or two about calculating the odds. He was perhaps the first person to fully realise that mathematical laws, which until then had been reserved for pristine subjects like celestial mechanics, could also apply to something as down-to-earth as the toss of dice.

Of course, as Cardano surely realised, not all of life's risks can be quantified in equations. He grew famous for his medical and mathematical achievements, but in 1560 his eldest son was found guilty of poisoning his wife, and was tortured and executed. His other son was a gambler and was repeatedly jailed for robbery. These events ruined Cardano emotionally and nearly destroyed his career. In 1570 he was imprisoned by the Inquisition for six months for publishing a horoscope of Jesus Christ.

His book on chance was found among his manuscripts, and was not published until nearly a century after his death. Perhaps for that reason, probability theory did not take another major lurch forward until 1654, when the Chevalier de Méré posed an urgent question to the greatest mathematical minds of France: how do you divide up the pot when a game of *balla* is interrupted by lunch?

Pascal's wager

Blaise Pascal is better known today for Pascal's wager – his statement that, even though God's existence cannot be rationally proved, the wisest course of action is to behave as if God does exist. The upside of this gamble is very good (salvation), the downside small. If instead you behave as if there is no God, then there's a potentially huge downside (damnation) and not much upside.

The stakes in the problem posed by de Méré were less critical, but people had been puzzling over it for a long time. The winner at *balla* was the first to six rounds (the rest of the rules have been lost to history). In 1494 the Franciscan monk Luca Paccioli had argued that, if one person was ahead 5 to 3 when the game was cut short, then the pot should be divided in the same proportion. In collaboration with the great French mathematician Pierre de Fermat, Pascal used (actually, invented) probability theory to show that this answer wasn't quite right.

To illustrate this, Figure 7 lists the different possible outcomes, were the game to be continued starting from 5:3. The outcome of the next game, denoted *G1* in the left column, can either be 6:3, in which case the first player wins, or 5:4, in which case the game continues for another round. The only way for the second player to win is by winning three games in a row (shown in bold). If the chances of winning a game are exactly even, then the chance of winning three games in a row is $1/2 \times 1/2 \times 1/2 = 1/8$.

Start		5:3			
G1	6:3		**5:4**		
G2		6:4		**5:5**	
G3			6:5		**5:6**

Figure 7. The different possible outcomes for a game of *balla*, starting from the case at the top where one player is ahead 5 to 3. The left column lists the games. The second player can win the match only by winning three consecutive games.

Since the probabilities must add up to 1, the chance of the first player winning is 1 minus 1/8, or 7/8, which is 7 times the probability that the second player can win. The stakes should therefore be divided in a ratio 7:1, which is far greater than the 5:3 proposed by Paccioli.

A novel feature of Pascal's method was that it was based not just on what has already happened, but on future events that have yet to happen. It therefore established the basic principles of risk management that are still in use today: consider all the possible different future outcomes, estimate the likelihood of each, then use the most likely outcomes as a basis for decision-making.

Pascal generalised his method to obtain what is now known as Pascal's triangle, shown in Figure 8 (the same figure was studied by the Chinese mathematician Yanghui some 500 years earlier, so there it is known as the Yanghui triangle). It is constructed in a very simple way: the numbers at the start and end of each row are 1, and the other numbers in the row are equal to the sum of the two nearest numbers in the row above. As we'll see, this figure is extremely instructive about financial risk, or at least how we model that risk.

The rows of the triangle correspond to separate coin tosses. In game *G1*, the possible results are one head (the 1 in the column labelled *1H*) or one tail (the 1 in the column labelled *1T*). An arrow points to each of these outcomes, which have equal probability.

Now suppose that we play another game, and keep track of the total score. If the result of game *G1* was a tail, then game *G2* will produce either another tail, so the score is two tails; or a head, so the score is a draw. If, on the other hand, game *G1* gave a head, then after game *G2* the total score will be either a draw or two heads. There are therefore two ways of producing a draw, which means that this result is twice as likely as that of two tails or two heads. This is indicated by the number 2 in the central column, with the two arrows pointing in to it from above. The total probabilities must sum to 1, so we need to divide each number in the row by the sum of the row. Here the sum is 4, so the probability of two tails is 1/4; the probability of a head and a tail is 2/4; and the probability of two heads is 1/4.

After the third round, the possible scores are three tails (which has one arrow pointing to it), a head and two tails (three arrows), two heads and a tail (three arrows), or three heads (one arrow).

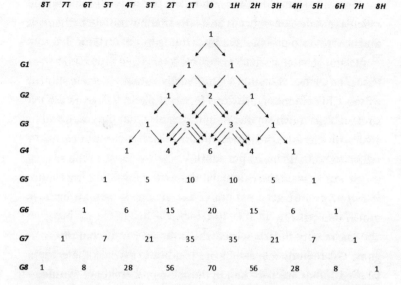

Figure 8. Pascal's triangle. The rows represent different games: *G1*, *G2*, etc. The columns represent a tally of heads or tails, so for example *2H* corresponds to the case where heads are winning by 2. The central column represents a tied result. The scheme for determining the entries is shown for the first four games. In each row, the number is the sum of the two nearest numbers in the row above. The summing process is indicated graphically by the arrows, so each number is equal to the number of arrows flowing into it from above. This triangle can be used to calculate the probability of any outcome from a sequence of coin tosses (or any other game in which the odds are even).

The arrows can be thought of as counting the number of possible paths to a result. Since each path is equally likely, the total number of arrows reflects the likelihood of the result. We again divide by the row total to get the probabilities. The chances of getting a mixed result are now 6/8, which is three times greater than the 2/8 chance of all heads or all tails.

Continuing in this way, we can read off the relative likelihood of any combination of heads and tails after any number of games, and convert into probabilities by dividing by the total for that row. For example, after six games, the row total is 1+6+15+20+15+6+1 = 64. The chance of tossing six consecutive heads is therefore 1 (the number in column *6H*) divided by 64, or about 0.016 (i.e. 1.6 per cent). This is much smaller than the chance that the result will be tied, which is 20 (the number in the central column) divided by 64, or about 0.31 (i.e. 31 per cent).

If we calculate these probabilities for the result of a large number of games, we get a bar graph like the one shown in Figure 9, which shows the result after 40 games. The height of each bar gives the probability of that score, which ranges on the bottom scale from −40, indicating 40 tails, to +40, indicating 40 heads. The shape of the graph is symmetrical, because the probability of winning a certain number of heads is always the same as winning a certain number of tails (we're assuming that the coin is fairly balanced). The graph is also bell-shaped, which means that the chances of a moderate result (a draw or a win by a small margin) are far greater than the chances of a lopsided outcome in favour of heads or tails. Note that after 40 games, the chances of tossing either all heads or all tails are nearly zero.

For whom the bell tolls

In 1733, the mathematician Abraham de Moivre showed that after an infinitely large number of games, the results would converge on the so-called bell curve (otherwise known as the normal or Gaussian distribution). This is shown by the solid line in Figure 9. The curve is specified by two numbers: the mean or average, which here is zero, and the standard deviation, which is a measure of the curve's width. In a normal distribution, about 68 per cent of the data fall within one standard deviation from the mean; about

Figure 9. Bar graph of the probabilities calculated by Pascal's triangle, for 40 games. Also shown is the corresponding normal distribution (solid line). The standard deviation is approximately 6.3.

95 per cent of the data are within two standard deviations; and about 99 per cent of the data are within three standard deviations. In Figure 9 the standard deviation is about 6.3, so after 40 games there is a 99 per cent probability that the score will be in the range −19 to +19. The odds are therefore only about 1 in 100 that someone will win by twenty games or more.

De Moivre was a respected mathematician and a friend of Isaac Newton, but he didn't have an academic position and supported himself by tutoring mathematics, playing chess for money, and occasional mathematical consulting to gamblers or the insurance industry. One of the first applications of the normal distribution was to the problem of estimating the revenue from annuities, because it turned out that human life spans also followed the bell curve quite closely. De Moivre's method for estimating his own life span was a little different. In later life, when his health was failing, he noticed that he was sleeping fifteen minutes longer every night. Doing the maths, he figured that by 27 November 1754 he would be sleeping for 24 hours. His prediction proved correct, and he died that day. (Girolamo Cardano also correctly predicted the day of his death, but it is believed that he cheated by committing suicide.)

The normal distribution also found many other applications in science and engineering (which is why it became known as normal). Scientists including Pierre-Simon Laplace, and particularly Carl Friedrich Gauss, used the method to analyse the errors in astronomical data (which is why its other name is the Gaussian distribution). They found that if many separate and independent measurements were taken of, say, a star's position in the sky, then the distribution of errors tended to follow the normal curve (yet another name at the time was the error law). The standard deviation of the errors therefore gave a measure of the accuracy.

The bell curve was adopted even more enthusiastically by social scientists, who found that it could be used to fit pretty much anything. For example, measurements of the height of English males were found to follow a near-perfect bell curve. One of the technique's greatest advertisers was the Victorian polymath Francis Galton, who wrote: 'I know of scarcely anything so apt to impress the imagination as the wonderful form of cosmic order expressed by the "law of error". A savage, if he could understand it, would worship it as a god. It reigns with severity in complete self-effacement amidst the wildest confusion. The huger the mob and the greater the anarchy, the more perfect is its sway. It is the supreme law of Unreason.'[1]

Mathematical justification for the ubiquity of the normal distribution came with the so-called Central Limit Theorem. This proved that the normal distribution could be used to model the sum of any random processes, provided that a number of conditions were met. In particular, the separate processes had to be independent, and identically distributed.

In his 1900 thesis *The Theory of Speculation*, Louis Bachelier used the normal distribution to model the variation of prices in the Paris bourse (Chapter 2). But it was only in the 1960s, with Eugene Fama's efficient market hypothesis, that the bell curve would really take its place as the 'supreme law of Unreason'.

The supreme law of unreason

According to the efficient market hypothesis, the market is always in a state of near-perfect balance between buyers and sellers. Any change in an asset's price is the result of small, independent, random perturbations as individuals buy or sell. The net result of many such changes will be like the final tally of a sequence of coin tosses, which de Moivre showed is governed by the bell curve. It follows that, even if the price change on a given day is unpredictable, one can still calculate the probability of a particular price change – just as insurance analysts can calculate the probability of a healthy male living to the age of 80, without knowing the exact day of death. It is therefore possible to derive a measurement of risk.

For example, suppose that we wish to calculate the risk in holding a particular asset such as stock in a particular company. According to the efficient market hypothesis, if we neglect longer-term effects such as growth and just concentrate on day-to-day price fluctuations, then the price changes are purely random. One day they will be up, the next they will be down, but there is no underlying pattern. We can therefore model them statistically with the normal distribution. A plot of the price changes should follow a bell curve, rather like Figure 9. The standard deviation is then one measure of the risk in holding that stock, because the larger it is, the higher the potential price swings. If another asset, such as a safer company, or a government bond, has a smaller standard deviation, then it appears to be less risky. (Of course, this assumes that volatility is a good measure of risk, a topic we will return to.) Since most people are willing to pay to avoid risk, it follows that the standard deviation should influence the asset's price. An optimal portfolio will maximise growth but minimise risk.

Economists of the 1960s and 70s began devising complex formulae to measure and control risk. William F. Sharpe's Capital Asset Pricing Model computed the value of any financial asset, taking into account its risk. It was based on Harry Markowitz's Modern Portfolio Theory, which presented a technique for minimising risk by choosing asset classes that are uncorrelated with one another. Fischer Black and Myron Scholes came up with a clever method for calculating the prices of options – financial derivatives that give one the right to buy or sell a security for a fixed price at some time in the future.[2] The field of financial engineering was born. Several of its founders, including those mentioned, were later awarded the economics version of the Nobel Prize.

These techniques all assumed the key economic myths: that investors are rational and independent; that markets are free and fair; that markets are stable and correctly reflect value and risk; and that, as a result of all this, price changes are random and follow a normal distribution. The techniques were therefore all based on formulae developed for 18th-century astronomy; which in turn were based on Pascal's triangle.

Even today, the normal distribution is the gold standard for risk calculation.[3] It was enshrined in the Basel II regulatory framework as a method for banks to calculate their risk (though the latest version, Basel III, also allows for other methods; see box, page 117). As we will see in Chapter 6, the assumption of normality, and the economyth that economic risk can be easily managed using statistics, also played an important role in valuing the complex financial instruments that brought about the credit crunch. The main attraction of the normal distribution is its convenience: it allows traders to estimate risk in a single parameter, the standard deviation. There is no need to make a complex judgement based on a detailed understanding of the asset or the market as a whole – just plug in a number and you're done. And if anyone asks, you can say it's backed by science. As one professor commented, 'We don't just assume normal distributions because it makes our life easier (although that is certainly part of it). The Central Limit Theorem gives us some cover for the pervasive normality assumption.'[4]

Of course most economists have long been aware that the assumptions behind normality do not hold perfectly, but it has generally been assumed that they hold well enough. As Fama put it in 1965, real data is unlikely to be 'characterized by perfect independence' and so the theory 'cannot be a completely accurate description of reality. For practical purposes, however, we may be willing to accept the independence assumption of the model as long as the dependence in the series of successive price changes is not above some "minimum acceptable" level.'[5]

The normal distribution has therefore played a key role in our financial system for the last half-century. That's enough time to compile a fair amount of data. So how's it doing so far?

The answer to this question would appear to be: not so well. The first big test came on 19 October 1987 (aka Black Monday), when the Dow Jones Industrial Index took everyone by surprise and dropped 29.2 per cent. According to theory, the chances of that happening were about 1 in 10 followed by 45 zeros – i.e. impossible.

In 1998, the firm Long-Term Capital Management used efficient market theory to make highly leveraged bets, by basically selling insurance against the possibility of extreme events. When such events materialised, courtesy of the Russian government defaulting on their bonds, the firm nearly self-destructed and had to be rescued in a $3.6 billion bail-out before it brought down the rest of the economy. According to theory, the chances of that happening were again incredibly small. At least they should have been, since the fund had a number of economic superstars on its payroll, including Myron Scholes. A memo from Merrill Lynch concluded that the models used 'may provide a greater sense of security than warranted; therefore reliance on these models should be limited'.[6]

In fact, orthodox risk-assessment techniques have failed to realistically assess the risk of every financial crisis of the past few decades, including the 1997 Asian crisis, the 2000 dot-com crisis, and of course the 2007–08 financial crisis. As a theory, it appears to have no backing from observational data. The reason is that, despite its obvious attractiveness and ease-of-use, the theory suffers from one major, overarching problem, which is that price changes don't actually follow a normal distribution. They're not normal.

Shaky grounds

While financial mathematics has its roots in games of chance, the truth is that real life does not follow the neat patterns of cards or dice. As author and former trader Nassim Taleb notes: 'The casino is the only human venture I know where the probabilities are known, Gaussian (i.e., bell-curve), and almost computable.'[7] The financial markets are not a kind of giant coin-tossing experiment – they are something far more complex, intractable, and extreme.

This is true even for everyday price changes. Panel A of Figure 10 shows daily price fluctuations in the S&P 500 index (a value-weighted index of the top 500 public companies in the

United States) from 1950. The record downward spike on Black Monday is clearly visible, as is the more recent turbulence from the credit crisis.

As a comparison, panel B shows what the price changes would have looked like if they had followed the normal distribution, with the standard deviation that would be calculated for the real price changes. You don't need to be an expert in statistics to see that these data have a very different appearance. The S&P 500 data has periods of calm followed by bursts of intense activity, while the normal data always fluctuates within a constant band. The real data also has much greater extremes than the normal data.

The lower panels of Figure 10 are histograms that express the probability distribution as in Figure 9. Panel D, for the normal distribution, reproduces the familiar bell curve as expected. The largest price swing in any one day is about 4.5 per cent. The real data, panel C, might not look that different; however, closer inspection reveals that it has what are known as fat tails: the extremes of the distribution extend to much higher and smaller values. As seen more easily in the upper panel, the price swing exceeded 4.5 per cent on 54 different days over the 60-year period – so an event that according to theory should almost never happen, actually happened about once per year on average.

Now, it has often been argued that the markets are normal most of the time, with only the occasional lapse into abnormal behaviour. Perhaps Black Monday and the credit crunch are inherently unpredictable events that come out of nowhere. If so, then there isn't much we can do about these 'Black Swans', to use Taleb's term. But if we look a little closer at the financial data, we see that it does have, not regularity, but a kind of character.

For example, financial crashes are often compared to earthquakes. This is no loose metaphor: in a very real sense, financial crashes feel like an earthquake happening in slow motion. The

Figure 10. Panel A shows daily percentage price changes in the S&P 500 index over a period of nearly 60 years. Panel B is what the price changes would look like if they followed a normal distribution

with the same standard deviation. Panel C is a histogram of price changes. Panel D is a histogram of the corresponding normal distribution.

top panel of Figure 11 is a zoomed view of the S&P 500 data for the period of the recent credit crunch. The lower panel shows 50 minutes of seismographic data recording during the earthquake of 17 January 1995 in Kobe, Japan. There is a strikingly similar appearance to the data. So when one of the traders at Lehman Brothers told a BBC reporter in September 2008 that 'It is terrible ... like a massive earthquake', she was being accurate.[8]

But the correspondence goes even deeper than that, for it turns out that the frequency of both phenomena is described by the same kind of mathematical law. If you double the size of an earthquake, it becomes about four times rarer. This is called a power law, because the probability depends on the size to the power 2. (A number raised to the power 2 is the number squared; a number raised to the power 3 is the number cubed; and so on.) Financial crashes are similar. Numerous studies have demonstrated that the distribution of price changes for major international indices follow a power-law distribution with a power of approximately 3.[9]

Power-law distributions are scale-free, in the sense that there is no 'typical' or 'normal' representative. There is only the rule that the larger an event is, the less likely it becomes. In many respects, power-law distributions are therefore the opposite of the normal distribution. The bell curve is concentrated about the mean, with a well-defined standard deviation. The power law, in contrast, is scale-free, but biased towards smaller events. (If economists were to do the job of a geophysicist, they would say that earthquakes don't exist – there is just a constant low level of vibration in the earth.)

Given that we can't predict earthquakes any better than we can predict financial crashes, it is again tempting to see crashes as isolated events. However, the scale-free nature of financial data implies that this is not the case. There is no clear boundary between normal and extreme: only the knowledge that, the bigger the change, the smaller the chance of it happening. To understand

Figure 11. Top panel is a zoomed view of the S&P 500 data from the preceding figure, showing the time period of the 2008 credit crunch. Lower panel shows seismological data from the 1995 earthquake in Kobe, Japan.[10]

this more clearly, it may help to take another look at Pascal's triangle, which also has a power law hidden within it.

Fractal markets

Figure 12 shows a modified version of Pascal's triangle in which the odd numbers are covered with triangles, leaving only the even numbers. Now imagine this extending to larger versions of the triangle (corresponding to more coin tosses). The result then converges towards a peculiar geometric object known as the Sierpinski gasket, discovered by the Polish mathematician Waclaw Sierpinski in 1916. This figure is shown in the lower panel.

The usual way to construct this figure is to start with a triangle; divide into four smaller triangles; and remove the central triangle. This process is then repeated for the three remaining triangles, and so on, *ad infinitum*.

The Sierpinski gasket is an early example of what mathematician Benoît Mandelbrot called fractals. These are geometric objects that have the property of self-similarity – no matter how far you zoom in, the object continues to reveal finer detail and structure, and different scales have a similar appearance. There is no preferred or 'normal' size for one of the white triangles.

As Mandelbrot noted, financial data is also self-similar – if you look at data taken over years, months, weeks, days, or even seconds, it is hard to know from the shape of the plot what the timescale is.[11] And it turns out that the gasket is close to being a visual history of stockmarket crashes.

To see this, suppose that each of the white triangles corresponds to a price change, with the size of the top edges equal to the size of the percentage change in a single day. The figure is dominated by a few large events, but as you zoom in further and further you can see that there are innumerable smaller triangles that correspond to much smaller fluctuations.

Figure 12. Top panel shows Pascal's triangle with the odd numbers covered. If you extend this pattern to larger versions of the figure, the result begins to resemble the Sierpinski gasket (lower panel). Market price fluctuations follow a similar pattern to the size of the triangles.

In real markets, the largest price changes tend to be crashes, which happen in times of panic. If the overall figure has sides of length 100, then the triangle at the centre has size 50. Let's say that corresponds to a fall of 50 per cent in one day – the worst imaginable crash, I hope, and the one we haven't had yet in a major index. Then there are three crashes of half the size (25 per cent); nine crashes of a quarter the size (12.5 per cent); and 27 crashes of an eighth the size (6.25 per cent). In general, every time we halve the size of the price change, there are three times as many that occur.

This relationship is equivalent to a power law, similar to that for earthquakes except that the power used is slightly different. It also captures the behaviour of the financial markets. Figure 13 shows the 100 largest price changes in the S&P 500, ranked in descending order (solid line). The dotted line is the result you would get by assuming that price changes follow the same distribution as the Sierpinski gasket. It is obviously not a perfect fit (this can be improved by adjusting the power). However, it is much better than the results calculated using the normal distribution, shown by the dashed line, which are clearly far too small. We therefore see that the presence of extreme market crashes is no more bizarre or inexplicable than the presence of the large triangles in the gasket: they all belong to the picture, and are created by the same processes.

It isn't just financial crashes and earthquakes that have these fractal patterns; the lengths of coastlines, the size of craters on the moon, the diameters of blood vessels, the populations of cities, the arrangements of species in ecosystems, and many other natural and man-made systems show fractal statistics. As we will see in Chapter 7, the sizes of businesses follow a fractal pattern – there are many smaller ones, and just a few big multinationals at the top. Pareto's 80–20 law was an observation that wealth scales fractally. Indeed, fractals are a kind of signature of complex organic systems

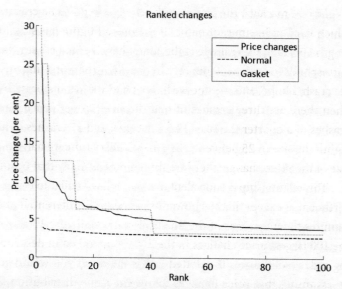

Figure 13. Plot comparing the 100 largest price changes in the S&P 500, ranked in descending order (solid line), with the 100 largest price changes from the normal distribution (dashed line), and the result you would get by assuming that price changes follow the same distribution as the Sierpinski gasket (dotted line). A largest crash of 50 per cent is assumed (not shown). The laddering effect is because the triangles in the gasket come in groups of the same size – for example there is one of the largest size, three of the next largest size, and so on.

operating far from equilibrium, which tend to evolve towards a state known as self-organised criticality.[12]

Going critical

The classic example of self-organised criticality is the humble sand-pile. Imagine a conical sandpile with sides of a certain slope. If the slope is too steep, then the pile will be unstable and adding just a single grain could cause it to collapse. This is the chaotic state, which shows sensitivity to initial conditions. On the other hand, if the slope is very shallow, then adding a few extra grains to the top of the pile won't cause much of a disturbance. In this state the system is stable. If you now continue to add grains of sand, then the sandpile will eventually converge, or self-organise, to a critical state. In a sense, this state is maximally efficient, because it has the steepest sides and reaches as high as possible without becoming fully unstable. However, it is not very robust. Adding further grains of sand will create avalanches that range in size from extremely small to very large, and that follow a power-law, scale-free distribution. The system is not chaotic or stable, but on the border between the two.

One can therefore hypothesise that markets, like the earth's crust or species in ecosystems, self-organise to a critical state, and so exhibit fractal statistics. This is an interesting insight, and one that links financial markets to the natural world. Unfortunately, it isn't much help in making precise predictions, or even calculating the odds of a crash in the future.[13] One reason is that we can know the exact distribution only by making a statistical sample of existing data. If you know that the data is normally distributed, then it is possible to quickly estimate the mean and standard deviation using standard techniques. But if the data is scale-free, then the largest and most important events occur extremely rarely. Even several decades of S&P 500 data gives us only a few major crashes. This makes it much more difficult to come up with accurate statistical estimates for the probability of similar events.[14]

Also, fractal statistics tell you only about the distribution of price changes, not the timing or the degree of clustering. We know that earthquakes follow a power-law distribution, but we still have no idea when the next one will strike.[15] (One useful tip, though, is that volatility does show clustering – if the markets are stormy, it's not safe to expect them to calm down soon.) Finally, a model that was valid in the 1960s or 1980s won't be valid in the 2010s, because the entire economy will be different – the mix of companies, investors, regulators, and so on will have changed.

Traders and investors like to have simple formulae that they can understand. The great appeal of the normal distribution is that it boils risk down to a single number, the standard deviation. It is possible to come up with more elaborate versions of the bell curve that include fat tails (extreme events), asymmetry, or temporal clustering, but this introduces extra complications and parameters, and the sampling problem means that the resulting estimates for extreme events are little better than guesses. Some hedge funds do use sophisticated statistical algorithms, but they tend to be focused on specialised trades that exploit isolated pockets of predictability. A dirty secret of quantitative finance is that the tools used are usually quite simple – those maths and physics Ph.D.s are largely for show. So in practice, the broader field of risk modelling hasn't moved on all that much since Pascal and his triangle.

A good example is the most widely used risk-modelling technique, Value at Risk or VaR, seen earlier. As the name suggests, it is used to estimate the worst-case loss that an institution could face on a given financial position. The method has been adopted and sanctioned by banks, regulators and credit rating institutions, and is important for investors and analysts. Risk is estimated by taking historical data over a time window ranging from a few months to several years, depending on the case, and applying standard statistical techniques to give a likelihood for a particular loss. This is usually expressed in terms either of standard deviation or percentage confidence level.

Despite its popularity, the model fails on a regular basis. As mentioned in the introduction, Goldman Sachs complained of

25-standard deviation events during 2007. On 29 February 2008, Bear Stearns reported a VaR of $62 million at 95 per cent confidence. By mid-March, its share price had dropped from $70 to $2, representing a loss of $8 billion. Bear Stearns were of course aware of the drawbacks of VaR, but as they stated in their final report to the Security and Exchange Commission, 'the company believes VaR models are an established methodology for the quantification of risk in the financial services industry despite these limitations'.[16] Indeed, it often seems that VaR is used as a device to sanction risk-taking behaviour and provide an excuse when things go wrong.

Even before the crisis, there have been many attempts to make VaR more robust by introducing extra variables (aka fudge factors) into the model to account for unseen risks. However, because the risks are unseen and therefore unobservable, there is no reliable way to forecast their future values.[17] The calculated risk will also depend on the exact values of these variables, making the techniques difficult to share on an industry-wide basis. Which is why risk still tends to be expressed in terms of standard deviations, even though the concept has little meaning for non-normal distributions.

The danger, as hedge fund manager David Einhorn put it, is that quantitative risk management give users 'a false sense of security ... like an air bag that works all the time, except when you have a car accident'.[18] And by downplaying the possibility of extreme events, it increases risky behaviour, thus making disaster more likely. The next way to improve economics, then, is to use the findings of complexity and fractal statistics, not to predict the timing or magnitude of the next crash, but to model the financial system and find ways to reduce the likelihood and impact of extreme events. We may not be able to build a perfect air bag, but we can make the roads safer in the first place.

Getting to normal

One useful observation from complexity theory is that, in complex organic systems, there is a trade-off between efficiency and robustness.[19] In the chaotic regime, the system fluctuates uncontrollably. In the stable regime, changes are small and follow the normal distribution. If left to their own devices, the systems will often evolve towards the critical state on the boundary between chaos and order. Here the fluctuations follow a power-law, scale-free distribution: the system is highly efficient, in the sense that it is being pushed to the maximum, but it is not robust because it is susceptible to extreme fluctuations.

In the same way, our financial system is very efficient, in the narrow sense that it generates big profits for banks and investors over the short term (this has nothing to do with the efficient market hypothesis, which is about normally distributed price changes). However, its fluctuations follow a power-law distribution, and it is susceptible to crashes that have a severe impact on the rest of society. Like a giant sandpile, investors are piling more and more money on to the top, in the hope that they can make a quick profit before the whole thing comes crashing down. In this state, extreme events aren't aberrations – they're part of the landscape.

An interesting question, then, is whether it is possible to improve the balance between stability and efficiency: to create a financial system that is less profitable in the short term, but also less prone to harmful collapses. After all, the financial system is not a natural system, but is something that we have created ourselves, so we should be able to engineer it in such a way that it behaves in a more stable fashion. Unlike a sandpile, we have at least some influence over our destiny.

Four steps immediately suggest themselves. The first is to better regulate the introduction of new financial products. The finance industry has become increasingly deregulated in the last few decades, based on the dogma that markets are stable and self-regulating. Whenever governments propose new rules, the banks complain that this will stifle innovation in the field of financial engineering. But in other kinds of engineering or technology, regulations are strictly applied because they save money and lives – they keep our systems operating in the stable regime, instead of veering off into chaos. This reduces efficiency by some measures because it means that new products take longer to get to market, but the benefits outweigh the costs.

As discussed further in Chapter 6, a major contributing factor to the credit crunch was the proliferation of new financial products (i.e. schemes) that allowed risk to be sliced and diced and sold off to third parties. The risk calculations were performed using standard techniques, which unsurprisingly weren't up to the job. In fact these new products, such as credit default swaps and collateralised mortgage obligations, turned out to have the same effect on risk as a sausage factory has on infected meat – instead of controlling risk, they disguised it and helped it propagate. Furthermore, they were not properly regulated by the financial authorities, which was a large part of their attraction. Their adoption was rather like the pharmaceutical industry introducing a new drug and claiming that there was no need to perform the necessary trials before bringing it to market.

Actually, some healthcare companies (or quacks) try to do this all the time, which is why regulatory bodies have to be on their toes. During the 2009 swine flu pandemic, the US Food and Drug Administration was forced to take action against 120 products that claimed to be able to cure or prevent the disease. These included a $2,995 'photon genie' to stimulate the immune system, and a bottle of 'Silver Shampoo' that would kill the airborne swine flu virus if it settled on your hair.[20] The FDA said that these claims were 'a potentially significant threat to public health because they may create a false sense of security and possibly prevent people from seeking proper medical help'.[21] Rather like risk models then.

It might seem that financial markets are so complex that they are impossible to regulate. However, this impression is largely due to the carefully maintained myths that markets are efficient and optimal, so any attempt to interfere with their function will be counterproductive. As Adair Turner, chair of the UK's Financial Services Authority, observes, 'the whole efficient market theory, Washington consensus, free market deregulation system' has resulted in 'regulatory capture through the intellectual zeitgeist'. The abandonment of this framework puts regulators 'in a much more worrying space, because you don't have an intellectual system to refer each of your decisions'.[22]

Effective regulation doesn't mean that regulators have to be smarter than hedge fund managers. The first step is to change their position, from allowing new financial products unless and until they are proven faulty, to (the default in other critical industries like medicine or nuclear energy) *not* allowing them unless they can be shown to provide a measurable improvement over other alternatives, with no dangerous side-effects.

Living on the edge
The next method to move the economy to a less risky regime is to reduce the incentives for bankers to make bets that have a high probability of paying off in the short term, thus generating fabulous bonuses, but are guaranteed to eventually blow up. The asymmetry in these bets is like that of Pascal's wager: they have a great upside (the bonuses) and a minimal downside (eventually the bet will go wrong, but there are no negative bonuses, and by that time the person will probably be on the beach anyway). After the credit crunch there was great public demand for measures such as pay

caps, and withholding a portion of bonuses for a few years to limit short-termism. However, at the time of writing, regulators have made only limited progress. As Mervyn King put it, paraphrasing Winston Churchill: 'Never in the field of financial endeavour has so much money been owed by so few to so many. And, one might add, with so little real reform.'[23]

The third suggestion, mentioned also in Chapter 3, is that credit creation and leverage should be controlled. The total amount of debt in the economic system in 2008, relative to gross domestic product, was approximately three times what it was in the 1980s.[24] That's fine when markets are rising, but any unexpected events quickly become amplified and create knock-on effects. Regulations shouldn't apply just to banks, but to any institution that creates credit, including derivative markets.

Leverage is of course linked to perceived risk: if you can convince a lending institution that a proposed investment has low risk, they will lend you more money. Finally, then, the risk models used by banks and financial institutions should be modernised to better reflect the fractal nature of the markets and the possibility of extreme events. Techniques from areas of mathematics such as fractal analysis can help, for example by generating realistic stress tests for financial products or institutions; however, it is equally important to acknowledge the limitations of mathematical models of any type.[25] The main implications are that banks need to hold larger reserves – i.e. keep some money under the mattress, even when risk seems low – and develop scepticism about their ability to predict the future. Just because a formula says it's safe, that doesn't mean it really is. Time-tested risk management techniques such as experience-honed intuition, common sense, and conservatism might even come back into vogue.

Perhaps the most important thing to realise with complex systems is that models can actually be counterproductive if they are taken too literally. Risk assessment based on faulty models may give a comforting illusion of control, but can turn out to be highly dangerous. Over-confidence in models makes us blind to the dangers that lurk below the surface. Just as engineers and biological systems exploit redundancy to provide a margin of safety, and boat-builders over-design their ships rather than build them to withstand only the 'normal' wave, so we need to buffer the economic system against unexpected shocks.

To summarise, the trade-off between efficiency and robustness in complex systems suggests that we can lower the risk level of the economy, if we are prepared to accept lower levels of short-term efficiency. Along with structural changes of the sort discussed in Chapter 2, this will also require a high degree of regulation. This shouldn't be surprising – all forms of life, from bacteria to an ecosystem, are closely regulated. Economists talk about the invisible hand, but if you look at your own hand, everything about it – the temperature, the blood pressure, the salinity of the cells, and so on – is subject to a fierce degree of regulation that would put any financial regulator to shame. Of course, it is possible to go too far in the other direction – we want to steady the economy, not stop it – and regulation should not be made unnecessarily complicated. A first step towards finding this balance is to change the 'intellectual zeitgeist' by absorbing new ideas from science.

It often feels that our financial system is living on the edge. Insights from complexity, network theory, nonlinear dynamics and fractal statistics may help us find our way back to a more stable and less nail-biting regime. Of course, finance is inherently risky, and when it comes to calculating the danger mathematical models are only one piece of the puzzle. Risk is ultimately a product of human behaviour, which has a way of eluding neat mathematical equations.

Straight versus crooked

As seen in this chapter, financial markets are characterised by fractal dynamics, so sharp (crooked) changes are the norm, as opposed to the linear dynamics of models used by economists, where changes tend to be proportional to the effects. (In mathematical terms, this assumption – which Keynes described as 'ridiculous' in 1939 – is related to the fact that economic models tend to be based on linearised equations around a stable equilibrium, rather than nonlinear equations which can lead to unstable behaviour and chaos.[26]) Most people managed to internalise this concept pretty well after the crisis. But there has been little progress with the problems noted here.

Consider for example the statement that 'credit creation and leverage should be controlled. The total amount of debt in the economic system in 2008, relative to gross domestic product, was approximately three times what it was in the 1980s.' To bring that up to date, banks may now hold higher reserves, but leverage in the wider economy has continued its heady ascent. In 2014, according to a study by the McKinsey Global Institute, global debt reached $199 trillion, an increase of $57 trillion in the seven years following the crisis.[27] Countries including Australia, Sweden and Canada have seen explosions in credit driven by low interest rates. Canada's banking system is no longer the envy of other developed countries as it was during the crisis; in fact with this build-up in debt it may be the most highly at risk, according to the Bank of International Settlements.[28] And of course the nonlinear dynamics behind credit creation, discussed in Chapter 3, continues to create dramatic booms and busts around the world (e.g. Chinese stocks in 2015). Conventional macroeconomic models struggle to make sense of this, in part because they ignore the role of debt and finance in general.

Bank regulators are now much more familiar with the drawbacks of the normal distribution, and are increasingly using alternatives to VaR which better account for extreme events: for example, scenario-based testing, where bankers are encouraged to think up worst-case scenarios. However, VaR still remains the gold standard for risk calculation. And while there has also been some tinkering with bankers' incentives, one of the main uses of mathematical models in finance, as Paul Wilmott and I show in *The Money Formula*, is exactly to make those incentives as wonderful as possible. Because concepts such as standard deviation and correlation are not very meaningful for financial data, risk calculations can be adjusted by cherry-picking the data. So, for example, a risky trade can be made to look less risky, which is very useful when bonuses are calculated.[29]

Traders continue to benefit from asymmetric bets using other people's money. And while there has been increased pressure to regulate banks, this has been complicated by the fact that the industry has only become more centralised since the crisis, as surviving banks took over their weaker competitors.

The system, in other words, remains as crooked as ever – and economists, with their linear thinking and their Central Limit Theorem and their basic understanding of mathematics, are still acting as naive enablers. As De Moivre's contemporary Alexander Pope put it in his *Essay on Criticism*, 'A little Learning is a dang'rous Thing; / Drink deep, or taste not the Pierian Spring: / There shallow Draughts intoxicate the Brain, / And drinking largely sobers us again'.

CHAPTER 5

The emotional economy

*In an insane world, the person who is rational has
the problem. Money is as addictive as cocaine.*
Andrew Lo, professor of financial engineering (2009)

If everything on Earth were rational, nothing would happen.
Fyodor Dostoevsky (1880)

**Mainstream economists see the economy as being on the whole
rational and efficient. This is based on the idea that individual
investors make decisions rationally. It has clearly been a while
since these economists visited a mall. While we do sometimes
apply reason and logic to financial decisions, we are also highly
influenced by the opinions of other people, advertisers, and
random compulsions that drift into our head for no particular
reason. Indeed, markets rely for their existence on emotions
such as trust and confidence: without trust there is no credit,
and without confidence there is no risk-taking. This chapter
shows that the emphasis on rationality in economic theory says
more about economists and their training than it does about the
real world, and discusses new approaches that take into account
the fact that money is emotional stuff.**

Market crashes often seem to happen in the autumn. The worst
days of the 1929 Wall Street crash were 24 October (known as
Black Thursday) and 29 October (Black Tuesday). The crash of
19 October 1987 gave us Black Monday. During the credit crunch,

there was an entire so-called Black Week: five days of trading that began on 6 October 2008, and that set records for volume and weekly decline. Historically, by far the worst month for US investors is actually September: the S&P 500 falls on average by 1.3 per cent during that month.[1] There is clearly something about the end of summer and the onset of winter that makes investors see black.

This pattern will be familiar to people who live in northern climates (I grew up in Edmonton, so I know what I'm talking about here). It's the time of year when the days are shortening at their fastest rate. I found it strangely comforting to realise this fact during the peak of the credit crunch. Of course, I thought: the markets are suffering from Seasonal Affective Disorder (SAD). They'll cheer up in the spring, when the sun starts to shine again.

Now, this might not be a very logical interpretation of stock market history. But the idea that markets have a life of their own, which includes patches of depression and elation, is hardly new. Even Alan Greenspan referred to the 'irrational exuberance' that preceded the dot-com bust.

Indeed, when you stand back and take a cool, hard look at the economy, it doesn't look like the most rational thing on earth. Those remaining traders, for example, who stand around in pits wearing brightly coloured shirts and shouting instructions over the phone to buy or sell shares or futures contracts – they seem a little, shall we say, over-excited. I suppose their actions could be driving prices back to equilibrium in an impartial, Newtonian sort of way, but I wouldn't want to bet on it.

Much trading these days is carried out by computerised trading algorithms, which are presumably immune to mood swings or psychological ailments. But it remains true that money brings out intense emotional reactions. A neurological study at University College London showed that the physical response of our brain when we experience financial loss is the same as that caused by fear or pain.[2] When the stock index spikes down, people the world over take it on the chin; when it spikes up, it's like a shot in the arm.

It is therefore strange that orthodox economic theory sees individuals as entirely cold, rational and emotionless. This is the economyth of *Homo economicus*: aka rational economic man.

The Logic Piano

Before he got into economics, the first love of William Stanley Jevons was the study of logic. He wrote a number of books and papers on the subject, including the bestselling textbook *Elementary Lessons on Logic*. In 1870 he even produced and exhibited at the Royal Society his 'Logic Piano', a kind of mechanical computer resembling a keyboard that could perform elementary logical tasks and show how conclusions are derived from a set of premises.

The aim of Jevons, and the other neoclassical economists, was to ground the study of money on a set of logical principles. The two main ingredients were the concept of the 'average man' and the utility theory of Jeremy Bentham (1748–1832).

According to Bentham, mankind was ruled by 'two sovereign masters – pain and pleasure … The principle of utility recognises this subjection, and assumes it for the foundation of that system, the object of which is to rear the fabric of felicity by the hands of reason and of law.'[3] The pursuit of pleasure was therefore a rational enterprise that could be explained in terms of logic. To question this was to 'deal in sounds instead of sense, in caprice instead of reason, in darkness instead of light'. (John Stuart Mill described Bentham as curiously naive about the complexities of the real world: 'Knowing so little of human feelings, he knew still less of the influences by which those feelings are formed: all the more subtle workings both of the mind upon itself, and of external things upon the mind, escaped him.'[4])

Of course, one person's pleasure is often another person's pain, but what counted was the response of the 'average man'. This hypothetical person was first proposed by the French scientist Adolphe Quetelet in his book *A Treatise on Man* (published in English in 1842). Quetelet found that many human statistics – such as mortality, height and weight, criminality, insanity, and so on – could be modelled using the bell curve, with a well-defined mean – the average man – and a certain spread, due to deviations from the average. His book even turned the idea of the average man into a kind of moral ideal – something to aspire to. As he put it: 'If an individual at any epoch of society possessed all the qualities of the average man, he would represent all that is great, good, or beautiful.'[5]

Armed with these ideas of utility and the average man, the neoclassical economists argued that, on average, investors would act rationally to maximise their own utility. Even if a few individuals had only a fragile grasp of logic, what counted was the average man, who could always be counted on to do the right and reasonable thing. It was therefore possible to build up a detailed mathematical model of the economy based on equations. Individual irrationality was seen only as a kind of random noise that could safely be ignored.

The model economy

The culmination of this effort was what many consider to be the jewel in the crown of neoclassical economics: the Arrow–Debreu model, created by Kenneth Arrow (the uncle of economist Larry Summers) and Gérard Debreu in the 1950s.[6] It finally proved, in a mathematically rigorous fashion, the conjecture of Léon Walras that idealised market economies would have an equilibrium.

The model consists of a number of ingredients:

- An inventory of available goods, with prices in arbitrary units. Money itself does not appear in the model.

- A list of firms, each of which has a set of production processes that describes its inputs and outputs.
- A list of households, each of which has a specified consumption plan, which describes how it intends to consume goods; an endowment, which includes things like goods and services (including labour) that it can sell; and other assets such as shares in companies.

The consumption plan for each household is determined by a unique utility function that reflects their preferences for the available goods (in fact it is necessary only for each household to rank the available goods in terms of preference). Preferences are assumed to remain fixed with time. For firms, the utility function is effectively their profits. Given a particular set of prices, it is possible to compute the optimal consumption plan for households, and the optimal production process for firms. From those one can calculate the total demand for the available products at the specified price, and also the total supply from firms.

The model therefore describes, in very general terms, a basic market economy. Its description may seem very dry and abstract and mathematical, but this is precisely the point. Just as the Pythagorean theorem works for any right-angled triangle, independent of the exact dimension, so the Arrow–Debreu model doesn't care what goods the economy produces or the exact preferences of the households – it can work for any goods and any preferences.

The achievement of Arrow and Debreu was to mathematically prove that, given certain conditions, there exists an equilibrium set of prices for which supply and demand are perfectly balanced. The model didn't say whether the equilibrium was stable, or unique, or explain how or if the market would attain it; but it did say that, in theory at least, one such point existed. Furthermore, according to the first fundamental theorem of welfare economics, any such equilibrium will be Pareto-efficient, meaning that it is impossible to reallocate the goods without making at least one household worse off.

To accomplish this level of generality, the model had to make a number of assumptions. One of them was the assumption of perfect competition, which states that no individuals or firms can influence prices except through the price mechanism – i.e. there are no monopolies or unions. As discussed further in Chapter 7, this ignores the power discrepancies in the real economy. But perhaps the biggest catch was that, to make the proof work, it required that all participants in the market act rationally to maximise their utility, now and in the future.

Since the future is unknown, the model assumed that households and firms could create a list of all possible future states, and draw up a consumption plan for each one. For example, a household's optimal consumption would depend on the price of food, which in turn would depend on the weather. So it would need a separate plan for each of the different weather states (flood, drought, cloudy with some rain, hurricane, etc.), now and for ever. The same would have to be done for other events, including the arrival of new technologies, changes in availability of commodities such as oil, and so on. The utility function of the household would be extended to cover all of these different contingencies.

Just to be clear, the claim here isn't that individuals do their best to make the right decisions based on the information that is immediately available to them. The claim is that, first of all, they can create a list of all the possible future states of the world. Then, they make the best decisions taking into account each of these separate future worlds. These people aren't just rational, they're hyper-rational.

In 1968, the American economist Roy Radner managed to weaken some of these conditions, but he still concluded that for the model to work, every participant in the economy needed to be endowed with infinite computational capacity.[7] The Arrow–Debreu model didn't represent an economy of human beings – it was an economy of gods.

Truth and beauty

While the Arrow–Debreu model obviously made some unreasonable assumptions – economist Mark Blaug described it as 'clearly and even scandalously unrepresentative of any recognizable economic system' – it wasn't easy to modify any of these too much without the whole thing falling apart.[8] Economists could adapt or extend it slightly to take into account 'distortions' such as asymmetric information (for example, buyers knowing less than sellers about the goods), or imperfect competition, or real currencies with fluctuating exchange rates. But these added complications, and it was easier and more elegant to treat the model as a perfect market economy to which real economies aspire. As such, the model soon became the core reference for neoclassical economic theory.

Some economists took it literally as a vision of perfectly efficient markets. Others concentrated on looking for instances of 'market failure' – i.e. situations where society or nature fail to provide the conditions for markets to attain perfection – that could potentially be corrected by government action. (Arrow, who died in 2017 at the age of 95, and whose youth was shaped by the Depression, originally thought like many of his generation that 'Socialism was the way in which the ideal market was to be achieved'; however, this fondness for government planning seemed to decline with time – in 1995 he said for example that 'I am not really inclined to think there is any very effective regulation of the derivative securities markets that would be useful'.[9]) The Platonic ideal of a perfect market with its naturally equilibrating invisible hand therefore remained in place, even if we could never quite attain it in practice.

So how much does this matter? An interesting defence of neoclassical economics was supplied by Milton Friedman, who said that the assumptions of a theory aren't important, so long as it makes accurate predictions.[10] Friedman was probably the most influential economist of the latter half of the 20th century. His interest in mathematics was inspired by a high-school geometry teacher who connected John Keats' poem 'Ode on a Grecian Urn' – 'Beauty is truth, truth beauty' – with the Pythagorean theorem.[11] He went on to become a leader of the Chicago School of Economics, based at the University of Chicago, which was famous for its free-market ideology, opposition to regulation – Friedman even opposed regulation of drug development – and general railing against taxes and big government. As Friedman said in a 1975 interview, 'thank God for government waste. If government is doing bad things, it's only the waste that prevents the harm from being greater.'[12] (Somewhat ironic, considering that Friedman and neoclassical economists in general were supported in large part by government grants.)

Friedman's main contribution to economic thought – and his most famous prediction – relates to his work on monetarism. The basic idea of monetarism is that markets are inherently stable, and the government's role in controlling the economy should be limited to making sure that the supply of money matches the increase in GDP. This contrasted with the views of John Maynard Keynes (probably the most influential economist of the first half of the 20th century), who believed that government policy was essential to moderate the business cycle – for example by boosting government spending during a recession to compensate for lack of demand.

According to Keynes, the economy was strongly affected by psychological factors. He believed that many of our decisions 'can only be taken as the result of animal spirits – a spontaneous urge to action rather than inaction, and not as the outcome of a weighted average of quantitative benefits multiplied by quantitative probabilities'.[13] Government policy could therefore act as a stabilising influence. Friedman, however, argued that governments couldn't understand the economy well enough to make such judgements. Instead, he predicted that people would learn to anticipate the government's actions, thus rendering them useless.

For example, if the government attempted to boost the economy by printing extra money during a recession, then this would cause prices to rise and stimulate supply. However, if price inflation persisted too long, then workers, being rational people, would build the expectation of future inflation into wage demands, and firms into planned price increases. This in turn would lead to loss of jobs and higher unemployment. The government cure was therefore worse than the disease.

Friedman's position appeared to be vindicated in the 1970s by the appearance in industrialised countries of stagflation – an unprecedented combination of high unemployment and high inflation – which defied Keynesian analysis or treatment. In the US, the so-called misery index – the sum of unemployment and inflation rates – reached 21 per cent. In the UK, the 1978–79 'winter of discontent' featured widespread strikes, with union leaders demanding higher pay agreements. Friedman and others blamed this disaster on Keynesian policies.

One result of stagflation was that President Carter in the US and Britain's prime minister, James Callaghan, were thrown out of power and replaced by Friedman's future friends and admirers, Ronald Reagan and Margaret Thatcher. Another was that economics came to be dominated by the paradigm of 'rational expectations' – the idea that participants in the economy act to maximise their long-term utility, based on their expectations for the future. As Naomi Klein documents in her book *The Shock Doctrine*, this Chicago School model was rolled out to countries around the world from Chile to South Africa.[14] Together with the Pareto optimality of the Arrow–Debreu model, and the efficient market hypothesis, it formed a compelling picture of the economy as intrinsically rational and efficient. One could argue that individual investors weren't completely rational all the time; but to all effective purposes, the economy behaved as if they were.

The prediction test

Inspired by all this rationality, institutions such as the US Federal Reserve set about building elaborate Computable General Equilibrium models to simulate the economy. These models were similar in principle to the Arrow–Debreu model, but were simplified versions in that they aggregated over large groups of consumers and other sectors of the economy. They assumed that the financial system works perfectly, so no need to worry about middlemen such as banks or hedge funds. The purpose of the models was to predict how the economy's equilibrium will react to changes in government policy, commodity prices, and so on.

Such models are still widely used by policy-makers and regulators.[15] More recent versions – the Dynamic Stochastic General Equilibrium models discussed on page 81 – take factors such as random shocks into account, but still assume the existence of an underlying equilibrium. The models crystallise economic theories into a single consistent framework that can be used to go out and make predictions about the real world. They have been around for long enough to have established a track record, so how do they match up with Friedman's test of making accurate predictions?

The answer, as we've already seen, is not so well. As discussed in Chapter 1, and illustrated in Figure 5, the ability of economic models to predict things like GDP growth is not much better than random. Nor have they proved successful at predicting the effects of major policy changes.[16] As the economist Alan Kirman noted: 'almost no one contests the poor predictive performance of economic theory. The justifications given are many, but the conclusion is not even the subject of debate.'[17]

The main effect of the models, in all their neat perfection, has been to desensitise policy-makers to the messy realities and lurking risks of the economy. David Blanchflower, a former member of the Bank of England's Monetary Policy Committee, wrote that although empirical data were signalling a downturn in the UK economy in mid-2007, the Committee 'ignored these data, and as late as August 2008 the majority were arguing that there was not going to be a recession.'[18] Let alone the longest recession on record. One problem, as discussed earlier, is that the models assume the existence of a stable equilibrium, so don't do crashes; another is that they do not properly account for the role of the financial sector (which in a perfect economy isn't necessary). The Bank of England's general equilibrium model, for example, omits banks.[19] We return to this topic later.

While Friedman was one of the first to see stagflation as a possibility, not all of his predictions were so prescient. His theory that inflation could be controlled through the money supply alone, for example, turned out to be a huge mistake when it led to high inflation and unemployment in the US and UK.[20] The claim that neoclassical economics can be defended on the basis of its ability to make predictions is the kind of extraordinarily counter-intuitive thing that people can say only when they are led by an unshakeable, almost religious belief that they are on the right path. Indeed, Friedman's mentor at the University of Chicago, Frank Knight, believed that professors should teach economic theories as if they were 'a sacred feature of the system' as opposed to mere hypotheses.[21]

Friedman's claim of predictive accuracy makes more sense if we see it as throwing down a gauntlet to other theories. Science traditionally evolves when a theory is replaced by one that makes better predictions. If no new and better theory comes along, but there are obviously problems with the existing one, then there is no clear rule on how to proceed. Whatever is in vogue, or has the strongest and most institutionalised support, tends to dominate.[22] 'To say something has failed,' says Myron Scholes, 'you have to have something to replace it, and so far we don't have a new paradigm to replace efficient markets.'[23]

So is there really no alternative economic model that can make better predictions than the neoclassical one? The answer is not yet clear, but an obvious first step is to take into account that we are humans rather than machines.

Irrational humans

One psychological quirk of human beings is that we like to find specific rational explanations for things. In the early 1970s, one of the most commonly cited causes for stagflation was the failure of the Peruvian anchovy fishery in 1972, which was due in large part to a severe El Niño event. Anchovies were a major source of livestock feed, so the effect was to push up food prices. Another contributor was the success of the Organisation of Petroleum Exporting Countries (OPEC) at constraining oil supplies, which also boosted prices. To the monetarists, the cause of stagflation was the inept government printing too much money.

While the exact causes are debated, though, one thing was for sure: the effect of stagflation was to make people unhappy. There's nothing like rising prices, and a risk of losing your job, to upset the electorate – which is why politicians keep a close eye on the misery index. They know that money is an emotional business. It may also turn out that the cause of inflation has less to do with things like oil, anchovies, or money supply, than with basic human emotions.

In 1971, the Israeli psychologists Daniel Kahneman and Amos Tversky published a paper that explored the difference between intuition, which they called System 1 thinking, and reasoning, or System 2. System 1, according to Kahneman, is 'fast, effortless, associative, and often emotionally charged'.[24] It is also governed by habit, which makes it hard to change or control. System 2, in contrast, is 'conscious, it's deliberate; it's slower, serial, effortful, and deliberately controlled, but it can follow rules'.

The paper, entitled 'Belief in the Law of Small Numbers', presented empirical results showing that their experimental subjects, when acting in System 1 mode, could not make accurate estimates of probability. They made extremely basic mistakes, and appeared to have no grasp of the rules of chance. This might not be surprising, except that the people they were studying were experienced statisticians.

The Law of Small Numbers in the title was a reference to the Law of Large Numbers. This is the name of a theorem, stated without proof by Girolamo Cardano and finally proved by the mathematician Jacob Bernoulli in 1713, which says that the accuracy of a statistical sample improves with its size. For example, the quality of an opinion poll will be much better if it is done for a thousand people, than if it is done for ten people.

Statisticians know this very well – or at least the System 2 side of their brain knows it very well. But Kahneman and Tversky found that, in practice, they didn't need large numbers of samples to jump to a conclusion – instead they 'view a sample randomly drawn from a population as highly representative, that is, similar to the population in all essential characteristics'. System 1 was leaping in with the answer before System 2 had even fired up its pocket calculator. As a result, people could be easily fooled.

During their long collaboration, Kahneman and Tversky found a number of results that directly question the neoclassical assumption that we make decisions rationally. If there is such a thing as the average man (or woman), then it turns out he has some distinct psychological quirks. For example, he has an asymmetric attitude towards loss and gain – he is roughly twice as sensitive to losses – so tends to avoid taking risks. He is biased by recent events, so if the market has been going up recently, then he expects that trend to continue. He dislikes change, prefers to keep what he has than trade it for something similar, and hates to give up a long-held belief. He underestimates the likelihood of extreme events, and overestimates his own ability to deal with them. And he labours under an 'illusion of validity', putting too much faith in his power of judgement, while tending to ignore or downplay information that doesn't agree.

One might think that a group of people would make better decisions, and in some ways they do. But as Kahneman explains, 'when everybody in a group is susceptible to similar biases, groups are inferior to individuals, because groups tend to be more extreme … In many situations you have a risk-taking phenomenon called the risky shift. That is, groups tend to take on more risk than individuals.'[25] Groups also tend to be more optimistic, suppress doubts, and exhibit group-think. In larger informal groups such as markets, this can translate into herd behaviour, in which investors all rush into the market, or out of it, at the same time.

The work of Kahneman and Tversky helped create the field of behavioural economics. The area has recently been supplemented by the even newer field of neuroeconomics, which uses techniques like brain scans to find out how our brains handle economic decisions. For example, scans have shown that the offer of a reward affects different parts of the brain depending on whether the reward is immediate or delayed. The former triggers a stronger response, known as the immediacy effect, which may explain why many people don't set enough aside for retirement.[26] In fact, studies of patients who for neurological reasons are unable to process emotional information show that it is extremely hard to make decisions without some emotional input.[27] If we really did have infinite computational capacity but no emotion, as the neoclassical model demands, we would be incapable of buying a pair of socks.

Don't mention the bubble

The findings of behavioural economics and neuroeconomics change the way we see the financial system. According to the monetarist argument, inflation becomes established, and is resistant to government control, because the rational expectation of workers is that inflation will continue, so they insist on pay hikes. But another way to look at it is as a System 1 phenomenon. Once inflation has been around for a few years, we tend to see it as an established trend rather than a random event (this is a typical example of the Law of Small Numbers, in which we create patterns based on insufficient data). At the same time our perception of rising prices is driven by anchoring – we compare the prices with those we have grown used to, and are sensitive to any change. Our asymmetric attitude towards loss means that our decrease in purchasing power outweighs any wage gains. The sight of other workers negotiating pay increases makes us afraid we are falling behind. The result is a positive feedback loop in which inflation breeds inflation. Other factors such as money supply and the overall state of the economy clearly play a role, but the problem on the human side isn't just rational expectations – it's also irrational expectations.

Similarly, asset price bubbles are driven as much by 'irrational exuberance' as by technical factors. General Equilibrium models assume that the economy reacts passively to external shocks, like an inert machine, but the reality is that the economy is capable of generating manic surges and despondent plunges all on its own. One study of the 100 largest daily price changes in the S&P index over four decades found that, rather than being driven by news, most of the large changes happened on days when there was little to report.[28]

While Kahneman was eventually awarded the economics version of the Nobel Prize for his work (Tversky had died), the findings of behavioural economics were long viewed suspiciously by the mainstream. To efficient market purists, things like bubbles, or irrational behaviour, are inventions of people who don't understand the wisdom of the market. As Eugene Fama said in 2007, at the height of the US housing bubble, 'economists are arrogant people. And because they can't explain something, it becomes irrational … The word "bubble" drives me nuts.'[29] Behavioural economist Robert Shiller wrote in 2009 that 'you won't find the word "bubble" in most economics treatises or textbooks. Likewise, a search of working papers produced by central banks and economics departments in recent years yields few instances of "bubbles" even being mentioned … the idea that bubbles exist has become so disreputable in much of the economics and finance profession that bringing them up in an economics seminar is like bringing up astrology to a group of astronomers.'[30]

After the credit crunch, this scepticism is beginning to change. Shiller was one of the few economists to have warned of the housing bubble. Another proponent is Richard Thaler, whose book *Nudge* was influential in the Obama administration. As he told the *Financial Times* in 2009, 'conventional economics assumes that people are highly rational – super-rational – and unemotional. They can calculate like a computer, and they have no self-control problems. They never over-eat, they never over-drink, they save for retirement, just the right amount – first by calculating how much they need to save, and then religiously putting the money aside.

Real people are not like that.'[31] Governments should therefore consider 'nudging' citizens into making healthy financial decisions. For example, enrolment in retirement programmes could be made the default option, so workers would have to choose to opt out if they didn't want to take part.

Of course, to some this all smacks of rampant Keynesianism and the idea that government knows best. Indeed, I suspect that part of the reason why behavioural economics has won a grudging degree of acceptance among our rational-thinking economists and government planners is because it tends to concentrate on the negative aspect of intuitive System 1 behaviour – of the sort frequently demonstrated by human beings – while downplaying the drawbacks of logical System 2 behaviour – of the sort frequently demonstrated by risk models, or government plans gone wrong (as we will see later, feminist economists and others who have assigned a more positive role to things like human feelings have found the going harder). Logic is not always superior to intuition, and behaviour that appears narrowly rational can turn out to be highly destructive and unreasonable, if divorced from an understanding of the larger context. That's one reason why nudging may be better than forcing.

The most eager adopters of behavioural psychology, it seems, are marketers and advertisers. As neuropsychologist David Lewis noted, purchase decisions are 'more emotional than logical and generated in the oldest part of the brain', though we may rationalise them after the fact.[32] Retailers and advertising companies are well ahead of economists at understanding this, because they have been nudging us into buying things since shopping was invented. Credit card firms have found, for example, that they get a better response rate to their mailings if they pay a marketing company to phone up a week or so in advance, and innocently ask the prospective customer if they are planning to make any large purchases in the near future.[33]

The imperfect economy

The next step to make economics more realistic, then, is to discard for ever the notion of rational economic man, and replace him with something that reflects empirical observations of how people actually behave. Economic agents should make decisions based on the information available to them, instead of a global bird's-eye view; should employ simple rules of thumb more than abstract reasoning; should be rational at times, but not always; and should be influenced by the context and by other agents. None of this comes easily in the framework of the neoclassical model, which is concerned with elegant mathematical representations of near-perfect markets; but it is the natural outcome in agent-based models.

The basic ingredients of a typical agent-based model are an inventory of available goods, which can be moved, changed, or traded; and a list of economic agents. These are people or firms who own, exchange, or transform goods, and provide or consume services. Their decisions are guided by a fuzzy and changeable set of needs and preferences that can be influenced by other agents or the passing of time (so no fixed utility function). Rather than being blessed with an Apollonian ability to look into the future and maximise utility, agents can make mistakes, and they can learn from them. Trades incur costs, and involve financial intermediaries such as banks (which can go bust). There are also external drivers and constraints such as inputs of energy and outputs of waste. The model parameters are tuned to agree with the wealth of empirical data that is now available for economic transactions of all kinds.

The behaviour of the economy is determined by computer simulations that track the interactions between economic agents as they buy, sell, and trade goods and services. The model economy therefore emerges from the actions of the individual agents, just as it does in real life. The aim is not to make abstract mathematical proofs of stability or other properties, as with the Arrow–Debreu model, but instead to use the model as a kind of experimental laboratory for trying out ideas.

Because agent-based models make no assumption of equilibrium, they are particularly useful at modelling highly dynamic phenomena such as price fluctuations. For example, models have been developed in which hundreds of agents buy and sell stocks in artificial markets. Each agent has an individual strategy that can change as the agent responds to changing markets and the psychological influence of other agents. As with real markets, the prices don't settle on a stable equilibrium, but are in a constant state of flux, with the ever-present possibility of extreme changes when investors flock into or out of the market in unison. The models also replicate statistical features such as volatility clustering and power-law distributions, and have provided a new framework for studying everything from inflation to the growth and death of companies.[34]

Why predict?

The question still remains of whether agent-based models will answer Friedman's critique, and make better predictions. It is one thing to be able to reproduce economic behaviour and statistics; another to correctly predict how the economy will react to a change in policy or regulation.

Another point made by Friedman, with which I agree, is that if models are to be predictive, they should remain as simple as possible: otherwise the result is an overly complicated structure that can fit past data but fail to predict the future. There is plenty of empirical evidence to show that simple models make better predictions than complicated models.[35] This is why hedge funds never use the DSGE models beloved of economists, and prefer to rely instead on relatively simple but robust trading strategies.

Agent-based models are clearly not immune to this problem, and are best seen as incomplete pictures that capture aspects of the real economy. However, while they often contain a large number of individual agents, that doesn't mean they are necessarily more complicated than traditional models, because the agents are usually described by a fairly short set of instructions. A property of complex systems is that the rules describing the system at the local level can be extremely simple, but the emergent behaviour can be rich and frequently surprising. Agent-based models can also help identify pockets of predictability, i.e. features that remain robust to changes in the parameters. One useful approach is to begin with a detailed model, and then use it to derive simpler models that capture aspects of the emergent behaviour.[36]

Indeed, another lesson of complexity science is that, because a complex system resists reduction, the unit of analysis should be chosen to match a particular problem. So, for example, rather than building a macroeconomic model up from individual people and firms, it may be more appropriate to concentrate on a few large-scale variables such as employment, gross domestic product, debt, investment, and so on, using a systems dynamics approach. If the equations are nonlinear, and there is no constraining assumption of 'rational' equilibrium, then as seen in Chapter 3 the resulting dynamics may be highly complex, even if the model captures only a portion of the real system. In general there is no one-size-fits-all, theory-of-everything solution, so modelling complex systems is as much an art as a science.

The main problem with economic prediction, though, has less to do with the simplicity or otherwise of the models than with the fact that many of the features of the economy, such as stock-market crashes, are inherently unpredictable. The aim of models should be not to predict the unpredictable, but to help design the financial system so that it is more robust. Orthodox models ignore effects such as investor irrationality, herding behaviour, destructive feedback loops, and so on, with the result that each failure of the financial system seems to come as a complete surprise. With their insistence on stability, normality and rationality, the models prevent us from learning from our mistakes, and therefore create their own form of risk.

No model will ever be able to realistically simulate the behaviour of real people with a few lines of code. The human brain is the most complex object in the known universe (at least that's what our brains say). But despite their drawbacks, even coarse models that account for phenomena such as trend-following and incomplete information may be good enough to yield substantial improvements over present methods.

Prove it

In mathematics, the highest kind of prediction is a mathematical proof. It doesn't just say that something will happen tomorrow, or next week, or in most situations – it says that it will *always* happen. There is also a kind of entropy law that ranks proofs according to the generality of their results, divided by their complexity. It is the mathematical version of 'Beauty is truth, truth beauty'. The aim is to explain as much as possible in the shortest and most elegant way. Pythagoras proved that in all right-angled triangles, the sum of the squares of the sides equals the square of the hypotenuse. Newton showed that the force which holds the moon in orbit is the same as that which makes an apple fall to the ground. The proofs in either case use simple, elegant, but extremely powerful arguments.

The Arrow–Debreu model was motivated by a desire to bring the same kind of beauty and clarity and permanence to economics. Gérard Debreu believed that the 'acid test' for economic theories should be that of 'removing all their economic interpretations and letting their mathematical infrastructure stand on its own'.[37] To accomplish this, though, their model had to grant the same kind of rational and prophetic powers to the economy.

Techniques such as agent-based modelling have none of this abstract appeal. An agent-based test of the Pythagorean theorem would be to run lots of simulations of different triangles and note that they all happen to satisfy the rule. Like an experimentalist, all the modeller can do is show that the result holds at the time, and in the manner, in which it is tested. Pythagorean harmony of the spheres, this is not. $E=mc^2$, it is not. Models are seen as toys, useful for exploring ideas but not for making detailed simulations or reliable predictions. If there is an advantage, it is that the modeller is less likely to become enraptured with the model, or confuse it with reality.

Such models do, however, provide a kind of negative proof. Because their behaviour is completely different from traditional equilibrium models – for one thing, they don't have an equilibrium – they prove that the neoclassical picture of rational utility optimisation cannot be right.

This view of models as inherently flawed creations also challenges the time-honoured tradition of preferring abstract theory over concrete data. Of course economists work with data all the time – the specialty known as econometrics focuses on just that – but as shown for example by the discussion of the demand curve (see box, page 30) or DSGE models, they rarely let it get in the way of a good theory. 'Existing economics,' said Nobel winner Ronald Coase in 1999, 'is a theoretical system which floats in the air and which bears little relation to what actually happens in the real world.'[38] According to economist Fischer Black, 'a theory is accepted not because it is confirmed by conventional empirical tests but because researchers persuade one another that the theory is correct and relevant'.[39] The adoption of theories and models that are less rigid or idealistic in their assumptions, but also more adaptable for handling different types of data, is helping to turn economics into a more empirical discipline, based on observations rather than just abstract theorising (though see 'How to succeed at economics' below).

What seems strange is that mainstream economics has held on to its picture of rational economic man for so long, despite all the evidence that people don't behave like that. Just as there are more ways to draw a crooked line than a straight line, so there are more ways to behave in an irrational fashion than a rational one (and we often seem to be bent on exploring them). This tenacity on the part of economists can be explained in part by behavioural psychology, and effects such as ownership bias, loss aversion, group-think, illusion of validity, and fear of change – we hold on to ideologies as tightly as we hold on to the most treasured possessions. Economists who have been educated to believe that people behave rationally find it hard to accept that, actually, the idea was pretty dumb all along.

As shown in the next chapter, though, the idea of *Homo economicus* runs even deeper than that. It is again part of a 2,500-year tradition with its roots in ancient Greece – so letting go of it may be the hardest thing in the world. At least for half of the population.

How to succeed at economics

The fascination of economists with rational behaviour also manifests itself as a preference for rational theory over real-world data. This was illustrated in the 1990 book *The Making of an Economist*, when Arjo Klamer and David Colander asked students at top graduate programmes to identify which of seven qualities were most important in order to succeed as an economist.[40] The results, from most important to least, were held to be:

1. Being smart in the sense of being good at problem-solving (65 per cent very important).
2. Excellence in mathematics (57 per cent).
3. Being very knowledgeable about one particular field (37 per cent).
4. Ability to make connections with prominent professors (26 per cent).
5. Being interested in, and being good at, empirical research (16 per cent).
6. Having a broad knowledge of the economics literature (10 per cent).
7. Having a thorough knowledge of the economy (3 per cent).

This is a little like saying that a successful doctor is one who is clever at passing exams, rather than one with actual hands-on experience of the human body. When Colander revisited the topic in 2007, he found the numbers had changed a little, with 9 per cent agreeing that knowledge of the economy was important, and more students (30 per cent) emphasising the importance of empirical research, but technical theory was still firmly on top.[41]

In his 2009 book *The Trouble With Markets*, Roger Bootle (founder of the leading consultancy Capital Economics) wrote that most academic economists 'practise a modern form of medieval scholasticism – of no use or interest to man or beast'.[42] And they seem intent on passing on this approach to their students: even today, according to Joe Earle et al. of Rethinking Economics, the urge of students to learn about society 'must be suppressed as they are confronted with a series of abstract concepts and ideas that have little to do with the actual economy. Students may wonder why it is necessary to detach the study of economics from reality in this way, but they must also learn to inhabit this parallel universe if they want any hope of passing their exams.'[43]

As discussed further in the box below, the love affair with theory is being challenged by what has been called the 'data revolution' in economics (though looking at data hardly seems a revolutionary concept). But while change is certainly under way in many areas of economics, the educational component is struggling to keep up – and if the human race is to succeed at economics, these traditional priorities need to be reversed. The financial crisis was not some tricky end-of-term exam question; and the people to solve the environmental crisis (see Chapter 8) must be very much of this world.

Light versus darkness

To question rationality, according to Jeremy Bentham, was to deal with 'darkness instead of light'. As noted in this chapter, one of the effects of the 'irrational' financial crisis was to turn behavioural economics into something of a growth area. An early endorser was the UK government, who in 2010 set up a group of economists and psychologists called the Behavioural Insights Team, or 'nudge unit' as it became known, with Richard Thaler as a consultant. One of their ideas was to send out court fines by text message rather than by mail. This electronic nudge improved compliance rates from one in twenty, to one in three.[44] Nudging has since been taken to a more advanced level by the Russian state, which allegedly used techniques including social media prompts to influence the 2016 US election, and the Chinese state, which is developing a 'Citizen Score' to prompt its own citizens into good behaviour.[45]

Behavioural economics has also become something of a

poster child for the integration between economics and other fields. It has been very useful in questioning the idea of rational economic man that still underpins many models (which is why it is still seen as a separate specialty, rather than a branch of the mainstream) and in helping to better understand the complex effects of things like money on the human psyche. Economic bubbles have even become an acceptable topic of discussion, though in 2016 Eugene Fama repeated that there was not 'any concrete evidence' for their existence.[46]

Of course, a cynic might be a little suspicious of the way that behavioural economics has been accepted, if only grudgingly, as a legitimate subject by mainstream economists, and point out that most of its insights seem – at least to the unindoctrinated – somewhat unrevolutionary in their scope, if not downright banal. Indeed, expressions such as 'bounded rationality' don't quite capture the extreme swings in sentiment which characterise financial crises; and one could argue that the emphasis on making irrationality sound computable, controllable and predictable (i.e. epicycle-able) limits the kinds of problems considered. Rather than taking human nature at face value, in other words, the field – at least in its current state – often seems to be more about making economics appear a little more sane, without disrupting it too much.

Something like the immediacy effect, for example, which makes us more likely to buy something when it is immediately accessible, can be handled mathematically through a technique known as 'hyperbolic discounting'.[47] But when you try to account for the fact that people are different from one another, but influence each other through social and other connections, then the entire equilibrium-based structure of mainstream economics falls apart rather quickly. It is like the ancient geometers trying to 'square the circle' – i.e. find a square with the same area as a circle using a compass and ruler. It just doesn't compute.

Also, if you make an honest assessment about the world economy, the most irrational thing about it is that we are destroying our natural environment (that wouldn't seem very logical or efficient, if it was your pet doing it). But acknowledging this and modifying our behaviour doesn't just rely on the light of reason. Instead it requires us to embrace humility, and accept uncertainty, in the face of a system we don't understand. We need to lose our fear of the dark.

But these are early days, at least by the time scales of economics. In the near term one of the greatest contributions of behavioural economics may be to help change the behaviour of economists. As Edward Fullbrook, co-founder of the heterodox World Economics Association, noted, 'Despite their atomist ideology, economists are, even more than most academics, herd animals'.[48] For too long, they have been labouring under an illusion of validity, confidently prescribing policies such as deregulation of the financial sector even when empirical evidence says they are not working, and justifying them with abstract mathematical models that only economists can understand. By helping to point out the fundamental inconsistencies in their approach, behavioural economics will hasten the development of true alternatives, which may even include a dose of humility. (Perhaps a nudge unit should be set up to alert economists by sending them a text.)[49]

A related growth area in economics which seems promising, if as usual a little overdue, is the application of data-driven techniques. Perhaps the most glamorous example is machine learning, which uses computer algorithms to search for patterns in large quantities of data. Research in the area goes back to the 1950s, but took off with the development of fast computers, and has since found many applications in areas from search algorithms to cancer diagnosis to self-driving cars. Hedge funds such as Winton Capital have used it for over 30 years to analyse financial data.[50] In academic economics it began to make an impact only around 2013, and has since become sufficiently popular that a backlash against this new-fangled technology is already appearing. (Economists prize themselves on their scepticism about new modelling approaches, though this scepticism doesn't seem to apply to older approaches such as DSGE modelling, which is still mentioned far more often in paper abstracts.[51])

There are again some caveats: any statistical technique including machine learning relies on the future resembling the past; and the difficulty in arranging controlled experiments means that models which try to generalise the data often have the same problem of parameter identification as the law of supply and demand, only on a larger scale. It is also easier to find short-term correlations of the sort exploitable by hedge funds than to generate theories of more general use. However, a focus on data should help to both come up with new ideas, and – equally useful – to falsify existing ones. The latter is important, since otherwise the danger is that abstract statistical models simply replace abstract mechanistic models.

While a shift in emphasis from abstract theory to more empirical approaches promises to profoundly change the way we understand and visualise the economy, this is not to say that economics will become the preserve of big-data specialists. In Canada, for example, real estate has become a systemically important industry, fuelled by massive price gains in cities such as Vancouver and Toronto, and encouraged (at least until recently) by government policy. Along with its success have come concerns about the influence of foreign ownership, money laundering, tax evasion, mortgage fraud, the shadow banking sector, realtor misconduct, debt management problems, difficulties in recruitment due to unaffordability, empty homes, hoarding of properties, 'fear of missing out', homelessness, inequality, intergenerational divisions over money, and all the other implications of housing being treated primarily as an investment commodity. This would seem to be a valid and interesting area for economic research, but perhaps because it wouldn't fit into a neat model, most investigations into the relevant data have been carried out by journalists, bloggers, and other non-economists.[52] (Most economists who do comment on the subject work for banks, which is an obvious conflict of interest.) Time for practitioners to get their hands dirty in the real world.

CHAPTER 6

THE GENDERED ECONOMY

*My voice was not popular. The financial markets had
been expanding, innovation was thriving, and the country
was prosperous. The financial services industry argued
that markets had proven themselves to be self-regulating
and that the role of government in market oversight and
regulation should be reduced or eliminated. All of us have
now paid a large price for that fallacious argument.*
Brooksley Born, former chair of the Commodity
Futures Trading Commission (2009)

They [Alan Greenspan, Robert Rubin and Larry Summers]
felt, I think, that they understood finance better than she did.
Jim Leach, co-author of
the 1999 Gramm–Leach–Bliley Act (2009)

Independent investors who know their minds and aren't influenced by the opinions of others; an emphasis on logic and reason over feelings and emotion; a belief in stability rather than flux and change: could it be that orthodox economic theory incorporates a gender bias? Could this be why the field is dominated at the upper levels of academia, business and government by men? What implications does this have, not just for economic theory, but for the economy itself? How would an economy designed by women differ from the present one? This chapter shows how feminist economists and business leaders are changing the way we think about money.

In August 1984, the economist Milton Friedman travelled to Reykjavik to give a lecture on Chicago School economics at the University of Iceland. While there, he also took part in a television debate with three serious-looking socialists. The moderator began by asking him to define his idea of a utopian society. He replied: 'My personal utopia is one which takes the individual – or the family, if you will – as the key element in society. I would like to see a society in which individuals have the maximum freedom to pursue their own objectives in whichever direction they wish, so long as they don't interfere with the rights of others to do the same thing.' The role of government should be minimal, and restricted to areas such as defence, justice, and legislating basic rules.

The debate was three against one, but Friedman – an excellent debater – more than held his own. One of the subjects that came up was the fact that people were being charged to attend, when normally such events were free. Friedman replied that all lectures have costs, so it was only fair that they should be covered by attendees, instead of being subsidised by other people. In a healthy economy individuals look after themselves, and buy their own tickets.

This argument must have rung a bell with some of those watching, because Friedman's positions were soon endorsed by young intellectuals in the aptly named Independence Party. One of them, Davíð Oddsson, went on to become Iceland's longest-serving prime minister (1991 to 2004) and later the governor of the central bank (2005 until April 2009). His radical reforms over that period turned Iceland from one of the world's most heavily regulated economies into a cold, volcanic version of Friedman's utopia.

State companies and banks were privatised, taxes were slashed, capital markets were liberalised, industrial subsidies were cut. In Iceland, if you wanted to see the show, then you had to buy your own ticket, just as Friedman said. This got a big thumbs-up from neoclassical economists, including those at the Fraser Institute, a

Canadian free-market think-tank. In 1980 they had ranked Iceland 67 (of 105 in the survey) in a list of the world's freest economies – just one above Sierra Leone.[1] By 2006 that had improved to 12 (out of 141).

Many of the reforms were indeed very successful, at first. Inflation was tamed through strict monetary control. The over-subsidised fishing industry was reined in. Businessmen like the flamboyant Jón Asgeir Jóhannesson, CEO of Baugur, led an Icelandic invasion of the British high street, buying stakes in retailers including French Connection, Debenhams, House of Fraser, and the toy store Hamleys. The lobby of Baugur's office in London featured a sculpture of a Viking carrying, for some reason, a guitar and a massive fishtank.

Icelandic banks were even more adventurous. Adopting free-market reforms and the latest ideas in financial engineering, they expanded into foreign markets and became a major lender to savers in the UK, the Netherlands, and elsewhere. Not bad for a tiny country of only 320,000 people, most of whom are related by blood.

That was when Iceland experienced a different kind of volcano.

Financial terror

One of the great but little advertised advantages of internet banking is that if you want to partake in a run on the bank, you don't need to physically queue like in the old days – you can do it all from the convenience of your own home. You might not get your money back, but at least you don't waste as much time, or get rained on.

This is the thought that simultaneously occurred to a large fraction of the British population in October 2008. The online bank Icesave, run by Landsbanki, had attracted hundreds of thousands of savers with its slick marketing and generous interest rates – 6.3 per cent for instant access and higher for fixed-term accounts.

And it wasn't just individuals who were stashing away their savings. Kent County Council had deposited some £50 million in Icelandic banks, and other local authorities had followed suit. But then word got out that the Icelandic economy was in trouble. The krona was losing value, inflation was spiking, banks were looking fragile, and the stockmarket was melting into the ocean. Articles appeared in the UK media saying that Iceland was on the verge of collapse. Savers got spooked and rushed online to get their money out.

Unfortunately, the Icesave website quickly iced up, which shows that even in the internet age, you have to be fast. The last people to catch on were, apparently, the UK county councils, who were still depositing tens of millions of pounds right up until the last moment (this fact was determined by the UK Audit Commission, which had itself deposited £10 million in the banks).

Things got worse when Oddsson, who was then governor of the central bank, told an Icelandic TV interviewer that: 'We have decided that we are not going to pay the foreign debts of reckless people ... of the banks that have been a little heedless.'[2] The UK treasury immediately invoked an anti-terror act to freeze billions of pounds' worth of Icelandic assets. This sealed the fate of the Icelandic economy. Only ten days after the start of the crisis, not one of its three main banks was still standing, and the country's brief reign as a financial power was over.

Foreign savers got their money back in the end, but in Iceland the consequences were devastating – the credit crunch bit harder there than in any other industrialised country. Interest rates, inflation and unemployment all soared, and the krona collapsed against other currencies. The result was stagflation squared. Home construction and car sales came to an abrupt halt. Widespread anti-government protests forced Oddsson and the prime minister Geir Haarde to step down. And people started to ask what had gone wrong.

One obvious problem was that Iceland's Financial Supervisory Authority had allowed the newly privatised banks to lend out too much money – about ten times the country's GDP, or half a million dollars for every man, woman and child. The central bank could not therefore act as a plausible lender of last resort. When the banks got into trouble, they were on their own.

During the boom years, many people and companies had also taken out large loans in foreign currencies (an example of the carry trade discussed in Chapter 3). As the krona soared, the loans became easier to pay off; but when the economy turned, they found themselves saddled with unpayable debts.

The UK government also played a part with its decision to use anti-terror legislation. Banking depends on trust, and it is considered poor form to have your central bank and ministry of finance appear on the UK's official list of terrorist organisations, right up there with al-Qaeda and the Taliban.

In Iceland, though, many believed that the roots of the problem lay in a particular culture and a particular group of people who had held power for far too long. As Halla Tómasdóttir from Audur Capital told *Der Spiegel*: 'The crisis is man-made. It's always the same guys. Ninety-nine per cent went to the same school, they drive the same cars, they wear the same suits and they have the same attitudes.' She described their focus on short-term profits, without any concern for the wider consequences, as 'typical male behavior' akin to a 'penis competition.'[3]

In other words – and I may be reading between the lines here – the credit crunch was some kind of *guy* thing.

Emotional capital

Of course, Iceland isn't the only country where women complain (not unfairly) that men are responsible for all the problems; however, in this case, it actually did something about it. The country has long been a world leader in measures of sex equality and female participation in the workforce, and when they realised what had happened to their money the women swung into action. Geir Haarde was replaced as prime minister by the world's first openly lesbian leader, Jóhanna Sigurðardóttir. Women took charge at two of the failed banks, and were given high-profile ministerial posts and positions in the Financial Supervisory Authority.

An example of the change in culture was the investment fund set up by Audur Capital together with famous-Icelandic-singer Björk, to focus on green start-ups. According to Halla Tómasdóttir, the fund is guided by 'core feminine values' that include risk aware-ness – 'we will not invest in things we don't understand'; profit with principles – 'a positive social and environmental impact'; and emotional capital – 'we look at the people, at whether the corporate culture is an asset or a liability'.[4]

To anyone used to the hard-driving, high-octane, dog-eat-dog world of finance, this might all seem a bit soft and fuzzy and feath-ery – like Björk in her famous swan costume, actually. It's hard to imagine Halla or her colleagues being invited to appear anytime soon on *Fast Money* – the manic, and very male, financial talk show on American cable TV, where they probably think 'core values' is a mining company.

So can we really say that the economy needs to become more feminine, less testosterone-driven? And – related question – is economic theory inherently biased towards a male perspective? To answer that delicate question, it's important that I first define some safe boundaries. I don't want to make the same mistake that Larry Summers made, when as president of Harvard University he implied that women didn't do as well at science and engineering because of innate biological differences.

So allow me to be perfectly clear: in the following discussion, I am not in any way implying that we men are incapable of doing economics, or should not be trusted with money, or suffer from some kind of innate biological flaw.

In fact, to be even safer, I will frame the problem as much as possible in terms of some very old concepts that predate our modern sexual politics: yin and yang. Or in numerical terms, even and odd.

Odd son

According to Greek mythology, the predictions at Delphi were originally due not to Apollo, but to the earth goddess Gaia. Her prophecies were sung out by a mythical figure referred to as Sybil. The site was guarded by Gaia's daughter, the serpent Python. However, the young god Apollo killed Python and took over the temple as his own. (His spokeswoman, the Pythia, was named after Python; as by implication was Pythagoras.)

Archaeological excavations tell a similar story. From 1500 to 1100 BC, the area was occupied by Bronze Age Mycenean settlements that were devoted to Mother Earth. The new god Apollo arrived via invading societies, and began to dominate. Religious art was modified accordingly. As the mathematician Ralph Abraham put it: 'the goddess submerged into the collective unconscious, while her statues underwent gender-change operations.'[5]

Pythagoras, whose followers believed he was descended directly from Apollo, can be viewed as the human incarnation of this switch in power. The Pythagoreans compiled a list of ten opposing principles that divided phenomena into two groups:

Limited	Unlimited
Odd	Even
One	Plurality
Right	Left
Male	Female

At rest	In motion
Straight	Crooked
Light	Darkness
Square	Oblong
Good	Evil

Limited and Unlimited were the two founding principles of the universe, and came together to form number. The former represented order, and was associated with the odd numbers; the latter signified chaos and plurality, and was associated with even numbers. The even numbers contained the number 2, which represented the initial division of the universe and was the symbol of discord and dissent.

It isn't known why the Pythagoreans chose this particular list of pairs, but there is an interesting correspondence between it and the Chinese concepts of yin and yang.[6] According to the Chinese scheme, which is equally ancient, odd numbers are yang, even are yin. Light is yang, darkness yin. Male is yang, female yin. In fact, the sole striking difference between the Pythagorean list and the Chinese equivalent is that the Pythagoreans explicitly associated one column with good and the other with evil. They believed that by associating themselves with yang properties, they could move closer to the gods.

As we'll see, the Pythagorean list permeates traditional economics in much the same way that yin and yang permeate traditional Chinese medicine. However, instead of seeing yin and yang as two aspects of a unified whole, as in Chinese culture, economics is fundamentally dualistic and emphasises always the yang. Gender bias isn't some kind of accidental feature of economic theory; it's built right into its DNA.

Dressing as Apollo

Ancient Greece in general wasn't a high-point for the feminist movement. The Pythagoreans did admit women into their cult, but they still associated the female archetype with darkness and evil. Thinking about numbers, notes science writer Margaret Wertheim, was 'an inherently masculine task. Mathematics was associated with the gods, and with transcendence from the material world; women, by their nature, were supposedly rooted in this latter, baser realm'.[7] In *Timaeus*, Plato described women as originating from morally defective souls. Aristotle saw the male archetype as being active, female as passive, and wrote in *Politics* that: 'the male is by nature superior, and the female inferior ... the one rules, and the other is ruled.' Women were capable of rational and deliberative thought, but it is 'without authority'.[8] Unsurprisingly, they were barred from entering his Lyceum.

Scientific thought continued to be dominated by men and by a narrow kind of left-brained masculinity emphasising objectivity and detached analysis. Francis Bacon, who is credited with establishing the empirical scientific method in the early 17th century, described the role of science in *The Masculine Birth of Time* as being to 'conquer and subdue Nature' and 'storm and occupy her castles and strongholds' – an activity clearly suited for 'a blessed race of Heroes and Supermen'.[9] When the Royal Society was founded in 1660, Henry Oldenburg defined its aim as being to construct a 'Masculine Philosophy' that would root out 'the Woman in us'.[10]

Things hadn't changed much in the late 19th century, when neoclassical economics was in its gestation phase. To the Victorians, science was as male an activity as moustache-waxing and bare-knuckle boxing. Theories abounded that women were less rational or intelligent than men, due to biological factors such as brain size or genetics. Many university departments did not admit women until the early 20th century. In 1959, when C.P. Snow gave his famous lecture on *The Two Cultures and the Scientific Revolution*, he ignored the role of women, adding in a footnote that: 'whatever we say, we don't in reality regard women as suitable for scientific careers.'[11] Harvard's physics department apparently agreed, since they didn't award a woman tenure until 1992.

While science in general still tilts towards the yang – in the numerical scheme of the Pythagoreans, it tosses more odds than evens – economics is something of an extreme case. This gender imbalance is manifested not just in head counts, but in ideas. For example, as feminist theologian and psychologist Catherine Keller notes, there is a strong correspondence between the theory of the Newtonian atom and the male sense of self: 'It is separate, impenetrable, and only extrinsically and accidentally related to the others it bumps into in its void.'[12] This view of atoms has long been abandoned in physics, but it lives on in orthodox economics with the concept of rational economic man.

According to the anthropologist Mary Catherine Bateson, 'The dangerous idea that lies behind "economic man" is the idea that anyone can be entirely rational or entirely self-interested. One of the corollaries, generally unspoken in economics texts, was that such clarity could not be expected of women who were liable to be distracted by such things as emotions or concern for others.'[13]

Because we see mathematics as inherently objective, we resist the idea that its use could incorporate a gender bias.[14] But as the economist Julie A. Nelson observes, mainstream economics remains characterised by an emphasis on 'detachment, mathematical reasoning, formality, and abstraction', which are culturally seen as masculine, as opposed to 'methods associated with connectedness, verbal reasoning, informality, and concrete detail, which are culturally considered feminine – and inferior'.[15] (When psychologist James Hillman defined the 'archetypal premise in Apollo' as 'detachment, dispassion, exclusive masculinity, clarity, formal beauty, farsighted aim and elitism', he could have been analysing an economist.[16])

The economist Deirdre (formerly Donald) McCloskey has described how her gender change related to her break with the 'main (i.e., male) stream in economics. It is to admit, indeed welcome, the role of love in the economy.'[17] A former 'positivist, straight-line scientist' herself, she once compared neoclassical economists to a motorcycle gang, 'strutting about the camp with clattering matrices and rigorously fixed points, sheathed in leather, repelling affection. They are not going to like being told that they should become more feminine.'[18]

The yang-like culture of economics – rather than anything to do with mathematical skills – may explain why female economists continue to be so poorly represented at the higher echelons of academia; and why it took until 2009 for the Nobel Prize in economics to be awarded to a woman, Elinor Ostrom, who is a political scientist and not an economist.[19]

Actually, strictly speaking, no economist has won the Nobel Prize, or should be called a Nobel laureate. The Sveriges Riksbank Prize in Economic Sciences in Memory of Alfred Nobel, to use its full title, was created in 1969, seven decades after Nobel's death, by *a bank* – the Bank of Sweden. Peter Nobel told author Hazel Henderson in 2004 that the bank had 'infringed on the trademarked name of Nobel. Two thirds of the Bank's prizes in economics have gone to US economists of the Chicago School who create mathematical models to speculate in stock markets and options – the very opposite of the purposes of Alfred Nobel to improve the human condition.'[20] At least the name is easy to pronounce, which is one reason it has caught on.

The story behind the word 'laureate' is also interesting. In ancient Greece, the laurel tree was the symbol of Apollo. He is often depicted in artworks with laurels in his hair, and laurels were used as a wreath to honour heroes. Today the word has become associated with the Nobel Prize, and by extension the Bank of Sweden version. So when economists crown their champions as laureates, they are dressing them up as Apollo.

The main problem with this male tilt and heroic posturing is that economic theory does more than study the economy – it also helps shape it, by endorsing and legitimising the 'typical male behavior' which in this case had the unfortunate side-effect of destabilising the economy not just of Iceland, but the entire world. To illustrate this, we next present a detailed feminist critique of the 2007 subprime mortgage crisis.

Household misrule

The word 'economics' was originally derived from the Greek words *oikos* (household) and *nomos* (law), and means something like household rule. It is ironic, therefore, that economic theory lay behind the household misrule of the subprime mess.

On 22 November 1999, the ever-cheerful Texan Republican senator Phil Gramm made a particularly happy announcement. He had obtained Senate approval for a gold medal honouring Milton Friedman 'for his enduring contributions to individual freedom and opportunity and for his steadfast support and efforts to champion free markets and capitalism. While many Americans will never know his name, the power of Milton Friedman's intellect has profoundly changed America and the world.'[21]

That turned out to be no overstatement. Just ten days earlier, Gramm had advanced Friedman's (male) values in a different way – by pushing through a controversial piece of legislation known as the Gramm–Leach–Bliley Act (all males). One of the few dissenters was Brooksley Born, the (female) chair of the Commodity Futures Trading Commission.

The Act's main function was to scrap Depression-era regulations that separated investment banks from ordinary commercial banks and that also prevented banks from operating as insurance companies. The reasons for signing this 'deregulatory bill', said Gramm, were that 'government is not the answer ... We have learned that we promote economic growth and we promote stability by having competition and freedom.'[22] Bill Clinton's treasury secretary at the time, the protean and ever-present Larry Summers, chimed in: 'With this bill, the American financial system takes a major step forward towards the twenty-first century.'

Gramm's next act, the following year, was the Commodity Futures Modernisation Act, which exempted futures and derivatives from any kind of regulation. 'Taken together with the Gramm–Leach–Bliley Act,' said Gramm, 'the work of this Congress will be seen as a watershed, where we turned away from the outmoded, Depression-era approach to financial regulation and adopted a framework that will position our financial services industries to be world leaders into the new century.'[23] In fact the two bills just continued a trend towards greater deregulation that had existed since the post-war years. A clause on energy futures had helpfully been drafted by lawyers from the energy company Enron. Gramm's wife was on the board, and the company also donated $97,000 to his campaign expenses.

America therefore went into the new century stripped of all its Depression-era baggage, and ready to do some cutting-edge, innovative financial engineering. Running ahead of the pack was Enron, which enjoyed itself making vast amounts of money off the deregulated energy futures markets for about another year, before straying a little too close to the wires and incinerating itself.

Undeterred by the sight of the smoking wreckage and billions of dollars in collateral damage, financial engineers pressed ahead with other new products, including the collateralised debt obligation (CDO), and the credit default swap (CDS). Together, these would change the way that Americans think about home-ownership.

Financial alchemy

In the old days, before the mortgage industry was modernised, and CDOs and CDSs were just a glimmer in a young geek's eye, the whole process of buying a house was incredibly painful. First of all, you had to come up with a sizeable deposit, around 20 per cent. Then you would have to physically go into your bank branch, and ask one of the human beings there for a loan. And to show you could pay the loan back, and ensure a successful response, you would need to provide evidence of some source of income. Like a job.

Obviously this was highly inefficient and went against the whole idea of economic freedom. It was equally bad for the bank. They would have to check your credentials, perhaps treat you like a person instead of a number etc., and at the end, assuming it went through, they were stuck with a long-term, inflexible loan on their books. To them, your home wasn't a symbol of security and stability and family evenings spent sitting around the fire – it was a festering risk and a liability, and furthermore the maximum interest rates chargeable were capped by regulations.

So to help with these problems, financial institutions went to work on the CDO, which had been around since the 1980s. A mortgage, like a bond, is a loan that is paid off through regular instalments, so it can be viewed as a financial instrument that gives a regular return in exchange for a certain risk of default. Banks can therefore trade mortgages the same way they trade other financial instruments. However, individual loans are relatively small and have a fixed payment schedule, and are therefore hard to trade, so the idea of the CDO was to bundle them all together into a large group; divide the group into tranches of varying quality; and then sell the tranches as separate instruments.

One advantage of this approach was that it got away from the whole messy problem of dealing with the details of people's lives.

If a bank took ownership of an individual mortgage, they would feel compelled to find out something about the homeowner and their ability to repay the loan. But with a CDO, they were dealing with the *average* homeowner. Some of the individual loans would default, but the average loan would be fine. This meant they could relax their lending standards, at least for the right price. As one former loan officer testified: 'If someone appeared uneducated, inarticulate, was a minority or was particularly old or young, I would try to include all the [additional costs] CitiFinancial offered.'[24]

Furthermore, because the loans were divided into tranches, it was possible to achieve a kind of financial alchemy and turn even the most subprime of mortgages into a high-quality security. Suppose that a CDO bundles together a thousand mortgages. Even if, taken individually, the loans look a bit dodgy, the bank may estimate that, in all, under 10 per cent will default. No one knows at the start which will default and which won't, but that doesn't matter, because tranches are defined by pecking order. The upper-tranche investors get the first call on any income, and because the top 90 per cent of loans can be considered safe, their risk is low. Lower tranches are the first to suffer when loans go into default, but also pay a higher rate of interest as compensation, which appeals to investors such as hedge funds who are in search of yield. The same idea could be applied to any kind of loan, such as commercial property, or emerging market debt.

The CDOs therefore provided a way to take a bunch of individual loans and abstract from them new investment products with a tailored degree of risk. The process could be repeated: groups of CDOs were combined, sliced into tranches, and turned into CDO^2s. Or even CDO^3s. The upper tranches of lower-quality CDOs could thus be turned into financial gold. The mortgage industry became increasingly specialised, so a broker would sell mortgages, a mortgage bank would compile them together, an investment bank would transform them into an investment product, and another firm would be responsible for managing payment collection. This led to some cost efficiencies, but also had the effect of severing the connection – the bond – between mortgage supplier and home-owner, so their interests were no longer aligned.[25]

Give us some credit

While CDOs made it easy to transform even the most dubious of mortgages into an easily-traded and valuable product, there were still a number of problems. The first was that banks were limited in the number of mortgages they could bundle together in this way, because of tedious banking regulations that capped the amount they could lend out. This was where Gramm's 'deregulatory bill' came in. One of its effects was to permanently deregulate a then-obscure financial product known as a credit default swap (CDS).

The credit default swap was invented in the 1990s by a team at J.P. Morgan, and is basically a form of insurance. A bank or other institution that owns a product such as a CDO can buy a CDS as insurance from a third party. This procedure removes the CDO risk from their balance sheets, because it is insured. They are then free to go out and create more loans.

The credit default swap is therefore similar to the insurance policy you might take out on your own home. If the house burns down, you get paid. However, there are a few key differences. One is that insurance companies are again limited by regulations that control how many policies they can write – they have to back up their liabilities with cash. This doesn't apply in the same way to credit default swaps, because they are not properly regulated. Also, you can take out insurance against your own home, but not against someone else's home. Reasons are that (a) it's weird, and (b) it might create a perverse incentive to burn the whole block down. With credit default swaps, on the other hand, multiple players can take out the same bets. This meant that the market was potentially unlimited.

While credit default swaps offered a way round balance-sheet regulations on CDOs, there still remained the problem of how to actually calculate what each of the tranches of the CDO was worth, so that it could get a credit rating and be sold at an appropriate price. To do that, the banks needed to come up with a number for the risk, i.e. the probability that many properties could go into default at the same time. And of course they needed to do it in a way that looked sufficiently technical and impressive, but was still workable.

Enter the mathematicians.

Heart-breaker

During the 1990s, I worked for a multi-billion-dollar particle accelerator project, known as the Superconducting Super Collider, near Dallas, Texas. In 1995, the project was inconsiderately cancelled by the US government, so I and about 2,000 other people had to look for new employment. Some of the more active recruiters picking over the bones of the project were Wall Street firms looking for analysts. At the time, most of us thought that sounded well-paid but dull, and we couldn't quite see the connection with building particle accelerators (unless it had something to do with wasting billions of dollars).

Plenty of young physicists, engineers and applied mathematicians did hear the siren call of cash, though, and went on to establish careers as quantitative analysts, or 'quants', and earn serious amounts of money. Their numbers roughly quadrupled between 1980 and 2005.[26] But did they ever win true happiness? As one poor quant told the *New York Times*: 'They sold their souls to the devil. I haven't met many quants who said they were in finance because they were in love with finance.'[27] The former trader Satyajit Das describes quants as 'prisoners of Wall Street', embroiled in a 'Faustian bargain'. Most of the work involved routine tasks like computer programming, developing databases and designing trading platforms, but a relatively small number of firms such as D.E. Shaw, Renaissance Technologies, and Citadel also put novel quantitative techniques at the heart of their trading strategies.

One fresh recruit to the cause was a young mathematician called David X. Li. In 2000, Li published a paper that included a novel and clever formula for valuing CDOs.[28] His method was based on actuarial science – specifically, something called the broken heart syndrome. Actuaries had long known that when couples have lived together a long time, if one dies, the other has a high chance of also dying within a short time. A study showed that a partner's death increased a woman's chance of dying in the following year by a factor two, and a man's chance of dying by a factor six. In mathematical terms, their deaths are correlated. This had implications for the pricing of annuities.[29]

Li realised that company bonds and household mortgages also behave a bit like married couples, because if one dies, it increases the chances of others dying. If a large retailer goes bankrupt, for example, then many of its suppliers are also affected. If one house on the block goes into foreclosure, that slightly increases the chance that the rest of the neighbourhood will go into decline as well. Of course, the situation in the economy is more complex because the connections and correlations are far more complicated, but in principle the same kind of mathematics could be used.[30]

The technique, called the Gaussian copula, provided a simple and elegant way of calculating the correlations between separate bonds or mortgages, based on the CDS market. There isn't much data on defaults available because it is a rare event.

However, according to mainstream economic theory, the price of an instrument like a CDS is supposed to reflect the chance of a loan defaulting. By analysing how the market priced different securities, Li's formula could tease out the correlations between them.

As with most risk models, the Gaussian copula technique incorporated all the usual economic assumptions. One, as indicated by the name, is that it was constructed using the Gaussian or normal distribution, which as seen in Chapter 4 works well for games of dice, less well for financial markets. Another is that it assumed that the complex relationships between a large number of separate mortgages could be expressed as a single average correlation, and that this number could be deduced from market prices. This is related to the efficient market idea that prices are right, and account for all relevant information. The formula also assumed that markets are stable, so that correlations are stable as well, and that the past is a good guide to the future. In particular, the model was calibrated on US housing data for a period which had never seen a nationwide housing decline. Defaults were rare and random occurrences with a low degree of correlation, and it was never foreseen that the entire market could suffer not just a few random heart attacks, but a massive collective coronary.

Perhaps the biggest flaw in the model, though, was that it didn't account for an extraordinarily powerful force.

Itself.

The house race

The whole point of objective, dualistic, 'masculine' science is that you are supposed to assume a detached stance and distance yourself from the system under study. As Evelyn Fox Keller observes, this presupposes 'an objective reality, split off from and having an existence totally independent of us as observers'.[31] With the economy, though, that's not easy, because you're involved. The copula

formula didn't just model the credit markets, it transformed them
– and in doing so, guaranteed its own failure.

In August 2004, the world's two main rating agencies, Moody's
and Standard & Poor's, both adopted the formula as a metric for
valuing CDOs (previously they had insisted on antiquated concepts
like loan diversity). This effectively gave the instruments a gold
stamp of approval, and removed any lingering uncertainty about
their worth. The market for CDOs and CDSs promptly exploded.
By the end of 2007, the value of the credit default swap market, in
terms of amount insured, had reached roughly $60 trillion – about
the same as world GDP. Credit default swaps evolved from a form
of insurance into a tool for hedge funds to make sophisticated bets
on just about anything – for example, the probability that another
hedge fund or investment bank would go bust (say Bear Stearns
or Lehman Brothers). Banks from all over the world joined in the
game.

The net effect of all this insurance activity was to move risk off
the banks' balance sheets, thus allowing them to lend even more
money. This meant that credit became cheap, further fuelling the
housing boom. Mortgage brokers enticed customers with cheap
teaser rates that would later reset to a higher level. Because risk
computations were based on historical data, the longer house
prices kept rising in tandem, the lower seemed the risk. A positive
feedback loop was therefore set up, in which rising prices lowered
the calculated risk, which increased the supply of credit, which
made loans more affordable, which drove further price increases.
In reality, of course, the risk was climbing all the time, but the
model couldn't see that because it didn't include the concept of
a price bubble. The situation was supported by interest rates that
had been set low after 9/11 and remained there, in part because
China – slogan: bank of America – was lending money cheaply to
the US government.

At the base of this vast international balloon of credit was the US housing market. As long as prices kept rising, everyone was making huge profits, at least on paper. In late 2006, when house prices dipped, the teaser rates started to expire, and the market began to turn, it was generally assumed that the global financial system would easily absorb any losses. As the IMF observed: 'The dispersion of credit risk by banks to a broader and more diverse group of investors, rather than warehousing such risks on their balance sheets, has helped to make the banking and overall financial system more resilient.'[32] Instead, the whole highly-connected structure came crashing down like a house of credit cards. The last one not holding the CDS was the loser. That would be companies like AIG. Or ultimately the taxpayers who bailed them out. Along with vulnerable economies around the world that were not directly involved but suffered as credit dried up. It wasn't just Iceland that turned out to be living next to a financial volcano.

So whose fault was this debacle? To blame US homeowners, or even predatory mortgage brokers, for the credit crunch is like blaming a horse for losing a race on which you've placed a huge wager: technically, it is their fault, but no one forced you to place the bet. Housing bubbles happen, but they don't usually take the whole world down with them when they pop.

The copula model also wasn't wholly to blame for the crisis. It just made the same mistakes as other conventional risk models, by assuming stability and market efficiency and ignoring nonlinear reflexive effects. And again, no one forced traders to use it. As Li said: 'The most dangerous part is when people believe everything coming out of it.'[33] The fact that the model was used in the way it was says as much about the traders, clients and quants who used it, as it does about the formula itself.

In fact, many traders probably *didn't* believe it but used it anyway, either to impress gullible clients with its apparent sophistication or to offload risk. Part of the appeal of methods like VaR or the Gaussian copula is that they ignore extreme events and consistently underestimate risk, thus enabling traders to justify highly aggressive and speculative bets. Clients, on their part, want numerical risk estimates to assuage their fear of the dark, and are reassured by scientific-looking formulae. Quants are happy to oblige because such formulae generate jobs. The model was therefore bound to be popular – but as discussed also in Chapter 4, whenever such a model becomes too widely adopted, it ends up influencing the market and therefore invalidating itself.[34]

The credit rating agencies, with the collusion of government regulators, clearly played a role in their failure to explore the limitations of the risk models. As Alan Greenspan testified to Congress in October 2008, the sector had for decades been dominated by a risk management paradigm created by Nobel Prize-winning economists. 'The whole intellectual edifice, however, collapsed in the summer of last year.'[35] He added: 'those of us who have looked to the self-interest of lending institutions to protect shareholders' equity (myself especially) are in a state of shocked disbelief.' (Though he went on to blame the problem on model calibration, rather than the models themselves.)

Gramm's Friedman-inspired deregulation of the markets also contributed.[36] Banks loved this deregulation because it allowed them to effectively lend out more money and make greater profits. If CDSs could only be used to insure debt that was actually held, as with usual types of insurance, then the market would never have grown so large.

The complexity and opaqueness of the products also meant that financial institutions could charge more for their consultancy services. People who work in finance often make a point of saying that they deal with reality, because everything boils down to money in the end, but the truth is that financial products have become

increasingly divorced from the real world. Someone selling derivatives contracts on equities or CDOs has no idea of the underlying
businesses or properties, so can't pick up on danger signals, such
as people on $18,000 a year moving into mansions. An econo-
mist or quantitative analyst could calculate the theoretical risk of
a CDO^2 prospectus using a single formula; but to truly understand
the underlying securities they would have had to read, according
to one estimate, over a billion pages of documentation.[37] This complexity added another source of risk and uncertainty.

As with the Icelandic crisis that it helped to create, though,
the problem may run even deeper. After all, you don't need to be a
hardcore feminist to see that the subprime crisis exhibits some of
the worst features of the yang economy:

- Taking dreams of home-ownership, converting into abstract
  financial instruments, dismembering into tranches, and selling
  off to highest bidder – check
- Reducing complex interdependencies to a single number
  – check
- Valuing mathematical formulae over common sense – check
- Figuring out ways to take maximum possible risks – check
- Turning economy into giant casino ruled over by rapacious
  hedge funds – check
- Breaking said economy – check

In other words – and we have to admit this – the credit crunch
really was a guy thing.

The power of yang

Obviously many other factors were involved, and it would be terribly reductionist to blame the credit crunch solely on people with a
tendency to grow facial hair. But to start with a basic observation,

if there is one aspect of the crisis that everyone can agree with, it is that just about everybody involved at a senior level was a male.

Consider, for example, Goldman Sachs – one of the few Wall Street firms to have done well out of the crisis. They made money in three ways: by packaging up subprime mortgages as CDOs; by insuring them (or betting they would blow up) with credit default swaps; and then by absorbing $13 billion of federal funds when the insurer AIG collapsed. In fact, with the demise of competitors like Bear Stearns, Merrill Lynch and Lehman Brothers, their position has never been stronger. Being far too big to fail, they also now enjoy an implicit government guarantee that they will never go bankrupt. In 2009, in the depths of a global recession, after showing 'restraint' in response to political pressure, they paid their 31,700 employees around $16 billion in compensation and bonuses. That works out to about half a million each, though of course it's not shared equally.

Goldman Sachs was one of the first Wall Street firms to get into quantitative finance, when in 1984 they hired Fischer Black – co-inventor of the Black–Scholes formula for valuing options – to explore mathematical methods for measuring risk. Even greater than their strength in mathematical models, however, is their extensive network of influential contacts. One of the more famous is former CEO Hank Paulson – treasury secretary under George W. Bush and the man responsible for administering the government bail-out funds. Perhaps the most yang-laden moment of the entire crisis was when ex-linebacker Paulson (nickname at Dartmouth, 'the hammer') appeared on TV to present to the American public a 'non-reviewable' three-page demand for a $700 million blank cheque to bail out Wall Street firms, as if he were addressing an opponent that had just been defeated in battle. Towards the end of his term, according to Bloomberg, Paulson brought on board 'a coterie of non-confirmed advisers from Goldman Sachs' on the basis that it was 'necessary to quickly bring in top talent when the financial system was on the verge of collapse'.[38] In 2010, Goldman alumni filled key posts including president of the New York Federal Reserve, economic advisor to the secretary of state, chief of staff to the treasury secretary, and chairman of the Commodity Futures Trading Commission. It's no surprise that one of the firm's nicknames is Government Sachs. (2017 update: the Goldman network has now expanded to include heads of four of the Federal Reserve's twelve regional banks, along with Mark Carney at the Bank of England and Mario Draghi at the European Central Bank. It was also first port of call for Donald Trump when it came time to fill the positions of director of the National Economic Council, treasury secretary, and chief strategist.[39])

The firm's secrecy rivals that of the Pythagoreans. When the playwright David Hare was researching his 2009 play *The Power of Yes*, he interviewed a number of bankers. As he told the *Financial Times*: 'I would get all these people saying things like, "I cannot talk about Goldman Sachs on the record." And I would think to myself: "What are you scared of? What would Goldman Sachs do?" I mean, I have talked with Palestinians who were living in a situation that was a matter of life and death. But Goldman Sachs?'[40]

While Goldman Sachs has many influential alumni, it's striking how few of them are women. The December 2008 issue of *Bloomberg Markets* magazine featured a fold-out page of 42 influential ex-partners, and eight honourable mentions. Out of all 50, only one of the ex-partners was female.[41]

This is not an unusual proportion – if anything Goldman appears to be relatively progressive in its efforts to include women. The stereotype of 'testosterone-filled, wild-eyed traders' is accurate.[42] To say that a macho culture predominates would not be an overstatement. David Hare's play has two women in a cast of twenty, but 'that is probably about right. It's shocking how few women there are in finance.' In his book *How I Caused the Credit Crunch*, Tetsuya Ishikawa describes it as 'the era of equality' when female colleagues occasionally go along to the lap-dancing clubs.[43]

As ex-Goldmanite Jacki Zehner wrote in 2008: 'Might this be one of many factors contributing to what is wrong with Wall Street leadership today? Arguably at this moment of financial and economic crisis, after approximately $10 trillion of global wealth has vanished, women remain virtually absent at the decision-making tables that count … In my 20 years of professional life I have seen very little to no progress for women in the financial services industry or in corporate America as a whole.'[44] According to Linda Tarr-Whelan, author of *Women Lead the Way*, women need to attain a critical mass of 30 per cent in order to have serious influence.[45]

There is plenty of empirical evidence to suggest that groups of males tend to engage in high-risk behaviour of the sort that characterised the subprime crisis. One paper entitled 'Testosterone and financial risk preferences' showed that testosterone levels are a predictor for risk-taking.[46] Trader testosterone levels soar during booms and fall during crashes, which helps amplify price swings. A study by Chicago-based Hedge Fund Research found that, while women manage only about 3 per cent of total funds, these fell half as much during the crisis as those managed by men, and also out-performed them over the past decade.[47] To balance your portfolio, you might want to consider having it managed by a company with women on its team. As Lu Hong and Scott E. Page wrote in *The Journal of Economic Theory*: 'There seems to be a strong consensus that diverse groups perform better at problem solving.'[48]

Note that these papers are not making generalisations about *all* men and *all* women, or even the average man and the average woman, who don't exist. Nor, I hope, are they saying that women are in some sense better than men. They are only making empirical observations about patterns in behaviour, which have complex causes and vary with time and context. Differences that are minor at the individual level can be amplified by group dynamics. One advantage of talking about abstract concepts like yin and yang is that we can recognise yin as being *associated* with female and yang as being *associated* with male, without confusing them with an individual person's gender. Margaret Thatcher and Ronald Reagan differed in X-chromosome status, but their Friedman-advised economic policies were both fairly yang (General Pinochet's Friedman-advised policies in Chile were even more yang).[49] Groups are affected by their makeup, and the yang quality of the financial industry is associated with the fact that it is largely made up of men.

If finance were to become less male-dominated, it might even have effects outside the industry. As Halla Tómasdóttir from Iceland's Augur Capital observes: 'If the institutions are under the control of a single group – and now it is men – and they all think the same way, we are not going to make positive changes. For the first time in 100 years we have the chance to create a company, a society, a country, and hopefully a world that is more sustainable, more fair for men as well as women. If we are not going to do that now, then when will we?'[50]

In the meantime, the rest of society has the right to ring-fence these activities so they can't bring down the rest of the economy. One step, as discussed in Chapter 2, is to revisit some of that Depression-era legislation that separated investment activities from ordinary commercial banking functions.[51] Another measure, which has often been discussed but has never caught on – banks describe it as unworkable, unsurprisingly – is a small global tax on financial transactions.[52] The aim would be to reduce speculative activity and shrink the bloated and self-important financial sector to a point where it services the real economy, instead of dominating it. Call it a punitive tax on a particular kind of toxic masculinity, if you like.

Myths and consequences

While the old-boy network, institutional sexism, and the under-representation of women in economics and finance are problems, however, they are not in themselves the main obstacle to a rebalancing of the economic system. A bigger factor is mainstream economic theory – the stuff they teach in universities. It is an entire view of the world, and pattern of thought, that reduces complexity to simple laws, and human motivations to cold calculations. It goes back to Julie Nelson's observation that economics values the 'masculine' methods of 'detachment, mathematical reasoning, formality, and abstraction' over the 'feminine' methods associated with 'connectedness, verbal reasoning, informality, and concrete detail'. Economics strives to be an impartial, detached, hard science like physics, but (in part for that reason) it condones and even glorifies a particular type of yang behaviour; and is blind to effects such as nonlinearity, fluidity, complex interdependence, and asymmetries in power. The subprime crisis, which was based on highly complex instruments such as CDOs that could be assessed only by relying on abstract mathematical tools, was a perfect example of this. As we will see in later chapters, the same emphasis on abstract theory over empirical reality is a major driver of everything from social inequality to the environmental crisis.

At Milton Friedman's 90th birthday bash, his former student Donald Rumsfeld said that 'Milton is the embodiment of the truth that "ideas have consequences"'.[53] The subprime crisis, in turn, is graphic proof that economic myths have consequences. These economyths, which again some economists may distance themselves from but are encoded in key models, include the ideas that:

- The economy is governed by mathematical laws, so risk can be controlled using equations
- Individuals or households act independently, and are immune to herd behaviour
- Markets are stable, so the future will resemble the past
- Investors or households or firms like Lehman Brothers act rationally, and don't make poor economic decisions that go against their best interests
- Economics is an objective, impartial mathematical science, rather than a cultural phenomenon that itself influences the economy in a gendered manner

Finally, there is the economyth – discussed further in the next chapter – that free markets are also fair. In many ways the subprime story was less about risk than about power. Friedman's utopia of a society of maximum individual freedom sounds attractive, until you see how it plays out in the real world. Giving companies like Goldman Sachs the maximum freedom to package subprime mortgages at teaser rates for financially illiterate people, construct multi-trillion-dollar balloons of credit out of thin air, and then extract money off the government when the scheme goes sour, probably isn't what he had in mind.

The crisis, whose consequences are still playing out, is unlikely to be the last demonstration of the power that these ideas still hold. Mainstream economists in academia and government remain entranced by their Pythagorean vision of a perfect economy, and therefore fail to learn from their mistakes. By continuing to propagate these myths, our universities and business schools sow the seeds for future financial catastrophes. Just as faulty risk models make the economy more risky, so a worldview that sees and treats the economy as inherently stable and self-regulating will – by loosening regulations – eventually turn it into the opposite. The point is not just that the economy is reflexive, and therefore hard to predict; but that our ideas and myths have shaped the economy in a particular way, and led to the *designing in* of instability. This is perhaps the clearest example of how economic theories influence the world, and therefore lose any pretence at objectivity. (As discussed later, this process also works in the other direction: the real economy affects theory by selecting ideas that suit its power structure.)

Indeed, it is ironic that, while economics has aligned itself as stereotypically masculine, the actual economy has become increasingly connected, changeable, and unpredictable – all traits that are culturally considered stereotypically female.[54] Economists are the jilted lovers of the science world – the more rigidly they approach their subject, the more it mocks them with spurious and headstrong behaviour.

Mathematical models are useful tools for simulating and understanding the economy, but they will never be able to accurately predict its course, or fully capture risk. To quote author and derivatives trader Pablo Triana: 'Reality is much more ferociously untamable. The randomness is not just wild; it's savagely uncageable, abominably undomesticated. No equations can subjugate it, control it, or decipher it. Where anything can happen, there are no mathematically imposed bounds.'[55] Or as science historian Evelyn Fox Keller puts it: 'Nature ... is not completely bound by Logos: it remains caught in an essential duality. If in some respects it is subject to the light of reason and order, it is also enmired in the dark forces of unreason and disorder. The forces of unreason, in Greek mythology and drama most often embodied in the earth goddesses or the Furies, are never fully vanquished, even when they are subdued.'[56] In its way, the subprime crisis was another manifestation of this eternal archetypal battle between chaos and order; and one in which chaos won.

In the 19th century, a band of outsiders sought inspiration from science and engineering to create a new theory of economics. It is time to do so again.

The Great Yinification

Scientists have long dreamed of a Grand Unified Theory that will explain all the known physical forces and the evolution of the universe. Some have even hoped for a theory that would unite physics, chemistry, biology, psychology, sociology – all the physical and social sciences – in a single model. The ultimate aim of the Enlightenment, according to philosophers Max Horkheimer and Theodor W. Adorno, was to make 'dissimilar things comparable by reducing them to abstract quantities. For the Enlightenment, anything which cannot be resolved into numbers, and ultimately one, is illusion; modern positivism consigns it to poetry. Unity remains the watchword from Parmenides to Russell. All gods and qualities must be destroyed.'[57] As Vilfredo Pareto wrote: 'It is only the imperfections of the human mind which multiply the divisions of the sciences, separating astronomy from physics or chemistry, the natural sciences from the social sciences. In essence, science is one. It is none other than the truth.'[58]

What seems to have happened instead, though, is a little different. Call it the Great Yinification. Since the 1960s, as we have seen, many of the most exciting developments in applied mathematics have been in areas such as nonlinear dynamics, network theory, and complexity. They are about systems that are connected, in flux, and resistant to reductionist logic. Rather than providing a single unified theory, these methods see models as imperfect patches; instead of elegant proofs, or reductive formulae, they offer only fuzzy glimpses of the complex reality. Science, I believe, is becoming more open, and less dogmatic. A degree of humility is even sometimes present. When sceptics say that science can offer little to economics – a view that has become popular since the crisis, as a counter-reaction to the antiquated pseudo-science of mainstream economics – they seem as unaware as neoclassical economists that science is moving on.[59]

As economists revise their field to reflect these developments, for example through the use of agent-based models discussed in previous chapters, or by a shift from overly abstract and theoretical treatments towards empirical knowledge, the field may lose its aura of homogeneity and stereotypical maleness and attract a broader range of talent. 'Because models by their nature represent only a partial viewpoint, partiality or bias cannot be eliminated from theories', wrote economist Paula England. 'A greater openness … is likely to lead to a multiplicity of perspectives that more adequately captures the complexity and diversity of economic activities.'[60]

For example, it has long been noted that measures of economic activity such as gross domestic product do not account for unpaid work, most of which is done by women. As the economist Cecil Pigou noted in 1920, 'if a man marries his housekeeper or his cook, the national dividend is diminished'.[61] In her 1988 book *If Women Counted: A New Feminist Economics*, New Zealand's Marilyn Waring totted up various types of unpaid labour such as bearing children, bringing them up and educating them; looking after the weak, disabled, sick, or aged; and running the household. She estimated that such work, about two-thirds of which was done by women, was equivalent to 25–40 per cent of the economy in industrialised countries.[62] In developing countries, the proportion was even larger.

One implication is that economic growth is illusory if it only represents a shift from unpaid to paid work. A paper from the

Bureau of Economic Analysis, for example, found that unpaid work increased GDP in the US by 39 per cent in 1965, but only by 26 per cent in 2010, thus lowering the average annual nominal growth rate from 6.9 per cent to 6.7 per cent.[63] This is more than an accounting detail, because it shows that biasing policy to favour paid work comes at a measurable cost. Feminist economists also point out that many of our choices, such as where we work, are determined as much by societal norms and government policies about things like daycare as they are about individual preferences.

While feminist economics is a growing field and has been influential in academic areas discussed in later chapters, such as alternatives to GDP, the role of women in economic development, and ecological economics, it has so far had little impact on the standard textbooks. As the professor of gender and economic development Lourdes Benería notes: 'Economics is a very hegemonic discipline, even though there are so many heterodox economists that protest this arrogance and this unwillingness to discuss criticisms. Compared to other social sciences that have integrated gender much more easily, conventional economics has been one of the most impenetrable disciplines. It has been difficult, if not impossible, for orthodox economics to incorporate feminist issues.'[64] Part of the problem, according to Benería, is that 'to deal with gender relations you have to incorporate power into the analysis. Neoclassical economics does not deal with power relations; it tends to focus on purely economic issues.'

To build a more balanced and just economy, we first need to rebalance our priorities, and our mental theories and mythologies. As the physician/gambler Cardano wrote: 'A man is nothing but his mind; if that be out of order, all's amiss, and if that be well, the rest is at ease.'[65] In the next chapter, we consider how this might apply to the greatest balancing act of all – that of social inequality.

Male versus female

Out of all the chapters in the original book, this one evoked the most polarised response. Some thought it was the worst, others the best. One issue is that the Western mind, steeped as it is in Aristotelian yes/no binary thinking, tends to rebel against, or dismiss as flaky, the concept of complementary dualities – which puts us at odds with everything from Chinese philosophy to the quantum nature of the universe, to the structure of the economy. Not to mention the question of gender.

When I wrote the chapter, prompted admittedly by allegiance to my Pythagorean chapter order, I was still surprised that I seemed to be one of the few people talking about the gender aspect of the crisis. That has since changed, especially after it was found that government austerity programmes such as benefit cuts and tax changes were having a disproportionate effect on women – in the UK they bore an estimated 85 per cent of the brunt, while the distribution of bank bail-out payments presumably had the opposite skew, and the former chancellor and 'architect of austerity' George Osborne himself obtained a £13,500-per-day part-time consultancy with US investment firm BlackRock.[66] (For some reason it seems easier to bring up the female-gendered nature of the fall-out, rather than what is to me the rather obviously male-gendered nature of the event itself.) As Margunn Bjørnholt and Ailsa McKay commented in 2013: 'Given the evidence emerging relating to the very gendered impact of the economic crisis it would seem that any attempt to render the economics discipline more effective as a tool for predicting, analysing and responding to economic phenomena should incorporate a gender perspective.'[67]

One way to do this is through the technique of 'gender budgeting', which considers such impacts and has been adopted in some fifteen countries from Iceland to Mexico.[68] Another step, though, is to counter what Bjørnholt and McKay call the continuing 'marginalization of women throughout the economics profession'. When the *American Economic Review* invited six (male) economists in 2011 to select the twenty most influential articles from the last 100 years, one of 30 authors was a woman.[69] When the *Economist* magazine did a similar exercise for the 25 most influential economists of 2014, zero were women (they excluded active central bankers, so Janet Yellen didn't make the list).[70] A 2014 study comparing gender balance in different academic fields concluded that 'Economics is an outlier, with a persistent sex gap in promotion that cannot be readily explained by productivity differences'.[71] In 2016 the *New York Times* reported that 'Economics remains a stubbornly male-dominated profession, a fact that members of the profession have struggled to understand'.[72]

As sociologist Elaine Coburn put it in a 2016 article, 'mainstream economics remains remarkably "pre-feminist"', and this is equally true of leading economic organisations such as the IMF and World Bank, where between them one of sixteen Chief Economists has been a woman (though Christine Lagarde has been Managing Director of the IMF since 2011).[73] Economics awaits its own version of the Guerilla Girls – the feminist artist collective which shook up the old-boy network, and the aesthetic, of the art world in the 1980s. The finance industry at least seems to be hiring more women, though one female hedge fund manager told Bloomberg in 2016 that sexism remains a 'huge, huge issue', as evidenced for example in the way that women are also more likely than men to be punished or fired for any infraction.[74] Megan Butler from the UK Financial Conduct Authority told an audience at the 2017 City & Financial Global's Women in Finance Summit that 'It's extremely rare that in my professional life I have a conversation with a head of desk at an investment bank or a global head of business that is anything other than a white male. I've increasingly come to find that a little bit difficult to take.'[75]

It was telling that one of the effects of the crisis was to boost the demand from people working in finance for testosterone treatments, in the form of injections, supplements, and creams. 'If you're going to be trading on Wall Street or dealing with large sums of money, you had better be confident', a Manhattan doctor explained in 2012. 'The man who is wishy-washy', he elaborated (still in 2012, as opposed to, say, 1962), 'is not going to be successful.'[76] Some female traders even take the therapy, but according to the *Financial Times* they 'get much smaller doses than men because there is a risk they might grow facial hair or display other male characteristics'. The testosterone presumably helps them worry less about such risks, though, in a scary kind of werewolfean feedback loop.

More controversial, perhaps, is the idea that mainstream economic thought itself incorporates a male bias. Consider for example the question of theory versus concrete data, discussed in the previous chapter, which is related to a broader dichotomy between abstract number and physical reality. 'Statistically, men and women are not drawn to the same fields within economics', write economist Miles Kimball and an untenured female economist who didn't want to be identified in case it hurt her career.[77] 'And even within a field, women are drawn to a different balance between immediate real-world relevance and theoretical elegance.' To encourage more female participation, economics therefore needs to 'become open to a wider range of scientific approaches and topics', and also promote 'a better power balance among colleagues. What we mean is that female economists should be encouraged to assert their power, but male economists should find it hard or impossible to exert illegitimate, sexist power over their female colleagues. If this sounds obvious, it's much harder than it seems.'

Strange, since I thought university campuses were bastions of political correctness, but maybe that doesn't apply to the 'hard' – cough – sciences like economics. Male professors may enjoy cultivating a 'rude' atmosphere, as discussed in the Appendix, but it sounds rather one-sided. Conversely, if and when more women go into economics, it will be interesting to see how this changes the profession.

But gender is a tricky subject, and it's getting trickier. I know this because I signed one of my daughters up for a summer rock camp for girls. On volunteers, the website features a 'special note to male-identified allies' which I think includes dads. The camp, it says, 'is primarily led by and for women and girls. We also value diversity, inclusion, and sensitivity towards all individuals, regardless of gender identity or expression. The organization welcomes the support of male-identified allies, and expects male-identified allies who would like to volunteer to respect the importance of leadership by women.'[78]

So in other words, someone like me who identifies as a male can volunteer but only if I respect the leadership of those who identify as female. It is like gender identity is important, but somehow flexible at the same time. Which perhaps is not a bad description. Maybe economists need to attend girls' rock camp.

CHAPTER 7

THE UNFAIR ECONOMY

*It's not that many young people do not have aspirations.
It is that they are blocked ... Such elitism is unjust
socially. And it can no longer work economically.*
Alan Milburn MP (2009)

History is a graveyard of aristocracies.
Vilfredo Pareto (1916)

**Economists are taught that, in principle at least, a well-run
market economy is fundamentally fair, so while luck and
random effects may be involved, our actual chance of success
depends only on merit. The whole point of a competitive market, after all, is that everyone has an equal shot. This belief in an
underlying equality influences everything from taxation policy
to the pay packages of CEOs. Yet in recent decades, the income
distribution has become increasingly skewed, with most of the
benefits of increased productivity accruing to the top few per
cent of the population. The reason, as this chapter shows, is
that markets are not fair and balanced, and the rich really do
get richer.**

The physicist Richard Feynman once said that the greatest of scientific facts was that all things are made of atoms. If there is a close
second, many scientists would choose the idea that the universe is
based on symmetry. Just as matter reduces to atoms, so physical
laws can be reduced to assertions of symmetry. And the discovery

of deep symmetries has motivated scientists since the time of the Pythagoreans.

The ancient Greeks believed that the celestial bodies moved around the earth in perfect circles, because those were the most symmetrical shapes – as Ptolemy put it, they alone were 'strangers to disparities and disorders'. Newton's laws of motion showed that every force creates an equal and opposite force; Maxwell's equations revealed a symmetry between electricity and magnetism.

The deepest theorems of physics are conservation theorems stating that some quantity remains stable and unchanged. These too are based on symmetry. Conservation of energy – which says that energy can be neither created nor destroyed in a process, but can only change its form – can be shown to reduce to a statement that the laws of physics are symmetrical in time: if an experiment is done at noon, and then repeated under identical conditions after lunch, the result will be the same. Conservation of momentum is equivalent to saying that the laws of physics do not depend on position: if the experimental apparatus is shifted a few feet to the side, the result will again be unchanged.

Symmetry and reductionism are two sides of the same coin, for only by exploiting deep symmetries can scientists reduce complex phenomena to simple equations. The search for new forms of symmetry still plays a guiding role in physics, as can be seen, for example, by the development of the theory known as supersymmetry, which hypothesises that every particle type has a kind of unseen mirror image. Many physicists even believe that, when the universe was born, at the moment of the Big Bang, all forces and all forms of matter were one, in a state of perfect symmetry. As the universe expanded and cooled, these symmetries gradually broke down in a process called symmetry breaking – the force of gravity separated from the force of electromagnetism, electrons separated from protons, and so on. The messy, asymmetric world we live in gradually took shape.

If physicists seem fascinated and enraptured by symmetry, then those physics groupies known as mainstream economists can't be far behind. In fact, they take the study of symmetry to a more advanced level. Their theories don't assume that the economy was once in a state of symmetry – they assume that it still is. This belief is the source of the economyth that the economy is inherently fair and balanced.

Mirror image

When economics began to be mathematicised in the late 19th century, economists were forced by the limitations of their mathematical and computational tools to simulate 'perfect markets' that included a high degree of symmetry. For example, the assumption of rational behaviour is a kind of symmetry, because it says that everyone, given the same preferences, would act in exactly the same way. When perfectly rational people (if they exist) look at one another, it's like looking in the mirror.

The markets were also assumed to be in equilibrium, which is symmetry in time: the past looks exactly like the future. And these perfect markets were fair and transparent, so individuals and firms were positioned symmetrically in terms of advantages: they all competed on an equal basis and had access to all necessary information, and no individual firm or person was powerful enough to affect prices on their own. The 'law of supply and demand', for example, assumed a large number of essentially identical firms all competing as equals in the same market. Statistical methods, based on statistical mechanics, could therefore be applied.

While these symmetry assumptions may originally have been essential for computational reasons, they have proved surprisingly resilient over the years. William Stanley Jevons defined the market as: 'persons dealing in two or more commodities, whose stocks of those commodities and intentions of exchanging are known to all … Every individual must be considered as exchanging from a pure regard to his own requirements or private interests, and there must be perfectly free competition.'[1] In the 1960s, Eugene Fama defined his efficient market as 'a market where there are large numbers of rational profit maximizers actively competing, with each trying to predict future market values of individual securities, and where important current information is almost freely available to all participants.'[2] About the only change, then, was the insertion of the word 'almost'. (As mentioned in Chapter 2, different versions of the hypothesis exist that relax this further, while still retaining the basic flavour.)

Economic models in general have continued to shy away from distinguishing economic agents based on power, influence, access to information, connections, gender, race, class, or any other characteristic. As Norbert Häring and Niall Douglas note in their book *Economists and the Powerful*, such imbalances are 'defined away by standard assumptions of most mainstream economic models'.[3] Milton Friedman even argued that properly functioning free markets would automatically render them irrelevant: 'There is an economic incentive in a free market to separate economic efficiency from other characteristics of an individual. A businessman or an entrepreneur who expresses preferences in his business activities that are not related to productive efficiency is at a disadvantage compared to other individuals who do not. Such an individual is in effect imposing higher costs upon himself than are other individuals who do not have such preferences. Hence, in a free market they will tend to drive him out.'[4] According to theory, sexism, racism or any other form of discrimination is inefficient, so in a pure (i.e. symmetrical) market it wouldn't exist. Economic transactions are more or less the same, regardless of who is involved or when they take place. (It is amusing to compare this picture with the highly ritualised, Vatican-like hiring practice standard in economics departments, which according to one sociological study is characterised by elitism, hierarchy, networking, and male-bias.[5])

Of course, no economist would claim that the real economy is *perfectly* fair or stable, or that each participant has access to *exactly* the same information. In 2001, the Sveriges Riksbank Prize in Economic Sciences was awarded to George Akerlof, Michael Spence and Joseph Stiglitz 'for their analyses of markets with asymmetric information' – in which, for example, sellers of used cars know more about the state of the items being sold than the buyers. One reason why mainstream economics has endured so long is that economists are willing to address what they consider to be isolated flaws in their models, and carry out detailed and apparently impressive research into phenomena such as 'bounded rationality', 'asymmetric information' or other 'market frictions' which interfere with perfectly competitive trade, while leaving their core theories, teachings and economyths essentially unchanged. The truth is that assumptions of symmetry or at best small departures from symmetry are implicit in theories such as the efficient market hypothesis, and the fascination with simplified, abstract, reductionist models explains what economists M. Neil Browne and J. Kevin Quinn describe as the 'almost complete absence of power from the toolkit employed by mainstream economists'. In a survey they performed of sixteen currently used introductory textbooks – major doorstoppers all – they found zero pages that dealt with topics directly related to power (and a total of only 25 pages dealing with issues related to women).[6] The trend towards increased deregulation is also based on the picture of free and fair competition between equals.

As seen with the subprime crisis, though, these assumptions soon begin to look ridiculous when you compare them with the real world. Markets aren't just slightly asymmetric, they're totally out of whack. Is it really OK to assume that Goldman Sachs and subprime mortgage holders are competing on a level playing field and have access to the same information? Is Wal-Mart versus the local corner store really a fair fight? And does it really make no difference where you are born, who your parents are, what schools you went to, who your friends are, or what your history is?

Circulation of the elites

The French statesman Georges Clemenceau is attributed with the saying that 'Any man who is not a socialist at age 20 has no heart. Any man who is still a socialist at age 40 has no head.'

Following a similar kind of trajectory, perhaps, neoclassical economics started off in an idealistic vein. The aim of people like Jevons, Walras and Pareto was to put economics on a rational basis, and thus improve the living standards of the general population. Jevons was brought up in a Unitarian tradition concerned with social conditions, and spent much of his free time walking the streets of the cities he lived in – Sydney, Manchester, London – observing the conditions of the poor and contemplating the connections between poverty and economics. Walras inherited his socialist ideals from his father, and spent a number of years working in the cooperative movement before taking up his professorship at Lausanne.

As a young man, Vilfredo Pareto was a dedicated democrat, and took pleasure in attacking the Italian government for corruption and corporatism. After the May 1898 riots in Milan, which were organised by the Italian Socialist Party and resulted in the deaths of hundreds of people, Pareto offered his home in Switzerland to socialist exiles and leftist radicals. Even by 1891, though, when Pareto was 43, it appeared that his head was pulling in another direction. He wrote to Walras: 'I give up the combat in defense of [liberal] economic theories in Italy. My friends and I get nowhere and lose our time; this time is much more fruitfully devoted to scientific study.'[7] He began to believe that his youthful passion for leftist ideals had been based on emotion rather than logic, and that all human societies were inherently corrupt and irrational.

Pareto's cynicism about human motivations was no doubt fuelled in 1901 when he returned home from a trip to find that his wife had run off with the cook and 30 cases of possessions. Under Italian law, Pareto couldn't get a divorce. He had inherited a large sum of money from an uncle in 1898, enough to make him financially independent. In 1907 he resigned his university position and retired to his villa near Lake Geneva, where he lived with a woman 30 years his junior called Jeanne Régis, a large stock of the finest wines and liqueurs, and eighteen Angora cats (the house was called Villa Angora).

Pareto continued to blast off incendiary books, articles and letters, but his aim switched from trying to change society, to analysing it from his detached vantage point – rather as an entomologist might analyse the social goings-on of an anthill, but with more spite and irony. In his million-word tome *Treatise on General Sociology*, he argued that human behaviour is driven by irrational desires, which are then justified by particular ideologies. To understand society, one therefore had to focus on the underlying irrational desires, which he classified into six types. The most important were innovation (Class I) and conservation (Class II). Everyone was motivated by a mix of these classes, but one could nevertheless speak of 'Class I' types, who are clever and calculating, and 'Class II' types, who are slower, more bureaucratic, and dependent on force.

Pareto had earlier discovered the power-law distribution of wealth (the 80–20 rule) in Italy and other countries, and wrote that it 'can be compared in some respects to Kepler's law in astronomy;

we still lack a theory that may make this law of distribution rational in the way in which the theory of universal gravitation has made Kepler's law rational'.[8] Today, we would describe it as an emergent property of the economy. In his retirement, Pareto came to see this highly-skewed power law as a kind of snapshot that revealed the underlying dynamics of any society.

At the top is a small elite consisting of a mix of Class I and Class II people who are engaged in a Machiavellian struggle for power. There is always a degree of social mobility, so the composition of the elite changes as people enter or leave. The balance between the two classes therefore varies with time, in a process Pareto called the circulation of the elite. If too many innovative and intelligent Class I people (Machiavelli's foxes) get in power, then the conservative Class IIs will plot a takeover. If the elite is dominated by Class IIs (Machiavelli's lions), then it will become overly bureaucratic and reactive and the Class Is will make their move. This process can be smooth and gradual; but, if the circulation becomes blocked, so that 'simultaneously the upper strata are full of decadent elements and the lower strata are full of elite elements', then the social state 'becomes highly unstable and a violent revolution is imminent'.[9]

Pareto demonstrated his argument with numerous case studies. Perhaps the best illustration, though, was the coming to power in Italy of Mussolini's Fascist government. Mussolini liked the idea of powerful lions taking over from foxes grown corrupt and ineffectual, and appointed Pareto Senator of the Kingdom of Italy. In 1923, Pareto finally managed to obtain a divorce and marry Jeanne Régis, before dying the same year.

How to get rich

While Pareto's sociological arguments have dated a bit in the last hundred years, his observation that wealth is distributed according to a power law has remained accurate – except that the elite has grown relatively smaller and more powerful. Figure 14 is a summary of how the world's wealth was distributed among the total 3.7 billion adults in the year 2000, according to a United Nations report. Adults required a relatively modest net worth of $2,138 to count themselves in the wealthiest 50 per cent. To be in the top 10 per cent (370 million adults) they needed $61,000. This group owned over 80 per cent of the total wealth. Anyone with $510,000 was in the top 1 per cent (that's 37 million adults). Together, this small sliver of the world population controlled 40 per cent of the world's financial assets. Contrast that with the bottom half, who collectively controlled about 1 per cent of the wealth. Someone

Figure 14. Bar graph showing the worldwide wealth distribution in 2000.[10] The top decile (10 per cent) controls over 80 per cent of the total wealth. Deciles 6 through 10, which represent the bottom 50 per cent of the population, control about 1 per cent in total.

born into the world at random would stand a 50 per cent chance
of ending up in that group of 1.85 billion adults. (As discussed in
the update on page 216, wealth distribution in many countries has
become considerably more skewed in recent years.)

Rather impressively, the power-law distribution of wealth
extends all the way up to the world's richest billionaires. In 2009
the world's richest person was Bill Gates, with a net worth of
$40 billion. To put that in perspective, suppose that you made a
plot of the wealth of everyone on the planet, in order from richest
to poorest. If you continued the plot up to the 99th percentile,
then the vertical scale of the graph would have to be around half
a million dollars (this will have changed slightly since 2000). But
if you wanted to contain Bill Gates, or his friend Warren Buffett,
then the vertical scale would need to expand by a factor of about
80,000 (see Figure 16 below).

Wealth is also of course not distributed evenly in geographical
terms. In 2000 the USA and Canada together had 34 per cent of
the wealth, Europe had 30 per cent, rich Asian-Pacific countries
had 24 per cent, and the rest of the world including Latin America
and Africa held 12 per cent. This mix is changing as countries like
China, India and Brazil continue to experience explosive growth
and claim a larger share of the world's economic pie.

From these data alone, one can therefore conclude that the
world economy is highly asymmetric. A small number of people
enjoy a huge proportion of the world's wealth, while billions live
in poverty. The same kind of pattern is seen repeating itself fractally over different scales. Every city has its own local elite, as does
every country or region. The sprawling metropolis of greater São
Paulo, Brazil, for example, now has some 500 helicopters, more
than any other city in the world. The rich find them a good way to
avoid traffic jams that can extend for over a hundred miles.[11] Also
they're hard to steal.

Apart from his discovery of the power-law wealth distribution, another aspect of Pareto's work to have passed the test of time was his insistence that humans act primarily on the basis of psychological motivations, and justify those actions on the basis of ideology. The ruling elite always has a very good argument as to why it should be in charge and have most of the wealth and be flying the helicopter. Today, that argument goes by names such as the invisible hand, the efficient market, or mainstream economics.

Broken symmetry

Adam Smith's concept of the invisible hand is usually taken to refer to the price mechanism. However, his first use of the expression, in his 1759 work *The Theory of Moral Sentiments*, is on the subject of wealth distribution: 'The rich ... divide with the poor the produce of all their improvements. They are led by an invisible hand to make nearly the same distribution of the necessaries of life which would have been made, had the earth been divided into equal proportions among all its inhabitants, and thus without intending it, without knowing it, advance the interest of the society, and afford means to the multiplication of the species.'[12] The invisible hand refers here not to the magic of the market, but to an early version of trickle-down economics.

Since the economy has patently failed to align itself with this happy picture, at the level of individual countries or the entire globe, one might ask what forces have created such a skewed distribution. According to Smith's later work *The Wealth of Nations* (1776), free markets tend to drive prices towards 'The natural price, or the price of free competition'. That applies to the price of labour, so it follows that an individual's earnings should reflect the person's inherent value to society. Efficient market theory similarly argues that markets allocate resources efficiently, and that includes wages. If Quetelet's picture of the 'average man' is correct, and our abilities are randomly distributed according to a normal distribution, then one might expect wealth to be symmetrically distributed in the same way – most people would be in the middle, and there would be only a few who are very poor or very rich. The reality in most countries is obviously very different, so either our financial elites are incredibly talented, or something else is going on.

As discussed in Chapter 4, one prevailing economyth is that the economy is inherently stable and at equilibrium – i.e., it is symmetrical in time – and so history doesn't matter. However, there is the old saying that 'the rich get richer', and it certainly seems that to make a lot of money, it helps to have some in the first place.

Imagine as a thought experiment that a city-sized group of people are given a windfall of $100 each, under the condition that they must keep it invested in a rather volatile and unproductive stockmarket. Each person makes their own investments, with an average real return of 0 per cent and a standard deviation of 5 per cent.

After one year, most people's nest eggs will be in the range $90 to $110, and will be distributed according to the bell curve with a peak at 100 and a standard deviation of 5. As time goes on, though, the distribution becomes increasingly skewed. If we follow the worth of the investments as they are passed down through generations for 150 years (about the age of economics), then the resulting wealth distribution looks like Figure 15, which is quite similar to the actual wealth distribution in Figure 14.

Obviously this is not a serious model of how wealth changes with time. It only tracks the value of imaginary investment port-folios, and ignores other kinds of economic transactions (more realistic agent-based models can be constructed, if desired). However, it does demonstrate the simple fact that, left to their own devices, investments will tend to concentrate themselves in

Figure 15. Bar graph showing the result from the computer simulation of the evolving wealth distribution described in the text. The skewed distribution is an example of symmetry breaking.

fewer and fewer hands. To use the physics term, it is an example of symmetry breaking. At the start of the simulation, everything is perfectly symmetrical. Each person has exactly the same initial amount of money. They also have identical chances of success with their investments – no one is assumed to be more talented at picking stocks. But over a period of time, some start to pull ahead of the pack. The reason is that there is a positive feedback effect at work. A person whose sum has grown already from the initial $100 to $1,000 can hope to make another $100 in the coming year. They might instead lose that much, but at least they have the opportunity. Someone whose savings fund has shrunk to $10 can only hope to make another dollar.

As the simulation is run for more years, the wealth becomes increasingly concentrated, until eventually only a few people are left gambling with the entire wealth of the community. If a person were born at random into such a population, their chance of being in the elite would be negligibly small. So even though the laws that govern this toy economy are symmetrical and non-discriminatory, the system tends to evolve towards an increasingly skewed state. Time matters.

Indeed, while we think of the current high degree of inequality as being a permanent feature of the human condition, it is actually relatively recent. For over 90 per cent of our existence, up until the development of agriculture, humans lived in highly egalitarian societies. For reasons discussed further below, the last few decades have seen a particularly large increase in inequality in many countries, even as the total number of people living in extreme poverty has declined globally. Pareto's power law was known as the 80–20 rule because he estimated that 20 per cent of the population owned 80 per cent of the wealth. In 2000, the share of wealth owned by the top 20 per cent of the world population was measured as 93.9 per cent. It is therefore impossible to assume, as mainstream economic theories do, that we are all on a uniform playing field, or that history can be ignored. It isn't just symmetries that have broken; it is an entire economic worldview.

CEO-nomics

While investment growth is a major factor in determining both income and wealth distribution, at least for those with investments, an equally important determinant is employment income. Here again we see marked differences within societies, between countries, and over time.

A typical measure of income inequality is the ratio of CEO compensation to the average worker's pay. This is currently highest in the United States, with the UK coming second, continental Europe trailing, and Japan far behind. In the 1930s, the ratio in the US was around 80:1. It declined to around 30:1 in the 1960s, partly as a result of increased regulations such as anti-trust laws and the growth of unions. The trend was reversed in the 1980s, with a relaxed regulatory environment under Reagan and the loss of union power with increased global competition. Today the number is about 350:1 (a survey showed that most people thought the real number was 30:1, and the ideal number 7:1).[13] The 2007 compensation of Wal-Mart CEO Lee Scott, Jr amounted to $31.2 million, well over 1,000 times what the average Wal-Mart employee could expect to earn. In 2009, one hedge fund manager pulled in $2.5 billion.[14]

While CEO pay in the US is headed for the stratosphere, median salaries have stagnated since the early 1980s.[15] Middle-income households work more hours; often rely on two incomes instead of one; hold far more debt; and have access in their jobs to powerful productivity-enhancing technology. But the benefits of this increased work and productivity have flowed upwards from workers to managers. As a result, said Harvard law professor (now politician) Elizabeth Warren, 'the middle class is under terrific assault'.[16] In contrast, the share of the top 1 per cent has more than doubled, and is now greater than that of the bottom 90 per cent. This represents a huge transfer of wealth.

According to the law of supply and demand, the price of a CEO should reflect his or her intrinsic value. As efficient market theory's Eugene Fama said in a 2007 interview: 'you're just look-ing at market wages. They may be big numbers; that's not saying they're too high.'[17] (Or as Harvard's Gregory Mankiw put it in a 2013 paper, 'the most natural explanation of high CEO pay is that the value of a good CEO is extraordinarily high'. As evidence he cites what its authors describe as 'a simple equilibrium model of

CEO pay'.)[18] Empirical studies have shown, though, that the success of a company is best seen as the emergent result of factors such as the state of the market, the contributions of all employees, the internal company culture, and so on. Having a good CEO is an important part of the mix, but far less critical than their pay packages would suggest.[19] The International Labour Organisation concluded that CEO compensation has 'only very moderate, if any, effects ... Moreover, large country variations exist, with some countries displaying virtually no relation between performance-pay and company profits.'[20] Indeed, CEO pay in Japan is less than half the levels in the US, but they appear to have some effective companies.

A better explanation for the huge rise in CEO pay is provided by behavioural psychology. For a company in trouble, hiring a new CEO is like a patient looking for a wonder drug. Studies have shown that painkillers are more effective if they are sold in an expensive package than if they are presented as cheap generics.[21] Similarly, the cachet of luxury goods is enhanced by an exorbitant price tag. So for CEOs, the 'invisible hand' of the market is a helping hand up, lifting them higher and higher. The more they charge, the better they look, and the healthier the company's shareholders feel. CEOs have come to resemble celebrities, like film stars or athletes, whose fame and appeal seem only to increase the more they get paid.

CEOs also benefit from their position as hubs in the business network. Positive feedback network effects mean that the more network connections they make with other business leaders, the more powerful they become, thus improving their position in the network, and so on.[22] This positional advantage might make them more effective in their jobs, but it is primarily a property of the network itself, rather than the individual – the whole rather than the atomistic part. If a CEO retires, the network will produce a replacement or rearrange itself into a new configuration. Conventional economics sees the economy as flat and level as an Illinois cornfield, while in fact the terrain is more like the mountains of Afghanistan. Position matters: the better it is, the easier it is to defend.

Of course, these behavioural psychology and network effects don't occur in quite the same way for, say, greeters at Wal-Mart (average salary, around $10 per hour) or those who actually make the items in third-world sweatshops (tens of cents an hour).[23] Low-level employees find it harder to capitalise on luxury cachet, media glamour, or powerful connections. For a typical business, payroll makes up about 70 per cent of their costs. There is therefore tremendous pressure, both from customers and from shareholders, to reduce employee pay. Even if executives are vastly overpriced, their compensation is still a relatively small proportion of the total wage bill, and of course they are the ones deciding how pay should be divided. The pressure is therefore transferred to workers at the bottom, for whom the invisible hand is not a helping friend, but a hand on their ankle holding them down.

Corporate power
Another reason cited for the increasing pay of CEOs is that the companies they govern have grown larger and more complex as a result of globalisation. (Oddly, the US military has also grown more complex, but generals still scrape by on about ten times a private's wages.) It is certainly true that, just as wages in the economy have grown increasingly asymmetric, so have the sizes of companies. These again follow a roughly power-law distribution. At one end of the scale are millions of tiny firms employing only a few people. Looming over them are a much smaller number of huge multinationals, the size of nation states. In 2009, the largest company in the world in terms of revenue was the oil company ExxonMobil, with estimated annual revenues of $390.3 billion. The second was Wal-Mart, at $374.5 billion. Out of the top ten, seven were in the oil and gas business. (In 2016, this number had reduced to five.)

The lower panel of Figure 16 shows the 100 largest companies as measured by annual revenue. It is interesting to compare the two plots with Figure 13, which showed the 100 largest price changes in the S&P 500. The similarity is a reminder that power-law distributions, and fractal scaling, apply not just to financial shocks but also to financial opportunities. Just as we don't know when the next crash will occur, so it is impossible to know from the outset which micro-company will grow into a global behemoth, or who will be the next Bill Gates or Warren Buffett. The business model of venture capitalists is to fund an ensemble of small firms in the hope that one or more will hit it big.

The large multinational companies, such as Wal-Mart, rely on global supply chains that source the cheapest suppliers from around the world. This has the beneficial effect of minimising costs for consumers and maximising profits for shareholders. They can exploit economies of scale, and can also invest large amounts of money in improving their products. The pharmaceutical industry, for example, is headed by Pfizer, with total annual revenues in 2008 of $71 billion. Its enormous size means that it could afford a research and development budget of $11 billion.

While there are certainly benefits to having large companies, there are also severe disadvantages. They fuel inequality in the larger economy by increasing the downward pressure on wages for ordinary workers, at the same time as executive compensation balloons. They influence consumers through enormous advertising campaigns. Companies such as banks that become too big to fail can take enormous risks under the implicit guarantee that the government will bail them out if they get into trouble. The companies can also employ armies of lobbyists to exert pressure on government bodies, for example to relax environmental or labour regulations (ironically, while corporations strongly regulate the behaviour of their employees, they oppose any external

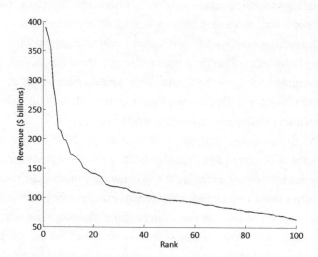

Figure 16. Top panel shows wealth (in billions of dollars) of the 100 richest people in 2009 according to *Forbes*.[24] Bill Gates is first with $40 billion, followed by Warren Buffett at $37 billion. Lower panel shows annual revenue in billions of dollars for the top 100 companies. ExxonMobil is top with $390.3 billion, followed by Wal-Mart at $374.5 billion.[25] Both plots follow a similar power-law distribution.

government regulation of their own behaviour on the grounds that it is inefficient). Economists learn about the dangers of monopolies in introductory classes, and see them as an example of 'market failure', but the situation here is more subtle and graded – Wal-Mart may not be a monopoly, but to a small competitor it can look like one. Skewed power is a natural feature of markets, rather than an aberration, and the problem is not market failure but theory failure.

Banks and financial institutions in particular hold enormous power over other companies, and the world economy in general. When complexity scientists from the Swiss Federal Institute of Technology performed a network analysis of the direct and indirect ownership links between 43,000 transnational corporations as of 2007, they found that 'less than 1 per cent of the companies were able to control 40 per cent of the entire network'.[26] Of the top 50 most powerful, 49 were related to finance (the exception at rank number fifteen was Walton Enterprises, which manages the fortunes of Wal-Mart's founding Walton family). Barclays, JPMorgan, and Goldman Sachs were all in the top twenty. Lehman was at 34, which explains why so much damage occurred when that particular node was removed from the network.

When companies are larger than many of the governments they deal with around the world, there is clearly a problem for democracy. The gulf between the average citizen and corporate power has never been greater, especially in developing countries. It's hard to make progress in addressing global climate change when some of the world's largest companies are in the oil and gas business; hard to reform the world finance system when faced with the political clout of firms like Goldman Sachs and JPMorgan; hard to negotiate labour conditions when the party on the other side of the table is Wal-Mart.

Neoclassical economists like Jevons argued that the market gains its power by aggregating the desires of a large number of people, thus increasing overall utility. However, it seems better at aggregating some things than others. As shown over the last few decades, markets can aggregate our power as consumers to force down prices of basic goods, and our power as investors to maximise profits. This restrains pay at the low end. They are much less good at aggregating our desire for a reasonable living wage, or a clean environment, or basic decency and justice. Now more than ever we need strong democratic institutions to temper the power of multinational corporations. We also need an economic theory to make sense of it all. Unfortunately, mainstream economics isn't it.

Unequal opportunities

Part of the enduring appeal of orthodox economic theory to our corporate leaders is that it provides a convenient intellectual argument for the programme of deregulation, privatisation of government assets, and social cutbacks that has been in place in many countries for the past few decades, and that has benefited large corporations at the expense of average workers. These changes have been justified by the economyth that the economic system is inherently fair, so people are paid what they are worth. But just as assuming that the market is stable actually makes it more risky, so the assumption of fairness ends up making the economy less fair.

In 2001, Harvard students performed a sit-in to demand a minimum hourly wage of $10.25 for the university's lowest-paid employees. *Harvard Magazine* formed a committee to debate the issue. One of the contributors was Gregory Mankiw, author of million-selling textbooks including *Principles of Economics*. Given an opportunity to put principles into practice, Mankiw wrote: 'Despite the students' good intentions, I cannot support their cause. If any institution should think with its head as well as its heart, it is a university.'[27] To quote from his book: 'The minimum wage is easily understood using the tools of supply and demand

... For workers with low levels of skill and experience, a high min-imum wage forces the wage above the level that balances supply and demand.'[28] He concluded that giving janitors an extra buck or so an hour 'would compromise the University's commitment to the creation and dissemination of knowledge'. (As economist Gilles Raveaud observed, the conversation wasn't extended to cover how academic tenure fits in with supply and demand.[29] Nor, one might also point out while we're on the subject, the economics of *Principles of Economics*: demand is enforced by professors so is rather insensitive to price – when reviews say 'required read-ing', they mean that literally – and the cost is often covered by government-subsidised student loans, which may explain why the book currently lists at $406.95.[30] It will be interesting to see what impact open-access alternatives such as CORE, mentioned in the Foreword, have on this publishing model.)

Given that neoclassical economics has been the dominant economic ideology since the late 1960s, it is no surprise that the inflation-adjusted minimum wage in the United States has declined over that period by about 25 per cent; or that wage inequality in general has exploded. While economics pretends to be an impar-tial science, it is also capable of being profoundly political. As the economist Joseph Stiglitz told *Adbusters* magazine: 'Mankiw was on the Council of Economic Advisors under President Bush and ... they tried to push forward a particular ideological view that markets work perfectly.'[31] The problem is that, while market forces will automatically assign janitors or professors a wage of some sort, there is no guarantee that it will be appropriate or reasonable.

This matters because, as documented by Richard Wilkinson and Kate Pickett in their book *The Spirit Level*, inequality is corre-lated, and not in a good way, with all kinds of other issues including community breakdown, mental and physical health problems, drug addiction, imprisonment rates, educational underperformance, teenage births, and so on.[32] Those rich-but-unequal countries the US and the UK, whose cultures have been strongly shaped by neoclassical thought, consistently top the charts on many of these areas, while more equal countries such as Japan, Norway and Sweden report fewer problems. Correlation is not the same as causation, but there is convincing empirical evidence that 'The more equally wealth is distributed the better the health of the society', as the *British Medical Journal* reported.[33]

Of course, as doctors know, anything is fine in moderation. Some people will always earn more than others, and a degree of inequality fosters entrepreneurship, so long as it is seen as fair. But when inequality, which is a function of wage differentials rather than just minimum wages, becomes too extreme, it violates at a basic level our sense of fair play. This is why cooperative human societies, such as ones in which men hunt large game, often take care to ensure equitable distribution. 'Without ever having heard calls for equality, these cultures are nevertheless keenly aware of the risk that inequity poses to the social fabric of their society', notes primatologist Frans de Waal, who sees the same behaviour in primates.[34] From a global perspective, inequality fuels problems such as ethnic violence – because wealth in many developing countries is controlled by small but economically dominant ethnic groups – and terrorism.[35]

Lack of power

Economists are of course aware of inequality and try to incorporate it into their calculations, but as Paul Krugman noted in 2016, 'we really don't know how to model personal income distribution'.[36] One problem is that it violates the symmetry assumptions at the heart of the models. As Olivier Blanchard wrote the same year, the derivation of distributional effects 'depends on the way distortions are introduced in the model. And, often, for reasons of practicality, these distortions are introduced in ways that are analytically convenient but have unconvincing welfare implications.'[37] Asymmetries are seen as 'distortions' to models, which were built around the idea of Quetelet's average man, so it makes sense that the models will behave better when they are kept small.

Another source of asymmetry and distortion, which remarkably escapes the attention of mainstream economists, is the role of money, which Friedrich Nietzsche described in *Thus Spoke Zarathustra* as 'the crowbar of power'.[38] According to analysis from Oxfam, 'over half the world's billionaires either inherited their wealth or accumulated it through industries which are prone to corruption and cronyism'.[39] In countries such as the UK and US, much of the wealth comes from the financial sector, whose crowbar-like effects on the economy and on wealth distribution don't even appear in orthodox models. As evidence of its power, consider for example how quant billionaire Robert Mercer helped reshape US politics by supporting the far-right Breitbart News and the campaign of Donald Trump.[40]

At the same time, even saying that inequality is a problem necessitates a judgement call. As economists Don Fullerton and Robert N. Stavins point out, 'An improvement in economic efficiency can be determined by a simple and unambiguous criterion – an increase in total net benefits. What constitutes an improvement in distributional equity, on the other hand, is inevitably the subject of considerable dispute.'[41] Indeed, Lionel Robbins argued in the 1930s that because the subjective utility of one person cannot be measured versus that of another, the whole question of fair distribution is 'entirely foreign to the assumptions of scientific Economics'.[42] The result is that economists have consistently tended to downplay or ignore distributional problems – or have even declared them off-limits, as Nobel laureate Robert Lucas did in 2004: 'Of the tendencies that are harmful to sound economics, the most seductive, and in my opinion the most poisonous, is to focus on questions of distribution.'[43]

As discussed in the box on page 215, this has not stopped all economists from thinking about inequality or looking for solutions; and nor does it imply that mainstream economics boils down to a right-wing, free-market ideology. Indeed, while their subject has long been associated with conservative politics, many academic economists see themselves as moderates, and would distance themselves from some of the harsher anti-government statements cited above from Friedman et al.[44] (see page 216. For perspective, a survey of the American professoriate found that about one-third of economists agree with the statement that corporations make too much profit, as opposed to two-thirds of those lefty sociologists, and basically no finance professors.[45]) Standard economic theory was inspired less by free markets than by the Pythagorean belief that everything can be reduced to number – or as Paul Romer put it, 'that math could tell you the deep secrets of the universe' – which introduces its own set of biases.[46]

However, a theme of this book is that what counts is the decisions that flow from the logic of economists' models, and these are related to their underlying assumptions, including core principles such as symmetry. I am sure that many economists dislike the power imbalance of the unfair economy, but their models and ideas have certainly helped to shape and enable it, if only by omission. It's not that their hearts are in the wrong place, it's that their heads are in the wrong place. And as we've seen, economyths have consequences.

Improving circulation

Although there is no single formula to create a more equal and fair society, some of the tools available are progressive taxation, wage controls, alternative company structures, and social policy. Hardcore neoclassical economists may see such measures as distortions to the free market, but they are as nothing compared to the distortions that are often produced *by* free markets.

Progressive taxation   This approach has been adopted by Nordic countries such as Denmark, which has a top tax rate of 60 per cent. Obviously such an eye-watering rate wouldn't play well in countries such as the United States – it's hard to see 'Tax the Rich!' and 'Redistribute the Wealth!' becoming popular political slogans anytime soon. Even there, though, Warren Buffett and Bill Gates have spoken out in favour of estate taxes on the wealthy.

Wage controls   At one end of the income scale, workers need protection in terms of a minimum wage. At the other end, we need protection from the workers. In 2009, President Obama imposed a $500,000 salary cap on bailed-out bank bosses. This was obviously justified by the fact that they were now glorified civil servants, but it opens up the question of whether caps are appropriate in other circumstances. Alternatively, shareholders could stop tolerating bloated pay packages when there is little or no correlation with performance. This appears to be the practice in Japan, where tax rates are low but so is pay inequality.

Company structure   The excesses of CEO compensation are also helping to fuel interest in alternative structures such as non-profits, employee-owned companies, and the cooperative movement. The non-profit sector in the US is already huge, and includes vital institutions such as universities, hospitals, and electric utilities.

According to political economist Gar Alperovitz, non-profit electricity companies are on average 11 per cent cheaper than profit-making companies, and are more likely to adopt sustainable technology.[47]

Social policy   One of the most important drivers of social inequality is a country's education system, including access to childcare. In unequal countries such as the UK or US, there is a huge difference in quality between the best and the worst schools. Rich families can buy their children a good education, either by sending them to a private school or moving to the catchment area of one of the better state-funded schools. Both of these options are expensive because there is competition from other families.

A UK study headed by Alan Milburn showed that parents send their children to good schools not just for academic reasons, but also so they can learn soft skills such as social confidence. Elite universities like Harvard or Oxford are valued for the quality of the education, but also because they allow access to powerful social networks (in 2007, just in time for the crisis, 47 per cent of Harvard graduates went into finance or consulting).[48] Inequality therefore gets frozen in – those born into poor families stay poor, and those born into rich families stay rich. General access to high-quality education and childcare is required to keep things fluid.

Tipping point

While there are many routes to a more equal society (see also box on page 215), an absolute prerequisite is an economic theory and worldview that acknowledges the huge discrepancies in power and influence that are present in the real world, and that points to ways of righting the balance. As with models of irrational behaviour, this is hard to accomplish in the classical framework, which is based on the reductionist, symmetrical methods of classical physics and assumes that the playing field is already roughly level. It does come easily in the complexity approach, whose models naturally tend to reproduce the power-law distributions of wealth distribution or company size; or with feminist economics, which is concerned with differences in power. Neither of these is featured in basic textbooks, which tend to focus on neoclassical theory.[49]

Just showing that the 'law of supply and demand' is not based on physics, or science of any type, will be enough to change the debate over things like inequality. As Charles Darwin observed: 'To kill an error is as good a service as, and sometimes even better than, the establishing of a new truth or fact.'[50] The best test for theoretical ideas is to compare them with empirical data, of which there is now plenty. Today, most economic transactions leave an electronic record. Credit rating agencies and other companies buy this information and use it to build sophisticated models of consumer behaviour. The information can also be used to test economic hypotheses. Consider, for example, Milton Friedman's prediction that free markets would tend to drive out businesses that discriminate on the basis of race or gender. A study of new car dealerships in the United States by law professor Ian Ayres back in 1991 showed that: 'White women had to pay 40 per cent higher markups than white men; black men had to pay more than twice the markup, and black women had to pay more than three times the markup of white male testers.'[51] Minorities were also targeted by predatory lenders during the US subprime mortgage scandal.[52] Studies of gender discrimination in the labour market show that women are over-represented in the poorest-paying jobs, under-represented in the highest-paying jobs, and are usually paid less than men for doing the same job.[53] (On the other hand, one 2016 empirical study based on data from Friedman's home town of New York claimed that 'employers who engage in hiring discrimination are less likely to remain in business six years later', but given that racism hasn't gone away it doesn't seem to have put anyone off.[54])

Pareto argued that if social structures become too rigid, so that 'the upper strata are full of decadent elements and the lower strata are full of elite elements', then eventually there will be a strong chance of 'violent revolution'. If he were around today – sitting in a comfortable chair with a cat on his lap and a glass of the finest brandy, watching Bloomberg on TV – I'm sure he would be monitoring the situation with interest. As he knew, ideologies are what the elites use to justify their inherently unstable position. It is ironic that the concept of Pareto optimality is now part of that ideology.

As discussed in Chapter 4, complex adaptive systems often tend to evolve towards a critical state – the slope of the sandpile increases until it approaches chaos. The same deregulatory ideology that allowed this instability to develop in the stockmarkets may also be pushing society towards an unstable tipping point. Markets crash, but societies can too.

To delay the day of reckoning, governments don't actually need to reduce inequality – they only need to perpetuate the illusion that (a) everyone's situation is improving, and (b) everyone has a shot at the prize. Above all, they need to keep the economy growing. As Henry Wallich, former governor of the Federal Reserve, said: 'Growth is a substitute for equality of income. So long as there is growth there is hope, and that makes large income differentials tolerable.'[55] As shown in the next chapter, though, that solution may be leading to a different kind of credit crunch.

Square versus oblong

The idea that the economy is fair and square has come under close examination since the Occupy movement made the '99 per cent' a rallying cry. In 2013, the French economist (and critic of mainstream economics) Thomas Piketty enjoyed an unlikely bestseller with his dense economics text *Capital in the Twenty-First Century*.[56] According to Piketty, who analysed extensive historical data to reach his conclusions, the reason that wealth in many countries has become increasingly concentrated in the hands of a few is because the rate of return on capital tends to exceed the rate of economic growth. Money therefore builds on itself as it is passed on within families through inheritance, in a manner rather like that sketched in Figure 15.

Possible solutions suggested by Piketty, along with his mentor the late British economist Tony Atkinson, include inheritance tax and a global tax on capital.[57] In 2016 the Panama Papers cast light on one problem with such approaches – illegal tax shelters. In 2017, Oxfam reported that eight men now hold as much wealth (legally) as half of the world's population.[58] The number has trended down from 388 people in 2010. How long will it take before it is just one trillionaire? At least billionaires don't control the armies, though, unless you count Donald Trump, or Vladimir Putin.

Corporate profits have also become more slanted in recent years, particularly in the US as epitomised by the success of network-economy giants such as Apple, Alphabet (Google), Microsoft, and Facebook, and increased concentration in the banking sector.[59] A report from the Economic Policy Institute in the US found that from 1978 to 2015, inflation-adjusted CEO compensation increased an impressive 940.9 per cent, and was up almost 50 per cent since the first edition of this book.[60] A Harvard Law School study rather undercut Mankiw's explanation that 'the value of a good CEO is extraordinarily high' when it discovered that the ten companies with the most overpaid CEOs 'underperformed the S&P 500 index by a gaping 10.5% and actually demolished shareholder value as a group with −5.7% financial returns'.[61] Median wages, meanwhile, have continued to stagnate.[62] (Though after years of protest the world's largest private employer, Wal-Mart, did raise the wages of its lowest-paid US workers to $9 per hour in 2015, and $10 in 2016.)

While this polarisation of wealth and power is normally considered a political issue, mainstream economics has also played a role by framing things like unions, trade restrictions, and financial regulations in terms of frictions and distortions to ideal markets. Orthodox economists, wrote (non-orthodox) economist John T. Harvey in 2012, 'were the ones who provided the intellectual justification for the transformation of our economy over the past thirty years. They stood idly by as jobs went overseas, demand was sapped by increasingly uneven distributions of income, competition was destroyed by lax attitudes towards antitrust laws, and safeguards were discarded in the financial sector ... Opposition would have slowed, if not stopped, these trends.'[63] Of course this would have meant standing up to the financial sector, but as MIT's Otto Scharmer and Katrin Kaufer wrote in 2013, the 'belief system' of mainstream economics 'has given Wall Street a de facto veto over public policy making that no other group or industry enjoys. Since the beginning of the financial crisis in 2008, this unparalleled influence of Wall Street on Washington has only increased.'[64]

These economic policies of globalisation and financialisation – which Sanjay Reddy from The New School for Social Research notes were 'legitimated' and 'aggressively peddled' by academic orthodoxy – all helped to fuel inequality in the countries affected, for example by undercutting the bargaining power of workers while protecting asset prices, which is why we are now seeing a political backlash against them.[65] In recent years social inequality has helped to fuel the rise of organisations such as the anti-austerity Podemos party in Spain, the anti-establishment Five Star Movement in Italy, and the pro-Brexit UK Independence Party. Inequality was also a theme during the 2016 US presidential election, with both Bernie Sanders on the Democrat ticket and Trump on the Republican side addressing many of their statements, in different ways, to those who feel that the power system, with its political insiders and Wall Street backers, is rigged against them. The rise of political populism, noted Ann Pettifor in 2017, is 'a phenomenon for which the economics profession bears considerable responsibility'.[66]

Of course, even if their models neglect power dynamics, economists know very well that benefits from things like trade are not evenly spread. In an article linking such failings to the election of Donald Trump, Dani Rodrik therefore described it as 'curious' that economists have 'consistently minimized distributional concerns'.[67] It seems less curious when you consider that the models have symmetry assumptions at their core (see box, page 209). But another factor, which needs to be taken into account, is that economics has itself been subtly distorted by financial power.

The 'flawed theories and models' of economics, according to Pettifor, 'are a great comfort to financial elites – which is why so many economists are hired and funded by big banks, corporations and the wealthy'.[68] Charles Ferguson, who directed the Oscar-winning documentary *Inside Job* in 2010, noted that 'the economics profession – in economics departments, and in business, public policy, and law schools – has become so compromised by conflicts of interest that it now functions almost as a support group for financial services and other industries'.

Economists are paid 'to testify before Congress, to write papers, to give speeches, to participate in conferences, to serve on boards of directors, to write briefs in regulatory proceedings, to defend companies in antitrust cases, and, of course, to lobby'.[69]

The problem is not particularly new: as the chemist-turned-economist Frederick Soddy wrote in 1934, 'orthodox economics has never yet been anything but the class economics of the owners of debts'.[70] However, the superficially scientific-looking nature of computer models makes them particularly easy to abuse. (Economists may leave power out of their mathematical models, but they are very aware of the power of mathematics to intimidate and confuse.) The tools of quantitative finance, for example, are as much about telling a particular story that suits the financial industry, and protects its pay structure, as they are about calculating risk (see *The Money Formula*). It is therefore unsurprising that mainstream economists have drawn a blank on the subject of inequality, which along with financial instability (sponsored by banks) and the environmental crisis (sponsored by oil companies) is one of the biggest issues of our time.

In a way, as economist Tyler Cowen points out, the fact that economic models 'treat all individuals as fundamentally the same' seems admirably egalitarian, and reflects the field's 'cosmopolitan perspective'.[71] But the paradoxical result, notes Michael Perelman, is that 'Economists consistently have upheld the power of elites. They have done this by ignoring or obscuring power, giving economics a veneer of science, in which the impact on people and the environment is hidden from public view ... As an economist, I am sensitive to the fact that radical analysis or curiosity about the exercise of power has been virtually banned from the discipline. Of course, this systematic exclusion is, in itself, an inexcusable exercise of power'.[72]

This may be beginning to change, as 'celebrity economists' such as Thomas Piketty, Joseph Stiglitz, and Paul Krugman (see box, page 271) lend their weight to the growing concern about reducing inequality, and new modelling techniques are adopted that take power imbalances at face value.[73] Institutions such as the World Economics Association, with a strongly international membership, are also helping to address another kind of power balance: the focus of research on the United States. A study of over 75,000 empirical papers published between 1985 and 2005 found that there were more about the US than the rest of the world combined, and only 1.5 per cent of all papers written about other countries were published in top-tier journals.[74]

In addition to the measures for combatting inequality suggested in this chapter, one other idea that is gaining traction around the world is the idea of a universal basic income. Of course paying people money for doing nothing doesn't align well with conventional economic principles, but most studies show that it seems to work rather well.[75] Finally, a major cause of income inequality comes down to the nature of the money system itself, both in the way it generates interest on loans, and in the way that profits are sequestered by 'money workers' such as bankers. To address this – and bring power back into economics – a first step is to recognise the importance of money. We return to this later.

CHAPTER 8

THE OVER-SIZED ECONOMY

Anyone who believes exponential growth can go on forever in a finite world is either a madman or an economist.
Kenneth Boulding, ecological economist (1910–1993)

If the climate were a bank, they would already have saved it.
Hugo Chávez, former president of Venezuela (2009)

Economists are taught that long-term economic growth should be maximised. However, ecologists and environmentalists believe you can have too much of a good thing. The models used by mainstream economists don't properly take into account a few details – such as melting icebergs, shrinking resource stocks, or the opinions on all this of future generations. In fact, the real credit crunch is not the one involving banks, but the one involving the environment. For centuries we have been depleting forests, oceans, fuel sources, and other species, and the bill is about to become due. This chapter shows how economists' cherished belief in economic growth is colliding with the reality that we are just one part of a larger ecosystem. It explores new economic approaches that aim to resolve the conflict and bring our financial system into balance with the rest of the world.

In November 2006, before the credit crunch got into full swing, another economic crisis had already begun to unfold. This crisis was not heralded on the front covers of the *Wall Street Journal* or the *Financial Times*. Pundits did not appear on financial TV shows to ruminate on its causes. Politicians did not exploit it to stir up envy or lambast their rivals. And it went completely unnoticed by economists.

The crisis began in America, where large numbers of agricultural workers suddenly stopped working. It wasn't that they went on strike, or demanded higher pay; they just left their jobs and didn't come back – even if it meant certain death. Some farmers said it was like mass suicide.

Businesses went bust or closed down; entire industries, such as Californian almond farming, were under threat. The crisis did not stay contained in the US, but propagated around the world as quickly as the credit crunch. By early 2007, farmers in Canada, the UK, mainland Europe, South and Central America and Asia were all reporting the same problem. But no one could figure out what was causing it. Why would these workers, who had served us so diligently for thousands of years, who had been celebrated throughout the ages in poems and myths for their industriousness and productivity, suddenly and collectively lose interest in living?

Were they suffering from a mysterious disease that affects their minds? Was it because, in their jobs, they are exposed to large amounts of chemical toxins? Could it be stress from overwork, or the constant need to travel around in search of the next job? Was it a result of climate change, or radiation from mobile phone masts, or working with genetically modified crops? Were there not enough flowers?

Scientists could not answer these questions – they had no idea why the bees were dying. But they did come up with a name: colony collapse disorder (CCD). And some believe it is a harbinger of things to come. As insect biologist E.O. Wilson said, the honeybee is nature's 'workhorse – and we took it for granted. We've hung our own future on a thread.'[1]

The Delphic bee

Bees and humans share a long history together. We started gathering honey in the wild around 10,000 years ago, and have kept bee colonies for at least 5,000 years. Bees and honey also feature prominently in our mythology. According to Homer, the god Apollo's gift of prophecy was granted to him from three bee maidens: 'There are three holy ones, sisters born ... From their home they fly now here, now there, feeding on honeycomb and bringing all things to pass. And when they are inspired through eating yellow honey, they are willing to speak the truth.' The oracle at Delphi was often called the Delphic bee. The Greeks associated honey with eloquence and the power of speech; Pythagoras was said to have been fed it as an infant, and the favourite food of the Pythagoreans was bread and honey.

Today, bees outnumber us on the planet by hundreds of times. They play a vital role in the world economy by pollinating crops including alfalfa (used for cattle feed), apples, almonds, citrus fruits, broccoli, carrots, onions and melons. Without them, large parts of our agricultural supply chain would fall apart. So if these winged prophets are trying to tell us something, then maybe we should listen.

Honeybees were brought to North America in the early 17th century by Dutch or British colonists, and reached a peak population of 5.9 million colonies in 1947. By 2006, that number had declined to around 2.4 million, and the wild population (though harder to measure) was estimated to be down by 90 per cent. According to congressional testimony, CCD has since knocked out a further 25 per cent of the remaining colonies.[2] Similar die-offs have happened in the past, but they have been smaller, and the bees have died in the hives rather than just flying away as with CCD.

The cause of the phenomenon is still being debated. Possible culprits include parasites, fungal diseases, and accumulated exposure to toxic chemicals such as pesticides. Another contributor is environmental stress: many of the colonies affected belong to large commercial operations, which regularly transport the bees around the country to pollinate crops. Climate change may also play a role, by changing the blooming times of crops.

The most likely scenario is that CCD has no single cause but is the cumulative result of many small stresses. Trying to analyse the collapse of a species is a little like trying to analyse the cause of a stockmarket crash – everyone has their own theory, but none of them quite add up on their own. As E.O. Wilson puts it: 'We are flying blind in many aspects of preserving the environment, and that's why we are so surprised when a species like the honeybee starts to crash.'[3]

While scientists are at a loss to explain the behaviour of bees, most economic models go a step further by eliminating them from consideration altogether. Bees play a pivotal and irreplaceable role in the world economy – in the US, the value of their services is estimated at $15 billion annually. However, they don't respond well to the usual range of economic incentives. Even though, in many respects, they appear to be quite intelligent – as shown, for example, by the intricate design of their hives, or the complex dance they perform to communicate the location of pollen sources – they seem to have no grasp of basic economic principles. The law of supply and demand eludes them altogether. They just don't get it. Maybe that's why they're so unmotivated.

In fact, this seems to be a property of the entire natural world. Take fish. Around 500 years ago, fishermen from Portugal and Spain started travelling to the Grand Banks off the coast of Newfoundland, Canada to catch cod. Everything went swimmingly for hundreds of years. Cod became a staple food in Europe and North America, and in 1968 the total catch from the Grand Banks was 810,000 tons. Then the fish population began to decline.

Scientists were brought in to determine the maximum allowable catch; but their models proved disastrously wrong, and in 1992 the most famous fishery in the world suddenly collapsed altogether, with the loss of 40,000 jobs.[4] It still hasn't recovered – for some reason, the remaining fish don't seem to be able to reproduce at the same rate.

Once again, the law of supply and demand was flouted. The *demand* for fish was increasing – one author described the situation as 'senseless, wild over fishing' – but the *supply* did not respond accordingly, or even adjust in a smooth manner.[5] It just suddenly disappeared. Other fisheries around the world have similarly collapsed. It makes you wonder what critical but economically-illiterate species will be next to throw in the towel without warning.

Could it be us?

The carbon question

The idea that the human race is approaching some kind of critical limit is probably premature. But if we take economics to be the study of 'household rule', then we have certainly failed to keep our house – this planet – in order, and it's fair to say that as a species we are economically illiterate.

When neoclassical economics was founded in the late 19th century, honeybees were still buzzing cheerfully about their work, and there were still plenty of fish in the sea. World population was only about a billion people, 15 per cent its current size. But even then, there were concerns that we were approaching fundamental limits of natural resources.

William Stanley Jevons first gained fame as an economist with his 1865 work *The Coal Question*, which drew attention to the fact that Britain's coal was running out. Britain had become the dominant world power by exploiting coal-based steam engine technology to drive its mines, factories, railways and ships.[6] As Jevons put it, coal 'is the material energy of the country – the universal aid – the factor in everything we do. With coal almost any feat is possible or easy; without it we are thrown back into the laborious poverty of early times.' The only problem with this 'miraculous' substance, formed from plant matter hundreds of millions of years old, was its limited supply. Britain's growing economy meant that the demand for coal was increasing exponentially. The country was therefore effectively accelerating towards a stop sign. Coal would never run out completely, but it would become near-impossible to extract what was left. 'In the increasing depth and difficulty of coal mining we shall meet that vague, but inevitable boundary that will stop our progress.'

Jevons reviewed a number of alternatives including wind, tidal, and solar power, but no suitable substitute for coal was available. Furthermore, technological innovation would only have the effect of lowering costs, thus increasing consumption even further. This phenomenon, sometimes known as the Jevons Paradox, was demonstrated by the fact that while steam-engine technology had continuously been improved by inventions such as the governor, any savings due to efficiency were more than offset by higher use.

Geologists at the time estimated that Britain had coal reserves of about 90 billion tons. Jevons argued that, if the exponential growth trend continued, the reserves would be severely depleted within half a century. The result would be that Britain would lose its dominant position in the world economy to low-cost producers like the United States. Labour and capital would emigrate, and 'all notions of manufacturing and maritime supremacy must then be relinquished'.

The Coal Question was very influential, and was cited in Parliament. As it turned out, coal production did peak 48 years later, though at 292 million tons it was about half what Jevons had estimated. Total production has since dwindled to about 20 million tons, and in 2003 the UK imported more coal than it produced for the first time.[7]

Of course, this isn't a problem, because unknown to Jevons, it turned out that coal did have a viable substitute. Britain has shaken off its reliance on solar energy stored in British coal, and is now reliant on solar energy stored in North Sea oil fields, which saw their peak production in 1999 and are now in decline.

So what about the oil question? Oil is clearly as important now as coal was in 19th-century Britain, and it too is a limited resource. Will market forces help us calibrate the correct price for this vital commodity – or are we instead accelerating towards another 'vague, but inevitable boundary'?

Closed economy

People have been worried about 'peak oil' for almost as long as we have been pumping it out of the ground. However, the fact that past predictions of supply exhaustion have been wrong does not inoculate us from it ever happening at all. It seems reasonable to suppose that we are approaching the later stages of our long relationship with carbon fuels; and as Jevons knew, our energy supplies are vital for our long-term future.[8] Weirdly, though, mainstream economic theory has almost as little to say about oil as it does about fish, or bees, or anything outside the human sphere. That is one reason why prices for these things don't reflect their real worth. And it is also what supports the economyth that the economy can, and should, grow for ever – or as ecological economist Robert Costanza puts it, the 'growth at all costs' economic model.[9]

Neoclassical economics represents a mathematical model of human behaviour. As the systems scientist John D. Sterman observes: 'The most important assumptions of a model are not in the equations, but what's not in them; not in the documentation, but unstated; not in the variables on the computer screen, but in the blank spaces around them.'[10] One of the things missing from neoclassical economics – and it's a big one – is the rest of the planet. It neglects the fact that the human economy is embedded in the biosphere, which consists of living things (including bees and wheat), the products of living things (including honey and oil), and necessary resources for living things (like fresh water).

Traditionally, economists had recognised three factors of production – land, labour, and capital. In neoclassical economics, though, only labour and capital have played an important role. Natural resources were either excluded from the list or paid lip-service to. Jevons' concerns about exponential growth in a world with limits were lost in the mix. Even in Gregory Mankiw's textbook *Principles of Economics*, as Gilles Raveaud pointed out in 2009, natural resources and energy were left out of the chapter on economic growth. As a result, 'they cannot become a problem – for economists, that is.'[11]

Underlying this omission has been a kind of denial. In his book *Beyond Growth*, the ecological economist Herman Daly relates a story about his work on a 1992 World Bank report whose topic was 'Development and the Environment'. An early draft contained a diagram of the relationship between the economy and the environment. It consisted only of 'a square labelled "economy," with an arrow coming in labelled "inputs" and an arrow going out labelled "outputs" – nothing more'. Daly suggested they should at least add a larger box around the one for the economy, to represent the environment. The following draft included the large box, but there was no label. Daly pointed out that 'the larger box had to be labelled "environment" or else it was merely decorative'. In the next draft, the entire diagram was left out.[12] It was as if economics had become so disembodied and detached from reality that it thought it could do without the physical world.

The reason for this peculiar attitude was rooted in the idea, derived from the work of Jevons et al., that the economy is a beautifully tuned machine – a closed system that operates according to perfectly calibrated laws. The machine will of course need fuel to keep it running, and oil to keep it lubricated, but these are freely available on the open market from a range of suppliers. The stock of these things in the ground was of no more concern to an economist than the stock of fuel is to the owner of a Lamborghini. They just know it's there.

Within this closed economic system, according to theory, the 'law of supply and demand' correctly allocates resources to each of the machine's parts. However, while this 'law' may be of some fuzzy use within the human economy, it breaks down completely at the boundaries of our economy with the natural world. The economy has no way to measure exactly how many fish are in the sea, or how much oil is in the ground. The costs of supply measure only the costs of extraction, which depend on a large number of factors, and do not smoothly adjust to give a measure of scarcity. Fishermen did not stop fishing the Grand Banks because it was too expensive – they stopped because one year there were no fish.

In fact, as Daly noted: 'resource prices are to a large extent arbitrary – a fact that is seldom recognized.'[13] The supposedly sensitive price signals of the free market turn out to be not just mildly paradoxical in their behaviour, but completely distorted. A good illustration is provided by the price perambulations in the commodities market in 2008.

Super spike
One of the irritating features of the 'law of supply and demand' is that, when you really need it, it gives confusing answers. The

more a CEO gets paid, the more he or she is in demand; but the more we need and use a valuable resource, the cheaper it may become. Or worse still, the price may just oscillate wildly for no apparent reason – as in 2008, when the price of crude oil increased by a factor three in a matter of months, before taking an equally sudden plunge.

At their peak, gasoline prices exceeded $4 a gallon in the United States, thus exacerbating the recessionary effects of the subprime mortgage crisis. The oil price increase also fed directly into higher prices for basic food supplies around the world. Some called it the worst food price inflation in history. It wasn't that people were finding it hard to fill their tanks – they were finding it hard to fill their stomachs.

As shown in Figure 17, the price of wheat also more than doubled in the twelve months from March 2007 to March 2008. Prices of bread, pasta and tortillas all soared. There were a number of factors behind this increase, including poor harvests, increased demand from countries like China and India, and speculation; however, the oil shock contributed by pushing up fertiliser and transportation costs. Oil and wheat are now also linked, because when oil is expensive, farmers are motivated to use land to grow biofuels for energy instead of wheat for food.

The people most exposed to the price shock were those in developing countries who spend as much as 75 per cent of their income on food. Sudden spikes are especially damaging because these people have little access to short-term credit that would see them through. Countries including Mexico, Egypt, Indonesia, Pakistan, Cameroon and Haiti experienced violent food riots. The director general of the International Food Policy Research Institute, Joachim von Braun, called the crisis 'a serious security issue'.[15] The World Bank warned that 100 million people were threatened with starvation.

Figure 17. Solid line shows the price of wheat, dashed line shows the price of oil, both normalised to a value of 100 at the start of 2000.[14]

It wasn't all doom and gloom, though. Some people did very well out of the price shock. One trader working for Citigroup was awarded a bonus of $100 million for his prescient timing of the oil market.[16] Citigroup at the time was part-owned by the US government after being rescued in November 2008, and the $100 million bonus was described by a White House spokesman as 'out of whack'. The 100 million people threatened with starvation may have agreed.

Nor did the commodities price shock have much to do with impending shortages – the world didn't suddenly run out of oil in the spring of 2008. As with the subprime mortgage crisis, the main cause or enabling factor for the surge in prices can be traced back to the dismantling of economic safeguards.

People involved in the commodities business have always been able to enter into futures contracts, in which they agree to buy or sell a certain amount of a commodity in the future for a set price. This gives some protection against future price swings. The Commodity Futures Trading Commission (CFTC) in the US put limits on this kind of speculative trade. However, in the 1990s, a subsidiary of Goldman Sachs asked for an exemption so that it could hedge the risk of oil price fluctuations. The CFTC agreed, and extended the exemption to other banks.

The net effect of this deregulation, as with subprime mortgages, was the creation of another casino, except that everyone was betting on oil and other commodities instead of houses. Goldman Sachs and other banks persuaded large institutional investors like pension funds and sovereign wealth funds to invest in commodity futures. Such funds tend to be long-term buy-and-hold investors, so the effect was to drive prices consistently higher. Between 2003 and 2008, the value of speculative oil future contracts grew by a factor of more than 20, until they added up to the equivalent of more than a billion barrels.

One of the more telling moments of the crisis came in May 2008, when the CFTC investigated the reasons for the commodity price spike and concluded that prices were 'being driven by powerful fundamental economic forces and the laws of supply and demand'.[17] Nothing, it seems, is beyond the explanatory abilities of the invisible hand. People around the world were dying of starvation as a direct result of the spike, but according to the CFTC there was nothing to investigate.

A year later, when prices had sunk back to a fraction of their peak, and with a new chairman working under the Obama administration, the CFTC changed its position and was once again considering caps on speculative activity. The truth is that markets or mainstream economic theory cannot tell us the correct price for oil, taking into account its future scarcity, any more than they know how to price a vanishing population of cod, or any other species or vital resource.

Selling futures

Just as the price mechanism fails to calibrate the economy to its available natural resources – the inputs – so it fails to account for that arrow going in the other direction – the effects of pollution.

Pollution does not fit easily with the framework of 'supply and demand' because while there is plenty of supply, there is not much demand – we just dump it where we can. Pollution and environmental damage therefore tend to be concentrated in poorer areas, such as developing countries. (As Larry Summers, who at the time was president of the World Bank, pointed out in a 1991 memo: 'the economic logic behind dumping a load of toxic waste in the lowest-wage country is impeccable and we should face up to that.'[18] He later claimed he was only kidding.) This acts as a hidden transfer of wealth from poor countries to rich countries.[19] Other soft targets include common areas, such as the atmosphere or oceans. Economists describe factors such as pollution in terms of 'negative externalities', which mean that the price of a product does not accurately reflect the true costs of its production – another kind of 'market failure'. One solution – first proposed by the British economist Arthur C. Pigou in his 1920 book *The Economics of Welfare* – is to tax the product accordingly. This makes sense in theory but the problem comes with the implementation (see box below).

Inside or out

As discussed above, economists can attempt to translate environmental 'externalities' such as pollution into monetary terms, and offset them with a tax as Pigou suggested. It obviously makes sense to tax the things you want less of – the concept of punitive taxes was invented by ancient rulers, and long predates the field of academic economics – and this approach has played a role in the development of environmental measures such as carbon taxes, discussed later. However, it is far from being a general solution.

One problem is that these adjustments tend to be viewed as optional epicycles that correct for 'market failures' and inefficiencies, rather than an intrinsic part of the approach. This introduces a bias towards making small distortions to the perfect model; but it also means that the numbers are easily rigged by whoever holds power and stands to profit (not something they mention in standard textbooks).

While economists tend to talk about externalities as if they are accidental side-effects, they are in fact designed into an economic system which puts profit maximisation above everything else. If you don't believe that, talk to anyone who has tried to take on a resource company. As one forester in India wrote: 'Perhaps the hard truth is that there may be areas of human activity that are so important for reasons other than financial gains, that the narrow criterion of individual economic gain cannot be the basis of decisions.'[20] When, as mentioned in the Appendix, economists went after environmentalist David Suzuki in 2012 for criticising their use of externalities, they should perhaps have reflected that he was speaking from experience.

At the same time, the logic of their economyths pushes economists towards an overly sunny belief in the power of self-regulation – especially, but not necessarily, when their work is funded by those being regulated.[21] These problems are seen clearly with the larger issue of climate change, whose costs economists have since the 1990s attempted to compute by linking climate models with economic models. The results usually seem suspiciously low, though it depends who is paying for the study.[22] In a 2016 article in the journal *Nature*, Nicholas Stern noted that current models are 'grossly misleading' because they 'underestimate seriously both the potential impacts of danger-ous climate change and the wider benefits of a transition to low-carbon growth'.[23]

The commodity price shock shown in Figure 17 paved the way for the Arab Spring that began in Tunisia in December 2010 – hard to think what the externality equation for that would look like.[24] Also, you may have noticed that when you go shopping there is no tax for things like species extinctions due to impact of economic activity on natural ecosystems. More than extending their models through externalities, economists need to internalise the lesson that the human economy is reli-ant on natural systems; and instead of calculating expenses or optimising numerical measures of efficiency, we need to better align our economic system with the organisation of nature.

The environment's ability to absorb pollutants may actually turn out to be a stronger constraint on the economy than have energy supplies. According to one estimate, to avoid dangerously destabi-lising the climate system in the foreseeable future, we need to limit total cumulative CO_2 emissions to 1 trillion tonnes of carbon.[25] Since the start of the industrial revolution we have emitted about half a trillion already, and at current rates we will spew out the next half trillion within 40 years. The amount of carbon in fossil fuel reserves exceeds that amount by several times, which implies we'll have to leave some in the ground.

Finally, another thing (mostly) missing from neoclassi-cal economics – and again it's a big one – is the future. Because neoclassical economics assumes that the economy is at or near equilibrium, it ignores or downplays the effect of time and concen-trates on maximising utility in the short term. When future events are incorporated they are assigned a discount rate, so they become

less important the further away they are, and dwindle to insignif-
icance beyond a few decades.[26] But with non-renewable stocks,
time does matter, because in the future there will be less of them.
For 'supply and demand' to be meaningful we should consider the
demand of future generations, but there is no pricing mechanism
in the market that will adequately take this into account.

To summarise, mainstream economics – the kind taught in
universities to undergraduate students, and the kind that dominates government policy and business strategy – struggles to
take into account the true value of natural resources, the effects
of pollution, or the rights of future generations. These biases are
reflected in the way that economic growth is measured using the
gross domestic product.

Appropriate measures

As Cambridge economist Partha Dasgupta wrote: 'we economists see nature, when we see it at all, as a backdrop from which
resources and services can be drawn in isolation. Macroeconomic
forecasts routinely exclude natural capital. Accounting for nature,
if it comes into the calculus at all, is usually an afterthought to the
real business of "doing economics". We economists have been so
successful in this enterprise, that if someone exclaims, "Economic
growth!", no one needs to ask, "Growth in what?" – we all know
they mean growth in gross domestic product (GDP).'[27]

The GDP is equal to the total amount spent for all final goods
and services produced within a country. (A final good such as a
bicycle may include intermediate goods such as tyres that are not
included separately.) Bees, fish or oil do not count unless they are
part of some economic transaction. Negative externalities such
as pollution are not included, but cleaning up pollution is, which
is why disasters such as the Deepwater Horizon oil spill can even
have a net positive effect on GDP.

While the GDP is often used as a proxy for standard of living by media and governments, it is actually a measure only of economic activity. If you believe in efficient markets, see the economy as a rational machine for optimising utility, and so on, then that makes sense. Governments also like it because it correlates with tax revenue. However, because it ignores the negative effects of growth, GDP gives a misleading impression of an economy's state of health. A number of alternative measures have therefore been developed in recent years, which typically address both environmental and social factors.

One such measure is the Index of Sustainable Economic Welfare (ISEW), developed by ecological economists Clifford W. Cobb and John B. Cobb, Jr in 1989. This corrects the GDP for factors such as uncounted household services, so it's the same if you clean the house yourself or pay a cleaner; and subtracts for effects such as environmental degradation and resource depletion. In the 1990s this was extended to form the Genuine Progress Indicator (GPI), which includes additional factors such as social inequality and crime rates. According to a paper in the journal *Ecological Economics*, global GPI peaked back in 1978, when the Bee Gees were topping the charts, and has since been in slow decline even as GDP has soared.[28]

The Happy Planet Index is defined by the New Economics Foundation in the UK as life satisfaction, multiplied by life expectancy, and divided by ecological footprint.[29] It therefore offers a kind of efficiency measure, in terms of happy years per unit of planetary area. In 2009 Germany scored about twice as high on this index as the US, because people in both countries have similar scores of life satisfaction and life expectancy, but Germans consume resources at about half the rate. Nine of the top ten countries were in Latin America, with Puerto Rico topping the rankings.

How to balance these different factors and combine them in a single indicator is obviously a difficult and ambiguous task, and the result is more like a report card, with a number of separate sections and a total overall grade, than a hard economic metric. The great appeal of the GDP is that it makes no such attempt – any transaction is the same as any other. As Herman Daly noted, economics is based on the 'Pythagorean analogy' between 'fuzzy' reality and 'well-defined, analytic number'.[30] However, economics has a long history of adopting models that are simple but wrong. Nobel laurel leaves have been sprinkled on risk formulae, based on the normal distribution, that are simple but wrong. The Gaussian copula used to value mortgage securities is simple but wrong. In exactly the same way, the GDP metric is simple but wrong, and by hiding the underlying complexity, it leads to the same kind of miscalculation.

If the alternative metrics seem fuzzy, ambiguous, and multi-dimensional, that's because the real world is too. In fact, one could argue that metrics of any type are over-used in our number-obsessed and target-driven society. Metrics can take on a life of their own, as they become the objects of government or corporate manipulation; and as with risk models, over-reliance on them can weaken our intuition and common sense. The best option may be to maintain a range of complementary metrics, but treat them with a grain of salt, and realise that each captures only a part of the full story.

The living economy

The term 'ecological economics' should be a little redundant, as both words share the Greek root *oikos* (household) and together mean something like household-study household-law. It is telling that the two fields of ecology and mainstream economics have grown so far apart in the century and a half since they were named that they now represent completely different sets of principles.

The basic idea of ecological economics can be summarised by Daly's argument with the World Bank economists: when you draw the box for the economy, you have to put it in a larger box called the environment. The human economy is a subset of the world system. Our inputs, in terms of natural resources, and outputs, including pollution, are like the metabolism of a kind of super-organism. We can analyse it using the same kinds of tools as we use to analyse other living systems, such as a cell, or a beehive, or a complete ecosystem.

Instead of being a closed system, like a machine, the economy is open to the environment. Attention therefore shifts from the inner mechanics of the economy to big-picture questions related to things like scale and timing and the flow of energy. Is the economy becoming too big relative to its environment? Is it consuming resources at too fast a rate? Is it adequately disposing of its own waste? Is it endangering the food chain on which it depends for survival?

One application of ecological economics is to estimate the value of 'services' provided by nature. In 1997, a group led by Robert Costanza came up with an answer of $33 trillion per year (about twice global GDP at the time).[31] A 2008 study estimated that the worldwide economic value of insect pollination services, provided mostly by bees, was $217 billion, which is about 9.5 per cent of the total value of the world agricultural food production.

An inherent problem with these reports is that, by necessity, they assign economic values to things that cannot be directly measured but only estimated or inferred. This might be reasonable for something like bee pollination; but we can weigh the rights of future generations only by making complicated value-based judgements of what they might want, what alternatives they might have, and so on. The future impact of climate change is also impossible to predict, because as discussed in Chapter 1, our models of the atmosphere aren't much more reliable than our models of the economy.[32] Even so, it is still possible to draw up reasonable targets, and monitor whether the situation is getting better or worse.

A different approach, sometimes known as environmental economics, is to let markets make the decision or, in cases where markets are absent, to infer price from consumers' choices. For example, if economists want to know the value of a public park, they can estimate it from signals such as its effect on the prices of nearby houses, or the travel costs that people will pay to visit it. If they want to know the value of an endangered species, they can ask people how much they would be willing to pay to protect it.

This approach shares many of the aims of ecological economics, but philosophically it is closer to mainstream economics, with a rather similar faith in the ability of 'Adam Smith's invisible hand to achieve what is best for society as a collective', as one textbook on environmental economics puts it, so long as market principles can be adequately applied.[33] But if markets cannot correctly price a CDO^2 mortgage contract, with its billion-page documentation, then it seems optimistic to think that they can price something like the CO_2 bond we hold with our billions of descendants.

Ecology vs economics

The different assumptions and worldviews behind ecological and mainstream economics mean that the two come up with very different policy recommendations. For instance, mainstream economists, along with most politicians and media, are almost religiously in favour of economic growth, as measured by GDP. The one thing every politician around the world could agree on after the credit crisis was that growth needed to be restored; less often was it mentioned what *kind* of growth. Some ideologues even argue that the best way to protect the environment is by growing the economy – as if a healthy planet is a luxury that only the rich can afford.[34] Yet there is now ample evidence that GDP growth is often associated with a decline in environment-sensitive indicators such as GPI. Quality matters.

Scale matters too. Ecological economists believe that when the human economy becomes too large relative to the natural systems that support it, then the problems caused by economic growth can outweigh any benefits. The world is already stretched to capacity to feed the current human population. We can increase production by improved efficiency, but there is always the trade-off between efficiency and robustness – intensive monoculture farming, for example, is inherently fragile and requires large amounts of fertilisers and pesticides to maintain it. Our agricultural system exhibits the same lack of modularity, redundancy, and diversity as our banking system (Chapter 2), but it is even more important for our survival. As the old saying goes: if you want to collect honey, don't kick over the hive.

Mainstream economists treat money in abstract numerical terms, as something that can grow and expand without constraints. Ecological economists see this as an illusion, and believe that money should be tied more closely to real physical wealth. Under fractional-reserve banking, banks can lend out far more money than they hold as reserves. The result is a debt-based financial system in which most of the money is in the form of credit, and everyone is running around frantically trying to pay it off. The situation is exacerbated by the existence of complex financial derivatives. The huge tower of money that was sitting uneasily on top of the world's oil supply in 2008 was an imaginary thing that could vanish as easily as it was created (though its effects on humanity were real enough). One of the biggest obstacles to a sustainable, controlled-growth economy is that governments would have to get out of debt in order to afford it. Ecological economists therefore argue that we should reduce the amount of credit in the economy, even to the extent of returning to full-reserve banking, in which the only money that can be lent out is backed by deposits.[35] This idea was proposed by Frederick Soddy in his 1926 book *Wealth, Virtual Wealth and Debt*, but as discussed in the final chapter it has failed to catch on.

Mainstream economists, or at least their models, often seem to treat the planet's resources and pollution sinks as if they were essentially infinite, but according to estimates from the World Wildlife Fund we are already living beyond our means. The ecological footprint of the human race – as measured in terms of the amount of resources we need to support ourselves sustainably – is now equivalent to 1.3 planets.[36] The extra 0.3 planets-worth of resources is being borrowed from future generations. If all countries had the same ecological footprint as the United States, the total would be equivalent to ten planets. We are building up a large and unsustainable debt of a different kind that far outweighs anything produced by the subprime housing market.

The healthy economy

To reduce this debt, a first step is to make both resource use and pollution reflect their real environmental cost. Key to this is the way we handle energy. The approach favoured by most economists, when asked how best to achieve this aim, is to shift the tax burden from things like salaries towards environmental negatives, through use of a carbon tax. This will not only make conventional carbon-based energy sources more expensive, but will affect the cost of all energy-intensive items, and therefore change price signals throughout the entire economy. Locally-produced goods, for example, will cost less than imported goods; housing and transport will be pushed to adopt energy-saving technologies. (An early version of the carbon tax was first proposed by the MIT engineer David G. Wilson back in 1973. He told the *Boston Globe*:

'I kept sending off articles about this scheme, and I couldn't get them published in the professional economic journals. They can't stand the idea of non-economists proposing things in their field. I tried to make them more mathematical, and that didn't work either.'[37])

While price signals will steer the economy towards a more sustainable path, they don't directly address the problem of resource depletion. As with fisheries, sometimes the only way to protect the resource is to put a hard physical limit on the extraction rate. This separates the problem into two parts: the extraction rate is determined according to ecological principles, while the use of the resources is determined by economics. For example, a cap-and-trade system can be used to auction extraction permits off to resource companies, in the same way that rights to bandwidth are auctioned off to mobile phone companies.[38]

Finally, we need to make the economy as a whole more robust to environmental shocks, even if this is at the cost of traditionally-defined efficiency. In previous chapters, I argued that in order to understand things like systemic risk, we need to adopt a systems approach to the finance system. A similar systems approach is adopted by ecologists in areas such as ecosystems-based fisheries management. Guiding principles, according to University of Washington fisheries professor Robert Francis and colleagues, include: 'Keep a perspective that is holistic, risk-averse and adaptive', and 'Maintain resilient ecosystems that are able to withstand occasional shocks'.[39] Similar principles could apply quite well to the human economy in general. Industries such as agriculture and retail are built around massive corporations and supply chains that circle the globe. These are highly efficient, in a narrow economic sense, and benefit from economies of scale, but also lead to uniformity, lack of regional self-reliance, and fragility. One benefit of a carbon tax is that it would make transport more expensive and lead to a greater diversity of local supply chains, therefore reducing systemic risk.

The main problem with the economy, after all, is not that it is hard to predict or is expanding insufficiently quickly, but that in many respects it appears to be in a state of ill-health. As Galen wrote in *On Medical Experience* (2nd century AD): 'In those who are healthy ... the body does not alter even from extreme causes; but in [the unhealthy] even the smallest causes produce the greatest change.' The extreme instability seen in the markets, the extreme inequalities in wealth, even the extreme weather that may become more common with climate change, are all signs that the system is out of balance. Economists will never be able to predict the exact timing of a crisis like the oil shock, any more than a doctor can predict the exact timing of a heart attack, but they can at least make general warnings, and detect whether a situation is getting better or worse. (Of course, one reason why doctors are less willing than economists to make unsound predictions is because they can be sued for malpractice.)

Models can play a useful role, by enabling us to picture and simulate the complex linkages within the economy–environment system.[40] As in biology or ecology, the predictive power of such models is usually low, because of the complexity and intractability of the system. As Evelyn Fox Keller noted, nature 'is not completely bound by Logos'. The main use of models is to elucidate basic principles, consider different future scenarios, and perhaps even make the system less stressed and unpredictable in the first place.

Our current approach to the economy is schizophrenic.[41] We design an unregulated system that is economically and ecologically unstable; model it using techniques that assume stability; try to make predictions of the future; and then react in surprise when something goes wrong. If instead we acknowledge that the system is unstable, that opens up the opportunity to actively improve it, rather than passively try to guess its next move.

It is often pointed out that growth is necessary in order for the economy, as currently structured, to avoid collapse. The whole point of capitalism, after all, is to use borrowed money to generate innovative products and services that increase productivity, raise standards of living, and pay off the debt. Consumers, for their part, are in a constant search for novelty and excitement. Social inequality guarantees that only the productive will be rewarded and prosper.[42] A low-growth economy would lead, it is claimed, to unemployment, mounting debt, inefficiency, and mass boredom. However, the current arrangement, in which the benefits of increased productivity are sequestered by the elite, as the middle classes sink deeper into debt, the poorest struggle to survive, and the planet comes under increasing stress, doesn't look very stable either. It will look even less stable if the world population reaches 9 billion people, as it is projected to do by 2050.

We therefore need to reorient our definition of growth away from GDP, and encourage innovation in strategically useful technologies and policies such as low-carbon housing and transportation. Given that this is not consistent with paying off massive debts, it seems that debt forgiveness or default – if not a major reworking of our monetary system; we return to this later – will probably be involved at some stage. We also need to rethink our approach towards consumption and the material world in general. The switch to an ecological perspective means that we can no longer pretend that optimality is somehow achieved by letting everything run free, or by naively assuming that the price is always right. When it comes to things like economic growth, the truth is a lot more complicated. In fact, as shown in the next chapter, we may already have overpaid.

Limited versus unlimited

Mainstream economics is based on the idea of scarcity (limits) and one would think this would extend easily to the idea of protecting nature. However, as seen in this chapter, there is a central contradiction between measures of the human economy, which are based on numbers, and nature, which is not – and economists naturally pay more attention to the former. As physicist and science writer Mark Buchanan noted in 2014: 'The irony is that economists love to talk about trade-offs and constraints. There are no free lunches, they like to say. Yet when it looks as if the unbridled optimism of economic growth itself is running into a wall, they prefer to look the other way.'[43] And as Jonathan Aldred notes, when it comes to orthodox economics, 'whatever the problem, markets are almost always the solution'.[44]

Now, clearly not all economists would agree with Northwestern's Robert Gordon when he told the author of a 2016 *Atlantic* piece that 'More growth is better, period', or think that markets will solve *all* problems.[45] Indeed, 'in the environmental domain, perfectly functioning markets are the exception, rather than the rule', note environmental economists Don Fullerton and Robert N. Stavins. 'Consequently, governments can take a variety of actions to try to correct these market failures. For example, the government may restrict pollutant emissions or limit access to open access resources. If undertaken wisely, government interventions can improve welfare, that is, lead to greater efficiency.'[46]

In recent years the economics of climate change has become a popular area of research. Leading economists including Gregory Mankiw have helped to promote carbon taxes, such as the one introduced in the Canadian provinces of British

Columbia in 2008 and Alberta in 2017, to be followed by a national tax in 2018.[47] While not representative of the mainstream, a survey of economists with climate expertise found that in 2009 some 57 per cent (of 144 respondents) said that the US should cut its carbon emissions independently of what other countries do, while a 2015 follow-up showed that number had increased to 77 per cent (of 365).[48] So credit where credit is due. But can environmental measures be bolted on to existing models or is something more radical needed? After all, we have already seen examples of the longstanding pattern in which economists modify their models in a minimal way and claim a problem is solved.[49] And as with questions of wealth distribution, climate change involves choices that are not purely economic, so beliefs and intentions matter.

In her 2014 book *This Changes Everything*, Naomi Klein asks: 'What is wrong with us? I think the answer is far more simple than many have led us to believe: we have not done the things that are necessary to lower emissions because those things fundamentally conflict with deregulated capitalism, the reigning ideology for the entire period we have been struggling to find a way out of this crisis.'[50] (In fact I think there is another, even simpler, reason as well, but we'll get to that in Chapter 11.) Mainstream economists may not all sign up to that ideology, but as a group they haven't exactly challenged it. As the environmental crisis has intensified over the last several years – the period 2011–15 was the warmest half-decade on record, and 2016 the warmest year so far – scientists have been up in arms, economists not so much. Which is why when former prime minister Stephen Harper was pursuing his dream to turn Canada into an 'energy superpower' (2006–15) he muzzled his scientists, not his economists, in what the journal *Nature* called 'nine years of censorship'. According to one communications officer, government science stories 'could only reflect economics, and what you could sell, not what you could save or conserve.'[51] After a temporary gag order was imposed by the incoming Trump administration, US government scientists working in e.g. the Environmental Protection Agency are at the time of writing concerned that similar restrictions may be imposed on them.[52]

Economic metrics such as GDP still don't include a negative term for things such as pollution or resource depletion, which seems to be a rather basic accounting error (why is oil worth something only when it's not in the ground?). For example, a 2016 report from the International Institute for Sustainable Development found that 'the value of Canada's minerals, fossil fuels, timber and agricultural land per person declined by a startling 25 per cent between 1980 and 2013', which means that much of the economy's apparent growth over that period was really based on a 'drawdown of natural capital'.[53]

Despite such problems, the growing consensus even among mainstream economists that environmental problems are both real and important is encouraging (and, ecologists and environmentalists might say, not a day too soon). Also on the good news front: commercial honeybee populations in some areas appear to be on the mend, helped by government regulations on pesticides and fungicides. Though as captive key workers I expect their reported career satisfaction levels (see next chapter) aren't very high. Modern debt-slave, gig-economy worker bees might know how they feel.

CHAPTER 9

THE UNHAPPY ECONOMY

One should never direct people towards happiness,
because happiness too is an idol of the market-place.
One should direct them towards mutual affection.
Aleksandr Solzhenitsyn, in *Cancer Ward* (1968)

I think you can reach a certain state of consciousness, a
state where you're not aware of anything ... you're just
being. The happiest people are those who are being, more
times a week than anybody else. It's just down to that.
John Lennon (1968)

According to the Victorian founders of economic theory, the main aim of growing the economy is to make people happy. But despite bigger houses, more cars, and a historically unprecedented abundance of material wealth in the richer countries of the world, measurements of happiness have actually declined slightly since the early 1960s. Meanwhile, countries with lower material standards of living often report higher happiness than those that are better off. It seems that we are working harder and longer, without becoming noticeably cheerier. This chapter explores the fuzzy and often contradictory relationship between money and happiness, and asks whether our future happiness depends on our ability to change the way we make economic decisions at the individual and societal level.

Neoclassical economics was forged during one of the most exciting periods of scientific history. Until the mid-19th century, scientists had a vague notion that there existed a mysterious quantity, energy, that permeated the universe but took many different forms. There was kinetic energy, the energy of motion, which Leibniz called the *vis viva*, or living force. Roll a ball down a ramp, and it gains kinetic energy as it speeds up. There was thermal energy stored in heat, which Leibniz and Newton believed was the energy of the random motion of atoms. And there was potential energy, which an object acquires in a force field – be it gravitational, mechanical, electrostatic, magnetic, or chemical. Alfred Nobel earned his prize-funding wealth by finding a way to store potential energy in the form of dynamite.

In 1845, the English physicist and brewer James Prescott Joule presented a paper, 'On the mechanical equivalent of heat', which described an experiment that shows how gravitational potential energy and heat energy are related. The apparatus consisted of a weight rigged up in such a way that, when it fell, it spun a paddle-wheel in an insulated barrel of water. The stirred water grew slightly warmer because the paddle's energy of motion was transferred to heat, just as your hands grow warm if you rub them energetically together. The potential energy of the weight in the gravitational field was therefore translated, as the weight fell, into thermal energy of the water (a small amount was also lost to friction or to kinetic energy of the weight). By measuring the change in temperature, Joule could quantitatively relate the amount of energy stored in heat to the energy in the gravitational field.

In 1847, the German physician and physicist Hermann Helmholtz, motivated by his study of muscle movement, postulated that mechanics, heat, electricity, magnetism and light were all different aspects of a single type of energy that was at all times conserved. The connection between the last three was made explicit by James Clerk Maxwell, who showed that light consisted of oscillating electrical and magnetic waves. Emmy Noether later showed that Helmholtz's principle of the conservation of energy was equivalent to a symmetry of the laws of physics in time.

The conservation of energy is the archetype of a successful physical law. It is stable and immutable – as far as we know, it holds for all times and all places. It unifies many disparate phenomena – motion, heat, light – into one theory. It embodies a deep property of symmetry. And it reduces complex reality to a single number. As the physicist Richard Feynman observed, the law is 'a most abstract idea, because it is a mathematical principle; it says that there is a numerical quantity, which does not change when something happens. It is not a description of a mechanism, or anything concrete; it is just a strange fact that we can calculate some number, and when we finish watching nature go through her tricks and calculate the number again, it is the same.'[1]

The physics of happiness

While these properties were remarkable enough, neoclassical economists believed that the power of the law extended even further. Helmholtz had been motivated by his studies of human muscles, which convert food energy into labour. So why not apply the law to human volition, which converts our labour into utility? Could it not even be used to describe all human behaviour? As Jevons wrote in *The Principles of Science*: 'No apparent limit exists to the success of the scientific method in weighing and measuring, and reducing beneath the sway of law, the phenomena of matter and mind … Must not the same inexorable reign of law which is apparent in the motions of brute matter be extended to the human heart?'[2]

The philosopher Jeremy Bentham had already shown how to compute the human tendency to action by summing up 'all the values of all the pleasures on the one side, and those of all the pains on the other' to give the total utility. And utility was like energy in that it could take different forms. For example, if a landowner orders a worker to dig a hole, then the worker will suffer a certain negative utility – the pain of labour – which will be compensated when he is paid. Suppose he then buys a loaf of bread with his earnings, and later eats it. Then over the cycle, utility will have transformed from the pain of labour, to money, to the purchase of food, to the pleasure of eating, in exactly the same way that Joule's mechanism transformed potential energy into heat.

Of course, a problem was that one could never directly measure utility or pleasure. However, Jevons argued that in reality we can never directly measure forces, only their effects: 'For instance, gravity cannot be measured except by the velocity which it produces in a body in a given time. All the other physical forces, such as light, heat, electricity, are incapable of being measured like water or timber, and it is by their effects that we estimate them. So pleasure must be estimated by its effects.'[3] Indeed, economics was in a fortunate position, because there was a wealth of data available – the markets: 'we may estimate the equality or inequality of feelings by the decisions of the human mind ... and its oscillations are minutely registered in the price lists of the markets.'[4]

To create a physics of happiness, the neoclassical economists therefore believed that they needed only to make a simple substitution between physical and economic quantities. In place of atoms, there were individuals or firms, and in place of energy, there was utility, in all its different forms. The result, claimed Jevons, would be 'a kind of physical astronomy investigating the mutual perturbations of individuals'.[5] Even if the available mathematical and statistical tools were not yet sufficiently refined, it would only be a matter of time: after all, 'Previous to the time of Pascal, who would have thought of measuring doubt and belief? Who could have conceived that the investigation of petty games of chance would have led to the creation of perhaps the most sublime branch of mathematical science – the theory of probabilities?'[6]

Léon Walras likewise described economics as 'a science that resembles the physio-mathematical sciences in every respect'. Vilfredo Pareto believed the theory was so deep that 'People who know neither mathematics nor rational mechanics cannot understand the principal conception of my book'.[7] In his 1881 work *Mathematical Psychics*, economist Francis Edgeworth wrote that 'The application of mathematics to the world of the soul is countenanced by the hypothesis ... that Pleasure is the concomitant of Energy'. The trajectory of each soul could be computed by assuming that its aim is to realise 'the maximum of pleasure'. Inspired by the work of 'psychophysicists' such as Ernst Weber, he hypothesised that utility could be directly measured using a 'psychophysical machine' called a hedonimeter which would register 'the height of pleasure experienced by an individual' or more technically 'the psychical side of a physical change in what may be dimly discerned as a sort of hedonico-magnetic field' (thus anticipating by 70 years Ron Hubbard's 'electropsychometer' for auditing the emotional state of Scientologists).[8]

Other economists such as Irving Fisher preferred to frame utility in terms of desire rather than pleasure, and saw it as something that had to be inferred from behaviour rather than directly measured using a probe. But either way, the net effect over a society would be to satisfy Bentham's 'greatest happiness principle', which was to provide the greatest happiness to the most people. The economy was nothing other than a mechanism for maximising (a word invented by Bentham) utility – a kind of giant pleasure machine.

In his 1920 *Principles of Economics*, which remained a standard textbook into the 1950s, Alfred Marshall wrote that: 'Utility is taken to be correlative to Desire or Want … the measure is found in the price which a person is willing to pay for the fulfilment or satisfaction of his desire.'[9] The more modern textbook *Economics*, by Ragan and Lipsey, similarly defines utility as 'The satisfaction or well-being that a consumer receives from consuming some good or service'.[10] So while today economists often treat utility as just a theoretical way of ranking preferences, and avoid comparing the subjective experience of one person with that of another, hidden away within the dry mathematical formalism of their models is the squishy idea that market value, as measured in monetary units, somehow quantifies pleasure, well-being, or the satisfaction of desire.[11] Or as economist Diane Coyle put it – in a section on the 'ten rules of economic thinking' – in her 2002 book *Sex, Drugs and Economics*: 'Economics is about happiness.' (In case you find this questionable, another handy 'rule' is: 'Where common sense and economics conflict, common sense is wrong.')[12]

In his 2009 book *The Skeptical Economist*, Jonathan Aldred points out, sceptically, that this leads to the core presumption, or economyth as we call it, that 'Economic growth increases happiness': 'Growth is good, because it leads to more consumption. Consumption is good, because it leads to more preference satisfaction. Preference satisfaction is good, because it makes people better off.'[13] Aldred adds that though 'this is clearly a simplified outline, it captures the essential argument for economic growth in developed economies that is so taken for granted that it goes unmentioned'. (Or sometimes economists do mention it, as Olivier Blanchard did in a textbook: 'Economists take for granted that higher output per capita means higher utility and increased happiness.'[14]) Far from being a 'dismal science', then, economics is the science of good times and easy living.

Bad energy

A recurrent theme of this book has been how ironic it is that economics gains its scientific credibility from its association with physics. It would make sense if, for example, its neoclassical founders had been physicists; or if they had at least shown a solid understanding of physics; or if their ideas had been endorsed by prominent physicists.[15] But they were really just grabbing ideas from the air and transplanting them into economics without any concern for basic principles, such as units of measurement or the fact that people are not machines. If you perform Joule's experiment, then the potential energy of a raised weight will transform into the thermal energy of a bucket of water as the weight falls, in a repeatable way. If you perform Jevons' experiment, and calculate the flow in utility as a man digs a hole and is rewarded, then you will get one answer if he's a union worker, another if he's doing it at gunpoint, and still another if he's digging a hole in his own garden for fun. As an analogue for energy – let alone as the basis for a grand theory of human behaviour – utility has limited use.

Jevons' argument that market mechanisms optimise utility, and therefore utility can be inferred from market prices, is an example of the circular logic that characterises neoclassical economics. As with the efficient market hypothesis, it boils down to the statement that markets know all and the price is right.

People did try to warn them. Replying to a letter from Walras, the French mathematician Henri Poincaré warned that the unrealistic assumptions of the theory might make the conclusions 'devoid of all interest'.[16] The mathematician Norbert Wiener later wrote that 'economists have developed the habit of dressing up their rather imprecise ideas in the language of the infinitesimal calculus … To assign what purports to be precise values to such essentially vague quantities is neither useful nor honest, and any pretense of applying formulae to these loosely defined quantities is a sham and a waste of time.'[17] Richard Feynman said of the tendency for social scientists in general to mathematicise their work: 'I have a great suspicion that they don't know, that this stuff is [wrong] and they're intimidating people.'[18] (This wasn't just non-economists being snobby: Thomas Piketty also noted more recently that 'This obsession with mathematics is an easy way of acquiring the appearance of scientificity without having to answer the far more complex questions posed by the world we live in.'[19])

The association with 19th-century physics doesn't explain how economics has managed to maintain its 'hard science' aura. All sorts of once-fashionable psychological and sociological theories have been built around hazy notions of energy, but have failed to qualify for Nobel Prizes. These days, people prefer to build flaky theories around something a little more recent, like quantum theory or relativity (see Chapter 11).

The main reason for the persistence of neoclassical economics is that it tapped into something much more enduring. As seen in previous chapters, it is based on ideas of unity, stability, and symmetry that have characterised Western science since the time of the ancient Greeks. Go back to the Pythagorean list of opposites (Chapter 5), or consider the latest theories of supersymmetry or strings, and you will see those same principles there. Economics therefore has the look and feel of traditional 'hard' science. It exploits this by 'dressing up' its ideas in mathematical equations that are inaccessible to those 'who know neither mathematics nor rational mechanics'.

The other reason that economics is considered a hard, mathematical science is of course because, as Jevons noted, there is a lot of data available. The economy is based on the idea of number – that's why coins have numbers on them. It is the realisation of the Pythagorean statement that 'number is all'. The ultimate aim of neoclassical economists was to put a number even on subjective experiences such as pleasure or happiness.

But can we really put a price tag on happiness? Are free markets really a machine for maximising pleasure? And if so, why aren't we getting happier?

Share the joy

In the neoclassical framework, money is seen as a store of utility – a kind of potential energy that can be transformed into pleasure just by spending it. I wonder how the early neoclassical economists would have seen the credit bubble of the early 2000s. A huge pleasure field that pervaded the atmosphere, perhaps. Or a massive, brewing electrical storm.

While money can certainly be used to buy pleasure, the two quantities – money and pleasure – are actually very different. For example, if you are given a large sum of money, it doesn't necessarily decay, because you can deposit it in an interest-bearing account. With pleasure, it lasts for a while, but soon dissipates. Studies have shown that lottery winners don't stay ecstatic for long, but soon return to something close to their previous levels of happiness. Conversely, we can learn to cope with most forms of misfortune, though of course some traumatic events never fade.[20]

Money also builds up in an additive fashion. If you have a million dollars, and earn another million, then you're twice as rich. But pleasures tend to saturate. Making the first million might make you very happy, but the second million is less of a thrill. In the terms of neoclassical economics, its marginal utility is lower. Materialistic desires therefore have an addictive quality – the more we have, the more we need.

Because money is lasting and additive, if left unspent it will tend to accumulate over time, which, as discussed in Chapter 7, is one reason for the extreme inequalities in world wealth. Pleasure is self-limiting, and short periods of great joy don't necessarily add up to lasting happiness. Happiness is more democratic than money in that it is more stable and equally shared. As Jevons wrote to his brother: 'I have a lurking suspicion that the sum total of a person's enjoyment is generally equal to what we should call in mathematics a "constant quantity."'[21]

The main determinants of long-term wealth include country of birth, education, ability, who your parents are, ambition, work, health, social networks, luck, opportunity, and whether or not you have access to a trust fund. Long-term happiness also depends to an extent on character traits, some of which may be inherited from your parents, and social networks, though they needn't be from the best school.[22] Health (mental and physical), family, a satisfying job, and societal trust are also important. However, the materialistic, acquisitive bent necessary to produce wealth doesn't correlate particularly well with happiness. One paper from the German Institute for Economic Research found that 'Nonzero sum goals, which include commitment to family, friends and social and political involvement, promote life satisfaction. Zero sum goals, including commitment to career success and material gains, appear detrimental to life satisfaction.'[23]

Furthermore, impressions of wealth are relative. If all of your friends and acquaintances and neighbours have more than you, then you feel poorer, which also affects happiness.[24] The easiest way to feel rich is therefore to move to an area where your neighbours all earn a little less. A problem with social inequality is that we tend to compare ourselves with those who have more than us rather than less – especially if we are constantly hearing about them through the media.

Pleasure, in contrast, is both an internal subjective experience and at the same time a shared emotion with positive network effects. According to a study of over 4,700 American people, who were followed over a twenty-year period from 1983 to 2003, happiness spreads between individuals rather like an infectious disease (but a nice one). Having a happy friend or neighbour boosts your own feelings of happiness by an estimated 9 per cent. If that's true, it would make sense for us all to take a half-day off work each week just to socialise. Even friends of friends have an effect. As one of the co-authors of the study, political scientist James Fowler, put it: 'The pursuit of happiness is not a solitary goal. We are connected, and so is our joy.'[25] To feel happier, you should move to a place where the neighbours look not less happy, but more.

While money and pleasure are closely related in some situations, e.g. while shopping, the linkages between the two are usually far more complex and ambiguous. Money doesn't always buy happiness – and even if it does, the happiness it buys may be offset by other effects. As one study by the behavioural psychologist Daniel Kahneman and collaborators pointed out, high-earners spend more time working and commuting, and less time relaxing and hanging out with friends. As a result, they concluded: 'People with above-average income are relatively satisfied with their lives but are barely happier than others in moment-to-moment experience, tend to be more tense, and do not spend more time in particularly enjoyable activities.'[26]

On a societal level, comparisons of 'subjective well-being' and wealth also appear only weakly related. Although measuring happiness across different societies and cultures is obviously much more difficult than measuring GDP, it appears that, while poor countries do report lower happiness than rich countries, the correlation is low once a basic threshold is met.[27] Countries such as Indonesia, Vietnam, El Salvador and Mexico report high levels of happiness, in total defiance of economic principles. This is one reason why, as discussed in the previous chapter, measures such as the Genuine Progress Indicator or the Happy Planet Index do not track with

GDP. Comparisons over time show the same thing. World GDP has grown enormously in recent decades, so if we were to insist that happiness and GDP are related, people must have been pretty damned miserable a hundred years ago, or a thousand years ago. But that doesn't seem to have been the case.

Another demonstration of the difference between pleasure/happiness and money is the fact that we are often happy to work for free – and in some cases, even happier than if we were paid. Volunteer work has been shown to bring many benefits, including the chance to make new friends, the satisfaction of seeing results, and even the sensation of being less selfish.[28] Achievements such as Wikipedia, or the open-source computer operating system Linux, stand testament to the power of unpaid labour. In fact, we often prefer to work for free than for a reduced wage – lawyers will work *pro bono*, but hardly ever *pro cheapo*. The reason is because happiness and money engage completely different parts of our brains and our personalities.

Warm and fuzzy

As the behavioural psychologist Dan Ariely observes in his book *Predictably Irrational*: 'we live in two worlds: one characterized by social exchanges and the other characterized by market exchanges.' Social exchanges are 'warm and fuzzy' and include offers of help, exchange of gifts, neighbourly collaborations, and volunteer work. The pleasure is in the action itself, and immediate reciprocity is not expected or demanded. Market exchanges, in contrast, are 'sharp-edged' and based on numerical calculations of wages, payments, and prices.[29] Social norms are more right-brained and intuitive, while market norms are left-brained and calculating.[30]

In most situations, we manage to keep these two worlds separate from one another, and it can lead to all sorts of misunderstandings when we mix them by accident or design. In one experiment, psychologists tested to see what would happen at a day care centre if parents were fined when they showed up late for their children. Under the usual system, parents felt guilty when they were late, so avoided doing it again in future – the situation was governed by social norms. When fines were imposed, the parents stopped feeling guilty and started calculating instead – with the unintended effect that many chose to show up late and pay the penalty.[31]

Interestingly, when the day care centre removed the fine after a few weeks and went back to the old system, the number of parents gone AWOL remained high. Instead of easily reverting to social norms, the parents were still operating under market norms – only now, being late was a really good deal. It seems there was a kind of hysteresis effect at work, in the sense that it was easy to go from social to market norms, but much harder to go back.

This preference for market norms is also shown by experiments in which subjects were primed to think about money, for example by seating them in view of a pile of Monopoly cash, before carrying out some tasks. The effect of the exposure to money was to make them less likely to ask for assistance, or make offers of help, or collaborate with others. They even preferred to sit further away from other people.[32] (Apparently the effect also applies when people are prompted to think about economics, so make sure you have plenty of elbow room while reading this book.[33])

Our ability to slip easily into market norms is perhaps because they have become so established throughout our society that they are now the default mode. People have always been interested in money, but we seem to be taking the obsession to new lengths. If we are taught and believe as a society that material success equates to happiness, and that market norms are in some sense more rational and real than social norms, then of course we will tend to favour them.

Unfortunately, though, getting stuck in market mode doesn't make us happy, because happiness relies more on social and psychological realities than a number in a bank account. A network of friends, a sense of purpose and harmony in life, the joy of 'just being' aren't available down at the mall.[34] Our economic theory promises us a road to happiness, but what it offers is an illusion. We built a machine for optimising happiness, only to find out we're not happy living in a machine.

The pursuit of unhappiness

According to the neoclassical model, the working life is a bit like Joule's experiment. You lift up a heavy weight (perform labour in exchange for money), then release the weight (drop some cash), thus stirring and warming the bucket of water (your soul). In practice, though, it often seems that we are left more stirred up than warmed; more agitated than content. Some aspects of our economic system seem designed to make us unhappy.

In the United States, reported happiness levels peaked some time back in the 1960s, and have remained fairly constant ever since, with a slight downward trend. Metrics of unhappiness, such as suicide and divorce rates, have shown the opposite tendency. One of the biggest profit-makers for pharmaceutical companies is antidepressant drugs. Given that the US was founded around the Jeffersonian ideas of 'life, liberty and the pursuit of happiness', this is something of a concern. Perhaps the problem is that those concepts aren't as compatible as they seemed.

Jefferson's phrase in the Declaration of Independence was based on Adam Smith's 'life, liberty, and the pursuit of property' (which was used directly in the 1774 Declaration of Colonial Rights). Milton Friedman's utopia of 'a society in which individuals have the maximum freedom to pursue their own objectives in whichever direction they wish, so long as they don't interfere with the rights of others to do the same thing' articulates the same idea. But if you forget all about supply and demand, Pareto optimality, etc., it seems a great leap of faith to assume that societal happiness is consistent with everyone selfishly trying to maximise their own utility. Instead, according to economist Richard Layard, our atomised societies suffer from 'extreme individualism ... We are unhappier as a result.'[35]

Indeed, the whole idea that individuals are in a competition for happiness is exactly the kind of thing that makes people unhappy. Everyone becomes paranoid that they're not rich and happy enough. The harder they chase happiness, the more it evades them. The net result is something akin to a mental disease. The psychologist Oliver James has described 'affluenza' as 'placing a high value on money, possessions, appearances (physical and social) and fame'.[36] The condition places people at increased risk of mental disorders including anxiety, depression, and drug abuse. It is worsened by social inequality, which highlights differences in status, and is exploited by advertisers who drum up envy to drive sales. It is the shadow side of the American Dream.

There is also a clear biological link between economic stress and mental and physical health. In a 2007 survey by the American Psychological Association, 73 per cent of the respondents cited money as a significant source of stress.[37] And that was before the housing crash. Stress affects the body in obvious and immediate ways, such as insomnia, or more subtle ways, such as increased blood pressure or even longevity. A study by a group of epidemiologists from Yale found that involuntary job loss more than doubled the risk of heart attack and stroke among older workers.[38] A graphic example of this was in Russia, when male life expectancy plunged by several per cent after the country experienced its traumatic shift to a market economy. (In a 2015 article, economists Anne Case and Angus Deaton suggested 'economic insecurity' as a possible cause for increased death rates for middle-aged white Americans.[39])

Part of the problem is that, while markets are very good at certain tasks, such as reducing costs and driving innovation, they are less talented in the social sphere. As the former US secretary of labour Robert Reich points out, in the 1950s and early 1960s 'issues of economic security, social equity, community, our shared environment, and common decency were central to democratic capitalism'. These have lost importance as power has moved away from public institutions to consumers and investors: 'Today's economy can give us great deals largely because it punishes us in other ways.'[40]

Businesses make their decisions based on cold calculations of profit and loss. That is to be expected. But this attitude has crept over so that it dominates decisions by governments as well. Reich notes that: 'Absent from any such calculus is consideration of ... inequality ... economic security ... civil or human rights ... public health or domestic tranquility ... community ... environment ... tolerance and global peace ... democracy. These attributes are clearly difficult to measure or to quantify, but that doesn't make them less worthy of consideration than consumer and investor welfare.'[41] The dominance of numerical market norms over fuzzy social norms means that we effectively devalue what is most important in life.

It seems that at the level of individuals, businesses or governments, we have become locked into a particular hard-edged, yang view of the economy as a battle between individuals or firms to maximise their own utility, where selfishness is the only rational behaviour. The aim is to achieve dominance and assert status over those around you. Yin values such as connectedness or altruism are downplayed, and associated jobs such as nursing and childcare are underpaid.[42] It is as if we are contorting ourselves to fit the model of rational economic man; to align with the economyth. The net result, though, is very far from Bentham's principle of the greatest happiness for the most people. It is also rather unreasonable; for as discussed in the previous chapter, our striving for growth at all costs has now reached a scale at which it threatens our viability on the planet. We need to call an end to the race. The best way to do that may be to reform our economic theories.

Reasons to be cheerful

The fact that money and happiness are totally different concepts somehow knocks the steam out of neoclassical theory, whose developers assumed precise and mathematical relationships between utility and price. If the economic machine isn't maximising utility, then what is it maximising?

The answer, of course, is nothing. The economy is what it is. Free markets have many splendid attributes, which must be protected. They are the best way that we have come up with to make a wide variety of economic decisions. They offer individuals and companies the opportunity to either succeed, or fail and make room for others.[43] Markets are a basic form of human interaction that existed before economics was invented, and they don't need neoclassical theories to justify them – any more than human cooperation must be justified by Marxism. But if we are to base our quest for the good life on empirical facts, rather than corny 19th-century ideas, then we need to rebalance our priorities.

As discussed above, one's happiness depends on a number of factors. It generally doesn't help if you're stressed out and working incredibly hard to pay off a mountain of debt. At the same time, what counts for happiness is relative rather than absolute salaries. It would therefore make sense to aim for lower debt and lower economic growth, as conventionally defined in terms of GDP. As shown in Chapter 8, economic growth also often subtracts from environmental quality, which itself is important for happiness. This doesn't of course mean that growth or progress should stop, only that they should be redefined.

In unequal societies, though, it is hard for anyone to be satisfied with what they have in material terms. So the first priority is to reduce inequality, which as discussed earlier is also strongly correlated with a range of social problems. The sociologist Robert Putnam observed that: 'Sometime around 1965–70 America ... started becoming both less just economically and less well connected socially and politically.'[44] Free markets, if left to their own devices for long enough, tend to concentrate wealth and power into the hands of a small number of individuals or firms. We therefore need non-market mechanisms, such as those discussed in Chapter 7, to limit this tendency.

Another plank of happiness is freedom from excessive levels of economic stress. So it is desirable that the economy be reasonably stable. Economic shocks such as financial crashes or unemployment have powerful emotional consequences. 'It's probably no accident that the economic term – depression – is the same as the psychiatric one', notes the psychiatrist David Spiegel. 'People tend to feel bad when what they have planned seems suddenly to come apart, when their ability to be effective in the world is challenged.'[45] To restore financial stability is not the same as arguing for continuous growth. A low-debt, low-growth economy with a smaller financial sector may turn out to be inherently more stable because it has less leverage.

As mentioned in Chapter 6, a large amount of labour – including much done by women – is unpaid. This work, which is performed according to social norms, is vitally important for maintaining the happiness of a society. It should therefore be acknowledged and rewarded. One way is to use tools such as local currencies or time banks, which allow one to earn credits for services performed, and offer a balance between social and market norms. The popularity of these schemes has exploded in recent years, with many areas adopting their own local version.[46] A shorter working week might lower GDP, but it would allow the informal sector time and space to expand, with increased involvement by both sexes.[47]

Finally, we have to acknowledge as a society that money and happiness are completely different quantities. The reason that GDP has soared in Western economies over the last few decades, but reported happiness levels have remained relatively static, is because they are *not the same thing*. The economy can't make us happy all by itself. We just need it to work. Happiness is a separate issue that eludes direct pursuit and instead emerges as the indirect result of other activities.

The neoclassical model for economic growth is unsustainable and unsatisfying, not just because it requires infinite resources and harms the environment, but also because it relies on an eternal desire for *more*, which can by definition never be satisfied. It offers, not happiness, but the eternal promise of happiness, if we can just work harder and upgrade our lifestyles to the next level before everyone else does. We therefore need a new model of a successful society, in which money and material possessions play a subordinate role. Part of that is a new model for what constitutes a full and satisfactory life. Who is to say that maximising individual pleasure is the guide to a good life – or that it is even appropriate, in a world where pain and suffering have yet to be banished? What about values and qualities like wisdom, humility, empathy, graciousness, justice, service, courage, loyalty, honour, spirituality and love, which cannot be reduced to simple calculations of short-term utility?[48]

One of the main obstacles to achieving this switch to a more balanced and pragmatic view of the economy is, I believe,

neoclassical ideology. Anyone who takes an introductory economics course is taught that the individualistic pursuit of pleasure will,
by a roundabout process involving the invisible hand, free markets and so on, somehow make life better for all humanity.[49] Since
many of these students then go on to become leaders in business
or government, where they perpetuate the same self-legitimising
fiction, it is no surprise that we live in an individualistic, materialistic culture dominated by market norms. As a society, we're all
sitting further away from one another.[50] It's time we started telling
a new story.

What's wrong with this picture?

Economics sees itself as an objective, impartial, detached science;
however, as already discussed, theories influence the world they
seek to describe, and sometimes in surprising ways. For example,
for a theory that emphasises qualities like stability and symmetry
and rationality, and ignores or downplays the role of the financial
sector, neoclassical economics seems destined to create a world
that is unstable and unfair and run by banks.

This points to perhaps the most puzzling fact about mainstream economic theory. On the one hand, it says that the economy
is fair and stable and optimal. On the other hand, companies in the
financial sector that actually control much of the world's wealth,
and should therefore understand how it works, don't seem to pay
any attention. They support all the correct neoclassical think tanks,
of course, but they also do everything they can to support inequality and instability. Such companies thrive on volatility, because they
make their money by speculating on changing prices. If markets
were really efficient, then price changes would be small and completely random, and it would be impossible to make a profit. It
would be as exciting as surfing in a puddle.

And for that matter: why do we need central banks? If

the economy is efficient and self-stabilising, and markets are all-knowing, what is the point in having a Federal Reserve tweaking interest rates? Wouldn't it be better to just let banks set their own interest rates according to the 'law of supply and demand'?

And finally, if neoclassical ideology is so rigid and widespread, and not just among economists, why is it that free markets and small government are OK when the economy is on the up, but as soon as a crisis comes the first companies to get supported by the taxpayer are the banks? Shouldn't they be allowed to fail according to the law of 'survival of the fittest'? Isn't it what their principles would *demand*? None of it makes sense.

In the final chapter, we therefore ask the inevitable, and entirely reasonable question: is neoclassical economics all part of a giant global conspiracy – an attempt to distract us from the real game that is being played behind the scenes?

Odd versus even

Continuing with the Pythagorean playlist, we talked a bit about the Pythagoreans' interest in even and odd numbers in other chapters. Even numbers (2, 4, etc.) were considered suspect because they could be broken into two equal parts. They lacked a kind of integrity. Odd numbers, in contrast, were considered hard and indivisible. According to his biographer Iamblichus, Pythagoras asserted that 'the right hand is the principle of what is called the odd number, and is divine; but that the left hand is a symbol of the even number, and of that which is dissolved'.[51]

This hard/soft duality carries over, in modified form, throughout all science.[52] We prefer hard equations over soft feelings, hard objectivity over soft subjectivity, gross domestic product over measures of well-being. As discussed in Chapter 11, this duality lies at the heart of money – best represented by ancient coins, with their hard numbers pressed into soft gold. Areas such as happiness economics attempt to address the disconnect between numerical price and the fuzzy idea of value.

To equate value with utility, as the founders of neoclassical economics did, may seem like a mere technicality, but it carries the message that economics is about optimising happiness, which is the economic equivalent of saying 'It's all good!' Perhaps the main lesson of happiness economics, though, is that happiness is not all about economics. The difference between them is like the difference between number and physical reality; between heads and tails. Money is a way to attach number to value, but we can never reduce happiness to a number.

As an example, the assumption that consumers make rational, independent choices to optimise their own utility leads naturally to what William Harold Hutt, in his 1936 book *Economists and the Public*, called 'consumer sovereignty' – the idea, on which much policy is based, that consumers drive the economy, and maximise their own welfare, by demanding the goods and services they want.[53] Yet as already seen, people make decisions that are based on things other than money, and they are influenced both by each other and by things like marketing or whatever is trending on Twitter. One reason economists have consistently miscalculated on Europe (e.g. Brexit) is because it turns out people have complex ideas about sovereignty that go far beyond the simplified consumer version.

This points to an interesting contradiction in economics, which is that people are assumed to do what makes them happy; but when they do something that economists disagree with, it is assumed they are behaving irrationally, so need to be corrected (or as Jonathan Aldred puts it, 'There is a widespread but implicit belief that non-economists are stupid').[54] In his 2007 book *The Myth of the Rational Voter*, economist Bryan Caplan for example wrote that: 'People do not understand the "invisible hand" of the market, its ability to harmonize private greed and the public interest.'[55] They also 'underestimate the benefits of interactions with foreigners' and are 'overly prone to think that economic conditions are bad and getting worse'. He asks: 'If people's views about economics are so irrational, how is persuasion possible?' and concludes that the us-or-them approach is the way to go with students: '"I'm right, the people outside this classroom are wrong, and you don't want to be like *them*, do you?" is, in my experience, fairly effective.' He also warns that 'professional humility is dangerous'.

This position seems strange, given that the whole point of the invisible hand is supposed to be that people don't have to know how it works, or attend economics seminars, in order for it to function. But it certainly helps explain why the Bank of England's forecasting errors at the time of the Brexit vote were blamed on 'behaviours that were deeply irrational', rather than on economists who were deeply confused (see box, page 35).

The idea that mainstream economists – with their 'hard' equations – know best how to make everyone happy, as opposed to just themselves, is on full display in the video of a 2015 event, 'The Genius of Economics', which features Thomas Piketty, Joseph Stiglitz and Paul Krugman discussing topics including inequality and societal happiness.[56] The host, journalist Alex Wagner, starts by politely – 'a philosophical question' – asking the panel – 'considered geniuses in the field of economics' – why economists had failed to predict the 'most disruptive thing that happened, economically speaking, globally … the years of 2007 and 2008'. Stiglitz interrupts: 'But both

Paul and I did.' ('And that's why you're the geniuses!', agrees Wagner, to much applause.) Krugman then clarifies that he personally 'didn't see the crisis coming' – indeed it 'came as a shock to me as to almost everyone' – but excuses the profession by saying that (a) 'there's always going to be something out there that you miss', and (b) of the few people who did predict it, 'they also saw five crises that didn't happen coming so it doesn't quite count'. (Knowing chuckles all round to these rather extraordinary statements, perhaps because none of the people who actually did accurately and specifically predict the crisis happened to be in the audience. It is also interesting to compare these comments with the remarks of the former head of the UK Treasury, who admitted on his retirement in 2016 that economists' failure to spot the build-up of risk prior to the crisis constituted 'a monumental collective intellectual error'.[57])

Krugman, again drawing his own conclusions from recent events, goes on to say that he feels vindicated because orthodox economic theory has 'worked remarkably well' during the aftermath of the crisis: 'I spent my life not entirely sure whether I was a fraud or not … it was only in the last six or so years that I said hey, you know, this stuff works.' Stiglitz agrees that 'if we were running Europe, we would know how to get it out of its troubles … same thing, if it were up to Paul and me, I think, in the United States' – to which Krugman happily quips, 'We're not geniuses, we're philosopher kings!'

While the two Nobel laureates, settled deeply in their upholstered armchairs, seem quite relaxed and comfortable about the 'genius' label, Piketty – perhaps because he was jet-lagged ('it's 2am in Paris') and thought he was at another event called The Monumental Collective Intellectual Error of Economics, or maybe just because he does not inhabit a Nobel-boosted bubble of delusion – refutes it completely; notes that mainstream economics is dominated by ideology and the desire to impress with impenetrable mathematical models, which he calls a 'joke'; and insists that: 'We have to be modest … if we want to be useful, and it's not always clear that economists are so useful.'

Happiness economics did make a number of advances following the 2008 crisis, some of them possibly useful. In 2009, a commission appointed by Nicolas Sarkozy, then French president, and chaired by Stiglitz, recommended that GDP should be replaced or augmented by measures which take into account factors including general well-being, educational standards, non-market activities such as childcare and leisure, and environmental sustainability. In the UK, the Conservative government decided to implement a survey of national well-being, which started in 2012. This happened at the same time that they pushed through their post-crisis austerity policies – maybe they wanted to find out whether it was hurting yet. The questions include (cue voice of Laurence Olivier in his dentist-torturer role in *Marathon Man*): 'Overall, how anxious did you feel yesterday?' (muffled scream).

By the way (spoiler alert!), note that this chapter's final sentence – the one asking whether neoclassical economics is 'part of a giant global conspiracy' – has a *question mark* at the end. It is a *playful question*. Perhaps unaware of things like context and humour – or perhaps to make the evidence fit their story – not all economists noticed that little question mark, apparently, with the result that I was soon being called a conspiracy theorist. Which I'm not – though I do sometimes wonder why every government bureaucrat who is important in finance seems to have worked at some point for Goldman Sachs.

CHAPTER 10

THE GOOD ECONOMY

The world over, citizens think we are lying to them, that the figures are wrong, that they are manipulated. And they have reasons to think like that. Behind the cult of figures, behind all these statistical and accounting structures, there is also the cult of the market that is always right.
French president Nicolas Sarkozy, speaking on the need for new economic metrics to provide alternatives to GDP (2009)

What's important when you are in that hedge-fund mode is to not do anything remotely truthful because the truth is so against your view, that it's important to create a new truth, to develop a fiction.
Jim Cramer, television personality and former hedge fund manager (2006)

Mainstream economics teaches that the market economy, if freed from distortions and isolated instances of market failure, will maximise the utility of each individual and lead to the best of all possible worlds. This chapter discusses how the mistaken assumptions and myths of economic theory mask our understanding of how the economy actually works. They persist not for scientific reasons, but because they serve a certain agenda. We see how a flood of new ideas is providing us with the tools to shape a better, fairer, and more sustainable economy. These ideas come from diverse sources: new areas of mathematics such as nonlinear dynamics, complexity, and network theory; social

movements like environmentalism or feminism; and also the ancient discipline of ethics. Current economic theory is less a science than an ideology peculiar to a certain period of history, which may well be nearing an end.

The Lipstick Building is an elegant 34-storey postmodern office tower in midtown Manhattan. Resting upon an oval array of pillars, the red granite and stainless steel construction tapers to the sky in three layers, like an opened tube of lipstick. The first two floors contain an impressive glass lobby, adjacent to a pedestrian plaza. The building's largest tenant is a huge law firm, Latham & Watkins. Until 2008, the 18th and 19th floors also played host to a thriving and unusually profitable stock-trading and investment operation known as Bernard L. Madoff Investment Securities.

Madoff started the firm in 1960, at the age of 22, on savings of $5,000. Initially, most of his clients came from family contacts – his father was a stockbroker, his father-in-law an accountant. Madoff was a pioneer at developing fast computer systems to make quotes, thus allowing him to siphon business away from rival companies that were members of the New York Stock Exchange. The technology later formed the basis of the NASDAQ exchange. By 1992, Madoff's trading volume was equivalent to 9 per cent of the NYSE.

Then in the mid-1990s, motivated at first by a desire to cover up an investment loss, this Wall Street insider took something of a left turn.[1] He set up what would become the largest investment fraud in history – a $65 billion Ponzi scheme, which sucked in money from private and corporate investors with the sole purpose, it appears, of enriching Bernie Madoff.

The 18th and 19th floors of the Lipstick Building were filled with the usual array of smart, college-educated traders, who gave the impression of urgent efficiency common to those who handle millions of dollars a day. They worked hard and long and were exceptionally well paid. Clients included Bear Stearns, Lehman Brothers, and Fidelity. The office was routinely audited by regulators. All in all, it was what you would expect from a successful financial company. That wasn't the whole story, though. Like a family with a secret in the basement, the whole operation had another level – the 17th floor – that clients, visitors, regulators, and even the other employees rarely got to see.

This floor was staffed with a different type of person – less educated, less experienced, less skilled. They dressed casually, and worked only regular nine-to-five hours. Their jobs were simple and routine, mostly clerical work, but still well paid. They were the ones running the 'hedge fund' that was the heart of Madoff's operation.

The scheme worked as follows. Madoff exploited his network of contacts in the business, philanthropic, and Jewish communities to take in money from wealthy investors, charities, or feeder funds. Advertising was by word-of-mouth, and referrals from the official business on the top two floors. The Madoff funds consistently delivered a high rate of return, and people asked few questions. If anyone wanted to withdraw money, they could at any time – there was always more cash coming in from new investors. But most preferred to allow it to grow. This was especially true of the charitable trusts that Madoff specialised in.

When asked how he managed to consistently beat the market, Madoff explained that his strategy was based on a combination of blue-chip stock investments and derivatives such as futures contracts. As he told the *Wall Street Journal* in 1992, this allowed investors 'to participate in an upward market move while having limited downside risk'.[2] The story was complicated but plausible enough to convince even major banks like HSBC or Spain's Banco Santander to invest billions. Intermediaries such as feeder funds were awarded high commissions, which discouraged too much analysis.

Madoff's operation came under suspicion from regulators a number of times and was investigated. But whenever they looked over the paperwork, and the reams of numerical data for all the stock transactions, it all looked OK. The only thing that brought it down was the crash in 2008, when too many investors tried to withdraw their funds at the same time, only to find that they had never really existed.

A new truth

So how did Madoff manage to perpetuate this illusion of growth for so long? Part of it was his skill at creating a compelling story – a 'new truth' – which according to Jim Cramer (host of CNBC's show *Mad Money*) is essential for any hedge fund, real or not. But technology – or rather the lack of it – also played an important role.

Madoff had built his original business around the innovative use of high-speed computerised trading. People on the top two floors had fast computers and real-time access to prices. But for the 'hedge fund' Madoff preferred to use an antiquated IBM AS/400 machine, which was kept in a special glass case. Its outdated hardware – the range first came out in 1988 – meant that it was not compatible with the other systems.

That wasn't an accidental drawback; in fact it was the entire point. Madoff, perhaps with help from his closest accomplices, would have to enter the data each day by hand. This procedure allowed Madoff to fabricate a history of stock transactions that would give whatever rate of growth was desired. Trade confirmations for each client were then prepared separately, each showing the fictitious gains calculated by the old IBM. In reality, no trades were taking place at all. There was a risk that clients would check, but it seems they never looked beyond the bottom line.

The key elements of this particular scam, then, were:

- **A complicated but plausible story**. The hedge fund strategy could have worked in principle, and the returns were never so large that they seemed impossible. Its apparent complexity deterred questioning.

- **Trust**. Madoff was an insider who had built a reputable business.

- **Incentives**. Intermediaries were kept happy with high commissions. Investors were kept happy, or at least optimistic, with dreams.

- **A network of rich and powerful contacts**. Madoff had many wealthy friends, including entrepreneur and philanthropist Carl J. Shapiro, who chipped in a quarter of a billion dollars months before the scheme collapsed.

- **Influence with regulators**. Madoff and his family had extensive ties with regulators. He was a former chairman of NASDAQ and on the board of directors of the Securities Industry Association.

- **The illusion of growth**. Madoff's funds showed consistent returns of around 10 per cent.

- **An ageing computer**. A machine that adjusts prices to agree with the story.

By 2006, Madoff had accumulated billions of dollars, which he mostly kept in cash accounts at Chase Bank. They financed a luxurious lifestyle for him and anyone in his gift-giving circle. But there was no investment, no real growth – all of that was a fiction. When the scheme collapsed, lives and institutions were destroyed. Madoff was sentenced to 150 years in prison – the judge labelled his crime 'extraordinarily evil'.

Logic Piano II

Now, it would of course not be correct to say that the scheme known as the 'world economy', with its accompanying neoclassical sidekick, is directly equivalent to a Ponzi scheme in which there is no actual investment or growth. However, there are a number of points in common, which are worth exploring.

First of all, the economy has a great story. Open competition between individuals in free markets lifting the world out of poverty and optimising the levels of happiness for all mankind – sounds good to me. The story also enjoys a great deal of trust and credibility. It has been endorsed by the best universities, and even the Nobel Foundation. Introductory textbooks make sure to downplay or smooth over difficult or frightening issues like financial instability (bubbles are debatable), social inequality (no chapters on power discrepancies), or environmental degradation (someone else's problem).[3] Anyone who remains unconvinced is referred to the elaborate and impenetrable mathematics that support the story. This usually deters further investigation.

The scheme has also made sure that participants are adequately incentivised. Anyone working at senior levels is well paid, sometimes extravagantly so. The neoclassical story means that ruthlessly pursuing your own objectives and amassing incredible wealth can be interpreted as virtuous behaviour – Goldman's CEO Lloyd Blankfein, for example, said his company was performing 'God's work' – which is an important motivational plus.[4] And the system has a powerful network of contacts at top universities, institutions like the World Bank and International Monetary Fund, and the highest ranks of world governments – all of which employ or are run by mainstream economists.

The 'investors' are kept in the game by the illusion that they can achieve happiness if they just work hard enough, along with the fact that most of them are heavily in debt. And many happy investors in emerging economies like China and India have seen huge increases in their material standards of living. (We'll leave aside the explosion in inequality in those countries, and also the fact that China hardly meets the usual definition of a free market economy.)

The scheme can point to an excellent track record of growth, with consistent year-on-year GDP increases. Finally, and perhaps most importantly, it has that essential device, the very secret of its success: the ageing computer in the corner, the equivalent of Madoff's IBM – the NeoClassic Logic Piano (Mark II).

The inner mechanical workings of this beautiful old machine date all the way back to the 19th century. It was designed by true pioneers – including William Stanley Jevons, inventor of the original Logic Piano. In the 1960s it was refitted with efficient market theory, and in the 2000s with the latest risk management techniques, but these were minor tweaks.

Again, it's no accident that the hardware is a little out of date, and incompatible with more recent technologies, because its role is purely cosmetic. The way it functions is very simple. The operator types in a price for whatever they want. The machine then makes a whirring sound, some cogs rotate, and it outputs: exactly the same number! Thus confirming, for all of a pseudoscientific bent, that the price is right. It will also print out a long disclaimer, written in tiny-print econom-ese, saying that the price may not be quite right due to the possibility of market failure, externalities, and so on, but hardly anyone reads this and it has little effect in practice (see box, page 283).

If anyone inquires how the machine works, they are referred to the original documents that explain how a pendulum housed inside measures 'minute oscillations' of an energy-like quantity called 'utility'. Huddled scholars can also print out complex mathematical equations proving that the answer is rational, efficient and optimal. But in reality, of course, the machine just gives the market price, which, following neoclassical theory, is right. As physicist J. Doyne Farmer and economist John Geanakoplos note: 'Economic theory says that there is very little to know about markets: An asset's price is the best possible measure of its fundamental value, and the best predictor of future prices.'[5]

For example: in March 1996, and October 2002, the NASDAQ was priced at 1,140. Between those two dates, in March 2000, it reached 5,048. That might seem like an error – but according to the NeoClassic Logic Piano, the prices were right. There are even academic references to back it up.[6]

Here's another: the oil spike of 2008. All due to the forces of supply and demand, according to the machine. So again, there was no error. At all times, the price was right.

The same applies to any asset or service, including human labour. Janitorial staff in Harvard not earning a 'living wage'? Sorry about that, the price is right.

Sweatshop workers making clothes for Wal-Mart for cents an hour? Tough. The price is right.

CEOs earning tens or hundreds of millions of dollars in compensation? Keep up the good work! The price is right.

Proportion of wealth owned by top 1 per cent of population, over 50 per cent and climbing? You're worth it. The price is right.

Bankers earning massive bonuses at the same time as they break their banks? Kudos. The price is right.

So if any member of the world economy is unhappy or unsure about their statement, or if regulators smell a fish, or if someone just thinks the system is a little out of whack, or unfair, or in danger of some kind of collapse, then the NeoClassic Logic Piano will assure them that everything is OK. Look, it says: the price is right. Everything is in order. It's logical.

It's found that this nearly always helps to restore peace of mind. People go home secure in the knowledge that their wealth is being cared for and all is right with the world.

Is the price right?

A number of readers of earlier editions took umbrage with this idea that economists claim that market prices are the 'right price'. One wrote in 2016: 'Neoclassical economics has no such concept as the right price. We have short run socially optimal price (the price that equates supply and demand in a perfectly competitive market, which equals marginal costs); we have long run socially optimal price (the price of a perfectly competitive market, in which the free entry and exit of firms has pushed the market price to long run average cost); we have the market price (the price that equates supply and demand in any market). None of these is ever called by Neoclassical economists "the right price".'[7]

Economists often respond to a criticism by translating it into their own jargon, replete with made-up concepts based on fictional markets, and writing it off by saying that it makes no sense within that framework. The point here is not that economists use the expression 'the right price'; it is that they talk about markets pushing prices towards a stable equilibrium that reflects some kind of 'inherent value', subject to the usual disclaimer about market failures and so on. This is explicit in key theories such as the efficient market hypothesis; and more generally it is what underpins e.g. Alan Greenspan's faith in 'the global "invisible hand"' to create relatively stable prices, with 'notably rare exceptions'; or most of the tools used in quantitative finance; or for that matter much of the Western worldview (another expression not used much in economics).

As remarked on earlier, neoclassical economists spend much of their time researching small deviations from perfectly competitive markets, and relaxing individual economyths such as rationality; but in doing so, they actually strengthen the hold of these economyths, by providing excuses when things go wrong. Of course no economy lives up to their idealised version with its perfectly balanced competition, its rational consumers, its freedom from burdensome regulation – but that's not the economists' fault! This is one reason why so many outsiders (and some insiders) are calling for fundamental reform, while most mainstream economists call for markets to be more like their models. Greenspan's Panglossian comment, for example, was part of a warning against excessive regulation in 2011, just a few years after the global invisible hand had nearly destroyed the world economy.

So no, economists don't literally shout out 'The price is right!' (and nor is there actually a NeoClassic Logic Piano). But the reason neoclassical economists have long been considered the bane of environmentalists (see box, page 218 and notes), but the pampered servants of the financial sector (see box, page 234), is because the core message of their economyths is that market price is a good estimate of intrinsic value, subject to disclaimer. Or in slightly brusque English: the price is right.

The money game

A key difference between the 'world economy' scheme and a Ponzi scheme such as Madoff's is that a Ponzi scheme is entirely supported by new investment money, while the world economy is clearly highly productive. Those rising GDP figures aren't an illusion, they represent real economic and technological progress:

we're richer, healthier, better educated, and more mobile than at any time in history. However, both schemes are eventually doomed to hit a wall. Economic growth, as traditionally defined in terms of production and consumption, is unsustainable – not in the sense that it will be bad for the planet, but in the literal sense that *it's not going to happen*.

As discussed in Chapter 8, the world economy can be viewed as a kind of super-organism that takes in energy and raw materials, generates various objects and services for internal consumption, and expels waste to the environment. If we think of capital in terms of natural resources – e.g. sources of energy and raw materials – then we are living off the existing stores. Not a good thing. (I'd say they teach that in introductory economics, but apparently they don't.)

At the same time, our waste products are actively degrading the world's forests, oceans and atmosphere, thus leaving a horrendous bill for future generations. As ecological economists point out, it's like a Ponzi scheme, except that the new investors – 'suckers' in investor parlance – who support the whole thing haven't been born yet. They say a sucker is born every minute, but in this case it's not quite true. As Herman Daly wrote in 1991: 'The current beneficiaries … try hard to keep up the illusion among those doubters at the end who are beginning to wonder if there are really sufficient resources in the world for the game to continue very much longer.'[8]

Like the Ponzi scheme, the world economy funnels wealth up to a tiny elite. The other investors think or hope that one day they will join that select group. But again, it's not going to happen. If everyone on the planet lived like Americans, with the same environmental footprint, then we would need ten planets to support us all – and we don't have them. It's about as likely and as feasible as Madoff suddenly deciding, before he got caught, to return all his money to the investors, with interest. If everyone lived like Wall Street bankers, we'd need an entire galaxy.

Of course, with the world economy there is no single mastermind or organisation at the top. The scheme is not being orchestrated by the World Bank, or Goldman Sachs, or Bernie Madoff from his jail cell. It wasn't designed by William Stanley Jevons or Vilfredo Pareto or Milton Friedman. It is better described as an emergent feature of our society. The masterminds/investors are you and I.

And while Madoff was called a monster by those he ripped off, the world economy does not have evil intent. It's more of a giant game that has run out of control. One of the more entertaining moments of the crisis came in March 2009 when *Mad Money*'s Jim Cramer was invited to appear as a guest on *The Daily Show* with Jon Stewart. For several days, Stewart had been mocking the financial forecasts of Cramer and his colleagues: 'If I had only taken CNBC's advice, I would have a million dollars today – provided I started with $100 million.' During the much-hyped showdown with Cramer, viewed by over 2 million people, Stewart accused him of trying to turn finance into entertainment, but 'it's not a [expletive deleted] game'. He also showed old videos of Cramer explaining, a little too clearly, how hedge funds manipulate the markets.

While Stewart's point is well taken, the truth is that markets are in large part a game – it's up to us to set the rules. Unlike Madoff, we may have the self-control and the motivation to wind the scheme up before it does more harm. Without the neoclassical 'price is right' machine, the scheme can't function. The story won't stand. The whole structure will come crashing down of its own accord.

All we need to do is break into the metaphorical 17th floor, open the glass case, pick up the old computer, and smash it into pieces.

The price is wrong

The tricky part, obviously, is that the machine is guarded and maintained by a dedicated group – the orthodox economists – whose sole function is to protect it from interference. Their loyalty is guaranteed by the special bond of tenure – described by Pablo Triana as 'perhaps the biggest incentive for toeing the official line ever invented by humankind' – along with a good salary supplemented by lucrative contracts in the private sector.[9] Plus of course the economyth that economic growth, as measured by them, is inherently good. (As Steve Keen put it in 2017, neoclassical economists 'sincerely believe they're doing good, which is why they're so dangerous'.[10])

Even the recent economic crisis, or the looming environmental catastrophe, is not enough to create more than a seed of doubt in their collective mind. Economist James K. Galbraith, a critic of conventional theory, notes that: 'I don't detect any change at all … It's business as usual.' Asked whether the crisis would lead to any big changes in economics, Eugene Fama replied, 'I don't see any'.[11] The behavioural economist Robert J. Shiller, who knows a thing or two about human behaviour, told the *New York Times*: 'I fear that there will not be much change in basic paradigms. The rational expectations models will be tweaked to account for the current crisis. The basic curriculum will not change.'[12]

So what we can do instead is build an alternative, based on 21st-century knowledge and technology. Or better yet: a number of alternatives, all reasonably plausible, all giving answers that, although not in perfect agreement, still make more sense than those of the machine. The sound of 'the price is right' being called out over and over will be drowned out by a cacophony of new voices.

These new theories will draw their inspiration from new areas of applied mathematics, such as network theory, complexity, and nonlinear dynamics. The economy has always been a complex, dynamic, networked system; but the development of the internet, increasingly globalised supply chains, and computerised finance mean that it is more necessary than ever to model it with the appropriate tools. By mining and exploiting the vast amounts of data now available on economic transactions, these techniques will revolutionise the way we understand and visualise the economy.

The theories will treat the economy not as an inert machine, but as a kind of living organism. The models and techniques will therefore resemble those developed for life sciences like systems biology or ecology or medicine. Instead of seeing the economy as a self-contained, closed box, the theories will include interactions with the environment over long timescales. They will also avoid over-simplifying complex issues such as inequality, happiness, or climate change.

As an example of this approach, an editorial published simultaneously by the *British Medical Journal* and the *Lancet* in 2009 wrote that our high-carbon economy is causing a range of environmental, political and health problems, particularly in poor countries. These include atmospheric pollution, deforestation, loss of biodiversity, extreme weather, drought, water shortages, spread of diseases, famine, and conflict. On the other hand: 'The measures needed to combat climate change coincide with those needed to ensure a healthier population and reduce the burden on health services. A low-carbon economy will mean less pollution. A low-carbon diet (especially eating less meat) and more exercise will mean less cancer, obesity, diabetes, and heart disease … This is an opportunity too to advance health equity, which is increasingly seen as necessary for a healthy and happy society.'[13] We need joined-up solutions to joined-up problems.

The theories will relax the neoclassical obsession with 'hard' equations and numbers, and adopt a more nuanced and multi-faceted approach. While they will take advantage of the new social and financial and environmental data being produced, they will not devalue things such as happiness or sustainability or the worth of other species just because they are hard to measure. They will consider new metrics, such as the Genuine Progress Indicator or the Happy Planet Index. They will also acknowledge the limitations of mathematical models and statistical measures, and balance them with words and narratives.

The theories will benefit from the insights of a diverse range of people including environmentalists, feminists, psychologists, and political scientists. Such collaborations will not be easily forged in traditional university settings, which divide researchers into finer and finer specialities. We therefore need new multi-disciplinary centres that place experts from diverse backgrounds into close proximity to work on shared projects.

And once we start to treat the economy as a living thing rather than a machine, we will have to consider a field that dates back even further than the 'price is right' logic machine: that of ethics.

Fuzzy logic

According to mainstream economics, both the economy and the entire planet are inert objects that blindly go about their actions, slave to the law of cause and effect. Apart from extreme cases like murder, there isn't much point in trying to second-guess whether an action is good or bad, because the answer is implicit in the market price. As economists M. Neil Browne and J. Kevin Quinn note: 'economists distinctly do not question the moral worth of market prices and wages.'[14] If something is good, then many people will want it, and its price will go up. The price is right. Neoclassical economics isn't a theory, it's an excuse.

If, however, we abandon the idea that the economy is an efficient machine, and the markets are as all-seeing as the eye that adorns the pyramid on the US one-dollar bill, then we need an alternative frame of reference. Unfortunately, our reliance on the 'price is right' principle seems to have atrophied our ability to make ethical judgements.

Taking market norms to their logical limit ends with situations like the mortgage mis-selling that contributed to the subprime crisis; or the commodity price spike of 2008, when the financial community transformed basic necessities like wheat and oil into volatile and unaffordable assets.[15] As investment manager Michael Masters testified to a US Senate committee: 'If Wall Street concocted a scheme whereby investors bought large amounts of pharmaceutical drugs and medical devices in order to profit from the resulting increase in prices, making these essential items unaffordable to sick and dying people, society would be justly outraged.'[16] (Martin Shkreli, who learned his trade working at Jim Cramer's hedge fund, did something a little like this in 2015 when as CEO of Turing Pharmaceuticals he famously raised the price of an anti-parasitic drug by a factor of 56, which some saw as parasitic behaviour.[17]) To address such issues we need a system of ethics that allows for fuzzy, graded statements instead of binary right/wrong, good/evil divisions. Trading for profit isn't always good or always bad, it's on a sliding scale that depends on the context. Adair Turner: 'It is much easier to proceed in life on the assumption that either all markets are axiomatically good, or all speculation evil. The reality is more complex and requires us to make trade-offs and judgements. But there is no alternative to that complexity.'[18] Economists can help us to navigate the terrain, but not before acknowledging the limitations of their models, which are no substitute for a moral compass.

That's entertainment

Consider for example the vexed issue of bankers' bonuses. After the crunch, these were defended by bank executives on the grounds that bankers are like entertainment stars, and firms have to pay whatever it takes to get the best talent. Their activities also make a significant contribution to GDP. Stuart Gulliver from HSBC compared his team to Hollywood actors. John Varley, the chief executive of Barclays, preferred the football analogy. 'There is simply no higher priority than to ensure we field the very best people. That in a sense is exactly the same as a football manager if they are going to win. Our obligation is to ensure we pay appropriately.'[19] Bill George, a director of Goldman Sachs, went for both: 'It's much like professional athletes and movie stars.'[20] Perhaps fearing a backlash, the London Investment Banking Association – which represents firms including Goldman Sachs, Morgan Stanley and JPMorgan Chase – criticised a plan to publish bonuses on the grounds that it would 'create the potential for ill-informed and populist public commentary on reasonable remuneration practices'.[21]

This topic might seem like a distraction, but it does bring up a number of interesting technical points that also apply to other aspects of the economy:

- The salaries of bankers do follow the same dynamics as those of CEOs or entertainment stars (Chapter 7). That doesn't mean they are appropriate or reasonable. According to one UK survey, 96 per cent of people believed that Premier League footballers are overpaid.[22]

- We are a little more willing to tolerate high salaries in the case of actors or sports stars because they are *entertaining* and don't *crash the economy*. Important hint: bankers don't get asked for autographs.

- Nonetheless, many sports leagues such as the National Football League and the National Hockey League in North America have instituted salary caps to level the playing field.

- In England, professional footballers today do earn massive salaries similar to those of top bankers. But they don't play that well as a team. The last time England won the World Cup was 1966, when salaries were orders of magnitude smaller.

- Mathematical models predicting movie box office returns have shown that actors and directors play a surprisingly small role in determining ticket sales.[23] Salaries therefore say more about the Hollywood star system than about profitability. Harrison Ford became famous because of *Star Wars*, not vice versa.

- Banks have an important positional advantage in the economy. For example, the fractional reserve system sanctions them the power to effectively produce money by lending out more than they have. Such rights and benefits are a property of the financial network as a whole, rather than individuals.

- Companies are also reliant for success on institutional reputation, not just lone stars. Lehman Brothers, for example, was founded in 1850 and had a formidable reputation which helped it attract business.

- In finance, skill is important, but so is luck. If 100 traders take high-risk leveraged bets over a period of several years, there will be a big spread in results by chance alone. That doesn't mean the winner is a genius.

- Large bonuses incentivise traders to make reckless decisions, resulting in 'negative externalities' such as global recessions.

- In the UK, the financial sector did make an outsized contribution to GDP before it had to be rescued following the credit crunch.[24] However, its growth coincided with a decline in manufacturing and technology – not surprising when the default destination for talented science students is finance – along with a rise in problems associated with social inequality.[25] Instead of needing protection, maybe it's just too big.

Finally, you don't need to be the Pope to see that there is an ethical dimension to all this. Although as it happens, Pope Benedict did speak out against the culture of greed, saying that: 'He who builds only on visible and tangible things like success, career and money, builds the house of his life on sand.'[26] As discussed in Chapter 4, when sand piles get too high they have a tendency to fall down. Rowan Williams, the Archbishop of Canterbury, told the BBC that bonuses should be capped, and said: 'What we are looking at is the possibility of a society getting more and more dysfunctional if the levels of inequality that we have seen in the last couple of decades are not challenged.'[27] When a sector like finance or natural resources becomes too large, it also fosters rent-seeking behaviour (extracting income without contributing to real productivity) and the growth of a corrupt and dependent political class.

At a speech to a banquet of dignitaries in 2009, the Lord Mayor of London, Ian Luder, said: 'It is banking activity, international banking activity, which makes the world go round.'[28] But the reality is that banking is just one of many vital services supporting the economy. The main thing that makes it unusual, for such an important profession, is its failure to develop sound ethical standards. Doctors and engineers have ethical codes; bankers have dress codes.

One positive aspect of the controversy over banker compensation was that it helped destroy the illusion that salaries accurately reflect a person's contribution to society, and showed the importance of ethics and fairness. A more important issue is of course the salaries earned by the bottom 50 per cent of the world's population. In terms of the movie analogy, they are currently the equivalent of the extras in a Hollywood film who get their appearance cut from the final scene. They are the children playing football on the Brazilian beach who don't get spotted by talent scouts and sold to Manchester United. But if we change our definition of economic efficiency to that of the Happy Planet Index – in which the aim is to be happy while consuming few resources – then they have more to teach us than our financial elite.

Dirty oil

Another example of an ethical quandary is from my home province of Alberta, whose boundaries happen to include the planet's largest reservoir of bitumen – a form of crude oil mixed with sand, minerals and water. Companies including Suncor, Syncrude and Shell have found that they can extract the crude oil, either by first scraping up the land or by using newer *in situ* techniques, and sell it on the open market at a profit. By normal economic accounting procedures, the operation makes a lot of money and boosts GDP. On the negative side, it also destroys vast swaths of the boreal forest, consumes incredible quantities of water, emits equally incredible amounts of pollution in the extraction process, and has blackened Canada's reputation as a green country.[29] The expression 'low-carbon economy' is not what comes to mind.

There has long been local opposition to oil sands development from environmental organisations, indigenous groups, academics, and others.[30] In August 2009, though, the oil sands became a hot political topic in, of all places, Norway. The Norwegian company Statoil started a $2 billion project in Alberta in 2007. But during the 2009 election campaign, most of the Norwegian political parties came out against the involvement. An editorial in the main newspaper *Aftenposten* wrote that Statoil and the government were showing a 'collective denial of responsibility' for oil sands emissions. The leader of the Christian Democrats party, Dagfinn Hoybraaten, said that: 'in our view, this is more than a regular business issue. It's an overall ethical issue.'[31]

The response of Alberta premier Ed Stelmach was: 'I'm not aware of Statoil. All I know is these last couple of weeks there has been just a huge renewed interest ... more and more news [is] coming from large pension fund managers that are looking at Alberta as a great place to invest.'

Albertans are famously resistant to suggestions from outsiders on how to manage said resources. It is also probably true that oil sand emissions are less of a threat to the planet than, say, Chinese or American coal. But two things are clear. First, Hoybraaten is right – there is an overall ethical issue, which needs to be discussed. Second, pension fund managers aren't paid to make ethical decisions or enforce standards. That's one of the jobs of governments. So when we delegate sensitive decisions to pension funds, there is a problem. Why should fund managers argue that we cap the rate of oil sands production, give the land time to repair, or spend money on improving the technology, if these harm short-term profits? Again, market norms are no substitute for ethics.

Nor can we delegate ethical decisions to our role as consumers or investors. One property of ethical violations is that their impact seems to decay with distance and separation. If we all bought our clothes directly from the people who made them, then their working conditions would probably loom somewhat larger in our consciousness than they presently do. With global supply chains, it's rarely clear where the objects we consume even come from, and we can't factor ethical decisions into judgements of price. We therefore need strong institutions and laws that enforce ethical standards at source in a uniform and democratic fashion.

It is encouraging that developments like the oil sands or

climate change are increasingly being framed in an ethical rather than a purely market context, because once ethical judgements are established, in the form of laws or social taboos, they tend to be long-lasting and will eventually outweigh even the profit motive.[32] Market forces may not be able to pick up the opinions of future generations, but our sense of ethics can. (Update: in December 2016 Statoil's Senior Vice President for Sustainability Bjørn Otto Sverdrup announced on Twitter their 'exit of oil sands which bends our cost and emissions curves'.[33] Ours too.)

Markets are enormously powerful tools for making a number of economic decisions. As someone who has spent almost his entire career in the private sector, I'm as involved in markets as most people. However, their strengths are overrated by ideologues. Markets by themselves are not responsible for innovation. Many of the technological advances of the 20th century – including the decades of development that led to the internet – actually took place in government labs or in heavily subsidised military programmes (economists should know this, given that the development of neoclassical economics also owes much of its success to funding by the US government during the ideological battles of the Cold War).[34] We live longer and healthier lives in large part because of work done at publicly-funded hospitals. Research and development is often best carried out in less competitive, less bottom-line, more cooperative environments. What markets excel at is selecting the best new technologies and turning them into successful products. The public, private, and non-profit sectors have synergistic roles – we need them all.

In fact, modern technology would be nowhere without the basic tools of mathematics and physics, which were also not developed by markets or private corporations. This points to the role of universities in shaping our attitudes towards the economy.

Book prize

Ethics is another tricky subject where it is sometimes hard to know what is up and what is down. For example: in 2011 this book, counter to most commonly accepted notions of literary taste, was nominated for the National Business Book Award in Canada. I was invited to a very nice event in Toronto, and put up with my family in a luxurious hotel suite, and wasn't in the least surprised or taken aback (and readers won't be either) that the award was given to another book that I hadn't heard of before, *Ethical Oil: The Case for Canada's Oil Sands*, by the Albertan lawyer and media personality Ezra Levant.

Levant's basic argument, I later learned, is that by a number of scores – including environmentalism and feminism – Canada is ethically superior to other big oil producers like Saudi Arabia or Venezuela, so our oil is too.[35] This logic made sense to the Conservative government headed by then-prime minister Stephen Harper, who immediately began using the 'ethical oil' angle to promote the oil sands. The fact that the book prize came with a large cheque also perked the interest of lawyer and former Conservative party staffer Alykhan Velshi, who according to *Maclean's* magazine 'told Levant that, in return for the $20,000 prize money, he would launch an Ethical Oil blog that would form the basis for a political movement'.[36]

One of the priorities for the duly-formed EthicalOil.org was to call for a review of the charitable status of leading environmental organisations, on the basis that they were involved in political activities. By 2014, according to the CBC, the Canadian Revenue Agency had assembled an 'A-team' to investigate Environmental Defence Canada, the Pembina Institute, the David Suzuki Foundation, and so on. John Bennett, of

Sierra Club Canada (targeted the following year), called it a 'war against the sector'.[37] As discussed further in the Appendix, the ethical oil movement found an ally of convenience with mainstream economists, who had other bones to pick with environmentalists.

So to summarise: the prize money for a book claiming that Canadian oil is ethical – in part because of the country's environmental protections – is used to set up a website, named after the book, that is largely devoted to combatting environmentalists. (I have no idea what I would have spent the money on, but I'm sure it wouldn't have been nearly as imaginative.) When I described it in the first edition of this book as 'encouraging that developments like the oil sands or climate change are increasingly being framed in an ethical rather than a purely market context', this isn't exactly what I had in mind. The question is not so much where the oil comes from, as where it goes (or stays). And rather than Canada's ethical standing in a number of areas acting to legitimise the oil sands, it is more that the oil sands issue is compromising that standing: polls showed a sharp deterioration in the way Canada was viewed in the world from around 2009, exactly because of 'our failure to move aggressively on climate change'.[38]

Since then, things have moved on. Alberta has a new provincial government which seems to tolerate environmentalists, and has even implemented a carbon tax. In 2015, Canada's new Minister of National Revenue mentioned in her mandate letter the need for 'charities to do their work on behalf of Canadians free from political harassment'.[39] At the same time, though, the federal government continues to dole out billion-dollar subsidies to oil and gas producers.[40] The IMF estimated in 2015 that around the world, global subsidies amount to $5.3 trillion, which is more than governments spend on health.

The question of how to balance these priorities – and here I agree with Levant – comes down to ethics; especially since, as the UN points out, many of the so-called negative externalities of climate change tend to fall on 'the poor and the vulnerable'.[41] I do wonder, though, how much they care if the carbon in their air was ethically-sourced – it's not like they are ordering it as an appetiser in an upscale Calgary restaurant. Similarly, in his 2015 encyclical *On Care For Our Common Home*, Pope Francis mentioned 'highly polluting fossil fuels', whose use needs to be 'progressively replaced without delay', but for some reason failed to bless ethical oil. Instead he said that it has become 'easy to accept the idea of infinite or unlimited growth, which proves so attractive to economists, financiers and experts in technology', and warned that we must 'reject a magical conception of the market, which would suggest that problems can be solved simply by an increase in the profits of companies or individuals. Is it realistic to hope that those who are obsessed with maximizing profits will stop to reflect on the environmental damage which they will leave behind for future generations?'[42] (Of course, orthodox economists might complain that he is a non-economist, is attacking a straw man, is promoting another magical system of thinking, and so on – but by so thoroughly scrubbing ethics from their field, they have rather disqualified themselves from the debate.)

'In war', said Seneca, 'there is no prize for runner-up'. But as Naomi Klein notes, it is 'our economic system and our planetary system' that are 'now at war'.[43] No prizes for figuring out who will win that one.

Breaking the piano

The NeoClassic Logic Piano owes its continued existence in large part to university academics, who keep it buffed and maintained and protected for the next generation. This involvement goes well beyond the economics departments. Universities divide subjects into minute specialities and have traditionally tried to keep them separate (there are signs that this is beginning to change).[44] Economic decisions affect most aspects of life in one way or another, though, so everyone else should at least have an opinion.

Some pending questions:

How does the physics department feel about economic ideas masquerading as laws of nature, or economists fostering a comparison between their own field and physics?

Do the humanities departments agree with the story that society is made up of individuals who act independently? If not, how is that being reflected in the education of future business leaders?

Is the mathematics department OK with the kinds of models used in economics classes? Are assumptions of things like stability plausible?

What do mechanical engineers think of the safety margin used by 'financial engineers'?

Is the gender studies department cool with the definition of *Homo economicus*?

Do sociologists agree that societies always behave rationally or almost rationally? Do neoclassical tools make sense in an increasingly networked society in which one of the most valuable commodities – information – can be distributed at near zero cost?

Are political scientists sure that economics is politically neutral? Are historians convinced that neoclassical economics is an objective science and not a cultural artefact shaped by a certain period of history? What will be the impact of non-Western countries with different political and economic ideas and agendas?

Do ecologists think that the environment is taken seriously enough in economics textbooks? If they seriously believe that we are in danger of a survival-threateningly huge environmental crisis, is the introductory economics class at their institution increasing or decreasing the risk?

What does the psychology department think of the definition of utility, or the economics of happiness?

Are philosophers in agreement that markets can make ethical decisions? Are university ethics committees concerned that the content of economics courses, and the types of questions being addressed, might be influenced when key staff members are moonlighting in the financial industry? And does anyone think it's acceptable or appropriate for academic economists – who have a special role in society as publicly-funded arbitrators of knowledge – to attempt to repress the ideas of heterodox economists or others, without giving them a proper hearing?

And finally, how do elite institutions like Harvard University, Oxford University, Massachusetts Institute of Technology, or California Institute of Technology feel about the fact that in 2007, at the start of the crisis, 20 or 30 or more per cent of their graduates went straight into the financial sector? Are these institutions being used as a filter or barrier of entry to select talented students for this overpaid and socially under-productive area?[45] If that is the case, shouldn't the universities at least revise their teaching to better reflect new theories and approaches, not to mention ethics?

Until university departments break down the artificial divisions that separate their subjects, the NeoClassic Logic Piano will be safe. The best hope for change probably comes not from university administrators, but from the ones with most at stake – the students. They are the ones who are being fed the story about the economy. If they decide not to buy in, then that will be it.

One excuse heard for the lack of progress in economics is that academia changes only slowly. But that isn't true at all. Nothing much happens for a long time, but when change comes, it is often sudden and violent – like an earthquake, or indeed a financial crash. Early in the last century, physics was completely rewritten in the space of a few years. Biology has been revolutionised by recent technological advances such as the human genome project.

So: students. Decision time. You live at what many believe is a bifurcation point in human history. You've seen all the graphs with lines curving up like a ski jump. Human population. Gross domestic product. Species extinction. Carbon emissions. Inequality. Resource shortages. You know that something has to give. You've got an idea that the price isn't right. Maybe you're even suspicious that, if the world economy does turn out to be a Ponzi scheme, you or your children are a little bit late in the game.

You therefore stand at a fork in the road. You can take the orthodox route – and risk ending up with a qualification as impressive as a degree in Marxist ideology right after the fall of the Berlin Wall. Or you can take a chance on regime shift, by speaking up, questioning your teachers, being open to disruptive ideas, and generally acting as an agent of change.

You can insist that the economy is a complex, dynamic, networked system – and demand the tools to understand it.

You can point out that the economy is unfair, unstable, and unsustainable – and demand the skills to heal it.

You can tell the oracles that they have failed.

You can go in and break the machine.

And then you can do something new.

A new economics
Of course, there's a risk to taking such a path. But it is no bigger than the one taken by those maverick outsiders Jevons, Walras and Pareto when they developed neoclassical economics.

For a theory to last 150 years is a triumph, of sorts. For it to last one more decade will be a disaster. It was perhaps the right story for a certain period of history, or the one that people wanted to hear, but it has far outlived its usefulness.

Since the credit crunch, stock markets have made back much of their losses. However, there is less oil in the ground, and more carbon in the sky. Debt levels have continued to climb, and inequality in many countries has increased. The financial sector is more concentrated than before. The real problems haven't gone away, only intensified slightly.

Where there are plenty of green shoots appearing is in the new economic ideas being developed by a range of scientists and thinkers and practitioners. Their theories may look scattered and unrelated, but if this book has one message, it is that they are all part of a semi-coherent movement. Instead of seeing the economy as an efficient, deterministic machine, running on automatic, they see it as a living thing that we can consciously influence, for better or worse.

The world economy has grown up, and the ancient myths are losing their power. The new story that's emerging isn't simple, or particularly flattering – we're less rational or efficient or fair or good in this version. It turns out that we're not all super-heroes with the ability to look far into the future and make perfect decisions. (Which is a shame, because those powers would be quite useful right now.)

We will never be able to perfectly model the economy, or eliminate the chance of another financial disaster. But we're living in a bubble, and we need to address our debt. I'm loath to make predictions, but in my opinion the next big crash won't be about money. It won't be triggered by bankers or mathematicians. It will be about something much more real. We have a line of credit with the rest of the planet, and it's flashing red. Soon it's going to get called in. We can't grow our way out, or work more hours. We can't hand back the keys and walk away. It's our home.

We need some household rule. We need a new economics.

Good versus evil

In his 2001 book *Economics as Religion*, the economist Robert Nelson argued that during the 20th century economists – exemplified by Paul Samuelson with his 'bible' textbook *Economics* – began to resemble 'the priesthood of a modern secular religion of economic progress that serves many of the same functions in contemporary society as earlier Christian and other religions did in their time'. Unlike other religions, though, ethics didn't play much of a role – or rather it was subsumed into mathematics. Who needs ethics when the model can decide what is good?

In 2010, when the first edition of this book came out, ethics was therefore decidedly absent from economics. As Tomáš Sedláček wrote in his *Economics of Good and Evil*, the topic had been neglected to the point where it was 'almost heretical to even talk about it'.[46] The economist George DeMartino similarly observed that there were 'no professional economic ethicists, or any texts, journals, newsletters, curriculum, regular conferences, or other forums that explore systematically what it means to be an ethical economist, or what it means for economics to be an ethical profession'. In 2016, he helped to fill the gap by co-editing *The Oxford Handbook of Professional Economic Ethics*, which included a chapter from Sedláček.[47] So economists at least now have a manual.

This is useful, because economic models are used all the time to make key ethical decisions involving complex trade-offs. Consider for example Larry Summers' memo about dumping toxic waste (Chapter 8). As Richard Denniss, Chief Economist for The Australia Institute, wrote in 2015: 'Summers claims that the memo was meant to be sarcastic and ironic, but, as anyone who has studied economics can assure you, the logic (if not the morality) is unquestionable.'[48] Such assumptions 'sit at the heart of the economic models' that are regularly used to 'prevent the introduction of environmental regulations or more generous welfare safety nets'. He also notes that 'Much of the power of economists is based on the public's (understandable) lack of desire to read reports written in algebra. That's why we like to use algebra.'

The economic priesthood plays a particularly important role in designing financial regulations, which raises the issue of another type of non-transparency. As one example, the blurb from Princeton University Press for a book called *The Squam Lake Report: Fixing the Financial System* says that: 'In the fall of 2008, fifteen of the world's leading economists – representing the broadest spectrum of economic opinion – gathered at New Hampshire's Squam Lake. Their goal: the mapping of a long-term plan for financial regulation reform … Arguing that there has been a conflict between financial institutions and society, these diverse experts present sound and transparent prescriptions to reduce this divide.'[49] Less transparent was the fact that most of the men behind this influential report (the 'broadest spectrum' was neither broad, nor inclusive of broads) were themselves highly involved in the sector they were supposed to be reforming. As economists Jessica Carrick-Hagenbarth and Gerald A. Epstein found, 'economists almost never reveal their financial associations when they make public pronouncements on issues such as financial regulation'.[50] This involvement might explain why, as Philip Mirowski describes, the report was 'more intently slanted toward codification of the minimum that the banking sector could get away with in the tense political aftermath of the debacle of the crisis, rather than any serious attempt to rethink the financial sector from the ground up'.[51]

Similarly, a Reuters study of '96 testimonies given by 82 academics to the Senate Banking Committee and the House Financial Services Committee between late 2008 and early 2010 – as lawmakers debated the biggest overhaul of financial regulation since the 1930s – found no clear standard for disclosure. In fact, roughly a third did not reveal their financial affiliations in their testimonies.'[52] Reuters uncovered a number of examples where economists listed academic affiliations, but neglected to mention that they also consulted for companies which would be affected by the regulation under discussion. Some economists have since become more forthcoming about declaring their affiliations, but as Carrick-Hagenbarth and Epstein observe, 'academic economists who offer economic medicine should reveal potential conflicts of interest just as readily as should medical doctors prescribing pharmaceuticals' (which is another issue).

Business schools also foster a cavalier approach towards ethical questions, with real implications for the economy. The problem, it seems, is not so much in *resolving* such questions, as in spotting them in the first place. According to ethicist Edward Queen, writing in 2015 after the Volkswagen emissions scandal, 'observational and anecdotal evidence suggests that business students are not only impaired in their moral judgments but that significant percentages of them have severely impaired moral imaginations ... Numerous interviews with business ethics faculty I have had over the past decade suggest that when business students are presented with an ethics case, that is a case where they have been told that there is an ethical problem, 20 percent to 30 percent of the students cannot find or identify the ethical issue.'[53] One case study would be the widespread fraud that contributed to the financial crisis, but received little attention because of everyone's faith in market forces. As James K. Galbraith told the US Senate back in 2010, 'Economists have soft-pedaled the role of fraud in every crisis they examined'.[54]

Julie Nelson wrote in 2016: 'We seriously undermine the ability of the economy to do its job – that is, to provide for the sustaining and flourishing of life – if we continue to imagine it as an ethics-free and care-free sphere. Economic dogmas, misleadingly presented as scientific and widely disseminated through education and the media, are largely to blame for this damage. The field of economics is far overdue for a thorough-going ethical wake-up call.'[55] The first place to start is perhaps with economics itself, and the numerous conflicts of interest that exist between academia and the financial sector. These are especially a problem given that an overly large financial sector both fuels inequality, and acts as a drag on the economy.[56] Economists are going to need that ethics handbook.

CHAPTER 11

THE TWO-FACED ECONOMY

Money plays the largest part in
determining the course of history.
Karl Marx, *The Communist Manifesto* (1848)

There cannot, in short, be intrinsically a more insignificant
thing, in the economy of society, than money.
John Stuart Mill, *Principles of Political Economy* (1848)

Our final economyth is not really an independent myth, but is better viewed as a justification or enabler for the other myths. The myth sounds fairly innocuous – it states only that the economy can be viewed as a kind of barter system. But without this key assumption, all the others fall apart – which may explain why it rarely gets discussed in proper economic circles. This new chapter looks at the role, or rather the lack thereof, of money in economics – and shows how bringing it back into the picture changes everything.

Reflecting on his spell serving as co-editor for the heterodox journal *Economic Thought*, the Mexican economist Alejandro Nadal wrote in 2015 that 'money, without doubt the most important economic object, remains a problem area where origin and nature are hotly debated. The fact that money was exiled from the analysis of market processes as the discipline was being born and that this tradition has been maintained until our days is one of the most outstanding facts of economic theory … the problem remains largely unsolved and microeconomics continues to be developed in terms of relative prices in a non-monetary context.'[1]

Umm, what? The problem of money is not just unsolved, it has actually been *exiled*? That does seem like a bit of an omission. Isn't economics supposed to be about money? It's one thing to miss out irrationality, instability, the planet, and so on, but the stuff you actually *buy things with*? I know I'm just a mathematician with no firm grasp of subtle details etc., but surely that is kind of a gaping hole in the theory, a blind spot in the expert knowledge, like saying that doctors haven't quite figured out the role of the red sticky stuff so are just going to ignore it for now, though it would be great if it stopped leaking out when people are being treated?

And anyway, there are plenty of university courses about money, banking, finance, and so on. So why would Nadal say that money was 'exiled' from the subject?

But Nadal, it seems, is not alone. Here is Martin Wolf, chief economics commentator for the *Financial Times*, saying that the teaching of economics leaves students thinking we operate in a 'barter system where money acts as a veil';[2] Steve Keen in a lecture, stating that the main reason central banks were surprised by the crisis was because their models include 'neither money nor banks nor debt';[3] Stephanie Kelton, in another talk, asserting that 'Money, debt and finance don't even fit into many economic models.'[4] Come to think of it, even I noticed in Chapter 5 that 'models do not properly account for the role of the financial sector (which in a perfect economy isn't necessary). The Bank of England's general equilibrium model, for example, omits banks.'

Sure, these are just commentators or heterodox economists working on the fringe of real mainstream economics. But why would former Bank of England governor Mervyn King, who spent his career dealing with money, state that 'most economists hold conversations in which the word "money" hardly appears at all'?[5]

Or complain that in standard macroeconomic models, 'money, credit and banking play no meaningful role'.[6] What, in short, is going on?

But wait, here is Paul Krugman to set us straight, and sum up the conventional mainstream view in plain language. Writing in his blog in 2015, he says: 'in some sense money is a really weird thing, which can look to individuals like a real asset – cold, hard, cash – but is ultimately, as Paul Samuelson put it, a "social contrivance" whose value is more or less conjured out of thin air. Mainstream macroeconomics acknowledges the weirdness – in particular, makes heavy reliance on the ability of central banks to create more fiat money at will – but otherwise treats money a lot like ordinary goods. But that intellectual strategy doesn't come naturally to many people, so there's always a constituency for monetary cranks.'[7]

Oh, I get it now! So this idea of treating the economy as a barter system, with money just another good (except that central banks have an infinite supply of the stuff), is an *intellectual strategy*! Like rationality, or equilibrium. How clever. The technicians have it under control. The idea that money, debt, finance, etc. have gone missing is a caricature, a misunderstanding caused by lack of seminars (see Appendix). And it explains why there are all those cranks. Like Frederick Soddy, the 'monetary crank' (as he was called) who turned his talents towards economics after winning a real Nobel in chemistry in 1921, muttering all that crazy stuff about the dangers of money creation by banks, and becoming a pioneer of ecological economics.

Actually, Krugman mentions money creation by *central* banks, which is what mainstream economists do tend to focus on. But the reality, as noted by the Bank of England, is that the vast majority of money is created by *private* banks, by issuing loans.[8] When you take a mortgage out from a bank, they don't go to the central bank and ask for the sum – they just create it as an entry in their accounts. The central bank only controls this process indirectly, by adjusting things such as the inter-bank interest rate. I think that was one of Soddy's points, when he described this ability to 'create and destroy money by adding and withdrawing figures in bank ledgers, without the slightest concern for the interests of the community' as being both unjust and a threat to democracy.[9] That's why he supported full-reserve banking.

Also, without wanting to come across as all cranky: if money is something like a commodity, an ordinary good, it does seem to have some highly unusual properties, for example the way it can suddenly disappear – as in the 2007–08 financial crisis – or act as a kind of straitjacket – as in the Eurozone Crisis. How did our intellectual strategy cope there?

Also – just a thought – should practitioners of a field based on the idea that prices measure an invisible energy-like quantity known as 'utility' really be calling other people cranks?

No, I still don't get it. I'm struggling here. What is money? Where did it come from? Where did it go, if it's not in the models? And how do you ignore something like that for so long?

Hit the books

To answer these questions, I first consulted a modern bestselling textbook on the subject: the thirteenth edition (!) of *Economics*, by Ragan and Lipsey. According to them, money emerged as a replacement for barter: 'If there were no money, goods would have to be exchanged by barter … The major difficulty with barter is that each transaction requires a double coincidence of wants … The use of money as a medium of exchange solves this problem.'[10]

Fortunately the book was free, because I'd happened to find it in a box of books being given away, probably by a student who had been forced to buy it under duress, so in this case neither barter nor money were involved. The authors went on: 'All sorts of commodities have been used as money at one time or another, but gold and silver proved to have great advantages ... The invention of coinage eliminated the need to weigh the metal at each transaction, but it created an important role for an authority, usually a king or queen, who made the coins and affixed his or her seal, guaranteeing the amount of precious metal that the coin contained.'

This seemed clear enough. Commodity money emerged from barter. The best commodities, for various reasons, were gold and silver. The only role of government was to come along at the end and put its stamp on the coins. It all made sense. And it would explain why no one cares about money – it is just a passive intermediary, a tool to facilitate barter.[11]

But reading it, something seemed a little familiar, as if I had heard it somewhere else. So I decided to find out what had been written about the subject elsewhere. A similar account is provided in Samuelson's 'bible' textbook *Economics*. William Stanley Jevons, it turned out, had also said much the same thing. As had Carl Menger, even Adam Smith, and for that matter countless other economists. But the trail eventually led all the way back to the philosopher himself: Aristotle.

In *Politics*, Aristotle wrote that the 'more complex form of exchange [money] grew, as might have been inferred, out of the simpler [barter] ... the various necessaries of life are not easily carried about, and hence men agreed to employ in their dealings with each other something which was intrinsically useful and easily applicable to the purposes of life, for example, iron, silver, and the like. Of this the value was at first measured simply by size and weight, but in process of time they put a stamp upon it, to save the trouble of weighing and to mark the value.'

So the official textbook story about the origins of money has remained essentially unchanged since antiquity. Which is strange, for two reasons. First, most textbooks have been updated since

Aristotle's time – we don't still think the planets are set in crystalline spheres that rotate around the earth. Second, the theory – as a little more research showed – turns out to be wrong.

One thing that struck me about these accounts was the lack of dates, references, or supporting details. The British economist Alfred Mitchell-Innes had a similar suspicion: 'So universal is the belief in these theories among economists that they have grown to be considered almost as axioms which hardly require proof, and nothing is more noticeable in economic works than the scant historical evidence on which they rest, and the absence of critical examination of their worth.'[12] He went on: 'Modern research in the domain of commercial history and numismatics, and especially recent discoveries in Babylonia, have brought to light a mass of evidence which was not available to the earlier economists, and in the light of which it may be positively stated that none of these theories rest on a solid basis of historical proof – that in fact they are false.'

Wow! So how has this 'modern research' impacted the field of economics? Not much, apparently. Because Mitchell-Innes wrote that over a century ago, in 1913. According to anthropologists, economies based purely on barter don't appear to ever have existed. Instead, money has its roots in a virtual credit system created 5,000 years ago in ancient Mesopotamia. Coin money came later, and ever since, money has alternated between spells where it is based primarily on credit (the Middle Ages, modern fiat currencies), and on precious metals (ancient Greece and Rome, the gold standard).[13]

It is perhaps understandable that Aristotle got it wrong, since his Lyceum didn't have an anthropology department, but why are economics textbooks still repeating the same story thousands of years later? Is the creation story of money some kind of super-economyth? And could it be related to the claim by Nadal and others that money has been exiled from economics? Is money just a score-keeping system, or is it something more? What, to insist again, is money, and why don't economists want to talk about it?

An insignificant thing

It isn't quite true, of course, that economists don't talk about money. Even when John Stuart Mill described money as an 'insignificant thing' in his seminal textbook, he still devoted several subsequent chapters to exploring its mechanics. As discussed in Chapter 5, monetarists such as Milton Friedman emphasised the importance of controlling the money supply. The point is that, when it comes to analysing exchange, money has been treated as an inert intermediary for barter, or a metric of value, rather than something with a life of its own.[14] This is reflected in our theories of money.

Just as money has oscillated, in emphasis at least, between real metal and virtual credit, so have our ideas about this mysterious substance. What is it, for example, that makes money valuable? Is it an intrinsic property, or an extrinsic property assigned by the state? Bullionists on the one side argue that money needs to based on a weight of precious metal, which gives it intrinsic value; while chartalists emphasise the role of the government, which backs the value of its money by accepting it for payments such as taxes.[15]

In 1912, the US banker J.P. Morgan testified that 'Money is gold, and nothing else'. But according to a paper from Mitchell-Innes that came out about six months later, 'Credit alone is money. Credit and not gold or silver is the one property which all men seek, the acquisition of which is the aim and object of all commerce.' Both these positions have their adherents today, with the difference that people who trust only in gold, which was the orthodox position under the gold standard, are now called 'gold bugs', while those who insist that money is based on government credit are known as 'neo-chartalists' (another name for this position is 'Modern Monetary Theory' – of course there is a range of opinions, but these are the two main opposing camps).

Most mainstream economists, though, prefer to keep out of the argument and take a neutral position. According to them, money has no unique or special qualities, but – following Jevons – is instead defined by its roles, e.g. as a medium of exchange, a store of value, and a unit of account.[16] In particular economists tend to emphasise the first: Samuelson, for example, defined money in *Economics* as 'anything that serves as a commonly accepted medium of exchange'. One consequence of this approach is that economic questions are reduced to abstract calculations of utility, which is assumed to be directly related to price. This is again consistent with the creation myth that money emerged as a facilitator of barter, and has no special importance in itself.

But it seems to be sidestepping the question of what makes money valuable – what alchemy it is that transfers a piece of paper, or for that matter a string of digital information in the form of a bitcoin (which is neither made of precious metal, nor mandated by the state), into something precious? To answer this question (as with many others in this book), we need to go back once again to the Pythagoreans.

Number is all

As stated in Chapter 1, 'Money is a way of assigning numbers to things, so it obviously fit with the Pythagorean philosophy that "number is all"'. In fact the relationship may be deeper than that. As the scholar W.K.C. Guthrie observed, it has been argued that Pythagoras was likely involved in the design of coinage for his region of southern Italy. Furthermore, according to contemporaries, 'Pythagoras derived his enthusiasm for the study of number from its practical applications in commerce. This is by no means an improbable supposition. The impact of monetary economy, as a comparatively recent phenomenon, on a thoughtful citizen of mercantile Samos might well have been to implant the idea that one constant factor by which things were related was the quantitative. A fixed numerical value in drachmas or minas may "represent" things as widely different in quality as a pair of oxen, a cargo of wheat and a gold drinking-cup.'[17]

If we dwell on that idea for a while, though, it actually says a very strange thing – for how does money assign numbers to things? Number makes sense for things like counting or weighing, but how does it work in general? How do you assign a number to something like the value of a holiday, or a human life, or even an apple?

Economists, when they have bothered to think about this at all, have usually said that money is measuring, via the magic of the invisible hand, something like labour (classical economists), or utility (neoclassical economists), or maybe 'economic value' (circular definition). Adam Smith, for example, based his ideas on a labour theory of value. In his *Wealth of Nations*, he identified the value of money with its weight in precious metal. He then defined the exchange value of a good as being 'equal to the quantity of labour which it enables [a person] to purchase or command'. The relative price of gold and silver could rise or fall depending on the labour required to produce it (he neglected the fact that much of this labour came from slaves). The economist's job was therefore to strip out this distracting effect and concentrate on 'real' rather than 'nominal' prices: 'The real price of every thing, what every thing really costs to the man who wants to acquire it, is the toil and trouble of acquiring it.' Value is labour, and the real price is labour, so they are one and the same. Money is just a medium of exchange, which drops out of the equation. The French economist Jean-Baptiste Say summed this up in his statement that 'money is a veil'.

When the neoclassical economists decided to put economics on a sound mathematical footing, they switched from relating value with labour, to relating it with the slightly more scientific-sounding notion of utility. As Jevons put it in his *Theory of Political Economy*: 'Repeated reflection and inquiry have led me to the somewhat novel opinion, that *value depends entirely upon utility*' (his emphasis). In practical terms this made little difference, since as Jevons admitted, utility could never be measured directly, only inferred from prices. So again, the economy could be seen in terms of mechanical exchange, with money as just a score-keeping device. What mattered was not so much the price, but the utility that the price was measuring.

Following this logic, we can understand Nadal's point about money being exiled, with few exceptions, from the analysis of market processes in mainstream economics. It explains how Samuelson could write that 'if we strip exchange down to its barest essentials and peel off the obscuring layer of money, we find that trade between individuals and nations largely boils down to barter'.[18] Or how the Arrow–Debreu model could ignore money altogether and deal only in exchange; or how Debreu's monograph on his 'Theory of Value' could announce that 'No theory of money is offered here'; or how modern macroeconomic models could leave out the financial sector, even if it is now one of the largest industries on the planet; or how sophisticated risk models can neglect the effect of finance, even when trading is dominated by highly-leveraged hedge funds.[19] Trade boils down to barter; money is a veil.

But again: how is it that money can represent the labour or utility embodied in an object, or for that matter the concept of value in general? For the fact is that number and real-world objects have completely different properties which make them incompatible. For example, numbers are exact and eternal, while qualities such as perceived value of an object depend on the context. Numbers can grow without limits, while natural processes tend to be bounded. Numbers are universal, while objects can be owned, or become scarce. Conventional theories of money don't offer any help: in bullionism, the role of number is reduced to the weighing of metal, in chartalism it appears as a unit of account, but the question of how we assign number to things is otherwise ignored. How does money work its magic of uniting these two things?

The 'how much' theory of money

To address this question, I believe that we need to start with the concept of number, and its relation to the world of things. To summarise this approach (I'm paraphrasing a bit from *The Evolution of Money*), we first define money objects to be transferable entities, created by a trusted authority, which have the special property of a defined monetary value, specified by a number and a currency unit.[20] They can be a coin, a sheet of paper, or a piece of electronic information sent over a phone (as in quantum physics with its virtual particles, the distinction between real and virtual objects is blurred). Money is treated as a fundamental quantity, with unit specified by the currency framework. The trade of money objects for goods or labour in a market means that those things attain a numerical value (in the money's units) as well, namely the price, by a kind of contagion. In this view, market prices are therefore an emergent property of the system, in the sense that they emerge from the use of money objects. While prices may reflect things such as utility, labour, etc. to a degree, they don't actually *measure* them. The price, for example, of a banker or a CEO or an 'undocumented worker' does not measure the worth of their labour, or their usefulness to society, or the happiness they create – it's just the number they get paid, which as we've seen might reflect a range of factors.

Money objects are unique in that their value is designed to

be objectively fixed and stable. For other goods, their values are indeterminate until the moment they are exchanged for money. This introduces an element of fundamental uncertainty – there is nothing solid like 'labour' or 'utility' to fall back on. This in turn means that prices are unstable, because people have to look to each other to help gauge something's worth. The special status of money objects as having a defined value, in contrast, makes them desirable in themselves. It is often said that money is just a medium of exchange so need have no value itself; but by attaching numbers to money objects, in a kind of alchemy, we make them valuable. A stack of hundred-dollar bills may only be paper, but it can evoke as much desire as a bar of gold. The distinction between intrinsic and external value, between real and virtual, is blurred.

Money objects harbour remarkable properties which feed into the economy as a whole – while simple, they create enormous complexity. In particular, they have both a physical aspect, and a virtual aspect which is expressed through interactions, in the same way that a subatomic object like an electron or photon has a dual wave/particle nature. The dualistic, two-sided nature of money – it is fitting that many early Roman coins featured the two-faced god Janus – means that it frequently shows paradoxical behaviour.

The dual properties of money also resonate with human psychology, and make it a strongly psychoactive substance which elicits powerful responses. On the one hand, the fact that money involves ownership makes it an effective emotional and motivational tool; but on the other hand, the fact that it is based on number encourages analytical thinking, and the tendency to reduce complex social exchanges to a one-dimensional computation. It is not surprising then that money has conflicting effects, or that our response to it is far from being purely mechanical, rational, or predictable.

I humbly refer to this as the 'quantum theory of money'. Now, I know I made fun of flaky theories back in Chapter 9, and readers may be worried that, like others before me, I have lapsed into a severe case of physics envy (though I did at least study and even once teach quantum physics, and knew it would come in useful one day). And discussing quantum physics in particular has long been a marker for pseud-ery, in no small part because of the way physicists have defended their turf; apparently the same is not true of the Victorian mechanistic analogies beloved by economists.[21] (Nassim Taleb, for example, describes someone who 'has mentioned quantum mechanics at least twice in the past 5 years in conversations that had nothing to do with physics' as a member of the 'intellectual-yet-idiot' class.[22] No one actually does that in my social circle.) But I didn't choose the name purely to annoy economists, so let me make the case for using it.

1. Money is seen as a fundamental quantity (from the Latin *quantus*, meaning 'how much').

2. Money objects contain a fixed amount of monetary value, in the same way that an electron contains a fixed amount of charge.

3. Money objects bind the virtual to the real, and abstract number to the fuzzy idea of value, in a way similar to the particle/wave duality in quantum physics.

4. Just as the properties of a substance such as water emerge from the quantum interactions of molecules, so prices emerge from the use of money objects.

5. Money serves as a means to quantify value, in the sense of reducing it to a mathematical quantity – but as in quantum measurement, the process is approximate.

Finally, I would argue that the word 'quantum' actually fits better here than it does in physics. The story goes how Max Planck invented the term to describe the idea that matter and energy is divided into discrete chunks. But why 'quantum' instead of 'discretum' or something (other than that it sounds better)? With money, though, it makes perfect sense, because, as noted above, it is from the Latin for 'how much' – as in 'how much is that?' It's a theory that does exactly what it says on the tin.

Now, if this makes me a 'monetary crank' all I can say is that I am honoured to share that description with the likes of Soddy, who not only helped to uncover the properties of radiation, but whose crazy economic recommendations (abandon the gold standard, allow exchange rates to float, etc.) are mostly standard practice today. In fact, the only one of his ideas that was not eventually accepted was to stop allowing private banks to create money out of thin air. (Maybe that's why he was called a crank?)

The other side of the coin

Viewed from this quantum perspective, the bullionist and chartalist schools are each focusing on one side of money, the real or the virtual. The debate between them resembles the debate over whether light was made of particles or waves, which was finally resolved when it turned out to be both. As with quantum matter, the central trick of money is that it combines both of these complementary, contradictory aspects into a single package; it is both real and virtual at the same time. (When people make the oft-repeated claim that 'money is not a thing', it feels like it is based on a misunderstanding of what *things* are – one consequence of not talking about quantum physics.)

The two faces of money are represented most graphically in the production of coins, where the virtual number is impressed into the real metal. In terms of Greek duality, the stamp represents the abstract, 'male' world of virtual forms, while the metal represents the material, 'female' body. The process of stamping coins resembles the Aristotelian view of procreation: 'The female always provides the material, the male provides that which fashions the material into shape; this, in our view, is the specific characteristic of each of the sexes: that is what it means to be male or female.'[23] The dualistic properties of money therefore reflect or embody the dualities of Greek philosophy, including of course the Pythagorean list of opposites.

It might seem that adopting a quantum view of money will have no more of an effect on the way we think about the economy than the discovery of the quantum properties of water molecules had on plumbing. But debates over the nature of money are not just theoretical, they go to the heart of how the economy is managed, as during the gold standard. The theory presented here emphasises that money is not just a static material, or a government-mandated accounting system, but is something that is actively created. One example of this process, which neither bullionism nor chartalism can address, is the emergence of cybercurrencies; but a more important one is the way in which the vast majority of money is today conjured out of nothing by private banks.[24]

Perhaps the main reason that mainstream economists didn't see the credit crunch coming was because they treat money as just an inert chip, or a passive accounting system, so the pluses and minuses all cancel out. According to Ben Bernanke, the debt cycle 'represent[s] no more than a redistribution from one group (debtors) to another (creditors)'.[25] Krugman again: 'Think of it this way: when debt is rising, it's not the economy as a whole borrowing more money. It is, rather, a case of less patient people – people who for whatever reason want to spend sooner rather than later – borrowing from more patient people.'[26] Eugene Fama (never strong on bubbles): 'People who get credit have to get it from somewhere. Does a credit bubble mean that people save too much during that period? I don't know what a credit bubble means. I don't even know what a bubble means.'[27] But these statements ignore the fact that private banks act as an amplifier on the supply of credit, boosting it in times of prosperity and reining it in during a crash.

Obviously you don't need to adopt a particular theory of money to understand the importance of credit, since others – particularly those of the neo-chartalist persuasion – have made similar points, but this viewpoint, by its nature, draws attention to the active, dualistic, and creative properties of money. And in the same way, it makes it very clear why money had to be excluded historically from the analysis. The reason is that all the other economyths depend on it.

The economy can be described by economic laws. The laws of economics are based on the idea that the economy is a computable system. However, price is an emergent property that only imperfectly reflects the fuzzy notion of value.

The economy is made up of independent individuals. Money can be understood as a medium not just of exchange, but also of communication, and as seen in Chapter 2 the monetary system is the epitome of a highly connected system, where information, and disinformation, propagate virally through the network.

The economy is stable. Most money is created by private banks through credit creation, and this is subject to highly nonlinear and unstable feedback loops as discussed in Chapter 3.

Economic risk can be easily managed using statistics. The 'normal' statistics of mainstream economics relies on a mechanistic view of the economy where individuals make rational decisions to optimise utility, which is supposed to be a meaningful and essentially stable quantity. But as we have seen, the dynamics of money are fractal and nonlinear, with periods of relative calm interspersed with moments of sudden change.

The economy is rational and efficient. As seen in Chapter 5, money is a psychoactive substance that arouses powerful emotions and often leads to irrational behaviour.

The economy is gender-neutral. Money – and the process of stamping number onto the world – is linked symbolically with Greek ideas about gender, which as demonstrated in Chapter 6 feed into the way we think about the economy; for example, in the preference for abstract number over physical reality, or for money-based output over unpaid work.

The economy is fair. As shown in Chapter 7, money tends to cluster over time, in part because the return on investments or loans grows exponentially even if the real world doesn't. But money is both debt and credit, and being on the wrong side of this numerical growth has historically been a major cause of debtors falling into bankruptcy, slavery or peonage.

Economic growth can continue for ever. Economic growth is necessary to pay numerical debts – but while debts can certainly grow for ever, the real world can't keep up. As argued in *The Evolution of Money*, it is this, rather than any particular ideology, that is the main driver of the environmental crisis.

Economic growth will make us happy. Mainstream economics assumes a direct link between price and utility, and therefore happiness. As seen in Chapter 9, happiness is a little more complicated – and so is money.

Economic growth is always good. Mainstream economics sidesteps ethical issues by focusing on apparently neutral,
number-based metrics such as GDP. In doing so it neglects the
other side of the ledger which includes non-numerical things such
as environmental damage that force us to take an ethical stance.

Post-Pythagorean economics

Collectively we have stamped these myths onto the world, in the
same way that coins are formed by pressing numbers into metal.
Changing these assumptions, and abandoning the economyths,
creates an ontological shift in the way we model the economy, in
two ways. The first is that it shifts our mental perspective from
seeing the economy as an essentially stable, optimal, mechanical
system to seeing it as a dynamic, organic system; and from treating it as a highly-tuned machine that occasionally breaks for no
apparent reason, to a lively system where change is the norm. This
in turn means that, as argued in this book, complicated mechanistic models based on detailed calculations of utility should be
replaced by simpler and more transparent models based on more
realistic assumptions, but which account for money, debt, and the
financial sector. Probabilistic risk models based on assumptions
of stability and efficiency, and traditional hedging instruments
which attempt to remove that risk, should be replaced by models
which acknowledge that risk is not something that can be precisely calculated or simply engineered away. Approaches such as
agent-based models or machine learning will widen the scope
of models available; but we also have to admit that the economy is not always amenable to mathematical techniques. The
Pythagorean preference for stability, linearity, rationality, and so
on was consonant with their desire – and that of modern-day
economists – to reduce the world to number. But number is only
half of the story.

Secondly, an appreciation of the fluid, dynamic nature of money points towards ways of making the economy more stable. Only by seeing risk can we do something about it. For example, we can learn from properties such as redundancy and modularity, which as discussed earlier lend stability to natural systems such as ecosystems. We also need to reduce the size of the bloated and mercurial financial sector.

The idea of a barter economy where money plays only an incidental role, along with the accompanying creation myth of money as a substitute for barter, is therefore the linchpin, the uber-economyth, that holds the other economyths together. The most direct way to refute and move beyond these economyths is to take money seriously. Doing so will turn economics into a genuinely exciting subject again, located at the nexus between science and art.

As we have already seen, addressing these economyths suggests a research programme that includes (following the chapter order) complexity economics, network theory, nonlinear dynamics/ evolutionary economics, fractal/extreme statistics, behavioural economics, feminist economics, economic inequality, ecological economics, happiness economics, and ethics, with money as a unifying thread. This doesn't mean that economics has to get larger – it may even shrink in size, as its imperialistic ambitions are reined in. Economics is supposed to be about optimising happiness, growth, power structures, financial stability, and so on, but it actually knows very little about any of these. The major lesson of the financial crisis was one of humility. Economics will benefit by importing techniques from other areas such as complexity science, but one outcome of an interdisciplinary approach will be to provide boundaries for economics, and reveal the problems that it cannot address.

As a name to describe this diverse yet at the same time stripped-down programme, heterodox economics doesn't work, because it suggests scattered variations on a central religion, rather than a direct, organised, multi-faceted system of thought. The new economics is post-Pythagorean rather than neo-Pythagorean, Gaian rather than Apollonian, quantum rather than atomistic, organic rather than mechanistic.[28] Its name should evoke a sense of being rooted in the ecology of living systems, but also a sense of active management. Let's not call it heterodox – it sounds like we've given up, and are resigned to being a slightly quirky alternative instead of a serious contender.

Oh, here's a good name. Let's call it – economics.

Of course, if we reclaim that name we will need a new one for the mainstream ('lamestream' is too Sarah Palin). But there is already a good one: neoclassical economics. In art and architecture, neoclassicism refers to a movement, originating in the 18th century, that was based on a revival of aesthetic principles from classical Greece and Rome, such as simplicity, balance and symmetry. That isn't the way economists currently use the label – and some apparently complain that it has become a 'term of near-abuse', which is surely an exaggeration – but it seems to fit.[29] If economic models are based on approximate versions of what amount to symmetry principles (stability, rationality, fairness, etc.) then neoclassical they are. Some of these models will no doubt continue to have a place, for example to give traders rough estimates of risk and reward, but should be viewed as useful only when carefully applied.

Follow the money

But this account still doesn't seem to quite explain how something as basic as money could have been downplayed or ignored for so long, with anyone pointing it out being called a monetary crank (a label that has apparently stuck for over a century). Economists are smart people, and even if they neglect money in their theoretical work, they do have some practical experience of the stuff. As we've seen, there has always been a close connection between economics and what Soddy and others called the 'money power'. For a field that ignores money, even academic economists do a pretty good job of raking it in, with their consulting gigs and a pay package which is already higher than that of other social scientists, or physicists and mathematicians for that matter.[30] If someone were to do the accounting exercise, those money-free DSGE macro-economic models might turn out to be one of the most expensive mathematical modelling projects in history, which is hardly a good example of utility optimisation. So again – how is it that the complex, dynamic properties of money have been excluded to such a degree from economics?

Well, you don't need to be a conspiracy theorist to know that money likes to work in the shadows. If a bank is going to sponsor economic research (see section on 'Nobel' prize, page 159), it doesn't want the research to be about what the bank has been up to! That's not the idea at all. This is ultimately why the subject of money, at least in its messier aspects, has been sent into exile, and why the core teachings of neoclassical/mainstream economics – rationality, efficiency, stability, and so on – have turned out to be so perfectly aligned with the public relations needs of the financial sector. Hillary Clinton came under enormous criticism for giving Goldman Sachs a series of talks at $225,000 a pop, but neoclassicists have been doing something similar for a long time, with the difference that they have released the lecture notes, and it's the same talk over and over. Robert Shiller, quoted in the previous chapter, was right: the basic curriculum remains unchanged.

As described in Chapter 10, the field of neoclassical economics is like the dusty old logic machine that equates price with value, that squares the books. But in the end (and I didn't quite get this back in 2010) it's just an enabler. It's like the moment in the movie when all the tantalising clues – the modern-day cult, the links to ancient mythology – turn out to have been concealing something even more powerful. The thing that is driving the system – and is the source of its emergence – is the power of money, a power that was first unleashed thousands of years ago in Mesopotamia when an ancient scribe scratched some numbers into a clay tablet, and that continues to reshape the world today. After all, it was money that influenced the Pythagoreans, and through them much of the way we see the world, not the other way round. Money may have been exiled as a way to protect economics, but really it's been in control all along.

We can and should rail against the distorting power of the financial sector, but to understand it we need to acknowledge that it is just expressing the true nature of money, doing everything it can to maximise the numbers, in the absence of a suitable ethical framework. And to understand problems such as wealth inequality, or societal happiness, or environmental destruction, it isn't enough to examine economic theories or capitalist ideology – we need to consider the role of this technology of money. Money is probably the most powerful thing we have invented, so we need to ask why we have granted private banks the right to produce most of it for us, while demanding so little in return for that extraordinary privilege. We need to consider ideas both old and new, from Solon's 6th-century idea of a debt jubilee, in which debts were periodically forgiven, to Soddy's full reserve banking, and from money-free commons to alternative currencies such as Bitcoin. A first step is to bring money out of exile – to bring it back into the fold.

Creation myth

Most societies have a creation myth. In capitalist societies, our creation myth – which our neoclassical priesthood continues to incant in their lectures and texts – is that the economy grew out of barter, with money arriving later as an inert facilitator. It has been kept in place exactly because it tells the story that they want us to hear. But if something good is to come out of the financial crisis, then we must abandon that myth, and the other economyths that it helps support, and start again. The result of this rebirth will be a new economics, which has money – and the delicate, unstable negotiation between price and value that money represents – at its very heart.

The Economist was right to point out (see box, page 29) that relaxing 'stark, crude theories about market efficiency or rational behaviour' with their 'defining numbers' will threaten the status of economics, and make it something closer to a soft science like sociology. It will also be less well-paid than before. But paradoxically, this may be the only way to avoid what Paul Romer called a 'regression into pseudoscience' (he was speaking of macroeconomics, though I would say the entire field has been a pseudoscience since the day they decided to leave money out of the equation).

A decade after the financial crisis kicked off, some of those graph lines mentioned in Chapter 10, such as species extinction and resource shortages, have presumably continued their heady (though hard to precisely measure) ascent. In other areas there has been progress: atmospheric carbon continues to accumulate, but annual emissions appear to have paused, thanks in part to the growing adoption of wind and solar power; inequality is higher in many countries, but at a global level the number of people living in extreme poverty continues to fall. And when it comes to economics, we don't stand at a fork in the road anymore. Neoclassical economists in dysfunctional university departments (see Appendix) are still playing with their epicycles and reciting from their overpriced textbooks, much as the Greek geocentric model was used and taught long after scientists knew that the earth rotated around the sun rather than vice versa.[31] But the number of people who believe in their central narrative of stability, rationality and efficiency is dwindling fast, the students (at least the ones who aren't just prepping for the financial sector) are past restless, and everyone knows the machine is broken.

Like neoclassical economics, the geocentric model was essentially static in nature – the celestial bodies were assumed to be fixed in crystalline spheres, but there was no theory about what made them move (apart from divine influence, the equivalent of economists' 'external shocks'). The model was overthrown only when it was discovered that the cosmos is in fact a dynamic system, driven by gravity and the laws of motion. Today, our task is to understand the dynamics of the economy, and to do so we need to explore the forces which move it. This task is in one sense much easier than Newton's – we don't have to prove that money and power exist, just point them out – but in another sense it is harder, because these forces don't obey neat equations, or even come down to number. The problem is in a different category. And the result of our inquiry will certainly be less far-reaching than Newtonian mechanics. But if there is one thing that the history of economics has taught us, it is that grand projects can be dangerous.

So here's to the new economics. May it be humble, wise, democratic, engaging, and grounded. Oh, and this time – let's not wait 150 years before we bring it in for an update.

Appendix
THE FIVE STAGES OF ECONOMIC GRIEF

It is just wrong to say that this financial crisis
caught modern macroeconomists by surprise.
Tom Sargent, winner of the 2011 economics Nobel,
speaking in a 2010 interview. No mention of whether
the non-modern macroeconomists saw it coming too

I think it [the efficient market hypothesis]
did quite well in this episode.
Eugene Fama, winner of the 2013 economics
Nobel, speaking in a 2010 interview

Blah blah blah.
Paul Romer, non-winner of the 2016 economics
Nobel (as his university later corrected[1]), in his
2016 paper 'The Trouble With Macroeconomics'

**Swiss psychiatrist Elisabeth Kübler-Ross, a pioneer in the field
of grief counselling, identified the five stages of grief as denial,
anger, bargaining, depression, and acceptance. This Appendix
draws on her model of grief as inspiration to chart the long,
arduous, but ultimately healthy and healing (we hope, it's not
over yet) process as the economics profession slowly comes to
terms with its role in the great financial crisis.**

The ten years since the first tremors of the crisis began in 2007 have
been a difficult journey, not just for the world economy, but also

for the economics profession. The status of the field had never been higher than in the two decades preceding the crisis, during what Ben Bernanke and others called the Great Moderation. Inflation and macroeconomic volatility seemed to be under control, and total national income was growing at an almost steady rate (the fact that total debt was growing even faster was less remarked upon). In 2002, Alan Greenspan received an honorary knighthood from the Queen for 'his outstanding contribution to global economic stability'.[2] The following year, Nobel laureate Robert Lucas, famous for his theory of 'rational expectations', told his audience: 'My thesis in this lecture is that macroeconomics in this original sense has succeeded: Its central problem of depression prevention has been solved, for all practical purposes, and has in fact been solved for many decades.'[3] With its firm grounding in mathematical rigour, economics was the undisputed queen of the social sciences. The zeitgeist was brilliantly captured in Steven Levitt and Stephen Dubner's 2005 book *Freakonomics: A Rogue Economist Explores the Hidden Side of Everything*, which saw Levitt ('considered a demigod' in the field, according to the book) cleverly apply fairly standard economic and statistical theory to offbeat areas such as prostitution and sumo wrestling (though not credit default swaps, which might have been more useful) in an effort that some compared to 'academic imperialism'.[4]

As we've already seen, economists were therefore more than a little surprised by what jurist and economist Richard Posner – author of books including the aptly-named *A Failure of Capitalism: The Crisis of '08 and the Descent into Depression* – inventories as 'the bursting of the housing bubble (they didn't know it was a bubble), the ensuing banking collapse, the stock market crash, the sharp decline in output and employment, the global scope of the crisis, and the onset of deflation in the late fall of 2008 that created fears of a depression comparable to the Great Depression of the 1930s'.[5] According to James Heckman from the University of Chicago,

'Everybody here was blindsided by the magnitude of what happened. But it wasn't just here. The entire profession was blindsided.'[6]

Indeed, the crisis came as a traumatic event that left mainstream economists in what Greenspan called 'a state of shocked disbelief'. Models which were based on assumptions of stability, equilibrium and efficiency were of little use when markets were cratering, real estate was sinking into the mud, and oil and food were spiking. And since that time, economists have been working their way slowly and painfully through the different stages or aspects of the grief process, as they realise that their elegant models not only failed to predict the crisis, but also helped to create it.[7]

Book-burning economists

When *Economyths* first came out, most economists were in a state of **denial** – especially those at the top of the profession such as Tom Sargent, quoted above (see also Chapter 10).[8] Robert Lucas preferred to see the unpredictability as a natural result of Eugene Fama's efficient market hypothesis (though as Posner notes, that didn't stop him from predicting, shortly after Lehman's collapse, that the crisis would soon go away).[9] When *The New Yorker*'s John Cassidy asked Fama in 2010 whether Posner was correct in his judgement that the crisis posed a serious challenge to Chicago economics, the response was: 'Er, he's not an economist. [Laughs] He's an expert on law and economics. We are talking macroeconomics and finance. That is not his area … I don't agree with him on this one. And I don't think the people here who are more attuned to these areas agree with him either.'[10] The similarly-attuned Nobel committee apparently agreed too.

As reality sank in, economists soon began lashing out in **anger** at anyone who dared criticise their field, including yours truly (I'm going to talk about this because it seems to be quite a general problem). At Canada's top-ranked economics blog Worthwhile

Canadian Initiative, for example, a group of prominent academics, including regular contributors to national publications (*Globe and Mail, National Post, Maclean's, Literary Review of Canada*, etc.), shared their professional thoughts about the book online.[11] Descriptors used included idiotic, ignorant, intellectually lazy, juvenile, random, rubbish, semi-articulated, and 'sort of like Malcolm Gladwell without the insight' – ouch. Someone even compared me to a climate change denier.

One commenter described the online book-burning as part of a widely-deployed 'shoot the messenger' strategy against critics. Which is fine – we give as good as we get, and at least they don't grade us. But what was interesting about their discussion was the way these academics, who hailed from top universities such as British Columbia, Carleton, Laval, and so on, managed to maintain the illusion that they were being incredibly tolerant and open to criticism. As one put it, 'Economists welcome criticism. In the academy, we are well-known, if not infamous, for being direct, abrupt, and rude in criticizing each other (and others). There is a very healthy discussion about methodology. Bring it on.' But they confused academic bickering with genuine criticism from people who share none of their biases.

Heterodox economists have long complained that mainstream economists are stifling or repressing their ideas without giving them a proper hearing, while mainstream economists insist that in fact they are totally open to new ideas and scientific discussion. So it was revealing to listen in to one of their group blog discussions, and see the process in action, for example in the way that commenters raising questions about orthodoxy are quickly slapped down. The most troubling part, though, was the author's final conclusion in the comments – 'Why should I care?'

The site linked to an even more vituperative blog review by an economics professor at the University of Victoria (quoted in the

Preface) who of course took pains to say that economics 'benefits from criticism', as long as it's the right type, a topic we discuss further below.[12] (Fortunately I was spared the electronic 'viruses and hate mail' which have apparently afflicted other critics of mainstream economics.[13]) And that was about it for thoughtful response from the country's economics establishment, at least until former Deputy Governor of the Bank of Canada William White (now at OECD) – one of the few people who warned of the financial crisis – cited the paperback edition as a Bloomberg Best Book of 2013, perhaps out of sympathy.[14]

It could be said that these academics were just sounding off on the internet, but they are also capable of more organised approaches. Another person in the 'shoot-the-messenger' firing line was the famed Canadian environmentalist David Suzuki, who the same group accused, first on blogs, then in the national media, of conducting a 'smear campaign' against them in 2012 after he insulted their treatment of environmental externalities and said that 'economics is not a science'.[15] (Though when economist and environmentalist Pavan Sukhdev said pretty much the same thing in 2016 no one seemed to react.[16]) In a number of articles they demanded that Suzuki apologise to economists, and (worse) take a course in economics, something that struck many as just a little tone-deaf, given that it seemed economists owed everyone an apology. Rather than address his point that economics tends to ignore natural services, their focus was on correcting him on the textbook definition of an externality (see box, page 234), saying that he 'displays a perplexing lack of understanding of basic economic concepts'.[17]

These articles and comments were presumably not politically motivated – and economists wouldn't admit it if they were – and economists have a right to defend their profession, within reason. But at a time when environmental concerns were colliding with the ramp-up in Alberta oil sands development, or 'ethical oil' as then-Prime Minister Stephen Harper was busy rebranding it (see box, page 297), their extended battle against its most visible opponent certainly played into political hands.[18]

Let's make a deal

As anger started to burn out, the next stage of the drawn-out and generally exhausting grief process involved **bargaining**: both with the future – perhaps we can put things right – and in a kind of retroactive bargaining with the past, saying that the event would not have occurred if only something had been done differently. One common argument, anticipated in the book's introductory chapter, was that there is nothing wrong with economics per se, the problem is one of *poor communication*: the field's critics just don't understand the full rich diversity of economic thought, and are attacking a simplified caricature.

A good illustration of this approach was the 2015 book *Economics Rules* by Dani Rodrik from Harvard. Echoing Lionel Robbins (see 1932 quote in the Preface), Rodrick explains that the reason student groups such as the one 'calling itself the Post-Crash Economics Society' are frustrated is that introductory economics courses offer only a pared-down version of the theory and give 'little sense of the diversity of conclusions in economics'.[19] Also most economists are poor at presenting their arguments to the public, because they 'see themselves as scientists and researchers whose job it is to write academic papers'. Rodrik does note the existence of a 'guild mentality' in economics which 'renders the profession insular and immune to outside criticism', and observes in a couple of places that 'Only card-carrying members of the profession are viewed as legitimate participants in economic debates'. Yet later he cites the influence of behavioural psychologists and so on to conclude that 'the view of economics as an insular, inbred discipline closed to outside influence is more caricature than reality'. (Pardon?) Rodrick also self-reports that 'even though I reach policy conclusions that differ from prevailing academic views … I have never really felt discriminated against in the profession'. The overall impression is one of bemusement at all the fuss.

After making a number of good points about models, the book concludes with 'Ten Commandments' (aka 'bargaining points') for economists, and ten for non-economists. Some of these are very sensible – #3 from the latter list, for example, says: 'Analysis requires simplicity; beware of incoherence that passes itself off as complexity.' Others are versions of common defences against critics, e.g. #9: 'If you think all economists think alike, attend one of their seminars'; and #10: 'If you think economists are especially rude to noneconomists, attend one of their seminars.' These are surely well-meant and sound fairly innocuous, unless you're afraid of economics seminars, but they come up all the time in different guises and it's worth inspecting them a little more closely.

The first is a polite variation of the 'caricature' or 'straw man' argument, implying that economics is far more diverse and complicated than it appears to an outsider. However, as already seen in this book, the fact that economists do not agree on every point does not somehow innoculate the field against criticism; and the claim or implication that non-economists don't fully understand the subject, and need to attend a seminar or take a course to appreciate its mysteries, often boils down to a debating or avoidance tactic (and obviously doesn't apply to the increasing number of critics from within the field's own ranks). It also leads to the Catch-22, perfectly expressed in a generally glowing 2017 review of Rodrik's 'marvelous book' by economist and game theory expert Ariel Rubinstein, published in the *Journal of Economic Literature*, that 'One needs to be an outsider to criticize Economics but one needs to be an economist to do it sufficiently well so as not to be drawn astray by stereotypes', which doesn't seem to leave many people.[20] Apparently Rodrik qualifies, despite or because of the fact that he 'belongs to the elite of the Economics academic establishment'.

But perhaps this desire to filter critics has more to do with the above-mentioned preference, also noted by Rubinstein, for academic economists 'to perceive ourselves as being open-minded. This is part of the group identity. Thus, "soft" criticism is sincerely welcomed in Economics. It contributes to our "sense of self-satisfaction". However, this open-mindedness often disappears once the critic is perceived as a threat to the profession. But *Economics Rules*, in spite of its occasionally harsh criticism, does not pose a real threat. It rarely criticizes a specific individual and leaves the reader with enough room to feel that at least he (though perhaps no one else) is doing good economics.' He warns presciently – while perhaps not reflecting quite hard enough on how this might apply to his own review; like ostriches, mainstream economists seem to think that just because they don't read non-economists, non-economists don't read them – that 'Some non-economists will probably take some spicy quotes from the book. However, I am not sure that the book can be fully appreciated by readers who lack advanced knowledge in Economics.'

Is there someone else we can talk to?

So to sum up – and I think I'm getting this right – a suitable critic is a card-carrying member of the guild who doesn't ruffle too many feathers; mainstream economists are open-minded with people of similar mind only; and even popular economic texts can only be properly understood by those with the correct form of advanced knowledge. Viewed this way, the communication problem is less a problem than a deliberately cultivated feature, that helps to protect the field from threats to its self-satisfaction. Mathematical jargon is exploited in the same way – as Julie Nelson notes, it is easy to intimidate outsiders with 'references to subgame-perfect equilibria or heteroskedasticity'.[21] According to Jonathan Aldred, policy-makers similarly 'preserve their special claim to expertise by encouraging the myth that economics is a mysterious science whose workings are unintelligible to the uninitiated'. Criticisms are arising not because economists are misunderstood, but because people are starting to understand them very well, as the mathematical smokescreen loses some of its magical concealment power.

If progress is to be made, then rather than faux-instructing the public to attend departmental seminars, it would surely be more constructive for academic economists to develop outreach programmes such as the community workshops and school events run by Rethinking Economics.[22] And instead of trying to define all the bargaining terms when it comes to reform, such as who is allowed to come to the table, the field should open itself further to insights from different disciplines. Indeed, it seems ironic that in Rodrik's book there is no corresponding 'commandment' unto the economic priesthood to attend seminars outside their own specialty, given that entire organisations and protest groups have sprung up in an attempt to make economists embrace pluralism; and that a sociological analysis from 2015 entitled 'The Superiority of Economists' concluded that 'economists, with their distinctive confidence in the superiority of their own discipline, are less likely to feel the need to rely on other disciplines or even to acknowledge their existence'.[23]

Commandment/bargaining point #10, meanwhile, echoes the idea, also expressed above, that rudeness between economists is evidence of a 'very healthy discussion about methodology'. I'm assuming this doesn't include hate mail. Five things ... First, the main objection to the arguments made by economists concerns not the style, but the content. Second: as seen below, economists are not rude at all when it comes to questioning their leaders – in fact obsequious deference would seem to be a better description.

Third: lack of civility (at least in itself) is not an indicator of healthy scientific debate, in the academy or in the playground. I'd say that advertising it probably reflects more an anxiety about appearing robustly scientific.

Fourth: in his 2006 book *The Trouble With Physics*, physicist Lee Smolin notes that string theorists cultivate a 'brash, aggressive, and competitive atmosphere', though he doesn't see it as an advantage.[24] He also detects a 'blatant prejudice' against hiring women. Could these be related – and could macho posturing be a similar problem in economics? According to the article quoted in the box on page 184 about sexism in economics, some male economists 'may not even realize all the ways they routinely put others down – especially those in vulnerable positions who dare not strike back'.[25]

Finally, and related, rudeness might be fine between equals, but one of the functions of social graces is to help deal with asymmetrical power relationships, of the sort encountered in economics departments (but less often in economics models, Chapter 7). The 2015 investigation at the University of Manitoba mentioned in the Preface, for example, concluded that while the department head, an orthodox economist, had insisted 'that he was committed to maintaining diversity', his subsequent actions resulted in a change of climate that had the opposite effect. This ultimately led among other things to 'a violation of academic freedom when orthodox members of the department behaved in ways that discriminated against doctoral students being supervised by heterodox economists'.[26] According to one professor there was 'serious bullying going on' including threats to interfere with the tenure process. No wonder the students are calling for revolt (they're so rude).

Economic depression

It therefore comes as something of a relief to us critics that some economists at least may be proceeding to the penultimate, more passive stage of the grief process, **depression**. Evidence is provided by a forthcoming paper by Paul Romer, 'The Trouble With Macroeconomics' (he had also been reading Smolin's book, hence the title), a 2016 preprint of which caused a considerable stir in economics circles.[27] Sounding almost *Economyths*-like in style, the first sentence of the abstract announces that 'For more than three decades, macroeconomics has gone backwards'. It goes on to describe the author's 'pessimistic assessment of regression into pseudoscience' and mention the 'serious failure' of top economists. Decidedly non-upbeat section titles include 'Post-Real Models', 'Loyalty Can Corrode The Norms of Science', 'Back to Square One', and 'The Trouble Ahead For All of Economics'. No concrete solutions are proposed for what sounds, to an outsider, like a rather dysfunctional state of affairs.

In the same way that elegant but unfalsifiable string theory has, as Smolin showed, taken over high-energy physics, so mainstream economics has increasingly emphasised elegant but unfalsifiable mathematical models over experimental reality (a point made in Chapter 5). Most of the parameters in the models cannot be determined from observations, but are simply made up to give the desired answers. Events such as crashes are assumed to be caused by external shocks, rather than internal dynamics. The models can't make sense out of even basic things like monetary policy, which according to theory – since money plays no significant role in these models – should have little or no effect.

However, the problems are as much sociological as they are mathematical. Just as string theory is characterised by what Smolin described as 'groupthink' about the correct way to approach problems, so some economists see it as 'an extremely serious violation of some honor code for anyone to criticize openly a revered authority figure ... neither facts that are false, nor predictions that are wrong, nor models that make no sense matter enough to worry about'.

Romer, who is now chief economist at the World Bank, notes that he sees himself more as a practitioner rather than an academic, so feels free to speak out and tell it like it is, but many people are afraid to criticise a 'revered leader' because of the 'unpleasant reaction' that it may evoke. He relates a story of running into a colleague who was so angry with him for criticising a paper by Robert Lucas that 'at first he could not speak. Eventually, he told me, "You are killing Bob."' Yikes. So much for that self-image of economists being open to criticism. And forget about the 'relentless self-criticism' called for by Simon Jenkins (see Preface). In fact Romer says he was inspired to write the paper after seeing a documentary about the Church of Scientology.[28]

Paul Mason observed in *The Guardian* that Romer's paper is important because he is not an outsider or a rebel, but 'a doyen of the profession, and from the heart of the US academic mainstream'.[29] As Bloomberg commented, 'along came one of the leading practitioners of his generation, to say that the skeptics were onto something'. Which, speaking as one such sceptic, is certainly appreciated. In fact in some respects Romer probably goes further – even I didn't sum an economic argument up as: 'Assume A, assume B, … blah blah blah … And so we have proven that P is true.'

However, while it is refreshing that some in the mainstream are facing up to these problems, and Romer's paper is written with great courage, a dose of dark humour, and an obvious concern for the state of economics, there is in fact little acknowledgement that these issues have long been debated and solutions proposed outside of the mainstream; and as argued in this book, it is exactly this deafness to other voices which is at the root of the 'trouble with economics', and the reason it has taken so long to confront the fact that there might be a serious problem, let alone actually do something about it.

The path to acceptance

Of course, depression is a state of mind that involves turning inwards. But for an area as insular as mainstream economics, the final stage of the grief process – **acceptance** – will only come when the field finally gets over itself and opens up to new ideas – or even the old ideas that have been there all along. This may be beginning to happen. In 2017 for example the UK's Economic and Social Research Council announced that it intended to set up a network with its remit being to 'revolutionise' the field of economics: 'It will be led by a team of 25 world leading experts taken not only from different branches of economics, but also from psychology, anthropology, sociology, neuroscience, economic history, political science, biology and physics.' Perhaps those experts can answer some of the questions we posed for them back in 2010 (see pages pages 300–1).[30] As seen in this revised edition of *Economyths*, ideas from areas such as complexity science and data analysis are starting to sink in and have an effect. And some high-profile economists are having a go at new approaches. Joseph Stiglitz, for example, recently contributed to a paper that uses an agent-based model to account for 'the complex adaptive nature of economic systems, and the implications of money endogeneity' (i.e. the fact that money is produced by banks).[31]

But one thing that mainstream economists won't go near – it doesn't fit with the models – is the idea that economists might not be quite so impartial, objective and unbiased as they appear. Rodrik, for example, notes that leading economists had bought into the dominant efficient market paradigm which saw markets 'not only as inherently efficient and stable, but also as self-disciplining', and that this 'legitimized and enabled a great wave of financial deregulation that set the stage for the crisis'.[32] He describes it as 'curious' that other models were not used. But why would they make that particular choice? Why were other models, such as

Minsky's model of the credit cycle, repressed? And did economists buy in or sell out? As we've seen, the field of economics has an unhealthily close dependency relationship with the financial sector, which may just have clouded its judgement.

Instead of acting out against critics in a way that embarrasses the profession, or ignoring those who want to help, it's time for mainstream economists to relax the defences and open up a little. A first step is to untangle those institutional effects and other motivations that have shaped their field and which continue to resist change. I'm sure there are plenty of sociologists and psychologists (even grief counsellors probably) who can help. Of course the process can't be rushed, so here is, not a commandment, but a gentle suggestion to economists in this difficult time: ten years is enough. Time to open the windows and let in the fresh air.

Assess your neoclassical economist!

Do you have a neoclassical economist in your life – as a colleague, a teacher, or even as a loved one? Then this simple test will allow you to assess the current status of their psychological progress, as they come to terms with the failure and collapse of their beautiful theories.

Just produce a copy of this book, and tell them it says that many economic models, used in everything from risk assessment to macroeconomics, are based or rely heavily on a number of key economyths. So for example a typical macroeconomic model uses made-up supply–demand curves; rational utility-maximising behaviour; existence of a stable equilibrium, and so on; but leaves out things like money and the financial sector. Ask them why these models are still being used in the 21st century. Then compare the response to the ones listed below to see where they are in the process. Note there is no fixed progression, and it is possible to be in more than one stage at the same time, or in some completely different stage.

1. If the response is 'I don't see a problem', then your neoclassical economist is in **denial**. He (or she) may have an oddly fixed smile and show an imperturbable optimism. If you press further, he might put his hands over his ears and hum quietly, or repeat 'Beauty is truth, truth beauty' over and over. It is important here to be patient and remember that your neoclassical economist's field has experienced a major loss of status which he may not be able to process. Even if he seems impossible to reach (and many will stay in this 'equilibrium state' at least until retirement), you shouldn't give up hope. At the same time you should watch out for influences that might enable his behaviour – for example the awarding of a Nobel prize has been shown to hinder progress, as have (other) payments from banks.

2. If your neoclassical economist becomes aggressive or insults you – spitting e.g. that 'You know nothing about the basic tenets of economics!' even when you kind of do – then he is in the **anger** stage. Beware that he may attempt to set the book on fire – this is especially dangerous if it is an electronic version. Try to stop him from composing rant-like inflammatory articles or sending harassing emails. Remember that the anger he is expressing is not really about you or even the book – instead it is 'shooting the messenger'. Sigmund Freud cited a story of the Moorish King Boabdil, who in the late 15th century was losing his Spanish territory to Christian invaders. On learning that his jewel city of Alhambra had fallen, he threw the letters in the fire and killed the messenger. As Freud pointed out,

such responses are a way of 'defending ourselves against things that are painful and unbearable'.[33] Compassion is in order, but keep your distance.

3. If your neoclassical economist says 'That is a straw man' or 'It is more complicated than that' or tries to get you to attend a seminar then he is in the **bargaining** stage. If you point out, for example, that equilibrium models assume the existence of an equilibrium – it's in the name – he may say 'There are plenty of other models'. And if you then point out that those models aren't actually used, he may agree it is a little strange but will come up with an excuse. He might appear somewhat confused, which could be a sign of progress (or just confusion). Rather than address your question in plain language, he is likely to lapse into incomprehensible jargon. In this stage, you should not expect him to seriously discuss alternative models, or acknowledge the existence of non-neoclassical economists, even if you produce pictures or YouTube videos of some. (Though if desperate, he may claim some kind of 'heterodox credentials' based on a paper he wrote during a period of youthful indiscretion.) There is an opportunity to make some progress here but it will be frustrating so don't waste too much energy. And don't become upset if he treats you like you are stupid.

4. If your neoclassical economist looks snarky or sad or what psychologists call 'down in the dumps' and appears to have lost all respect for the field of economics, then he may be in the **depression** stage. One way to look at this stage is as anger turned inwards. Your neoclassical economist is upset because deep down he knows, in a rational, utility-maximising kind of way, that the models he and his colleagues have been working on were a waste of time or

were actively counterproductive. He may also be disappointed in his leaders, or himself. And it may bother him that other people often appear unsympathetic, or even seem to be holding him responsible for something. Back to King Boabdil: after losing the war he was sent into exile. The spot where the king paused his horse to view his beloved Alhambra for the last time is now known as the Suspiro del Moro, the Moor's Sigh. Your neoclassical economist is feeling the same way, except instead of a beautiful city he's thinking about his elegant models (and he still hasn't got on his horse). The best medicine at this stage may be tea and sympathy, perhaps a gentle back rub. Telling him that he should cheer up and stop the sighing – at least he hasn't lost his job or even suffered a pay cut, unlike other victims of the financial crisis – will not help.

5. If your neoclassical economist lifts himself to his feet and says, 'All right, let's try another approach, God knows people have been trying to get us to do that for years', then congratulations, he appears to be on the road to recovery and **acceptance**! Warning: this may take ten years or more – giving up on a belief system is not easy. Be careful to ensure that the change is genuine, rather than a ruse to make you go away. Alternatively, it is possible that he was only pretending to be neoclassical all along, so as not to offend a Dear Leader. Don't expect an apology – that is asking too much. Also don't be too disappointed if your neoclassical economist never reaches this stage. He might just lack the necessary skill-set to make the transition. And as the author Upton Sinclair once observed: 'It is difficult to get a man to understand something, when his salary [or tenure application] depends on his not understanding it.'

NOTES

Preface
1. Lasn, Kalle (2011), 'Paradigm Shift', *Adbusters* 94, March 2011.
2. DelReal, Jose A. (2011), 'Students Walk Out of Ec 10 in Solidarity with "Occupy"', *The Harvard Crimson*, 2 November 2011.
3. Concerned students of Economics 10 (2011), 'An Open Letter to Greg Mankiw', *Harvard Political Review*, 2 November 2011.
4. See http://economieautrement.org/pour-un-enseignement-pluraliste -de-leconomie-au-quebec. ISIPE has its own open letter – agreed upon after an epic twelve-hour Skype conference – at http://www .isipe.net/open-letter/
5. Chang, Ha-Joon, and Aldred, Jonathan (2014), 'After the crash, we need a revolution in the way we teach economics', *The Observer*, 11 May 2014.
6. Though financial sector involvement in INET's own funding raises questions. It was initially funded by a pledge of $50 million from George Soros, and its executive director is Robert Johnson, who was previously the managing director at Soros Fund Management. Haering, Norbert (2014), 'George Soros' INET: A conspiracy theory assessment', *World Economics Association Newsletter*, 4(2): 4–5.
7. Lavoie, Marc, 'Should heterodox economics be taught in economics departments, or is there any room for backwater economics?', paper prepared for the session 'Teaching Economics', at the 2015 INET Annual conference, Paris, April 2015. Available at: https://www .ineteconomics.org/uploads/papers/Lavoie.pdf
8. Trimarco, James, 'Students for Economic Pluralism, Unite!' *Yes!* Magazine, 20 February 2015.
9. Ruccio, David (2016), 'Crash and learn?', Real World Economic Review blog, 7 October 2016, https://rwer.wordpress.com/2016/10/07/ crash-and-learn/
10. The Rethinking Economics network (2016), 'Economics teaching is still neglecting critical thought', *The Guardian*, 17 November 2016.
11. Inman, Phillip (2017), 'Chief economist of Bank of England admits errors in Brexit forecasting', *The Guardian*, 5 January 2017.

12. Pettifor, Ann (2017), 'I was one of the only economists who predicted the financial crash of 2008 – in 2017 we need to make urgent changes', *The Independent*, 6 January 2017. See her books *Real World Economic Outlook: The Legacy of Globalization: Debt and Deflation* (Palgrave Macmillan, 2003) and *The Coming First World Debt Crisis* (Palgrave Macmillan, 2006). Ha-Joon Chang quoted in: Milne, Seumas (2013), 'Orthodox economists have failed their own market test', *The Guardian*, 20 November 2013.

13. Jenkins, Simon (2017), 'Economists have completely failed us. They're no better than Mystic Meg', *The Guardian*, 6 January 2017.

14. Shipley, David (2017), 'Why Not Make Economics a Science?', Bloomberg.com, 6 February 2017.

15. Smith, Noah (2017), 'Economics Gets a Presidential Demotion', Bloomberg.com, 14 February 2017.

16. Phillips, F. et al. (2016), 'Business schools in crisis', *Journal of Open Innovation: Technology, Market, and Complexity* 2(1).

17. There is a list of reviews at https://futureofeverything.wordpress .com/2013/05/28/reviews-of-economyths-by-david-orrell/

18. The quote is from Auld, Christopher (2011), 'A review of *Economyths: Ten Ways Economics Gets it Wrong*, by David Orrell', https://chrisauld dotcom.wordpress.com/2011/09/29/a-review-of-economyths-ten -ways-economics-gets-it-wrong-by-david-orrell/

19. As economist Narayana Kocherlakota wrote in 2016: 'Despite the shocking experience of a global financial crisis and prolonged economic slump, most macroeconomic research is guided by the same paradigms that prevailed ten years ago. I think this might have more to do with professors' salaries than with the state of the broader economy.' Kocherlakota, Narayana (2016), 'Professors Aren't Feeling the Economy's Pain', Bloomberg.com, 22 September 2016.

20. Lee, Frederick (2009), *A History of Heterodox Economics: Challenging the Mainstream in the Twentieth Century* (London: Routledge), pp. 5–6.

21. Mandelbrot B. (1971), 'When can Price be arbitraged efficiently? A limit to the validity of the Random Walk and Martingale Models', *Review of Economics and Statistics*, 53, 225–36.

22. Hannam, James (2009), *God's Philosophers: How the Medieval World Laid the Foundations of Modern Science* (London: Icon Books), p. 174.

23. Stewart, Ian (2012), *17 Equations That Changed the World* (London: Profile Books), p. 134.

24. Sedláček, T., Orrell, D. and Chlupatý, R. (2012), *Soumrak Homo Economicus* (Prague: 65.pole). I did receive a transcript two years later, but didn't read the whole thing.

25. Wilmott, Paul and Orrell, David (2017), *The Money Formula: Dodgy Finance, Pseudo Science, and How Mathematicians Took Over the Markets*, (Chichester: Wiley).

26. Yates, Michael D. (2011), 'The Emperor Has No Clothes But Still He Rules', *Monthly Review* 63 (2).

27. Keynes, John Maynard (1936), *The General Theory of Employment, Interest and Money* (London: Macmillan), p. 383.

28. Quoted in comments to Auld, Christopher (2011), 'A review of *Economyths: Ten Ways Economics Gets it Wrong*, by David Orrell', chrisaulddotcom.wordpress.com

29. Manson, A., McCallum, P., and Haiven , L. (2015), *Report of the Ad Hoc Investigatory Committee Into the Department of Economics at the University of Manitoba* (Manitoba: Canadian Association of University Teachers). The term 'gaslighting' comes from a 1938 play, *Gas Light*.

30. Robbins, Lionel (1932), *An Essay on the Nature and Significance of Economic Science* (London: Macmillan), p. 112.

31. Earle, J., Moran, C., and Ward-Perkins, Z. (2016), *The Econocracy: The Perils of Leaving Economics to the Experts* (Manchester: Manchester University Press), p. 178.

32. Jonathan Aldred describes as a basic misunderstanding 'the view that the perfect free market of pure economic theory (and every undergraduate textbook) could, if governments so wished, be introduced into real economies'. Jonathan Aldred (2009), *The Skeptical Economist: Revealing the Ethics Inside Economics* (London: Earthscan), p. 81.

33. See https://en.oxforddictionaries.com/definition/myth

34. Simpson, J. and Roud, S. (2000), *Dictionary of English Folklore* (Oxford: Oxford University Press), p. 254.

35. An example of this usage is when economists call something like 'efficiency' a myth because economists sometimes depart from it, which somehow misses the point. Fullerton, D., and Stavins, R. (1998), 'How economists see the environment', *Nature*, 395 (6701), 433–4.

36. Galbraith, James K. (2010), 'Why the "Experts" Failed to See How Financial Fraud Collapsed the Economy', AlterNet, 14 May 2010.

Introduction

1. Thomasson, Lynn (2009), 'Strategists See 17% S&P 500 Rise on Fed Cuts After Saying "Buy"', Bloomberg.com, 5 January 2009.
2. Whitehouse, Kaja (2007), 'One "Quant" Sees Shakeout For the Ages – "10,000 Years"', *Wall Street Journal*, 11 August 2007.
3. Tett, Gillian and Gangahar, Anuj (2007), 'Limitations of computer models', *Financial Times*, 14 August 2007.
4. Giles, C. (2008), 'The vision thing', *Financial Times*, 25 November 2008.
5. Ferguson, Charles (2010), 'Larry Summers and the Subversion of Economics', *The Chronicle of Higher Education*, 30 October 2010.
6. Appelbaum, Binyamin (2012), 'Inside the Fed in 2006: A Coming Crisis, and Banter', *New York Times*, 12 January 2012.
7. 'It appears scandalous,' notes Taleb, 'that, of the hundreds of thousands of professionals involved, including prime public institutions such as the World Bank, the International Monetary Fund, different governmental agencies and central banks, private institutions such as banks, insurance companies, and large corporations, and, finally, academic departments, only a few individuals considered the possibility of the total collapse of the banking system that started in 2007.' Taleb, Nassim Nicholas (2009), 'Errors, robustness, and the fourth quadrant', *International Journal of Forecasting*, 25, 744–759. See also: Mihm, Stephen (2008), 'Dr Doom', *New York Times*, 15 August 2008; Taleb, Nassim Nicholas (2007), *The Black Swan: The Impact of the Highly Improbable* (New York: Random House); Galbraith, James K. (2009), 'Who Are These Economists, Anyway?', *The NEA Higher Education Journal*, Fall 2009.
8. Clark, Andrew (2009), 'Massive bet on RBS and Lloyds helped financier earn $2.5bn', *Guardian*, 22 December 2009.
9. Abbey, E. (1975), *The Second Rape of the West* (Chicago, IL: Playboy), p. 183.
10. See: http://news.bbc.co.uk/1/hi/programmes/hardtalk/default.stm

Chapter 1

1. Burnet, John (1920), *Early Greek Philosophy* (3rd edn; London: A. & C. Black Ltd).
2. As economists M. Neil Browne and J. Kevin Quinn note, 'perhaps unlike any other social science, economics does have an orthodoxy that is so dominant that few economists see themselves as even

having a perspective or as being part of a school of thought'. I will describe this dominant strain variously as mainstream, orthodox, or neoclassical. Browne, M.N. and Quinn, J.K. (2008), 'The Lamentable Absence of Power in Mainstream Economics', in John T. Harvey and Robert F. Garnett (eds), *Future Directions for Heterodox Economics* (University of Michigan Press), 240–61.

3. The full definition was 'the science which studies human behaviour as a relationship between ends and scarce means which have alternative uses'. Robbins, Lionel (1932), *An Essay on the Nature and Significance of Economic Science* (London: Macmillan), pp. 15, 110.

4. DeLong, Brad (2011), 'The Sorrow and the Pity of Another Liquidity Trap', Bloomberg.com, 5 July 2011.

5. Kling, Arnold (2002), 'Efficiency, Supply and Demand, and Market Clearing', arnoldkling.com, http://arnoldkling.com/econ/markets/efficiency.html

6. Ragan, Christopher T.S., and Lipsey, Richard G. (2003), *Macroeconomics*, 10th edition (Toronto: Pearson Education Canada), p. 62.

7. Housing data from the *Financial Times* House Price Index. See: http://www.acadametrics.co.uk/ftHousePrices.php; inflation data from http://www.statistics.gov.uk

8. Lionel Robbins for example said that 'Nobody in his senses would hold that the laws of mechanics were invalidated if an experiment designed to illustrate them were interrupted by an earthquake'. Robbins, Lionel (1932), *An Essay on the Nature and Significance of Economic Science* (London: Macmillan), p. 112. But as the philosopher Hans Albert et al. noted, the *ceteris paribus* clause 'here produces something of an absolute alibi, since, for every apparently deviating behavior, some altered factors can be made responsible. This makes the statement untestable, and its informational content decreases to zero.' Albert, H., Arnold, D., and Maier-Rigaud, F. (2012), 'Model Platonism: Neoclassical economic thought in critical light', *Journal of Institutional Economics*, 8(3), 295–323.

9. McCauley, Joe (2004), *Dynamics of Markets: Econophysics and Finance* (Cambridge University Press), p. 25.

10. Taibbi, Matt (2009), 'Inside The Great American Bubble Machine', *Rolling Stone*, 1082–83.

11. Bernanke, Ben S. (2009), 'Commencement address at the Boston College School of Law' (Newton, Massachusetts): http://www.federal reserve.gov/newsevents/speech/bernanke20090522a.htm

12. Kerr, R.A. (2004), 'Second thoughts on skill of El Niño predictions', *Science*, 290, 257–58.

13. Source: http://www.cgd.ucar.edu/cas/catalog/climind/TNI_N34/index.html#Sec5

14. Mill, John Stuart (1843), *A System of Logic: Ratiocinative and Inductive*, (London: Longmans, Green). Mill, John Stuart (1909), *Principles of Political Economy with some of their Applications to Social Philosophy*, William J. Ashley, ed. (London: Longmans, Green and Co.), III.9.11.

15. Menger, C. (1892), 'On the origin of money', *Economic Journal* 2, 239–55. Hayek, F.A. (1948), *Individualism and Economic Order* (Chicago: University of Chicago Press).

16. Caballero, Ricardo J. (2010), 'Macroeconomics after the Crisis: Time to Deal with the Pretense-of-Knowledge Syndrome', *Journal of Economic Perspectives*, 24(4): 85–102.

17. For cancer therapy, see for example: http://www.physiomics-plc.com/services/schedules-and-combinations

18. Orrell, David and McSharry, Patrick (2009), 'A Systems Approach to Forecasting', *Foresight*, 14, 25–30. See also the commentary in the same issue by Paul Goodwin and Robert Fildes.

19. Woolley, Frances (2010), 'Another rant about the *Globe and Mail*'s coverage of economics', Worthwhile Canadian Initiative, 20 September 2010.

20. Auld, Christopher (2011), 'A review of *Economyths: Ten Ways Economics Gets it Wrong*, by David Orrell', chrisaulddotcom .wordpress.com; Smith, Noah (2017), 'Economics Gets a Presidential Demotion', Bloomberg.com, 14 February 2017.

21. Katzner, Donald W. (2015), 'A Neoclassical Curmudgeon Looks at Heterodox Criticisms of Microeconomics', *World Economic Review* 4, 63–75. He describes demand and supply functions as 'abstractions that are not reflected in actuality'.

22. Anonymous (2016), 'The emperor's new paunch', *The Economist*, 24 September 2016.

23. Dubner, S. (2016), 'Why Uber Is an Economist's Dream', Freakonomics.com, 7 September 2016. Produced by Harry Huggins. The textbook is Goolsbee, A., Levitt, S.D., and Syverson, C. (2013), *Microeconomics* (New York: Worth).

24. Cohen, Peter et al. (2016), 'Using Big Data to Estimate Consumer Surplus: The Case of Uber', 30 August 2016.

25. Samuelson, P.A. and Nordhaus, W.D. (2010), *Economics* (New Delhi: Tata McGraw-Hill), p. 57.

26. McGilchrist, Ian (2009), *The Master and His Emissary* (New Haven, CT: Yale University Press), p. 330. See also Orrell, David (2007), *Apollo's Arrow: The Science of Prediction and the Future of Everything* (Toronto: HarperCollins), p. 30.

27. Karabell, Zachary (2013), 'The "Laws of Economics" Don't Exist', *The Atlantic*, 11 April 2013.

28. Which is ironic given that heterodox approaches such as stock-flow consistent models make more use of accounting principles than do mainstream approaches. Pilling, David (2016), 'Crash and learn: should we change the way we teach economics?', *Financial Times*, 30 September 2016. See comments to: Ruccio, David (2016), 'Crash and learn?', Real World Economic Review blog, 7 October 2016, https://rwer.wordpress.com/2016/10/07/crash-and-learn/ In his classic 1948 textbook *Economics*, Paul Samuelson asks: 'Is the law of supply and demand immutable?' He concludes that, while factors such as government action confuse the picture, their effects are felt through these quantities, so in general 'it is still true that price is determined by supply and demand'. Samuelson, Paul (1997), *Economics: The Original 1948 Edition* (New York: McGraw-Hill), p. 461.

29. The theory is therefore 'fully immunized to facts'. Albert, H., Arnold, D., and Maier-Rigaud, F. (2012), 'Model Platonism: Neoclassical economic thought in critical light', *Journal of Institutional Economics*, 8(3), 295–323.

30. McGilchrist, Ian (2009), *The Master and His Emissary* (New Haven, CT: Yale University Press), p. 82.

31. McGilchrist, Ian (2009), *The Master and His Emissary*, (New Haven, CT: Yale University Press), p. 217. See also Orrell, David (2012), *Truth or Beauty: Science and the Quest for Order* (New Haven, CT: Yale University Press), p. 267.

32. Average results were skewed somewhat by a collapse in sales of the highest-priced properties. Tencer, Daniel (2016), 'Vancouver Average House Price Plunge Is Largest On Record: BMO', *The Huffington Post Canada*, 11 October 2016.

33. Dmitrieva, Katia and Hertzberg, Erik (2017), 'Toronto Home Sellers Vanish as BMO Warns of Housing Bubble', Bloomberg.com, 15 February 2017. The rationale given is that people have 'nowhere

cheaper to move to', though it is not clear why this only applies now: for example, if your house was worth very little you might think it was hard to find somewhere cheaper too. A more likely reason is that some owners 'hold off listing because they believe prices will continue to escalate': Gordon, Josh (2017), 'In High Demand: Addressing the demand factors behind Toronto's housing affordability problem', CBI Policy paper, 13 March 2017.

34. Inman, Phillip (2017), 'Chief economist of Bank of England admits errors in Brexit forecasting', *The Guardian*, 5 January 2017. Paul Wilmott and I made the same comparison in *The Money Formula*, p. 44.

Chapter 2

1. Newton, Isaac (1952), *Opticks; or, A treatise of the reflections, refractions, inflections & colours of light*. Based on the 4th edn, London, 1730 (New York: Dover Publications), p. 400.

2. See Nelson, Robert (2002), *Economics as Religion: From Samuelson to Chicago and Beyond* (Pennsylvania State University Press).

3. For a discussion, see: Malkiel, Burton G. (2016), *A Random Walk Down Wall Street: The Time Tested Strategy For Successful Investing*, eleventh edition (New York: W.W. Norton & Company), pp. 182–4.

4. Cooper, George (2008), *The Origin of Financial Crises: Central banks, credit bubbles and the efficient market fallacy* (Petersfield: Harriman House), p. 11.

5. Soros, George (2008), *The New Paradigm for Financial Markets: The Credit Crisis of 2008 and What It Means* (New York: PublicAffairs), p. 216.

6. See Putnam, R.D. (2000), *Bowling Alone: The collapse and revival of American community* (New York: Simon & Schuster).

7. Wilkinson, Richard and Pickett, Kate (2009), *The Spirit Level: Why Greater Equality Makes Societies Stronger* (London: Bloomsbury), p. 4.

8. Energy Information Administration (2015), Annual Energy Outlook Retrospective Review, Report DOE/EIA-0640(2014), (Washington, DC: EIA). See Table 2 in https://www.eia.gov/outlooks/aeo/retrospective/

9. See Orrell, David (2007), *Apollo's Arrow: The Science of Prediction and the Future of Everything* (Toronto: HarperCollins), p. 242.

10. Ahir, H. and Loungani, P. (2014), 'Can economists forecast recessions? Some evidence from the Great Recession', *Oracle*, March 2014.

11. Edge, Rochelle M. and Gürkaynak, Refet (2010), 'How Useful Are Estimated DSGE Model Forecasts for Central Bankers?', *Brookings Papers on Economic Activity*, 41(2): 209–59.

12. Surowiecki, J. (2004), *The Wisdom of Crowds: Why the Many Are Smarter Than the Few and How Collective Wisdom Shapes Business, Economies, Societies and Nations* (New York: Random House). Prediction markets such as Betfair provide a systematic means of tapping into collective knowledge.

13. US–Canada Power System Outage Task Force, Final Report on the Implementation of the Task Force Recommendations, Natural Resources Canada, US Department of Energy, September 2006. http://www.ferc.gov/industries/electric/indus-act/.../09-06-final-report.pdf

14. Anonymous (2009), 'House proud?', *Economist*, 3 October 2009.

15. Bianchi, Stefania (2009), 'Dubai Debt Freeze to Hit Property Recovery', *Wall Street Journal*, 27 November 2009.

16. Delli Gatti, Domenico, et al. (2008), 'Financially Constrained Fluctuations in an Evolving Network Economy', NBER Working Paper No. W14112.

17. By 'design principles' I am not implying there is a designer – these are emergent properties that have evolved in natural systems. See also: De Atauri, Pedro, et al. (2004), 'Evolution of "design principles" in biology and engineering', *IEE Syst. Biol.*, 1, 28–40.

18. Kubelec, C. and Sa, F. (2009), 'The Geographical Composition of National External Balance Sheets: 1980–2005', Bank of England Working Paper (forthcoming). Available at http://econ-www.mit.edu/files/3232. Haldane, A.G. (2009), 'Rethinking the Financial Network', speech delivered at the Financial Student Association, Amsterdam, April 2009, available at: http://www.bankofengland.co.uk/publications/speeches/2009/speech386.pdf. For a discussion of network connectivity, see Orrell, David (2008), *The Other Side of the Coin: The Emerging Vision of Economics and Our Place in the World* (Toronto: Key Porter), p. 96.

19. May, R.M., Levin, S.A., and Sugihara, G. (2008), 'Ecology for bankers', *Nature*, 451, 891–93.

20. Csete, M. and Doyle, J. (2004), 'Bow ties, metabolism and disease', *Trends in Biotechnology*, 22 (9), 446–50.

21. Bair, Sheila (2007), 'Remarks', 2007 Risk Management and Allocation Conference (Paris), 25 June 2007.

22. Canada had the world's soundest banking system in 2008, according to the World Economic Forum. Taylor, Rob (2008), 'Canada rated world's soundest bank system: survey', Reuters, 9 October 2008.

23. Martin, Eric and Tsang, Michael (2009), 'Cash Best as Record Correlation Hints Herd Collapse', Bloomberg, 29 June 2009.

24. As an example, see: Lillo, Fabrizio, et al. (2008), 'Specialization of strategies and herding behavior of trading firms in a financial market', *New Journal of Physics*, 10, 043019.

25. Giles, Chris and Parker, George (2009), 'Transcript: Interview with Alistair Darling', *Financial Times*, 14 September 2009.

26. Kambhu, J., Weidman, S., and Krishnan, N. (2007), *New Directions for Understanding Systemic Risk* (Washington DC: National Academies Press).

27. House of Representatives, Committee on Oversight and Government Reform, 'The Financial Crisis and the Role of Federal Regulators, Preliminary Transcript', 36–37, 23 October 2008, available at: http://oversight.house.gov/documents/20081024163819.pdf; Greenspan, Alan (2011), 'Dodd-Frank fails to meet test of our times', *Financial Times*, 29 March 2011.

28. As Bank of England governor Mervyn King said in October 2009: 'Anyone who proposed giving government guarantees to retail depositors and other creditors and then suggested that such funding could be used to finance highly risky and speculative activities would be thought rather unworldly. But that is where we are now.' Vina, Gonzalo and Ryan, Jennifer (2009), 'King Opens Rift With Brown on Whether to Split Banks', Bloomberg, 21 October 2009.

29. Network scientists were among the first to spot the possibility of cascading failures in the financial system. Barabási, Albert-László (2003), *Linked: How Everything is Connected to Everything Else and What it Means for Business, Science, and Everyday Life* (Cambridge, MA: Plume), p. 211.

30. In the UK, at the height of the crisis, the sight of financiers 'scrawling on pieces of paper' gave the treasury department 'the feel of a particularly crowded kindergarten during art class', according to the *Observer* newspaper. Treanor, Jill and Elliott, Larry (2009), 'Dark days when banks reached brink of oblivion', *Observer*, 6 September 2009.

31. See: 'Rep. Kanjorski: $550 Billion Disappeared in "Electronic Run On the Banks"', http://www.liveleak.com/view?i=ca2_1234032281

32. Haldane, A.G. (2009), 'Rethinking the Financial Network', speech delivered at the Financial Student Association, Amsterdam, April 2009, available at: http://www.bankofengland.co.uk/publications/speeches/2009/speech386.pdf

33. Eichengreen, Barry (2015), 'Time to get serious about bank reform', *Prospect Magazine*, February 2015.

34. Jopson, Barney and McLannahan, Ben (2015), 'Bank living wills reveal Wall St victims', *Financial Times*, 6 July 2015.

35. See letter from senators Elizabeth Warren and Tammy Baldwin to Goldman Sachs, 9 February 2017, at: https://www.baldwin.senate.gov/imo/media/doc/2.9.17%20Letter%20to%20Goldman%20Sachs%20on%20Cohn.pdf. Perhaps they will at least make it shorter and simpler – at 848 pages, it seems a little wordy compared to 37 pages for Glass-Steagall.

36. See for example: Massad, Timothy, 'Remarks of Chairman Timothy Massad before the Conference on the Evolving Structure of the U.S. Treasury Market', 21 October 2015. Available at: http://www.cftc.gov/PressRoom/SpeechesTestimony/opamassad-30. See also *The Money Formula*, p. 199 for a discussion of flash crashes and high-frequency trading.

37. For a survey of complexity modelling, see Bruno, B., Faggini, M. and Parziale, A. (2016), 'Complexity Modelling in Economics: the State of Art', *Economic Thought*, 5(2): 29–43.

38. Shiller, Robert (1984), 'Stock Prices and Social Dynamics', *Brookings Papers on Economic Activity* 2: 457–510.

39. Wilmott, Paul and Orrell, David (2017), *The Money Formula: Dodgy Finance, Pseudo Science, and How Mathematicians Took Over the Markets* (Chichester: Wiley), p. 118.

40. Nietzsche, Friedrich (1967), *The Birth of Tragedy, and The Case of Wagner*, translated by Walter Kaufmann (New York: Vintage Books), p. 36. The trend towards increasing individualism has been going on for centuries; see: Orrell, David (2012), *Truth or Beauty: Science and the Quest for Order* (New Haven, CT: Yale University Press), pp. 57–8.

41. Monbiot, George (2016), 'Neoliberalism is creating loneliness. That's what's wrenching society apart', *The Guardian*, 12 October 2016.

Chapter 3

1. Bouchaud, J.-P. (2008), 'Economics needs a scientific revolution', *Nature*, 455, 1181.

2. These may take the form of probability laws, as in quantum theory.

3. The economist Alfred Marshall said that Jevons' work 'will prob-ably be found to have more constructive force than any, save that of Ricardo, that has been done during the last hundred years'. Marshall, Alfred and Whitaker, John King (ed.), (2005), *The Correspondence of Alfred Marshall, Economist: Climbing, 1868-1890* (Cambridge University Press), p. 164.

4. Anonymous (2008), 'Léon Walras', *The Concise Encyclopedia of Economics* (Library of Economics and Liberty). Retrieved 17 July 2009 from: http://www.econlib.org/library/Enc/bios/Walras.html

5. Schumpeter, J.A. (1954), *History of Economic Analysis* (London: Routledge), p. 827.

6. Powers, Charles H. (1987), *Vilfredo Pareto*, ed. Jonathan H. Turner (Masters of Social Theory, 5; Newbury Park, CA: Sage Publications), pp. 13-20.

7. Dani Rodrik (2015), *Economics Rules: The Rights and Wrongs of the Dismal Science* (New York: W.W. Norton & Company), p. 50.

8. Jevons, William Stanley (1909), 'The Solar Period and the Price of Corn (1875)', in H.S. Foxwell (ed.), *Investigations in Currency and Finance* (London: Macmillan), pp. 194-205.

9. Image from: http://www.history.rochester.edu/steam/thurston/1878/f29p115.gif

10. Soros, George (2008), *The New Paradigm for Financial Markets: The Credit Crisis of 2008 and What it Means* (New York: PublicAffairs), p. 6.

11. Boyle, Catherine (2009), 'Bank of China starts to offer mortgages in the UK', *The Times*, 25 July 2009.

12. Adrian, Tobias and Shin, Hyun Song (2008), 'Financial Intermediary Leverage and Value-at-Risk', Staff Report No. 338 (Federal Reserve Bank of New York).

13. For example, MIT economist Andrew Lo described economists as suffering from a 'peculiar psychological disorder known as "physics envy"'. Anonymous (2002), 'Bubble trouble', *Economist*, 16 May 2002.

14. Minsky, Hyman P. (1972), 'Financial instability revisited: the eco-nomics of disaster', *Reappraisal of the Federal Reserve Discount Mechanism* (Washington, DC: Board of Governors of the Federal Reserve System), 95-136.

15. Mihm, Stephen (2009), 'Why capitalism fails', *Boston Globe*, 13 September 2009.

16. As noted at http://www.sndeecon.org: 'In the last decade, many have come to realize that nonlinearity [including feedback loops] is an inherent feature of economic and financial markets'. Despite this, mainstream economics retains a conceptual framework that, as systems scientist Jay W. Forrester observed, 'is narrow, is based on unrealistic assumptions, emphasizes equilibrium conditions, and is committed to mostly linear mathematical methods'. Forrester, Jay W. (2003), 'Economic Theory for the New Millennium', plenary address at the International System Dynamics Conference, New York, 21 July 2003.

17. John Sterman of the MIT System Dynamics Group, for example, has developed 'management flight simulators' that allow business leaders to accustomise themselves to the effects of feedback. Sterman, J.D. (2000), *Business Dynamics: Systems thinking and modeling for a complex world* (New York: McGraw Hill).

18. 'Tests of market efficiency are tests of some model of market equilibrium and vice versa', according to Eugene Fama. 'The two are joined at the hip'. Clement, Douglas (2007), 'Interview with Eugene Fama', *The Region*, December 2007.

19. According to Arthur Levitt Jr. (former chairman of the Securities and Exchange Commission). Goodman, Peter S. (2008), 'The Reckoning – Taking Hard New Look at a Greenspan Legacy', *New York Times*, 8 October 2008.

20. Kitano, H. (2004), 'Cancer as a robust system: implications for anti-cancer therapy', *Nature Reviews Cancer*, 4, 227–35.

21. As an example of how removing regulatory control loops can disrupt a biological system, see: Orrell, David, et al. (2006), 'Feedback control of stochastic noise in the yeast galactose utilization pathway', *Physica D*, 217, 64–76.

22. As George Soros notes, central banks can 'take a step and then they get a feedback from the market and so the feedback will tell them whether they've done enough or whether they have to do more. So this feedback helps to correct and get close to maintaining balance'. Soros, George and Freeland, Chrystia (2009), 'George Soros interview', *Financial Times*, 23 October 2009. Another proposed stabilising mechanism, known as regulatory hybrid securities, is a kind of debt, to be issued by banks, that can be converted into equity during a crisis. See: Shiller, Robert (2009), 'Engineering financial stability', *World Finance*, 16 February 2010.

23. Mirowski, Philip (2013), *Never Let a Serious Crisis Go to Waste: How Neoliberalism Survived the Financial Meltdown* (London: Verso), p. 178.
24. White, William R. (2013), 'Is Monetary Policy A Science? The Interaction of Theory And Practice Over The Last 50 Years'. In *50 Years of Money and Finance – Lessons and Challenges*, edited by Balling, Morten and Gnan, Ernest (Vienna: SUERF).
25. Haldane, Andrew (2014), 'The Revolution In Economics', in *Economics, Education and Unlearning: Economics Education at the University of Manchester* (Manchester: Post-Crash Economics Society), pp. 3–6.
26. British Academy (2015), 'Reflections on Economics'. See http://www.britac.ac.uk/node/4180/
27. Caballero, Ricardo J. (2010), 'Macroeconomics after the Crisis: Time to Deal with the Pretense-of-Knowledge Syndrome', *Journal of Economic Perspectives*, 24(4): 85–102.
28. See http://www.ideaeconomics.org/minsky/. The group also received funding from the Institute for New Economic Thinking.
29. Munchau, Wolfgang (2015), 'Macroeconomists need new tools to challenge consensus', *Financial Times*, 12 April 2015.
30. Keen, Steve (2016), 'Olivier Blanchard, Equilibrium, Complexity, and the Future of Macroeconomics', Forbes.com, 4 October 2016.

Chapter 4
1. Galton, Francis (1889), *Natural Inheritance* (London: Macmillan).
2. Clever, but not completely original or reliable, according to: Haug, Espen Gaarder and Taleb, Nassim Nicholas (2009), 'Why We Have Never Used the Black–Scholes–Merton Option Pricing Formula (fifth version)'. Available at SSRN: http://ssrn.com/abstract=1012075
3. As Pablo Triana wrote: 'all the Nobels awarded to financial economics are heavily grounded on the Normal assumption; remove such tenet, and the prized theories crumble and crash.' Triana, Pablo (2009), *Lecturing Birds on Flying: Can Mathematical Theories Destroy the Financial Markets?* (New York: Wiley).
4. See comments by Kevin Milligan to blog post: Woolley, Frances (2010), 'Another rant about the *Globe and Mail*'s coverage of economics', Worthwhile Canadian Initiative, 20 September 2010.
5. Fama, E.F. (1965), 'The behavior of stock-market prices', *Journal of Business*, 38(1): 34–105.

6. Overbye, Dennis (2009), 'They Tried to Outsmart Wall Street', *New York Times*, 9 March 2009.

7. Taleb, Nassim Nicholas (2007), *The Black Swan: The Impact of the Highly Improbable* (New York: Random House), p. 127.

8. Barford, Vanessa (2008), '"It's like a massive earthquake"', *BBC News*, 15 September 2008.

9. Lux, T. (1996), 'The Stable Paretian Hypothesis and the Frequency of Large Returns: An Examination of Major German Stocks', *Applied Financial Economics*, 6, 463–75; Gopikrishnan, P., et al. (1998), 'Inverse cubic law for the distribution of stock price variations', *European Physical Journal B*, 3, 139–40; Gopikrishnan, P., et al. (1999), 'Scaling of the distribution of fluctuations of financial market indices', *Physical Review E*, 60, 5305–16; Plerou, V., et al. (1999), 'Scaling of the distribution of price fluctuations of individual companies', *Physical Review E*, 60, 6519–29.

10. Seismograph (vertical acceleration, nm/sq. sec) of the Kobe earthquake. Recorded at Tasmania University, Hobart, Australia on 16 January 1995 beginning at 20:56:51 (GMT). Source: Data management centre, Washington University. Downloaded from: http://robjhyndman.com/TSDL/

11. Mandelbrot, Benoît and Hudson, Richard L. (2004), *The Misbehavior of Markets: A Fractal View of Financial Turbulence* (New York: Basic Books).

12. Bak, Per (1996), *How Nature Works: The science of self-organized criticality* (New York: Springer-Verlag).

13. One person who uses fractal methods to make predictions is econophysicist Didier Sornette, who foresees a 'singularity around 2050, signaling a fundamental change of regime of the world economy and population'. Of course this assumes we survive 2012, predicted by the Mayans to be an equally eventful year. (Update: we did!) Sornette, Didier (2002), *Why Stock Markets Crash: Critical Events in Complex Financial Systems* (Princeton University Press), p. xvii.

14. As Nassim Taleb points out: 'Parametrizing a power law lends itself to extremely large estimation errors.' Taleb, Nassim Nicholas (2009), 'Errors, robustness, and the fourth quadrant', *International Journal of Forecasting*, 25, 744–59.

15. As geophysicist Susan Hough wrote: 'Scientists have been chasing earthquake prediction – the holy grail of earthquake science – for decades ... Yet we have little to no real progress to show for our efforts.'

Hough, Susan (2009), 'Confusing Patterns With Coincidences', *New York Times*, 11 April 2009.

16. Quoted in Triana, Pablo (2009), *Lecturing Birds on Flying: Can Mathematical Theories Destroy the Financial Markets?* (New York: Wiley), p. 137.

17. An example is so-called 'frailty factors'. See Duffie, Darrell, et al. (2006), 'Frailty Correlated Default', Swiss Finance Institute Research Paper.

18. Nocera, Joe (2009), 'Risk Mismanagement', *New York Times*, 2 January 2009.

19. According to Hiroaki Kitano, this is similar to the law of conservation of energy in physics. See for example: Csete, Marie E. and Doyle, John C. (2002), 'Reverse Engineering of Biological Complexity', *Science*, 295, 1664–69.

20. http://www.fda.gov/ICECI/EnforcementActions/WarningLetters/ucm165237.htm

21. Birchall, Jonathan (2009), 'Ionic shampoo and photon genies offer phantom cures for swine flu', *Financial Times*, 8 August 2009.

22. Tett, Gillian (2009a), 'Could "Tobin tax" reshape financial sector DNA?', *Financial Times*, 27 August 2009.

23. Sunderland, Ruth (2009a), 'We can put a stop to huge, undeserved bank bonuses', *Guardian*, 25 October 2009. As an illustration, here's a quote from the chief executive of the Royal Bank of Scotland, in his 2009 letter to shareholders: 'We are in the limelight – understandably but uncomfortably so … we especially, but all banks too, have become regrettably high profile. We sometimes feel as if commentators variously want us to go back to over-lending, to operate on a "not-for-profit" basis, to never entertain a client and to offer employment conditions that deter the best and brightest. Oh yes, and at the same time to pull off a recovery enabling taxpayers to recoup the support given.' The tone seems a little self-pitying, from a person on a £9.6m salary package, at a company that is majority owned by the UK government. The argument that banks need to pay enormous salaries to pay the 'best and brightest' is also disingenuous – if they're so smart, why are they on government support?

24. Taleb, Nassim Nicholas and Spitznagel, Mark (2009), 'Time to tackle the real evil: too much debt', *Financial Times*, 13 July 2009.

25. For my take on this topic, see Orrell, David (2007), *Apollo's Arrow:*

The Science of Prediction and the Future of Everything (Toronto: HarperCollins).

26. Keynes, J.M. (1939), 'Professor Tinbergen's Method', *The Economic Journal*, 49(195), 558–77.

27. Dobbs, Richard et al. (2015), 'Debt and (Not Much) Deleveraging', McKinsey Global Institute.

28. Canada is the only country studied by BIS that has triggered three of their four 'financial crisis early earning indicators'. It is close to triggering the fourth as well. Bank of International Settlements, 'Highlights of global financial flows', *BIS Quarterly Review*, March 2017.

29. Wilmott, Paul and Orrell, David (2017), *The Money Formula: Dodgy Finance, Pseudo Science, and How Mathematicians Took Over the Markets* (Chichester: Wiley), pp. 177–80.

Chapter 5

1. Kearns, Jeff and Tsang, Michael (2009), 'VIX Signals S&P 500 Swoon as September Approaches', Bloomberg, 10 August 2009.

2. Seymour, Ben, et al. (2007), 'Differential Encoding of Losses and Gains in the Human Striatum', *Journal of Neuroscience*, 27, 4826–31.

3. Bentham quoted in Jevons, William Stanley (1879), *Theory of Political Economy* (2nd edn; London: Macmillan), p. 24.

4. Mill, John Stuart (2002), *'Utilitarianism' and 'On Liberty': Including 'Essay on Bentham' and Selections from the Writings of Jeremy Bentham and John Austin* (introd. Mary Warnock), (2nd edn; Oxford: Blackwell).

5. Bernstein, Peter L. (1996), *Against the Gods: The remarkable story of risk* (New York: Wiley), pp. 159–60.

6. Arrow, Kenneth J. and Debreu, Gérard (1954), 'Existence of a Competitive Equilibrium for a Competitive Economy', *Econometrica*, 22, 65–90.

7. Radner, Roy (1968), 'Competitive equilibrium under uncertainty', *Econometrica*, 36, 31–58. Quoted in Ormerod, Paul (1994), *The Death of Economics* (London: Faber and Faber), p. 90.

8. Blaug, Mark (1998), 'Disturbing currents in modern economics', *Challenge*, 41 (3), 11–34.

9. Klein, Daniel B. (2013), 'Kenneth J. Arrow [Ideological Profiles of the Economics Laureates]', *Econ Journal Watch*, 10(3): 268–81.

10. Friedman, Milton (1953), *Essays in Positive Economics* (University of Chicago Press).

11. Noble, Holcomb B. (2006), 'Milton Friedman, 94, Free-Market Theorist, Dies', *New York Times*, 17 November 2006.

12. *The Open Mind: Milton Friedman interview* (WNBC, 1975), Heffner, Richard (dir.). For opinions on drug regulation, see: Friedman, Milton and Friedman, Rose (1990), *Free to Choose: A Personal Statement* (New York: Harvest Books), pp. 207–10.

13. Keynes, John Maynard (1936), *The General Theory of Employment, Interest and Money* (London: Macmillan), pp. 161–2.

14. Klein, Naomi (2008), *The Shock Doctrine: The Rise of Disaster Capitalism* (London: Penguin).

15. The *Economist* noted in 2006 that governments rarely make big decisions without 'turning to CGE models to forewarn them of the consequences'. Anonymous (2006), 'Big questions and big numbers', *Economist*, 13 July 2006.

16. In the 1990s, for example, CGE models were used to assess the economic impact of the North American Free Trade Agreement (NAFTA). A 2005 study by Timothy Kehoe of the University of Minnesota showed that: 'The models drastically underestimated the impact of NAFTA on North American trade.' Kehoe, Timothy J. (2005), 'An Evaluation of the Performance of Applied General Equilibrium Models of the Impact of NAFTA', in Timothy J. Kehoe, T.N. Srinivasan and John Whalley (eds), *Frontiers in Applied General Equilibrium Modeling: Essays in Honor of Herbert Scarf* (Cambridge University Press), pp. 341–77.

17. Quoted in Beinhocker, Eric D. (2006), *Origin of Wealth: Evolution, Complexity, and the Radical Remaking of Economics* (Boston, MA: Harvard Business School Press), p. 59.

18. Blanchflower, David (2009), 'It's good to go walkabout', *New Statesman*, 16 November 2009.

19. Anonymous (2009), 'The other-worldly philosophers', *Economist*, 16 July 2009.

20. As even he admitted: 'The use of quantity of money as a target has not been a success.' London, Simon (2003), 'Lunch with the FT: Milton Friedman', *Financial Times*, 7 June 2003.

21. Knight, Frank H. (1932), 'The Newer Economics and the Control of Economic Activity', *Journal of Political Economy*, 50, 455.

22. A good example of this is the popularity of string theory in physics,

despite the fact that it enjoys no experimental support. See Woit, Peter (2006), *Not Even Wrong: The Failure of String Theory and the Continuing Challenge to Unify the Laws of Physics* (New York: Basic Books). Also: Smolin, Lee (2006), *The Trouble With Physics: The Rise of String Theory, the Fall of a Science, and What Comes Next* (Boston, MA: Houghton Mifflin).

23. Anonymous (2009), 'Efficiency and beyond', *Economist*, 16 July 2009.

24. Michael Schrage (2003), 'Daniel Kahneman: The Thought Leader Interview', *Strategy+Business*, Winter 2003.

25. Michael Schrage (2003), 'Daniel Kahneman: The Thought Leader Interview', *Strategy+Business*, Winter 2003.

26. McClure, Samuel M., et al. (2004), 'Separate Neural Systems Value Immediate and Delayed Monetary Rewards', *Science*, 306, 503–07.

27. Bechara, A. (2004), 'The role of emotion in decision-making: Evidence from neurological patients with orbitofrontal damage', *Brain and Cognition*, 55, 30–40.

28. Cutler, D.M., Poterba, J.M., and Summers, L.H. (1989), 'What moves stock prices?', *Journal of Portfolio Management*, 15, 4–12.

29. Clement, Douglas (2007), 'Interview with Eugene Fama', *The Region*, December 2007.

30. Shiller, Robert (2009), 'Reinventing economics', *World Finance*, 23 October 2009.

31. 'Long View Part 3 – "Real people" economics', *Financial Times* (online video), 31 April 2009.

32. Quoted in Moye, Catherine (2007), 'All in the mind', *Financial Times*, 16 September 2007.

33. Ayres, Ian (2007), *Super Crunchers: How Anything Can Be Predicted* (London: John Murray), p. 50.

34. See, for example: LeBaron, B. (2006), 'Agent-based Financial Markets: Matching Stylized Facts with Style', in D. Colander (ed.), *Post Walrasian Macroeconomics: Beyond the DSGE Model* (Cambridge University Press), pp. 221–35; and Howitt, P. and Clower, R.J. (2000), 'The emergence of economic organization', *Journal of Economic Behavior and Organization*, 41, 55–84.

35. An extensive comparison of forecasting techniques found that 'simple methods … do as well, or in many cases better, than statistically sophisticated ones'. Makridakis, Spyros and Hibon, Michele (2000), 'The M3-Competition: results, conclusions and implications', *International Journal of Forecasting*, 16, 451–76.

36. Orrell, David and McSharry, Patrick (2009), 'A Systems Approach to Forecasting', *Foresight*, (14), 25–30. See also the commentary in the same issue by Paul Goodwin and Robert Fildes.

37. presidential address to the American Economic Association. See: Debreu, Gérard (1991), 'The Mathematization of Economic Theory', *American Economic Review*, 81, 1–7.

38. Coase, Ronald (1999), 'Interview with Ronald Coase', *Newsletter of the International Society for New Institutional Economics*, 2 (1).

39. Derman, Emanuel (2004), *My Life as a Quant: Reflections on Physics and Finance* (New York: Wiley), p. 268.

40. Klamer, A., and Colander, D.C. (1990), *The Making of an Economist* (Boulder, CO: Westview Press), p. 18.

41. Colander, D. (2007), *The Making of an Economist, Redux* (Princeton: Princeton University Press), p. 24.

42. Bootle, R.P. (2009), *The Trouble with Markets: Saving Capitalism from Itself* (London: Nicholas Brealey), p. 248.

43. Earle, J., Moran, C., and Ward-Perkins, Z. (2016), *The Econocracy: The Perils of Leaving Economics to the Experts* (Manchester: Manchester University Press), pp. 35–6.

44. Benedictus, Leo (2013), 'The nudge unit – has it worked so far?', *The Guardian*, 2 May 2013.

45. Strohm, Chris (2016), 'Russia Weaponized Social Media in U.S. Election, FireEye Says', Bloomberg.com, 1 December 2016; Dirk Helbing et al. (2017), 'Will Democracy Survive Big Data and Artificial Intelligence?', *Scientific American*, 25 February 2017.

46. Gisiger, Christoph (2016), 'The business of central banks is like pornography', *Finanz und Wirtschaft*, 18 May 2016.

47. Ainslie, G. (1991), 'Derivation of "rational" economic behavior from hyperbolic discount curves', *American Economic Review*, 81: 134–40.

48. Fullbrook, Edward (2010), 'How to bring economics into the 3rd millennium by 2020', *real-world economics review*, 54: 89–108.

49. For a critique of behavioural economics, see: Berg, Nathan and Gigerenzer, Gerd (2010), 'As-If Behavioral Economics: Neoclassical Economics In Disguise?', *History of Economic Ideas*, 18 (1): 133–65.

50. David Harding, founder of Winton Capital, told the *Financial Times* that 'we have used techniques that would be described as machine learning for at least 30 years'. Cookson, Clive (2016), 'Winton Capital's

David Harding on making millions through maths', *Financial Times*, 25 November 2016. Another pioneer in the area was Renaissance Technologies.

51. 'Of all the tools at the discipline's disposal, the practitioners' scepticism is the most timeless.' And their sense of humour. Anonymous (2016), 'Trend growth', *The Economist*, 26 November 2016.

52. One useful study by an academic economist is: Gordon, Josh (2017), 'In High Demand: Addressing the demand factors behind Toronto's housing affordability problem', CBI Policy paper, 13 March 2017.

Chapter 6

1. Fraser Institute, 'Index of economic freedom', http://www.free theworld.com/

2. Anonymous (2008), 'Excerpts: Iceland's Oddsson', *Wall Street Journal*, 17 October 2008.

3. Ertel, Manfred (2009), 'Iceland's Women Reach for Power', *Der Spiegel*, 22 April 2009.

4. Sunderland, Ruth (2009), 'After the crash, Iceland's women lead the rescue', *Observer*, 22 February 2009.

5. Abraham, Ralph (1994), *Chaos, Gaia, Eros: A chaos pioneer uncovers the three great streams of history* (New York: HarperCollins), p. 92.

6. Guthrie, W.K.C. (1962), *A History of Greek Philosophy, Vol. 1* (Cambridge University Press), p. 252.

7. Wertheim, Margaret (2006), 'Numbers Are Male, Said Pythagoras, and the Idea Persists', *New York Times*, 3 October 2006.

8. Aristotle (350 BCE), *Politics*, trans. Benjamin Jowett: http://classics .mit.edu/Aristotle/politics.html

9. Fox Keller, Evelyn (1985), *Reflections on Gender and Science* (Yale University Press), p. 53.

10. Roszak, Theodore (1999), *The Gendered Atom: Reflections on the Sexual Psychology of Science* (San Francisco: Conari), p. 56.

11. Snow, C.P. and Collini, Stefan (1993), *The Two Cultures* (Cambridge University Press), p. 103.

12. Roszak, Theodore (1999), *The Gendered Atom: Reflections on the Sexual Psychology of Science* (San Francisco: Conari), p. 88.

13. Bateson, M.C. (1999), 'What is the most important invention in the past two thousand years? From: Mary Catherine Bateson', Edge.org, edited by J. Brockman, 10 February 1999.

14. Or what Evelyn Fox Keller calls 'gender ideology'. Keller, Evelyn Fox (1985), *Reflections on Gender and Science* (Yale University Press), p. 20.

15. Nelson, Julie A. (1996), 'The Masculine Mindset of Economic Analysis', *Chronicle of Higher Education*, 42, B3.

16. Hillman, James (1975), *Re-Visioning Psychology* (New York: Harper Perennial), p. 132.

17. McCloskey, D. (2000), 'Crossing economics', *International Journal of Transgenderism*, 4 (3). See also: McCloskey, D. (1999), *Crossing: A memoir* (Chicago: University of Chicago Press).

18. Gabor, Andrea (2006), 'Deirdre McCloskey's Market Path to Virtue', *Strategy+Business*, 43 (summer). McCloskey, D. and Ziliak, S.T. (2001), *Measurement and meaning in economics: The essential Deirdre McCloskey* (Cheltenham: Edward Elgar), p. 303.

19. According to *Freakonomics* author Steven Levitt, the vast majority of economists hadn't heard of Ostrom before she won the prize: 'I have no recollection of ever seeing or hearing her name mentioned by an economist. She is a political scientist, both by training and her career.' Levitt, Steven D. (2009), 'What This Year's Nobel Prize in Economics Says About the Nobel Prize in Economics', *New York Times*, 12 October 2009.

20. Henderson, Hazel (2004), 'The "Nobel" Prize That Wasn't', *Le Monde Diplomatique*, December 2004. An example was Myron Scholes, who in 1997 won for his work on the very risk models that contributed to the spectacular collapse, a year later, of his employer Long-Term Capital Management. Lowenstein, Roger (2000), *When Genius Failed: The Rise and Fall of Long-Term Capital Management* (Random House).

21. Senate Banking Committee (1999), 'Gramm Wins Senate Approval For Gold Medal Honoring Nobel Laureate Milton Friedman': http://banking.senate.gov/prel99/1122met.htm

22. Senate Banking Committee (1999), 'Gramm's Statement at Signing Ceremony For Gramm–Leach–Bliley Act': http://banking.senate.gov/prel99/1112gbl.htm

23. Senate Banking Committee (1999), 'Gramm Calls Commodity Futures Modernization Act "A Major Achievement of the 106th Congress"': http://banking.senate.gov/prel00/1215cofu.htm

24. Younge, Gary (2008), 'Bad cheque for black America', *Guardian*, 7 February 2008.

25. It is debatable whether these cost efficiencies were very significant. Paul Volcker, who is chairman of President Obama's Economic Recovery Advisory Board, said: 'I wish someone would give me one shred of neutral evidence that financial innovation has led to economic growth – one shred of evidence.' Any reduction in the cost of mortgages also fed through to higher home prices, which was not universally perceived as a good thing. Hosking, Patrick and Jagger, Suzy (2009), '"Wake up, gentlemen", world's top bankers warned by former Fed chairman Volcker', *Times*, 9 December 2009.

26. Bannon, Lisa (2009), 'As Riches Fade, So Does Finance's Allure', *Wall Street Journal*, 21 September 2009.

27. Overbye, Dennis (2009), 'They Tried to Outsmart Wall Street', *New York Times*, 9 March 2009.

28. Li, David X. (2000), 'On Default Correlation: A Copula Function Approach', *Journal of Fixed Income*, 9, 43–54.

29. Spreeuw, J. and Wang, X. (2008), 'Modelling the short-term dependence between two remaining lifetimes of a couple' (London: Cass Business School).

30. 'Default is like the death of a company', Li later told the *Wall Street Journal*, 'so we should model this the same way we model human life.' Whitehouse, Mark (2005), 'How a Formula Ignited Market That Burned Some Big Investors', *Wall Street Journal*, 12 September 2005.

31. Fox Keller, Evelyn (1985), *Reflections on Gender and Science* (Yale University Press), p. 141. Philospher Mary Midgley also notes that 'social scientists ... have often pursued a very powerful and confused notion of "objectivity" as requiring, not just the avoidance of personal bias, but a refusal to talk or think about subjective factors at all. The word "subjective" then becomes a simple term of abuse directed at any mention of thoughts or feelings, and the word "objective" a potent compliment for any approach which ignores them.' Midgley, Mary (1985), *Evolution as a Religion: Strange Hopes and Stranger Fears* (London: Methuen), p. 25.

32. International Monetary Fund (2006), 'Global Financial Stability Report: Market Developments and Issues' (Washington, DC: International Monetary Fund), April 2006, p. 51.

33. Whitehouse, Mark (2005), 'How a Formula Ignited Market That Burned Some Big Investors', *Wall Street Journal*, 12 September 2005.

34. Another example of this, apart from VaR and the Gaussian copula, is the famous Black–Scholes formula which played a key role in the

Black Monday crash. See Triana, Pablo (2009), *Lecturing Birds on Flying: Can Mathematical Theories Destroy the Financial Markets?* (New York: Wiley).

35. Committee of Government Oversight and Reform (2008), 'Testimony of Dr Alan Greenspan', 23 October 2008: http://oversight.house.gov/documents/20081023100438.pdf

36. Bill Clinton admits that: 'I very much wish now that I had demanded that we put derivatives under the jurisdiction of the Securities and Exchange Commission and that transparency rules had been observed ... That I think is a legitimate criticism of what we didn't do.' Baker, Peter (2009), 'The Mellowing of William Jefferson Clinton', *New York Times*, 26 May 2009.

37. Haldane, A.G. (2009), 'Rethinking the Financial Network', speech delivered at the Financial Student Association, Amsterdam, April 2009, available at: http://www.bankofengland.co.uk/publications/speeches/2009/speech386.pdf

38. The same pattern is true for Paulson's successor: 'Some of Treasury Secretary Timothy Geithner's closest aides, none of whom faced Senate confirmation, earned millions of dollars a year working for Goldman Sachs Group Inc., Citigroup Inc. and other Wall Street firms, according to financial disclosure forms.' Schmidt, Robert (2009), 'Geithner Aides Reaped Millions Working for Banks, Hedge Funds', Bloomberg, 14 October 2009.

39. Regional Fed presidents Robert Kaplan, Neel Kashkari, and William Dudley are alumni, as are Gary Cohn, Steven Mnuchin and Stephen Bannon. Philadelphia Fed President Patrick Harker was the trustee of the Goldman Sachs Trust.

40. Tett, Gillian (2009), 'Lunch with the FT: David Hare', *Financial Times*, 25 September 2009.

41. Zehner, Jacki (2008), 'Why Are Goldman's Women Invisible? (Asks a Former Goldman Sachs Partner)', *The Huffington Post*: http://www.huffingtonpost.com/jacki-zehner/why-are-goldmans-women-in_b_139650.html

42. Triana, Pablo (2009), *Lecturing Birds on Flying: Can Mathematical Theories Destroy the Financial Markets?* (New York: Wiley), p. 88.

43. Ishikawa, Tetsuya (2009), *How I Caused the Credit Crunch* (London: Icon), p. 177.

44. Zehner, Jacki (2008), 'Why Are Goldman's Women Invisible? (Asks a Former Goldman Sachs Partner)', *The Huffington Post*:

http://www.huffingtonpost.com/jacki-zehner/why-are-goldmans
-women-in_b_139650.html

45. Tarr-Whelan, Linda (2009), *Women Lead the Way: Your Guide to Stepping Up to Leadership and Changing the World* (San Francisco: Berrett-Koehler).

46. Apicella, Coren L., et al. (2008), 'Testosterone and financial risk preferences', *Evolution and Human Behavior*, 29 (6), 384–90.

47. Sunderland, Ruth (2009), 'Woman's touch helps hedge funds retain their value', *Guardian*, 19 October 2009.

48. Hong, Lu and Page, Scott E. (2001), 'Problem Solving by Heterogeneous Agents', *Journal of Economic Theory*, 97, 23–163.

49. See: Klein, Naomi (2008), *The Shock Doctrine: The Rise of Disaster Capitalism* (London: Penguin).

50. Sunderland, Ruth (2009), 'After the crash, Iceland's women lead the rescue', *Observer*, 22 February 2009.

51. A version was proposed by the Obama administration. Bowley, Graham (2010), 'Strong Year for Goldman, as It Trims Bonus Pool', *New York Times*, 22 January 2010. Vekshin, Alison and Sterngold, James (2009), 'War on Wall Street as Congress Sees Returning to Glass–Steagall', Bloomberg, 28 December 2009.

52. This idea was suggested by John Maynard Keynes and is sometimes known as a Tobin tax after economist James Tobin, who also championed a version of it. Most bankers say that the system is too complex to be regulated in such a naive way – but they would say that, wouldn't they? Rodrik, Dani (2009), 'The Tobin tax lives again', *World Finance*, 23 October 2009.

53. Rumsfeld, Donald H. (2002), 'Secretary of Defense Donald H. Rumsfeld speaking at Tribute to Milton Friedman (transcript)', US Department of Defense: http://www.defenselink.mil/speeches/speech.aspx?speechid=216

54. Jay Griffiths, for example, describes 'chance, caprice and unpredictability' as things that 'for good and for bad, have been associated with the female'. Griffiths, Jay (2004), *A Sideways Look at Time* (New York: Tarcher/Penguin), p. 167.

55. Triana, Pablo (2009), *Lecturing Birds on Flying: Can Mathematical Theories Destroy the Financial Markets?* (New York: Wiley), p. 163.

56. Fox Keller, Evelyn (1985), *Reflections on Gender and Science* (Yale University Press), p. 22.

57. Horkheimer, Max and Adorno, Theodor W. (2002), *Dialectic of Enlightenment: Philosophical Fragments*, trans. Edmund Jephcott (Stanford University Press), pp. 4–5.

58. Pareto, Vilfredo (1897), *Cours d'économie politique* (Lausanne: Rouge).

59. As Nassim Taleb put it at Edge.org: 'I urge all you scientists to go take your "science" where it may work – and leave us in the real world without more problems. Please, please, enough of this "science". We have enough problems without you.' Taleb, Nassim Nicholas (2008), 'Can Science Help Solve The Economic Crisis?' Edge.org: http://www.edge.org/3rd_culture/brown08/brown08_index.html#taleb. Understandable under the circumstances, though somehow I've never thought of finance as being the real world.

60. Ferber, Marianne A. and Nelson, Julie A. (eds) (1993), *Beyond Economic Man: Feminist theory and economics* (University of Chicago Press), p. 65.

61. Pigou, Arthur C. (1932), *The Economics of Welfare* (London: Macmillan); fourth edition; first published 1920.

62. Waring, Marilyn (1988), *If Women Counted: A New Feminist Economics* (San Francisco: Harper & Row).

63. Bridgman, Benjamin, et al. (2014), 'Accounting for Household Production in the National Accounts, 1965–2010', Bureau of Economic Analysis Report.

64. Green, Tom (2009), 'Lourdes Benería', *Adbusters*, 15 July 2009.

65. Bernstein, Peter L. (1996), *Against the Gods: The remarkable story of risk* (New York: Wiley), p. 46.

66. Effects of austerity were estimated over the period 2010 to 2015. Cracknell, Richard and Keen, Richard (2016), 'Estimating the gender impact of tax and benefits changes', Briefing Paper Number SN06758, House of Commons Library, 13 December 2016; Neate, Rupert and Mason, Rowena (2017), 'Striver? Tory architect of austerity George Osborne banks £1m fortune', *Guardian*, 10 March 2017.

67. Bjornholt, M. and McKay, A. (2013), 'Advances in feminist economics in times of economic crisis' in Bjornholt, M. and McKay, A. (eds), *Counting on Marilyn Waring: New Advances in Feminist Economics* (Bradford, ON: Demeter Press).

68. Downes, Ronnie and Gentili, Elena (2016), 'Gender Budgeting', presentation at the 37th Annual Meeting of OECD Senior Budget Officials, Stockholm, 9–10 June 2016.

69. Arrow, Kenneth et al. (2011), '100 Years of the *American Economic Review*: The Top 20 Articles', *American Economic Review*, 101: 1–8. The sole woman was Anne Krueger, who has held important posts in the IMF and the World Bank.

70. Anonymous (2015), 'Shifting clout', *The Economist*, 3 January 2015.

71. Ceci, Stephen J. et al. (2014), 'Women in Academic Science: A Changing Landscape', *Psychological Science in the Public Interest*, 15(3) 75–141.

72. One factor is that they get less credit for team publications than their male counterparts. Wolfers, Justin (2016), 'When Teamwork Doesn't Work for Women', *New York Times*, 8 January 2016.

73. Coburn, Elaine (2016), 'Economics as Ideology: Challenging Expert Political Power', in *State of Power: Annual Report 2016* (Amsterdam: The Transnational Institute).

74. Porzecanski, Katia (2016), 'This Election Shines a New Light on Wall Street's Bro Culture', Bloomberg.com, 4 November 2016. See also: Steverman, Ben (2016), 'Proof Wall Street Is Still a Boys' Club', Bloomberg.com, 14 March 2017.

75. Ring, Suzi (2017), 'White Male Bank Culture "Difficult to Take", U.K. Regulator Says', Bloomberg.com, 24 January 2017.

76. Wallace, Charles (2012), 'Keep taking the testosterone', *Financial Times*, 9 February 2012.

77. Kimball, Miles and Anonymous (2015), 'How big is the sexism problem in economics? This article's co-author is anonymous because of it', *Quartz*, 6 January 2015.

78. See http://www.girlsrocktoronto.org/about/. Highly recommended, by the way.

Chapter 7

1. Jevons, William Stanley (1879), *Theory of Political Economy* (2nd edn; London: Macmillan), p. 86.

2. Fama, Eugene F. (1965), 'Random walks in stock-market prices', *Selected Papers*, 16 (University of Chicago, Graduate School of Business).

3. Häring, Norbert and Douglas, Niall (2012), *Economists and the Powerful* (London: Anthem Press), p. x.

4. Friedman, Milton (1962), *Capitalism and Freedom* (University of Chicago Press), pp. 109–10.

5. Fourcade, M., Ollion, E. and Algan, Y. (2015), 'The Superiority of Economists', *Journal of Economic Perspectives*, 29(1), 89–114.
6. Browne, M.N. and Quinn, J.K. (2008), 'The Lamentable Absence of Power in Mainstream Economics', in John T. Harvey and Robert F. Garnett (eds), *Future Directions for Heterodox Economics* (University of Michigan Press), pp. 240–61.
7. Coser, Lewis A. (1977), *Masters of sociological thought: Ideas in historical and social context* (2nd edn; New York: Harcourt Brace Jovanovich), p. 404.
8. Pareto, Vilfredo (1897), 'The New Theories of Economics', *J. Pol Econ*, 5, 485–502.
9. Quoted in Kimmel, Michael S. (1990), *Revolution, a sociological interpretation* (Philadelphia: Temple University Press), p. 54.
10. Davies, James B., et al. (2006), 'The World Distribution of Household Wealth' (World Institute for Development Economics Research of the United Nations University).
11. Phillips, Tom (2008), 'High above São Paulo's choked streets, the rich cruise a new highway', *Guardian*, 20 June 2008.
12. Smith, Adam (1759), *The Theory of Moral Sentiments* (London: A. Millar).
13. Sorapop, Kiatpongsan and Norton, Michael I. (2014), 'How Much (More) Should CEOs Make? A Universal Desire for More Equal Pay', *Perspectives on Psychological Science*, 9 (6): 587–93.
14. Clark, Andrew (2009), 'Massive bet on RBS and Lloyds helped financier earn $2.5bn', *Guardian*, 22 December 2009.
15. Sawhill, Isabel and Haskins, Ron (2009), '5 myths about our land of opportunity', *Washington Post*, 1 November 2009.
16. Romano, Lois and Warren, Elizabeth (2009), 'Voices of Power: Elizabeth Warren', *Washington Post*, 8 October 2009. As the *Economist* magazine observed in 2006: 'every measure shows that, over the past quarter century, those at the top have done better than those in the middle, who in turn have outpaced those at the bottom.' Anonymous (2006), 'The rich, the poor and the growing gap between them', *Economist*, 15 June 2006.
17. Clement, Douglas (2007), 'Interview with Eugene Fama', *The Region*, December 2007.
18. Mankiw, N. Gregory (2013), 'Defending the One Percent', *The Journal of Economic Perspectives*, 27 (3), 21–34.
19. A study by McKinsey & Company showed that 'from 1991 to 2000,

market and industry factors drove about 70 per cent of the returns of individual companies, company-specific factors only about 30 per cent'. De Swaan, J.C. and Harper, Neil W.C. (2003), 'Getting what you pay for with stock options', *McKinsey Quarterly* (1). See also: Bebchuk, L. and Fried, J. (2004), *Pay Without Performance: The unfulfilled promise of executive remuneration* (Harvard University Press).

20. International Labour Organisation (2008), 'World of Work Report 2008: Income inequalities in the age of financial globalization': http://www.ilo.org/public/english/bureau/inst/download/world08.pdf

21. Ariely, Dan (2009), *Predictably Irrational: The Hidden Forces That Shape Our Decisions* (London: HarperCollins), p. 183.

22. One study showed that directors of Fortune 1000 companies formed a small and highly connected group, bound together by the approximately 20 per cent of directors who serve on more than one board. Newman, M.E.J., Strogatz, S.H., and Watts, D.J. (2001), 'Random graphs with arbitrary degree distributions and their applications', *Physical Review E*, 6402, 6118.

23. Cleeland, Nancy, Iritani, Evelyn, and Marshall, Tyler (2003), 'Wal-Mart wrings efficiency from Third World factories', *Los Angeles Times*, 28 November 2003.

24. 'The World's Billionaires 2009', *Forbes*, 11 March 2009: http://www.forbes.com/lists/2009/10/billionaires-2009-richest-people_The-Worlds-Billionaires_Rank.html

25. Source: http://en.wikipedia.org/wiki/List_of_companies_by_revenue

26. Vitali, S., Glattfelder, J.B., and Battiston, S. (2011), 'The network of global corporate control', *PLoS ONE*, 6 (10): e25995. James Glattfelder quoted in: Coghlan, A., and MacKenzie, D. (2011), 'Revealed – the capitalist network that runs the world', *New Scientist*, 19 October 2011.

27. Anonymous (2001), 'Ways and Means: Harvard's Wage Debate', *Harvard Magazine*, November–December 2001.

28. Mankiw, N. Gregory (2008), *Principles of Economics* (Cincinatti, OH: South-Western College).

29. Raveaud, Gilles (2009), 'Neocon Indoctrination – The Mankiw Way', *Adbusters*, 85.

30. Read, Richard (2015), 'A $280 college textbook busts budgets, but Harvard author Gregory Mankiw defends royalties', *The Oregonian*, 12 February 2015; Richardson, Craig (2015), 'The $250 Econ 101 Textbook', *The Wall Street Journal*, 13 January 2015.

31. Stiglitz, Joseph (2009), 'Joseph Stiglitz', *Adbusters*, 85.
32. Wilkinson, Richard and Pickett, Kate (2009), *The Spirit Level: Why Greater Equality Makes Societies Stronger* (London: Bloomsbury).
33. Quoted in: Wilkinson, Richard and Pickett, Kate (2009), *The Spirit Level: Why Greater Equality Makes Societies Stronger* (London: Bloomsbury), p. 81.
34. De Waal, Frans (2009), 'Fair play: Monkeys share our sense of injustice', *New Scientist*, 11 November 2009.
35. Chua, Amy (2007), *World on Fire: How Exporting Free Market Democracy Breeds Ethnic Hatred and Global Instability* (New York: Doubleday).
36. Krugman, Paul (2016), 'Economists and Inequality', nytimes.com, 8 January 2016.
37. Blanchard, Olivier (2016), 'Do DSGE Models Have a Future?', Policy Brief 16-11, Peterson Institute for International Economics, August 2016.
38. Nietzsche, Friedrich (2008), *Thus Spoke Zarathustra: A Book for Everyone and Nobody* (Oxford: Oxford University Press), p. 44.
39. Oxfam, 'Just 8 men own same wealth as half the world', 16 January 2017, http://oxf.am/ZLE4
40. Mayer, Jane (2017), 'The Reclusive Hedge-Fund Tycoon Behind the Trump Presidency', *New Yorker*, 27 March 2017.
41. Fullerton, D., and Stavins, R. (1998), 'How economists see the environment', *Nature*, 395(6701), 433–4.
42. Robbins, Lionel (1932), *An Essay on the Nature and Significance of Economic Science* (London: Macmillan), p. 125.
43. Lucas, Robert E. (2004), 'The Industrial Revolution: Past and Future – 2003 Annual Report Essay', Federal Reserve Bank of Minneapolis, 1 May 2004. 'The standard approach to policy-making and advice in economics implicitly or explicitly ignores politics and political economy.' Acemoglu, D., and Robinson, J.A. (2013), 'Economics versus Politics: Pitfalls of Policy Advice', *Journal of Economic Perspectives*, 27(2), 173–92.
44. Economist Noah Smith, for example, notes the subject's 'historical identification with conservative politics'. Smith, Noah (2014), 'Economics Is a Dismal Science for Women', Bloomberg.com, 21 November 2014.
45. Fourcade, M., Ollion, E. and Algan, Y. (2015), 'The Superiority of Economists', *Journal of Economic Perspectives*, 29 (1), 89–114.

See also: Gross, Neil (2013), *Why Are Professors Liberal and Why Do Conservatives Care?* (Cambridge, MA: Harvard University Press).

46. Mayeda, Andrew (2016), 'The Rebel Economist Who Blew Up Macroeconomics', Bloomberg.com, 18 November 2016.

47. Alperovitz, Gar (2004), *America Beyond Capitalism* (Hoboken, NJ: Wiley).

48. Bannon, Lisa (2009), 'As Riches Fade, So Does Finance's Allure', *Wall Street Journal*, 21 September 2009.

49. For example, economist Gilles Raveaud notes that Mankiw's text 'presents economics as a unified discipline, entirely committed to the neoliberal agenda'. Raveaud, Gilles (2009), 'Neocon Indoctrination – The Mankiw Way', *Adbusters*, 85. See also the survey of textbooks in: Browne, M.N. and Quinn, J.K. (2008), 'The Lamentable Absence of Power in Mainstream Economics', in John T. Harvey and Robert F. Garnett (eds), *Future Directions for Heterodox Economics* (University of Michigan Press), 240–61.

50. Darwin, Charles (1903), *More Letters of Charles Darwin, Volume II* (New York: D. Appleton and Company), p. 422.

51. Ayres, Ian (2007), *Super Crunchers: How Anything Can Be Predicted* (London: John Murray), pp. 130–1. See also: Ayres, Ian (1991), 'Fair driving: Gender and race discrimination in retail car negotiations', *Harvard Law Review*, 104, 817–72.

52. Younge, Gary (2008), 'Bad cheque for black America', *Guardian*, 7 February 2008.

53. In the UK, for example, women working full time earn on average 18 per cent less per hour than males. The difference is 25 per cent less when part-time workers are included. Steed, S., et al. (2009), 'A Bit Rich: Calculating the real value to society of different professions', New Economics Foundation: http://www.neweconomics .org/publications/bit-rich. See also: Olsen, W. and Walby, S. (2004), 'Modelling the Gender Pay Gap in the UK', CSSR Working Paper No. 17 (Manchester: University of Manchester).

54. Pager, Devah (2016), 'Are Firms That Discriminate More Likely to Go Out of Business?', *Sociological Science*, 3: 849–59.

55. Quoted in: Wilkinson, Richard and Pickett, Kate (2009), *The Spirit Level: Why Greater Equality Makes Societies Stronger* (London: Bloomsbury), p. 221.

56. Piketty told the Paris-based *Potemkin Review* that 'I do not believe

in the basic neoclassical model'. Dolcerocca, Antoine and Terzioglu, Gokhan (2015), 'Interview: Thomas Piketty Responds to Criticisms from the Left', *Potemkin Review*, January 2015.

57. Piketty, Thomas (2014), *Capital in the Twenty-First Century* (Cambridge, MA: Belknap Press), p. 515. Atkinson, Anthony B. (2014), *Inequality: What Can Be Done?* (Cambridge, MA: Harvard University Press). See also: Piketty, Thomas (2017), 'Passing of Anthony B. Atkinson', http://piketty.blog.lemonde.fr/2017/01/03/passing-of-anthony-b-atkinson/

58. Elliott, Larry (2016), 'World's eight richest people have same wealth as poorest 50%', *The Guardian*, 16 January 2017. You can argue that the numbers change if factors such as purchasing power parity are taken into account, but the trend is clear.

59. Anonymous (2016), 'The rise of the superstars', *The Economist*, 17 September 2016.

60. Mishel, Lawrence and Schieder, Jessica (2016), 'Stock market headwinds meant less generous year for some CEOs', Economic Policy Institute, 12 July 2016.

61. Weaver, Rosanna Landis (2017), 'The 100 Most Overpaid CEOs: Are Fund Managers Asleep at The Wheel?', www.asyousow.org, February 2017. The ranking used a formula that compared factors such as total shareholder return with the CEO's pay.

62. According to one report, for example, half of Americans have been 'completely shut off from economic growth since the 1970s'. Piketty, T., Saez, E. and Zucman, G. (2016), 'Economic growth in the United States: A tale of two countries', Washington Center for Equitable Growth, http://equitablegrowth.org/research-analysis/economic-growth-in-the-united-states-a-tale-of-two-countries/

63. Harvey, John T. (2012), 'How Economists Contributed to the Financial Crisis', Forbes.com, 6 February 2012.

64. Scharmer, C.O., and Kaufer, K. (2013), *Leading from the Emerging Future: From Ego-System to Eco-System Economics* (San Francisco: Berrett-Koehler), p. 71.

65. Reddy, Sanjay (2016), 'Trumpism Has Dealt a Mortal Blow to Orthodox Economics and Social Science', INETeconomics.com, 23 November 2016.

66. Pettifor, Ann (2017), 'I was one of the only economists who predicted the financial crash of 2008 – in 2017 we need to make urgent changes', *The Independent*, 6 January 2017.

67. Rodrik, Dani (2016), 'Straight Talk on Trade', *Project Syndicate*, 15 November 2016.

68. Pettifor, Ann (2017), 'I was one of the only economists who predicted the financial crash of 2008 – in 2017 we need to make urgent changes', *The Independent*, 6 January 2017.

69. Ferguson, Charles (2010), 'Larry Summers and the Subversion of Economics', *The Chronicle of Higher Education*, 30 October 2010.

70. Soddy, Frederick (2003), *The Role of Money: What It Should Be, Contrasted with What It Has Become* (repr. London: Routledge).

71. Cowen, Tyler (2013), 'A Profession With an Egalitarian Core', nytimes.com, 16 March 2013.

72. Perelman, Michael (2015), 'How economics bolstered power by obscuring it', in *State of Power: Annual Report 2015* (Amsterdam: The Transnational Institute), p. 97.

73. Stiglitz, J.E. (2016), *Rewriting the Rules of the American Economy: An Agenda for Growth and Shared Prosperity* (New York: W.W. Norton & Company). Krugman, Paul (2013), 'Why Inequality Matters', *New York Times*, 15 December 2013.

74. Das, Jishnu et al. (2013), 'U.S. and them: The Geography of Academic Research', *Journal of Development Economics*, 105: 112–30.

75. Even Milton Friedman supported a version, on the basis that it would shrink the size of government and therefore pay for itself. See *The Evolution of Money*, p. 178.

Chapter 8

1. Anonymous (2007), 'Bee Colony Collapses Could Threaten US Food Supply', *Associated Press*, 3 May 2007.

2. Johnson, Renée (2007), 'Recent Honey Bee Colony Decline: Congressional Research Service Testimony given before 110th Congress', 26 March 2007: http://www.fas.org/sgp/crs/misc/RL33938.pdf

3. Higgins, Adrian (2007), 'Saving Earth From the Ground Up', *Washington Post*, 30 June 2007.

4. Pilkey-Jarvis, Linda and Pilkey, Orrin H. (2006), *Useless Arithmetic: Why Environmental Scientists Can't Predict the Future* (New York: Columbia University Press), p. 6.

5. Chantraine, Pol (1993), *The Last Cod-Fish: Life and Death of the Newfoundland Way of Life* (St John's, Newfoundland: Jesperson Press).

6. Jevons, William Stanley (1865), *The Coal Question: An Inquiry Concerning the Progress of the Nation, and the Probable Exhaustion of Our Coal-Mines* (London: Macmillan).

7. Vidal, John (2008), 'Downward spiral', *Guardian*, 5 March 2008.

8. According to Fatih Birol, chief economist of the International Energy Agency, conventional oil will plateau around 2020, 'which is, of course, not good news from a global-oil-supply point of view'. Monbiot, George (2008), 'When will the oil run out?', *Guardian*, 15 December 2008.

9. Costanza, Robert (2010), 'Toward a New Sustainable Economy', in Steven Kates (ed.), *Macroeconomic Theory and Its Failings: Alternative Perspectives on the Global Financial Crisis* (Cheltenham: Edward Elgar), p. 49.

10. Sterman, John D. (2002), 'All Models are Wrong: Reflections on Becoming a Systems Scientist', *System Dynamics Review*, 18 (4), 501–31.

11. Raveaud, Gilles (2009), 'Neocon Indoctrination – The Mankiw Way', *Adbusters*, 85.

12. Daly, Herman E. (1996), *Beyond Growth: The Economics of Sustainable Development* (Boston, MA: Beacon Press), p. 5.

13. Daly, Herman E. (1977), *Steady-state Economics: The economics of biophysical equilibrium and moral growth* (San Francisco: W.H. Freeman), p. 33.

14. Wheat price source: International Monetary Fund. Oil price source: Energy Information Administration.

15. Walt, Vivienne (2008), 'The World's Growing Food-Price Crisis', *TIME*, 27 February 2008.

16. Clark, Andrew (2009), 'US government faces pay challenge with one of Citigroup's biggest earners', *Guardian*, 16 August 2009.

17. 'Written Testimony of Jeffrey Harris, Chief Economist and John Fenton, Director of Market Surveillance Before the Subcommittee on General Farm Commodities and Risk Management, Committee on Agriculture', United States House of Representatives, 15 May 2008.

18. 'Furor on Memo at World Bank', *New York Times*, 7 February 1992: http://www.nytimes.com/1992/02/07/business/furor-on-memo-at-world-bank.html

19. Dasgupta, Partha (2010), 'Nature's role in sustaining economic development', *Phil. Trans. R. Soc. B*, 365, 5–11. Accounting for such effects changes the perceived growth rates of developing countries.

For example, Dasgupta estimates that per capita GDP in Pakistan grew at an average rate of 2.2 per cent a year between 1970 and 2000, but total wealth, including natural capital, declined by 1.4 per cent per annum.

20. Kumar, Dilip (2015), 'Applying Economics to Sustained Yield Forestry: Why Foresters Don't Listen to Social Scientists', Forest Matters blog, 26 February 2015, http://forestmatters.blogspot .ca/2015/02/13 -applying-economic-analysis-to.html

21. In an interview for the Sun News Network, Canadian economist Mike Moffatt, for example, explained that: 'What happens is when companies log for instance they replant trees so they can have more wood to use in the future.' No need for logging protests or government regulations, then. See also box on page 297. Moffatt, Mike (2012), 'Suzuki vs. Reality', interview by Charles Adler (television broadcast), 18 October 2012 (Toronto: Sun News Network). See also the interview with Richard Denniss in: Mary O'Connell and Paul Kennedy, 'It's The Economists, Stupid' (Toronto: CBC), 9 September 2015, http://www.cbc.ca/radio/ideas/it-s-the-economists -stupid-1.3219471

22. One early effort claimed that acting to minimise climate change would yield a cost savings of only 5 per cent. Nordhaus, W.D. (1994), *Managing the Global Commons: The Economics of Climate Change* (Cambridge, MA: MIT Press). See also Orrell, David (2007), *Apollo's Arrow: The Science of Prediction and the Future of Everything* (Toronto: HarperCollins). As Richard Denniss pointed out in 2015: 'Many economists have calculated that it will be cheaper for the world to endure climate change than to prevent it. The models they use to draw this bizarre conclusion are built on thousands of assumptions about everything from the value of human life to the willingness of consumers to buy smaller cars if petrol becomes more expensive. If any one of those assumptions is wrong, the answer will be wrong.' Denniss, Richard (2015), 'Spreadsheets of Power', *The Monthly*, April 2015.

23. Stern, N. (2016), 'Economics: Current climate models are grossly misleading', *Nature*, 530(7591): 407-09.

24. Zurayk, Rami (2011), 'Use your loaf: why food prices were crucial in the Arab spring', *The Observer*, 17 July 2011.

25. Allen, Myles, et al., 'The Exit Strategy', *Nature Reports Climate Change*, 30 April 2009, 2. The authors estimate that a trillion tonnes

of carbon leads to about two degrees of warming. As discussed later, there is huge uncertainty in such calculations, but they are still useful for generating rules of thumb about maximum emissions.

26. An example is the DICE model of the economic effects of climate change, available at: http://www.econ.yale.edu/~nordhaus/homepage/dicemodels.htm. The welfare of anyone around in 2025 was weighted at less than 2 per cent of the 1995 value.

27. Dasgupta, Partha (2010), 'Nature's role in sustaining economic development', *Phil. Trans. R. Soc. B*, 365, 5-11.

28. Kubiszewski, Ida et al. (2013), 'Beyond GDP: Measuring and Achieving Global Genuine Progress', *Ecological Economics*, 93: 57-68.

29. New Economics Foundation (2009),'The Happy Planet Index 2.0': http://www.happyplanetindex.org/

30. Daly, Herman E. (1968), 'On Economics as a Life Science', *Journal of Political Economy*, 76, 392-406.

31. Costanza, Robert et al. (1997), 'The value of the world's ecosystem services and natural capital', *Nature*, 387, 253-60.

32. See Orrell, David (2007), *Apollo's Arrow: The Science of Prediction and the Future of Everything* (Toronto: HarperCollins). As Spyros Makridakis and Nassim Taleb note: 'it must be accepted that accurate predictions are not possible and uncertainty cannot be reduced (a fact made obvious by the many and contradictory predictions concerning global warming), and whatever actions are taken to protect the environment must be justified based on other reasons than the accurate forecasting of future temperatures.' Makridakis, Spyros and Taleb, Nassim Nicholas (2009), 'Decision making and planning under low levels of predictability', *International Journal of Forecasting*, 25, 716-33.

33. Hanley, Nick, Shogren, Jason E., and White, Ben (1997), *Environmental Economics in Theory and Practice* (New York: Oxford University Press), p. 358. See also: Nadeau, Robert (2008), 'Brother, Can You Spare Me a Planet? (extended version)', *Scientific American*, April 2008.

34. The idea that getting rich will fix our environmental problems is a business-as-usual approach that is not backed by empirical evidence. Economic growth, of the sort measured by GDP, uses resources and tends to create environmental damage. That's why we're in this mess in the first place. For an example of the pro-growth approach, see: Bjørn Lomborg (2001), *The Skeptical Environmentalist* (Cambridge University Press).

35. See: Daly, Herman (2007), *Ecological Economics and Sustainable Development, Selected Essays of Herman Daly* (Northampton, MA: Edward Elgar), p. 114.

36. World Wildlife Fund (2008), 'Living Planet Report 2008': http:// assets.panda.org/downloads/living_planet_report_2008.pdf

37. Berdik, Chris (2014), 'The unsung inventor of the carbon tax', *Boston Globe*, 10 August 2014.

38. See: Daly, Herman (2007), *Ecological Economics and Sustainable Development, Selected Essays of Herman Daly* (Northampton, MA: Edward Elgar), p. 114.

39. Francis, R.C., et al. (2007), 'Ten commandments for ecosystem-based fisheries scientists', *Proceedings of Coastal Zone 07* (Portland, OR). See also: Pikitch, E.K., et al. (2004), 'Ecosystem-Based Fishery Management', *Science*, 305, 346–7, and May, R.M., Levin, S.A., and Sugihara, G. (2008), 'Ecology for bankers', *Nature*, 451, 891–3.

40. An early example along these lines is the LOWGROW model of the Canadian economy, which uses a standard macroeconomic approach to explore how the economy could function in a low-growth, low-carbon mode. Victor, P.A. (2008), *Managing without Growth: slower by design, not disaster* (Cheltenham: Edward Elgar).

41. The author and psychologist Iain McGilchrist describes schizophrenia as 'an excessively detached, hyper-rational, reflexively self-aware, disembodied and alienated condition'. Sufferers see themselves as a 'passive observer of life'. Their artwork often features 'an all-observing eye, detached from the scene it observes, floating in the picture'. Rather like the one on the back of a US dollar bill, come to think of it. McGilchrist, Iain (2009), *The Master and his Emissary: The Divided Brain and the Making of the Western World* (London: Yale University Press), pp. 332–5. The design of the dollar bill features a single eye above a pyramid: http://en.wikipedia.org/wiki/File:United_States_ one_dollar_bill,_reverse.jpg

42. And the unfit will perish, especially if they can't afford healthcare. The 2009 healthcare debate in the US seemed to have some elements in common with the Social Darwinism of the 19th century. As Herbert Spencer wrote: 'It seems hard that widows and orphans should be left to struggle for life or death. Nevertheless, when regarded not separately, but in connection with the interests of a universal humanity, these harsh fatalities are seen to be full of the highest beneficence – the same beneficence which brings to early graves the children of

diseased parents.' Spencer, Herbert (1851), *Social Statics* (London: John Chapman).

43. Buchanan, Mark (2014), 'Economists Are Blind to the Limits of Growth', Bloomberg.com, 5 October 2014.

44. Jonathan Aldred (2009), *The Skeptical Economist: Revealing the Ethics Inside Economics* (London: Earthscan), p. 3.

45. Semuels, Alana (2016), 'Does the Economy Really Need to Keep Growing Quite So Much?', *The Atlantic*, 4 November 2016.

46. Fullerton, D., and Stavins, R. (1998), 'How economists see the environment', *Nature*, 395(6701), 433–4.

47. Mankiw, N. Gregory (2009), 'Smart Taxes: An Open Invitation to Join the Pigou Club', *Eastern Economic Journal*, 35, 14–23.

48. Nuccitelli, Dana (2016), '95% consensus of expert economists: cut carbon pollution', *The Guardian*, 4 January 2016.

49. See also Earle, J., Moran, C., and Ward-Perkins, Z. (2016), *The Econocracy: The Perils of Leaving Economics to the Experts* (Manchester: Manchester University Press), p. 178, and Chapter 3.

50. Klein, Naomi (2014), *This Changes Everything: Capitalism vs. the Climate* (New York: Simon & Schuster), p. 33.

51. Ogden, Lesley Evans (2016), 'Nine years of censorship', *Nature*, 3 May 2016.

52. Maron, Dina Fine (2017), 'USDA Calls Scientist Gag Order a "Misunderstanding"', *Scientific American*, 25 January 2017.

53. Smith, Robert et al. (2016), 'Comprehensive Wealth in Canada: Measuring What Matters in the Long Run', International Institute for Sustainable Development, November 2016. See: http://www.iisd .org/library/comprehensive-wealth-canada-measuring-what -matters-long-run

Chapter 9

1. Feynman, Richard (1964), *The Feynman Lectures on Physics; Volume 1* (Reading, MA: Addison Wesley).

2. Jevons, William Stanley (1874), *The Principles of Science: A Treatise on Logic and Scientific Method, Vol. 2* (London: Macmillan), p. 428.

3. Letter to J.L. Shadwell, 17 October 1872. Jevons, William Stanley (1886), *Letters and Journal of W. Stanley Jevons* (London: Macmillan).

4. Jevons, William Stanley (1879), *Theory of Political Economy* (2nd edn; London: Macmillan), pp. 11–12.

5. Quoted in Mirowski, Philip (1989), *More Heat than Light: Economics*

as *Social Physics, Physics as Nature's Economics* (Cambridge University Press), p. 219.

6. Jevons, William Stanley (1879), *Theory of Political Economy* (2nd edn; London: Macmillan), p. 8.

7. Walras, Pareto and Edgeworth quoted in Mirowski, Philip (1989), *More Heat than Light: Economics as Social Physics, Physics as Nature's Economics* (Cambridge University Press).

8. Edgeworth, Francis Ysidro (1881), *Mathematical Psychics: An Essay on the Application of Mathematics to the Moral Sciences* (London: Paul), p. 101.

9. Marshall, Alfred (1920), *Principles of Economics. An introductory volume*, 8th edn (London: Macmillan), p. 78.

10. Ragan, Christopher T.S., and Lipsey, Richard G. (2003), *Economics*, 13th edition (Toronto: Pearson Education Canada), p. 121.

11. Modern economists speak in terms of 'ordinal' utility, which just ranks preferences, instead of 'cardinal' utility, which is seen as something that can in principle be measured.

12. Coyle, D. (2002), *Sex, Drugs and Economics: An Unconventional Introduction to Economics* (New York: Texere).

13. Jonathan Aldred (2009), *The Skeptical Economist: Revealing the Ethics Inside Economics* (London: Earthscan), p. 22.

14. Blanchard, Olivier (2006), *Macroeconomics* (Upper Saddle River, NJ: Pearson Prentice Hall).

15. Alfred Marshall, for example, wrote that: 'Jevons was, as he frankly confessed, not a skilled mathematician. Truly mathematical as was the tone of his best work, he was not at his ease when using mathematical formulae.' Marshall, Alfred and John King Whitaker (ed.), (2005), *The Correspondence of Alfred Marshall, Economist: Climbing, 1868–1890* (Cambridge University Press), p. 164.

16. Beinhocker, Eric D. (2006), *Origin of Wealth: Evolution, Complexity, and the Radical Remaking of Economics* (Boston, MA: Harvard Business School Press), p. 49.

17. Wiener, N. (1964), *God and Golem, Inc.* (Cambridge, MA: MIT Press), p. 89.

18. Feynman, Richard P. (2000), *The Pleasure of Finding Things Out: The Best Short Works of Richard P. Feynman* (New York: Basic Books), pp. 22–3.

19. Piketty, Thomas (2014), *Capital in the Twenty-First Century* (Cambridge, MA: Belknap Press), p. 32.

20. Frey, Bruno S. and Stutzer, Alois (2002), *Happiness and Economics: How the economy and institutions affect human well-being* (Princeton University Press).

21. Jevons, William Stanley (1886), *Letters and Journal of W. Stanley Jevons* (London: Macmillan).

22. Lykken, D. (1999), *Happiness: What studies on twins show us about nature, nurture and the happiness set-point* (New York: Golden Books).

23. Headey, Bruce (2006), 'Life Goals Matter to Happiness: A Revision of Set-Point Theory', *Discussion Papers of DIW Berlin*, 639.

24. When a US Gallup poll asked people: 'What is the smallest amount of money a family of four needs to get along in this community?', the answer simply tracked the average income. Rainwater, L. (1990), 'Poverty and equivalence as social constructions', *Luxembourg Income Study Working Paper*, 91 (Syracuse, NY: Center for Policy Research, The Maxwell School).

25. Anonymous (2008), 'Joy to the world is contagious: study', CBC News, 4 December 2008.

26. Kahneman, Daniel, et al. (2006), 'Would You Be Happier If You Were Richer? A Focusing Illusion', *Science*, 312, 5782. Money can also be hard on relationships. Here, for example, is the story of the wife of a UK banker: 'I know some people look at our lifestyle and cringe and it does sometimes embarrass me. We have the obligatory double-fronted house in a communal garden in Notting Hill, with a gardener, a housekeeper/cook, a cleaner, a chauffeur, a nanny and a tutor. But it has come at a huge price. Most of the time I feel like a single mother – my husband comes home now and again, repacks his suitcase and is off to another European city. We do use Netjet for our Ibiza summer holidays but that is because he gets only one holiday a year, and even then he spends most of the time pacing up and down the beach on his BlackBerry in his Vilebrequins. He can never make our son's parents' evenings and missed our daughter playing the lead in the school play. I don't think he has ever swum with the children in our pool ... If it wasn't for the bonus, it wouldn't be worth it.' Thomson, Alice (2009), 'City workers: "We're worth our bonuses"', *Times*, 22 October 2009.

27. Helliwell, J.F. et al. (2012), 'World Happiness Report' (New York, NY: Earth Institute, Columbia University).

28. Frey, Bruno S. and Stutzer, Alois (2002), *Happiness and Economics:*

How the economy and institutions affect human well-being (Princeton University Press), p. 106.

29. Ariely, Dan (2009), *Predictably Irrational: The Hidden Forces That Shape Our Decisions* (London: HarperCollins), pp. 68, 76.

30. As Iain McGilchrist notes: 'Money changes our relationships with one another in predictable ways. These also clearly reflect a transition from the values of the right hemisphere to those of the left.' McGilchrist , Iain (2009), *The Master and his Emissary: The Divided Brain and the Making of the Western World* (London: Yale University Press), p. 279. See also: Orrell, David (2008), *The Other Side of the Coin: The Emerging Vision of Economics and Our Place in the World* (Toronto: Key Porter), p. 131.

31. Gneezy, Uri and Rustichini, Aldo (2000), 'A Fine is a Price', *Journal of Legal Studies*, 29.

32. Vohs, Kathleen D., Mead, Nicole, and Goode, Miranda (2006), 'The Psychological Consequences of Money', *Science*, 314, 1154–6.

33. Grant, Adam (2013), 'Does Studying Economics Breed Greed?', *Psychology Today*, 22 October 2013, https://www.psychologytoday .com/blog/give-and-take/201310/does-studying-economics-breed -greed

34. The John Lennon quote at the start of the chapter is from: Hindle, Maurice (2009), 'Christmas with John and Yoko', *New Statesman*, 21 December 2009.

35. Jeffries, Stuart (2008), 'Will this man make you happy?', *Guardian*, 24 June 2008.

36. James, Oliver (2007), 'Blind feminism has hurt our children', *Times*, 15 February 2007. See also: James, Oliver (2007), *Affluenza: How to Be Successful and Stay Sane* (London: Vermilion).

37. APA Press Release (2007), 'Stress a Major Health Problem in the US, Warns APA': http://www.apa.org/releases/stressproblem.html

38. Gallo, W.T. et al. (2006), 'The impact of late career job loss on myocardial infarction and stroke: a 10 year follow up using the health and retirement survey', *Occupational and Environmental Medicine*, 63, 683–7.

39. Case, A., and Deaton, A. (2015), 'Rising morbidity and mortality in midlife among white non-Hispanic Americans in the 21st century', *Proceedings of the National Academy of Sciences*, 112(49), 15078–83.

40. Reich, Robert (2008), *Supercapitalism: The battle for democracy in an age of big business* (London: Icon), p. 98.

41. Reich, Robert (2008), *Supercapitalism: The battle for democracy in an age of big business* (London: Icon), p. 161.

42. According to a report from the New Economics Foundation, child-care workers contribute almost ten times their salary in positive benefits to the rest of society, while highly-paid bankers *subtract* about seven times their salary. Steed, S., et al. (2009), 'A Bit Rich: Calculating the real value to society of different professions', New Economics Foundation: http://www.neweconomics.org/publications/bit-rich

43. Schumpeter, Joseph A. (1942), *Capitalism, Socialism and Democracy* (New York: Harper & Row).

44. Putnam, R.D. (2000), *Bowling Alone: The collapse and revival of American community* (New York: Simon & Schuster), p. 359.

45. Elmhirst, Sophie (2009), 'Hard times', *New Statesman*, 24 August 2009.

46. For a discussion, see: Orrell, David, and Chlupatý, Roman (2016), *The Evolution of Money* (New York: Columbia University Press), pp. 185–90.

47. Many women now earn more than their husbands – in Canada, the number is around 30 per cent – so it often makes sense for fathers to look after the kids. Anonymous (2006), 'More Canadian women bringing home the back bacon: StatsCan', CBC News, http://www.cbc.ca, 23 August 2006.

48. Of course, some still try. A good example is: Bueno de Mesquita, Bruce (2009), *The Predictioneer's Game: Using the Logic of Brazen Self-Interest to See and Shape the Future* (New York: Random House), which manages to reduce Mother Teresa's motivations to a cold calculation of utility.

49. As economist Neva R. Goodwin notes: 'every year, 1.4 million undergraduates in the US take an introductory economics course that teaches that only selfishness is rational.' Monaghan, P. (2003), 'Taking On "Rational Man"', *Chronicle of Higher Education*, 49, A12.

50. The quality and extent of social networks appears to be in decline in many rich countries. One study found that the average number of people with whom Americans can discuss important matters dropped from about three people in 1985 to about two in 2004. McPherson, Miller, Smith-Lovin, Lynn, and Brashears, Matt (2006), 'Social Isolation in America: Changes in Core Discussion Networks Over Two Decades', *American Sociological Review*, 71, 353–75.

51. Iamblichus (1918), *The Life of Pythagoras*, translated by T. Taylor (Kila, MT: Kessinger).

52. See: Midgley, Mary (1985), *Evolution as a Religion: Strange Hopes and Stranger Fears* (London: Methuen), p. 98.

53. Hutt, W.H. (1936), *Economists and the Public; A Study of Competition and Opinion* (London: J. Cape).

54. Jonathan Aldred (2009), *The Skeptical Economist: Revealing the Ethics Inside Economics* (London: Earthscan), p. 226. As a non-economist, I have sometimes had a suspicion that something like that was going on – see Appendix.

55. Caplan, B.D. (2007), *The Myth of the Rational Voter: Why Democracies Choose Bad Policies* (Princeton: Princeton University Press). See pages 10, 201, and 204. See also discussion in Aldred (2009).

56. MSNBC, 'Thomas Piketty, Paul Krugman and Joseph Stiglitz: The Genius of Economics', YouTube, 6 March 2015. Available at: https://www.youtube.com/watch?v=Si4iyyJDa7c (accessed 27 January 2017). The same video is discussed in: Earle, J., Moran, C., and Ward-Perkins, Z. (2016), *The Econocracy: The Perils of Leaving Economics to the Experts* (Manchester: Manchester University Press), p. 160.

57. Parker, George (2016), 'Veteran of Treasury battles tots up a decade's wins and losses', *Financial Times*, 14 April 2016.

Chapter 10

1. Henriques, Diana B. and Berenson, Alex (2009), 'The 17th Floor, Where Wealth Went to Vanish', *New York Times*, 14 December 2008; Arvedlund, Erin (2009), 'How Bernard Madoff escaped detection', *Financial Times*, 4 September 2009; Frean, Alexandra (2009), 'Madoff started Ponzi scheme to "cover losses"', *Times*, 30 October 2009.

2. Smith, Randall (1992), 'Wall Street Mystery Features a Big Board Rival', *Wall Street Journal*, 16 December 1992.

3. When these issues are mentioned, it is usually in a kind of pretend-impartial baby language that presents them as beyond the scope of the book. For example, Mankiw's *Principles of Economics* (p. 610) does acknowledge 'the possibility of speculative bubbles' but gives the last word to the efficient market hypothesis: 'if the market were irrational, a rational person should be able to take advantage of this fact; yet ... beating the market is nearly impossible.'

4. John Arlidge (2009), 'I'm doing "God's work". Meet Mr Goldman Sachs', *Sunday Times*, 8 November 2009.

5. Farmer, J. Doyne and Geanakoplos, John (2009), 'The virtues and vices of equilibrium and the future of financial economics', *Complexity*, Vol. 14, No. 3, 11–38.

6. As George Cooper notes: 'The intellectual contortions required to rationalize all of these prices beggars belief, but the contortions are performed, none the less, in the name of defending the Efficient Market Hypothesis.' Cooper, George (2008), *The Origin of Financial Crises: Central banks, credit bubbles and the efficient market fallacy* (London: Harriman House), p. 10. See also Pastor, L. and Veronesi, Pietro (2006), 'Was there a NASDAQ bubble in the late 1990s?', *Journal of Financial Economics*, 81.

7. From a 2016 review at Amazon.com. The book seems to have polarised readers at that site, with most reviews being either 5-star or 1-star.

8. Daly, Herman (1991), *Steady-State Economics: Second Edition with New Essays* (Washington, DC: Island Press), p. 9.

9. Triana, Pablo (2009), *Lecturing Birds on Flying: Can Mathematical Theories Destroy the Financial Markets?* (New York: Wiley), p. 44. This is ironic, since tenure is supposed to protect academic freedom. But in some fields it seems that anyone who doesn't fall in line early in their career won't get tenure.

10. Keen, Steve (3 February 2017), 'I've spent 40 years dealing with Neoclassical economists. They sincerely believe they're doing good, which is why they're so dangerous', https://twitter.com/ProfSteveKeen/status/827559583363252225

11. Cassidy, John (2010), 'Interview with Eugene Fama', *The New Yorker*, 13 January 2010.

12. Cohen, Patricia (2009), 'Ivory Tower Unswayed by Crashing Economy', *New York Times*, 4 March 2009.

13. Jay, M. and Marmot, M.G. (2009), 'Health and climate change', *British Medical Journal*, 339, b3669.

14. Browne, M.N. and Quinn, J.K. (2008), 'The Lamentable Absence of Power in Mainstream Economics', in John T. Harvey and Robert F. Garnett (eds), *Future Directions for Heterodox Economics* (University of Michigan Press), 240–61.

15. In 2009, one hedge fund manager even went to the lengths of renting a tanker, filling it with a million barrels of oil, and paying it to float for six months, on the bet that the oil price would go up in the meantime. Gandel, Stephen (2009), 'How Citi's Andrew Hall Made $100 Million Last Year', *TIME*, 19 October 2009.

16. Testimony of Michael W. Masters, managing member/portfolio manager, Masters Capital Management, LLC, before the Committee on Homeland Security and Governmental Affairs, United States Senate, 20 May 2008.

17. Thomas, Zoe and Swift, Tim (23 September 2015), 'Who is Martin Shkreli – "the most hated man in America"?' (London: BBC News).

18. Turner, Adair (2009), speech by Adair Turner, chairman, FSA, the City Banquet, the Mansion House, London, 22 September 2009: http://www.fsa.gov.uk/pages/Library/Communication/Speeches/2009/0922_at.shtml

19. Treanor, Jill and Inman, Phillip (2009), 'Banks defend bonus culture as profits jump', *Guardian*, 3 August 2009.

20. See 'Big Think Interview with Bill George', available at: http://bigthink.com/videos/big-think-interview-with-bill-george

21. Ungoed-Thomas, Jon (2009), 'Banks resist government plan to publish bonuses', *Sunday Times*, 25 October 2009. Another complaint was that they would infringe on privacy, but the plan was to release them anonymously.

22. Fabian Society (2009), 'Public Attitudes Towards Economic Equality: Report for the Joseph Rowntree Foundation'.

23. Ayres, Ian (2007), *Super Crunchers: How Anything Can Be Predicted* (London: John Murray), p. 147.

24. As London mayor Boris Johnson pointed out, 'the leper colony in the City of London produces 9 per cent of UK GDP', and so needs protection. Hughes, David (2009), 'Bankers "vital" for recovery, says Johnson', *Independent*, 5 October 2009.

25. Another impact is to distort housing markets. In the UK, one 2007 report found that 'the average house price in 99 per cent of towns was too rich for the typical nurse'. Chisholm, Jamie (2007), 'House price rises show signs of slowing', *Financial Times*, 13 April 2007.

26. Krause-Jackson, Flavia (2008), 'Pope Says Credit Crunch Shows Money Is "Nothing"', Bloomberg, 7 October 2008.

27. Murphy, Megan (2009), 'Archbishop chastens City for failure to repent', *Financial Times*, 16 September 2009.

28. Masters, Brooke (2009), 'Turner tells bankers to focus on core roles', *Financial Times*, 22 September 2009.

29. Author and environmentalist Mark Lynas described it as 'the world's most environmentally destructive industrial project'. Of course, coal

is a pretty destructive project too, if taken over a country the size of China. Lynas, Mark (2009), 'We need to go cold turkey to kick our addiction to oil', *New Statesman*, 12 November 2009.

30. See, for example: http://www.greenpeace.org/canada/en/campaigns/ Energy/tarsands/; http://oilsandstruth.org/

31. Weber, Bob (2009), 'Oil sands may feel effect of Norway election', *Globe and Mail*, 9 September 2009.

32. If you don't think the Albertan government can ever be made sensitive to environmental pollution, just try lighting up a cigarette in one of their offices. That wouldn't have been a problem either, not so long ago.

33. Sverdrup, Bjørn Otto (3 February 2017), 'Today we announced @Statoil exit of oil sands which bends our cost and emission curves. Building resilience', https://twitter.com/bsverdrup/ status/809335312069644288

34. For example, in 1965 the Pentagon-affiliated RAND corporation began funding economics fellowships at Harvard, Stanford, Yale, Chicago, Columbia, Princeton and California universities. Those institutions (plus MIT) have since dominated the field of economics.

35. Levant calls Alberta 'the most environmentally obsessive jurisdiction there is' because 'voters consider the environment a priority'. Levant, Ezra (2010), *Ethical Oil: The Case for Canada's Oil Sands* (Toronto: McClelland & Stewart), p. 126. See also: Vanderklippe, Nathan (2010), 'Blood diamonds, blood oil?', *The Globe and Mail*, 13 September 2010.

36. Wells, Paul (2012), 'Canada's crude awakening', *Maclean's*, 20 January 2012.

37. Solomon, Evan and Everson, Kristen (2014), '7 environmental charities face Canada Revenue Agency audits', CBC News, 6 February 2014.

38. Bob Johnson of the Canadian International Conference, quoted in: CBC News (2010), 'Canada's reputation worsens: global poll', CBC, 11 February 2010. See http://www.cbc.ca/news/canada/canada -s-reputation-worsens-global-poll-1.892750

39. See Diane Lebouthillier's mandate letter at: http://pm.gc.ca/eng/ minister-national-revenue-mandate-letter. See also: Anderson, Mitchell (2015), 'Time to clean house at the Canada Revenue Agency', *iPolitics.ca*, 30 November 2015.

40. Milman, Oliver (2016), 'Canada gives $3.3bn subsidies to fossil fuel producers despite climate pledge', *The Guardian*, 15 November 2016.

41. Carrington, Damian (2015), '"Fossil fuels subsidised by $10m a minute", says IMF', *The Guardian*, 18 May 2015.

42. Available at http://w2.vatican.va/content/francesco/en/encyclicals/documents/papa-francesco_20150524_enciclica-laudato-si.html

43. Klein, Naomi (2014), *This Changes Everything: Capitalism vs. the Climate* (New York: Simon & Schuster), p. 21.

44. One example is the Smith School for Enterprise and the Environment, based at the University of Oxford, which conducts research on the public and private sector responses to environmental challenges.

45. Bannon, Lisa (2009), 'As Riches Fade, So Does Finance's Allure', *Wall Street Journal*, 21 September 2009. A 1990 study by economists Kevin M. Murphy, Robert W. Vishny and Andrei Schleifer concluded that: 'Some professions are socially more useful than others, even if they are not as well compensated.' Murphy, Kevin M., Shleifer, Andrei, and Vishny, Robert W. (1990), 'The Allocation of Talent: Implications for Growth', *NBER Working Papers*, 3530. Adair Turner also pointed out that much of the work performed by the financial sector is 'socially useless'. Monaghan, Angela (2009), 'City is too big and socially useless, says Lord Turner', *Daily Telegraph*, 26 August 2009.

46. Sedláček, Tomáš (2011), *Economics of Good and Evil: The Quest for Economic Meaning from Gilgamesh to Wall Street* (Oxford: Oxford University Press), p. 210.

47. DeMartino G., McCloskey D., eds (2016), *The Oxford Handbook of Professional Economic Ethics* (Oxford: Oxford University Press).

48. Denniss, Richard (2015), 'Spreadsheets of Power', *The Monthly*, April 2015.

49. See http://press.princeton.edu/titles/9261.html

50. Carrick-Hagenbarth, Jessica and Epstein, Gerald A. (2012), 'Dangerous interconnectedness: economists' conflicts of interest, ideology and financial crisis', *Cambridge Journal of Economics* 36(1): 43–63.

51. Mirowski, Philip (2013), *Never Let a Serious Crisis Go to Waste: How Neoliberalism Survived the Financial Meltdown* (London: Verso), p. 199.

52. Flitter, Emily, Cooke, Kristina and Da Costa, Pedro (2010), 'Special Report: For some professors, disclosure is academic', *Reuters*, 20 December 2010.

53. Queen, Edward L. (2015), 'How could VW be so dumb? Blame the unethical culture endemic in business', *The Conversation*, 26 September 2015.

54. Galbraith, James K. (2010), 'Why the "Experts" Failed to See How Financial Fraud Collapsed the Economy', AlterNet, 14 May 2010.

55. Nelson, Julie (2016), 'Ethics in economics: or, more precisely, the lack thereof', in *ISRF Bulletin Issue XI: The Ethical and/is the Social*.

56. The Bank for International Settlements, for example, notes that 'a bloated financial sector can also suck in more than its share of talent, hampering the development of other sectors'. Bank for International Settlements (2012), '82nd Annual Report, 1 April 2011–31 March 2012', Basel.

Chapter 11

1. Nadal, Alejandro (2015), 'Some Thoughts on my Experience as Co-Editor of *Economic Thought*', *World Economics Association Newsletter* 5(4), pp.6–7, August 2015.

2. Jones, Claire (2013), '"Dismal science" seeks fresh thinking after failure in crisis', *Financial Times*, 11 November 2013.

3. Keen, Steve (2015), 'Will We Crash Again? FT/Alphaville Talk', YouTube: https://www.youtube.com/watch?t=130&v=JKy6_yy3C3U

4. Kelton, Stephanie (2012), 'Money Is No Object: Accounting for Deficits, Taxes, and Trust in the 21st Century' (presentation at the Financial Planning Association Annual Retreat Conference, 5–8 May 2012).

5. Martin, Felix (2013), *Money: The Unauthorised Biography* (London: Random House), p. 224.

6. King, Mervyn (2012), 'Twenty years of inflation targeting', The Stamp Memorial Lecture, London School of Economics, 9 October 2012.

7. Krugman, Paul (2015), 'There's Something About Money (Implicitly Wonkish)', nytimes.com, 10 February 2015; http://krugman.blogs.nytimes.com/2015/02/10/theres-something-about-money-implicitly-wonkish/

8. McLeay, M., Radia, A., and Thomas, R. (2014), 'Money Creation in the Modern Economy', *Quarterly Bulletin* (Bank of England), no. 1, 14 March 2014.

9. Soddy, Frederick (2003), *The Role of Money: What It Should Be, Contrasted with What It Has Become* (repr. London: Routledge).

10. Ragan, Christopher T.S., and Lipsey, Richard G. (2011), *Economics*, 13th edition (Toronto: Pearson Education Canada), pp. 672–3.

11. This section is partly based on my 2015 Marshall McLuhan Lecture, 'Money is the Message', hosted by Transmediale and the Canadian Embassy in Berlin. The YouTube video is in four parts; part one is at https://www.youtube.com/watch?v=ZqsNx-3Thyc

12. Mitchell-Innes, A. (1913), 'What is Money?', *The Banking Law Journal*, May 1913, pp. 377–408.

13. David Graeber (2011), *Debt: The First 5000 Years* (Brooklyn, NY: Melville House).

14. An example is the paper: Kocherlakota, Narayana R. (1996), 'Money Is Memory', Staff Report 218 (Federal Reserve Bank of Minneapolis). This describes money in terms of 'barren tokens' that serve only as a kind of memory aid.

15. Knapp, G.F. (1924), *The State Theory of Money* (London, NY: Macmillan and Company), pp. 38–9.

16. Jevons, William Stanley (1875), *Money and the Mechanism of Exchange* (New York: Appleton).

17. Guthrie, W.K.C. (1962), *A History of Greek Philosophy: The earlier Presocratics and the Pythagoreans*, vol. 1; (Cambridge: Cambridge University Press, 6 vols), pp. 221–2. Design of coinage: p. 176.

18. Samuelson, Paul (1973), *Economics*, 9th edition (New York: McGraw-Hill), p. 55.

19. Debreu, G. (1971), *Theory of Value: An Axiomatic Analysis of Economic Equilibrium*, fourth printing (New Haven: Yale University Press), p. 28. As John Geanakoplos observed, 'Money does not appear in the Arrow–Debreu model ... There is no point in making the role of money explicit in the Arrow–Debreu model, since it has no effect on the real allocations.' Geanakoplos, John (1987), 'Arrow–Debreu model of general equilibrium', *The New Palgrave: A Dictionary of Economics* (1): 116–24.

20. This section is based on material in Orrell, David, and Chlupatý, Roman (2016), *The Evolution of Money* (New York: Columbia University Press), as well as: Orrell, David (2016), 'A quantum theory of money and value', *Economic Thought*, 5(2): 19–36, and the second part available as a working paper at: http://etdiscussion.world economicsassociation.org/?wea_paper=a-quantum-theory-of-money -and-value-part-2-the-uncertainty-principle

21. I have argued elsewhere that our shyness to discuss quantum physics is unfortunate: Orrell, David (2012), *Truth or Beauty: Science and the Quest for Order* (New Haven, CT: Yale University Press), pp. 109–14.

22. Durden, Tyler (2016), 'Nassim Taleb Explains Who Just Got Buried', *ZeroHedge*, 9 November 2016; http://www.zerohedge.com/news/2016-11-09/nassim-taleb-explains-who-just-got-buried. I would prefer Arnold Zellner's expression 'sophisticatedly simple'. Zellner, A., Keuzenkamp, H.A., and McAleer, M.J. (2001), *Simplicity, Inference and Modelling: Keeping it Sophisticatedly Simple* (Cambridge: Cambridge University Press).

23. Aristotle (1943), *Generation of Animals*, trans. A.L. Peck (Cambridge, MA: Harvard University Press), p. 184.

24. Orrell, David (2016), 'A quantum theory of money and value', *Economic Thought*, 5(2): 19–36.

25. Bernanke, Ben (1995), 'The Macroeconomics of the Great Depression: A Comparative Approach', *Journal of Money, Credit, and Banking*, 27(1): 1–28.

26. Krugman, Paul (2012), *End This Depression Now!* (New York: Norton), p. 112.

27. Cassidy, John (2010), 'Interview with Eugene Fama', *New Yorker*, 13 January 2010.

28. For post-Pythagorean, see Orrell, David (2009), 'Post-Pythagorean Economics', *Adbusters* #85, 15 July 2009. See also Orrell, David (2012), *Truth or Beauty: Science and the Quest for Order* (New Haven, CT: Yale University Press).

29. Pilling, David (2016), 'Crash and learn: should we change the way we teach economics?', *Financial Times*, 30 September 2016.

30. Fourcade, M., Ollion, E. and Algan, Y. (2015), 'The Superiority of Economists', *Journal of Economic Perspectives*, 29(1), 89–114.

31. In search of a suitable example, I perused the Worthwhile Canadian Initiative blog (not to pick on them or anything), where they were wrestling with the question of how to bring money into the standard 'New Keynesian' macroeconomics model without actually modifying it. The trick is to *reinterpret* it as a model of a monetary exchange economy in a way that 'leaves the equations of the model unchanged'. After all: 'No sensible New Keynesian macroeconomist should object to this reinterpretation. It's a friendly amendment – and not even really an amendment.' So how to begin? 'Simplify massively, to clear the decks of anything that is not required for me to make my points. Large number of identical infinitely-lived self-employed agents who produce and consume haircuts (the only good).' And so on. Rowe, Nick (2016), 'My Cunning Plan to reform New Keynesian Macro',

Worthwhile Canadian Initiative, http://worthwhile.typepad.com/
worthwhile_canadian_initi/2016/11/my-cunning-plan-to-reform
-new-keynesian-macro.html

Appendix

1. In 2016, New York University was so convinced that Romer would be awarded the prize that they accidentally posted a document announcing the win.

2. Anonymous (2002), 'Greenspan to be knighted', *Agence France-Press*, 7 August 2002.

3. Lucas, Robert E. Jr. (2003), 'Macroeconomic Priorities', *American Economic Review*, 93(1): 1–14.

4. Rubinstein, Ariel (2006), 'Freak-Freakonomics', *The Economists' Voice*, 3 (9).

5. Posner, Richard A. (2009), 'Economists on the Defensive – Robert Lucas', *The Atlantic*, 9 August 2009.

6. Cassidy, John, 'Letter From Chicago: After The Blowup', *The New Yorker*, 11 January 2010.

7. This section draws on a series of articles I wrote for *World Finance*; see: Orrell, David (2016), 'Economists are still bargaining with the financial crisis', *World Finance*, 4 October 2016.

8. Art Rolnick (2010), 'Interview with Thomas Sargent', *The Region*, Federal Reserve Bank of Minneapolis, September 2010.

9. Lucas, Robert (2009), 'In defence of the dismal science', *The Economist*, 6 August 2009.

10. Cassidy, John (2010), 'Interview with Eugene Fama', *The New Yorker*, 13 January 2010.

11. Woolley, Frances (2010), 'Another rant about the *Globe and Mail*'s coverage of economics', Worthwhile Canadian Initiative, 20 September 2010. See: http://worthwhile.typepad.com/worthwhile_canadian_initi/2010/09/another-rant-about-the-globe-and-mails-coverage-of-economics.html. The site was ranked eighth worldwide among economics blogs at the time, and first in Canada, according to Palgrave. The initial topic – which was prompted by an interview I gave with the *Globe and Mail* – was that economics is unfairly portrayed to the public (ironic, given that these economists enjoy regular access to the media). My response to the post is in the comments section.

12. Auld, Christopher (2011), 'A review of *Economyths: Ten Ways*

Economics Gets it Wrong, by David Orrell', chrisaulddotcom. wordpress.com. Auld devotes much of his site to a discussion of 'anti-economists' who he describes variously as 'staggeringly ignorant', 'anti-intellectual', 'technically incompetent', 'spectacularly wrong', and even 'vitriolic'.

13. Fullbrook, Edward (2002), 'A Brief History of the Post-Autistic Economics Movement', paecon.net, August 2002, http://www.autisme-economie.org/article155.html. Fullbrook went on to co-found the World Economics Association.

14. Kennedy, Simon (2013), 'Buffett, Slim, Greenspan, El-Erian, Lew Pick Best Books of 2013', Bloomberg.com, 14 December 2013.

15. Suzuki told an interviewer that when economists call something an externality, what they really mean is 'We don't give a shit'. Which was obviously an over-the-top remark, but nothing compared to the reaction. Christopher Auld of the University of Victoria wrote a blog post saying that 'David Suzuki owes the community of economists, and his audiences, an apology and an unequivocal retraction'. Mike Moffatt from Ivey Business School followed with a *Globe* article, in which he claimed that Suzuki 'owes economists an apology'. And Laval's Stephen Gordon, who like Moffatt blogs for Worthwhile Canadian Initiative, followed *that* with a piece in *Maclean's* magazine where he accused Suzuki of conducting a 'smear campaign' against economists. The next step would have been an encyclical denouncing him as a heretic, unless he says sorry.

16. See https://www.facebook.com/evonomics/videos/1788016561469125/

17. Moffatt, Mike (2012), 'David Suzuki needs an economics refresher course', *The Globe and Mail*, 10 October 2012. For a riposte to Moffatt's article, see: Salustri, Filippo A. (2015), 'Mike Moffatt Needs An Ethics Refresher Course', filsalustri.wordpress.com, 9 February 2015. Moffatt followed his article up with an interview on the now-defunct, right-wing Sun News Network; see Chapter 8 note 21 (page 385).

18. For example, it helped the 'ethical oil' angle that politicians were promoting with the help of the Sun News Network, where Ezra Levant was a regular host (see box, page 297). See also previous note, and: Pullman, Emma (2012), 'The Harper government, Ethical Oil and Sun Media connection', Rabble.ca, 20 January 2012. These attacks from academic economists also helped set the tone for what the David

Suzuki Foundation later called 'false allegations' and 'mud-slinging' from political opponents. Robinson, Peter (2013), 'False allegations pollute the well of public discourse', DavidSuzuki.org, 17 October 2013.

19. Dani Rodrik (2015), *Economics Rules: The Rights and Wrongs of the Dismal Science* (New York: W.W. Norton & Company). See pp. 80, 168, 171, 198, 207, 214.

20. Rubinstein, Ariel (2017), 'Comments on Economic Models, Economics, and Economists: Remarks on *Economics Rules* by Dani Rodrik', *Journal of Economic Literature*, 55(1), 162–72.

21. Nelson, Julie A. (2003), 'Clocks, Creation, and Clarity: Insights on Ethics and Economics from a Feminist Perspective', *GDAE Working Papers 03-11*, Tufts University (Medford, MA).

22. See http://www.ecnmy.org/act/ for more information.

23. Fourcade, M., Ollion, E. and Algan, Y. (2015), 'The Superiority of Economists', *Journal of Economic Perspectives*, 29 (1) 89–114.

24. Smolin, L. (2006), *The Trouble with Physics: The Rise of String Theory, the Fall of a Science, and What Comes Next* (New York: Houghton Mifflin), pp. 263, 336.

25. Kimball, Miles and Anonymous (2015), 'How big is the sexism problem in economics? This article's co-author is anonymous because of it', *Quartz*, 6 January 2015.

26. Manson, A., McCallum, P., and Haiven, L. (2015), *Report of the Ad Hoc Investigatory Committee Into the Department of Economics at the University of Manitoba* (Manitoba: Canadian Association of University Teachers).

27. Available at https://paulromer.net/wp-content/uploads/2016/09/WP-Trouble.pdf

28. Mayeda, Andrew (2016), 'The Rebel Economist Who Blew Up Macroeconomics', Bloomberg.com, 18 November 2016.

29. Mason, Paul (2016), 'It's time to junk the flawed economic models that make the world a dangerous place', *The Guardian*, 19 September 2016.

30. www.esrc.ac.uk/news-events-and-publications/news/news-items/innovative-new-network-will-revolutionise-how-we-study-the-economy/

31. Caiani, Alessandro et al. (2016), 'Agent based-stock flow consistent macroeconomics: Towards a benchmark model', *Journal of Economic Dynamics and Control*, 69, August 2016, 375–408.

32. Dani Rodrik (2015), *Economics Rules: The Rights and Wrongs of the Dismal Science* (New York: W.W. Norton & Company), p. 158.

33. Freud, Sigmund and Phillips, Adam (2006), *The Penguin Freud Reader* (London: Penguin).

Acknowledgements

Thanks to everyone at Icon Books, especially Simon Flynn and Duncan Heath for helping get the manuscript into shape; and to Karen Milner, Thomas Hyrkiel, Robert Lecker, and my family.

Thanks also to Emmeline Skinner, Patrick McSharry, Cahal Moran, and Beatriz Leon for their close reading of portions of the manuscript and valuable comments.

INDEX

Note: page numbers in italics refer
to illustrations or graphics.